Additional publications may be ordered from:

American Correctional Association
4380 Forbes Blvd.
Lanham, MD 20706-4322
1-800-ACA-JOIN

ACA Staff:

Bobbie L. Huskey, President
James A. Gondles, Jr., Executive Director
Gabriella M. Daley, Director, Publications and Communications
Leslie A. Maxam, Assistant Director, Publications and Communications
Alice Fins, Managing Editor
Michael Kelly, Associate Editor
Mike Selby, Production Editor

Cover by Mactronics, Washington, D.C.
Printed in the United States by Graphic Communications, Inc., Upper Marlboro, MD.

ISBN 1-56991-044-8

Table of Contents

Adult Examples

Juvenile Examples

Program Components

Staff Training

Women in Boot Camp Programs

Cost and Evaluation Factors

Preface

James A. Gondles, Jr.

Executive Director
American Correctional Association
Lanham, Maryland

We are pleased to present the ideas and program descriptions of some of the best minds and practitioners operating and conceptualizing boot camps. As the popularity of boot camps continues, it is important for those implementing new programs to understand what boot camps can do best and for whom. This volume presents the answers, which include: preplanning, staff training, considering special populations, evaluating, and choosing from among program elements.

This volume adds a further dimension to the two videos we have on boot camps—juvenile and adult boot camps. We have long recognized the increasing number of boot camps and last year issued standards for both adult and juvenile correctional boot camp programs. We recommend that those instituting boot camps review these standards and accredit their facilities with the Commission on Accreditation for Corrections.

We are particularly grateful to the authors who wrote these essays. Special appreciation and thanks to Cheryl L. Clark and Doris Layton MacKenzie for their help in guiding the development of this project.

Introduction

Doris Layton MacKenzie, Ph.D.

Associate Professor, Department of Criminology and Criminal Justice
University of Maryland
College Park, Maryland

Often as I travel around the country to visit correctional boot camps and talk with individuals responsible for designing or implementing the programs, I find they have very similar questions: How do I select and train staff? Do I develop a coed program or separate programs for men and women or boys and girls? What offenders are appropriate candidates? How long should the program be? Are the programs effective? This book, in combination with the recently published National Institute of Justice book, *Correctional Boot Camps: A Tough Intermediate Sanction*, provide planners with information to answer these questions. While the National Institute of Justice book focused on descriptive and impact evaluations of correctional boot camps, this book fills the need people have for specific information about the design, operation, and staffing issues of the camps. Chapters are written by a variety of individuals knowledgeable about different aspects of the boot camp programs. During the development phase of the programs, these authors learned the hard way what worked and what did not. They share these experiences with the reader.

A Place Where Positive Development and Change Occurs

A quick review of the chapters shows numerous agreements among the authors. First, and perhaps foremost, is the emphasis in the camps on the positive development and change of the participants. The camps have moved from what has been referred to as the "first-generation camps" to second-, third- or even fourth-generation camps. As happens with generations, it is difficult to identify the specific characteristics of this change. What is clear in this book is that the move has been toward a leadership model away from an old-style confrontational Marine boot camp. The chapter by Command Sergeant Major Joshua Perry (Retired), describes the training available at Fort McClellan that emphasizes the military leadership model.

Research supports this positive view of the boot camp experience. In interviews and surveys, the participants report being drug free and physically healthy in the camps. They also recount supportive interactions with staff and constructive activities. In comparison to those in prisons, they view the experience as beneficial and they believe that they have changed for the better. Surprisingly, even those who are expelled or who voluntarily drop out often have positive things to say about their experiences in the camps. Of course, it is imperative that the reader understands that these positive reports from participants are from particular types of camps that provide close administrative oversight, a caring staff, and a focus on positive change.

Correctional Officers as Agents of Change and Models for Behavior

One side benefit that has occurred from this new emphasis on the correctional officers as behavior change agents is the development of professional pride and training for a new type of correctional officer. These officers take responsibility for more than providing security for inmates. Instead, they view themselves as change agents and models. Prior to this book, little has been written about the expectations and training for these "new-style" officers.

Frequently, around the country, boot camps are begun without sufficient planning for the training and education of the staff. Those who have been in the military attempt to replicate what they thought happened to them when they went through boot camp. They do not realize, as is obvious in chapters throughout this book, that the drill sergeant-correctional officers must be leaders, teachers, counselors and, most important, they must really care about the people with whom they work (see chapters by Command Sergeant Major Joshua Perry (Retired) and Colonel Thomas H. Cornick (Retired)). In the experience of most of these authors, staff with past military experience can be an asset, but experience in correctional settings as officers, counselors, or staff is more important than the military experience (see chapters by John F. Wertz and Ronald D. Griffith and Dr. Corby Myers).

Innovative Ideas and New Perspectives

Another obvious change in the boot camps is in the variety of philosophies on which the camps are based. The early, first-generation camps all had physical training, structure, and discipline in an environment that emphasized military drill and ceremony. This is not the case in these more recent camps. Take, for example, Washington's "Work Ethic" camp (see the chapter by Jackie Campbell) or Vermont's emphasis on restorative justice (see chapters by John Perry and Dr. Gordon Bazemore and Thomas J. Quinn). These new generation camps are testing innovative ideas that hold promise for effectively changing the offender participants. The commonality among the camps today appears to be a long, intensive daily schedule of activities in a program that emphasizes discipline and structure. Other than these basic qualifications, the programs differ dramatically. In this book, the American Correctional Association has worked to obtain chapters by authors who can describe the variety of different philosophies and practices of these camps.

Focus on Skills and Behaviors Needed to Make It on the Outside

Another change that has occurred in these boot camps is the emphasis on the outside and what the participants need to live crime-free lives after leaving the camps. Each element in the boot camp is evaluated specifically for what it will give the participants or the program. If marching and drill provides an opportunity for teamwork or physical health, then it is viewed as appropriate, but if it is just an activity that keeps them busy, it is viewed as much less useful. As Colonel Cornick writes in his essay, "The boot camp should not become an end in itself, and the protocols associated with it should not take over for important treatment interventions."

Boot camps that expect to change offenders so that they live crime-free lives after they return to the community must evaluate every aspect of the daily schedule to insure that the focus is on the changes that will be required for this to happen. There is a consensus among the authors in this book that these changes will not occur as a result of the demeaning confrontations that have become part of the media representation of the camps. Activities in the boot camp need to be carefully planned and analyzed to insure that they relate to the overall program mission and not just occur because "it's a boot camp" (see the chapter by Cheryl L. Clark, Ronald Moscicki, and Joshua Perry). The initial chapter, the planning guide by Cheryl Clark, provides an aid to assist jurisdictions in the careful planning of a boot camp.

The chapters by Dr. Ernest L. Cowles and Lisa Matheson describe different methods of providing drug treatment and education to offenders participating in the boot camps. This is an important component of many boot camps because so many of the participants are drug-involved. Another type of program that is becoming increasingly popular for offenders is cognitive skills. This is a strong emphasis of the Oregon Summit program described by William Beers and Chris Duval.

Focus on Rewards, Good Behavior, and Successful Accomplishments

One aspect of the camps that has been controversial is the emphasis of many camps on punishment. Psychologists familiar with behavior change emphasize the fact that programs that are successful in changing behavior use a high ratio of rewards to punishments. That is, rewards for good behavior are offered ten or more times for each punishment given for misbehavior. Correctional boot camp planners and staff struggle with methods for evaluating the behavior of participants, but, frequently, these evaluations are unreliable (one person scoring the performance of a participant gives very different scores than another person scoring the same performance of the identical participant). Such evaluations are frustrating for the participants because they are never quite sure what is required of them. Furthermore, the scores frequently are viewed as punishment for misbehavior (they are unable to progress in the program if they receive negative scores).

There are so many other possibilities for rewarding good behavior. Participants could receive weekly or biweekly rewards for such things as:

- "Most Improved" in math or language arts based on test scores
- "Most Helpful" to other students in class based on teachers' votes
- "Best Accomplishment in Academic Area" (writing, math, art work, computer skills, or other areas) based on teachers' votes
- "Achieved Math and/or Language Arts Goal" (set for each individual) based on individual tests
- Completed Marathon (or some outstanding physical accomplishment)
- "Most Improved Cadet" based on drill instructors' vote
- "Best Overall Cadet" based on drill instructors' vote
- "Best Boot Camper" based on boot camp participants' vote
- "Hero" (unusual award for some outstanding heroic feat) nomination from staff or participants
- "Best Citizen" (caring and helpful to others, role model for others) based on a vote by all staff.

All of these rewards encourage the type of behavior that will be important after the participants leave the facility.

The military rewards behavior with medals. There is no reason that correctional boot camps could not give medals or at least certificates to reward behavior. Another excellent example of a system of rewards is that used at the Sergeant Henry Johnson Youth Leadership Academy (see the chapter by Colonel Tom Cornick (Retired)). They give recognition for clearly identified skill acquisition.

Juveniles in Boot Camps

As correctional boot camps have moved from the adult prisons to local jails and juvenile detention centers, it has become crucial that those developing the programs identify a clear philosophy describing the mission, objectives, and goals of the programs. For example, while adult programs could target nonviolent offenders in prison, nonviolent juveniles are much less apt to be incarcerated. Thus, net widening and the associated costs become critical issues for juvenile programs. This is particularly relevant given the concern with the destructive environment of detention centers for nonviolent juveniles or status offenders. The deceptively seductive idea of providing discipline and structure for disruptive juveniles means that there is a real threat that increasingly large numbers of juveniles will be placed in boot camps, whether or not it is a suitable alternative sanction. We know that adjudication and incarceration, even as a juvenile, carry a stigma. If these programs increase the number of adjudicated and incarcerated juveniles, we have to question whether this is in the best interest of these children. After working so hard to remove status offenders from facilities, it will be a real disadvantage if the boot camps result in increasing the numbers of status offenders who are incarcerated.

As our chapter (MacKenzie and Rosay) shows, the number of boot camps for juveniles is growing rapidly. It will be dangerous if these camps borrow too heavily from adult boot camps because many of the issues are very different for juveniles. For example, while it may be reasonable to have a six-month boot camp for adults, it may not be sensible for juveniles if the target population's average length of stay is only four months. If a complete analysis of the target population and their length of stay is not completed prior to the initiation of the program to determine the numbers of appropriate and eligible participants, jurisdictions often find that they are unable to fill the allotted beds. This has implications for both the cost of the camp and its very existence. It is hardly cost effective to keep a program that is operating well below capacity. This appears to be the reason for the closure of Maryland's juvenile boot camp which held only eight participants.

Boot Camps in Local Prisons and Jails

Length of stay and the identification of appropriate participants has been a particular problem with jail boot camp programs. As pointed out by Susan McCampbell, in her discussion of the Broward Sheriff's Office Boot Camp, most jails do not hold individuals serving long sentences. Furthermore, offenders who are serving time in jail may not be appropriate candidates for the program due to criminal history, physical or mental health, or a history of violence. Jail programs can become a very costly alternative if they keep the offenders in jail for a longer period, particularly if the time in jail involves enhanced therapeutic programming as is happening in many boot camps. These are the factors that were responsible for shutting down the Los Angeles boot camp program (Regimented Inmate Discipline, RID).

Equity and Equality for Women and Girls

There is still a great deal of controversy about these boot camps. Some individuals are still against them because, in their views, the camps are a poor way to rehabilitate offenders. Other controversies revolve around the details of how the camps should be run and who are appropriate candidates for the program. One important issue is whether women and girls should be given equal opportunities for participating in the boot camps or whether different types of programs should be developed for them. Voncile Gowdy discusses the issues and the complexities surrounding decisions about whether boot camps are appropriate for women.

In the interest of fairness there ought to be programs for women that offer equal opportunities for programming, aftercare, early release, physical training, or other positive aspects of the boot camps. But equity is not always accomplished by offering identical programs, particularly since these programs are often developed for males and not for females. Such programs may have unintended consequences that are damaging for the women or that do not address the specific problems they have. This is particularly true in the boot camps that are developed for males. Females are admitted, frequently as an afterthought, in the interest of equality (and most likely with the fear of lawsuits). Cheryl Clark describes some of the problems New York has encountered during the implementation of the program for women, and how they resolved these problems in the existing model. Jurisdictions planning boot camps must examine fairness and equity issues and decide how they will address these concerns.

Return to the Community and Aftercare

There is some research examining the impact of the correctional boot camps on the later criminal activities and prosocial activities of the participants. The boot camps can be examined from one of the following two perspectives:

1. The boot camp experience changes offenders; without the boot camp these offenders would not change;

2. The boot camp does not necessarily change offenders, but it identifies those who want to change; those who are identified are willing to work hard to try to change and thus those who will be less apt to recidivate.

In general, there is little research evidence that the boot camp actually changes the behavior of the participants (item one above). In the majority of cases, no differences have been found in recidivism or positive social activities between boot camp offenders and comparison samples. Exploratory analyses suggest that there may be some differences in programs that are voluntary, focus on therapeutic activities, and have some type of aftercare, but this is still not documented with strong research support.

However, in the view of many of those responsible for developing the boot camps, aftercare is a necessary component of the programs. Many program developers focused first on the implementation of the in-prison phase of the program. When they realized how difficult it was for the participants to return to their home community, program administrators began to look for ways to provide help and support to the boot camp graduates during the difficult transition to the community. In their chapter, Dr. Thomas C. Castellano and Susan M. Plant provide an overview of aftercare programs, the difficulties many jurisdictions have had in implementing such programs, and the importance of the programs as a follow-up to the in-prison phase.

A second perspective on the potential impact of boot camps is as a mechanism for identifying offenders who are ready to change. The boot camps may be successful in selecting those participants who are ready to change, give them the opportunity to work hard to demonstrate this readiness, and to provide them an experience that will help them in making the change. Some offenders are not ready to change and refuse to enter, drop out, or are expelled from the program. There is more research support for this perspective than evidence that the boot camp actually changes offenders. If the boot camp were not there, the successful boot camp participants probably would not have recidivated, but the corrections' system would not be able to identify which prison inmates would recidivate and which would not. The research generally shows that the offenders who complete the boot camps do better than others who either do not complete it or who refuse to enter. We cannot conclude that offenders who completed the program were changed by their experiences, but we can conclude that the boot camp separated those who would succeed in the community from those who would not. Research examining the New York Shock Program for adults presents particularly strong evidence of this "signaling" effect.

The Political Nature of the Boot Camps

From the beginning, the public has enthusiastically supported boot camps for offenders. In fact, the initiative for developing the camps in most jurisdiction has come from the legislature or policy makers not from correctional administrators. At first, naively, many of us believed that this support came from the public's desire for punitive reactions to young offenders. Yet, recent surveys suggest that the public is not as punitive as originally thought. They also appear to want cost-effective correctional programs that will successfully change offenders. However, not all boot camps are cost effective (see the chapter by Dr. David Aziz and Peter Korotkin).

Many of the boot camps have provided a method for corrections to demonstrate its positive side and the advantages of this should not be overlooked. Boot camp graduations are public ceremonies; policy makers are asked to give public addresses to the graduates. This works to educate policy makers and the public about the positive side of corrections. The benefit for the graduates is that they are recognized for their hard work in completing the boot camp. The participants in many of the boot camps provide service to local communities. They have been particularly valuable in helping during emergencies such as the

Midwest flood relief efforts in 1993 in Illinois (see the chapter by Robert J. Jones). This is the type of positive image that benefits the field of corrections. Another way of ensuring quality in the boot camps is through their accreditation (see Carole Knapel's chapter). The Appendix contains a list of contacts in accredited boot camps. It may be helpful to call and visit these sites.

Planning Guide

Cheryl L. Clark

Director of Shock Incarceration
New York State Department of Correctional Services
Albany, New York

In this Planning Guide, you will . . .

❑ Identify the purpose, methods and intended results of a boot camp.

❑ Identify the who, what, when, where, why, and how of the boot camp.

❑ Identify evaluation and monitoring strategies for boot camps.

❑ Learn about the history and current practices of model boot camp programs.

❑ Learn strategies for designing effective boot camp and aftercare programs to maximize benefits.

❑ Review model programs, training designs and treatment interventions.

Introduction

This manual is a guide for policy makers and planners for designing an effective boot camp program and for program administrators to help them assess and evaluate operating programs. Since the beginnings of modern boot camps in 1983, boot camps have grown from the two initial programs in Georgia and Oklahoma to more than fifty-five at the beginning of 1995. Generally, boot camp programs are an alternative to incarcerating young, nonviolent offenders for longer periods of time. They are characterized by their short duration, intensity, and structure. Most have some type of military flavor, whether it is the uniforms that staff and offenders wear, the use of military drills and ceremonies, a structured physical training component, military courtesies and titles, and/or grooming standards and procedures.

In response to this growing phenomenon, the American Correctional Association has established accreditation standards for both adult and juvenile boot camp programs. Those standards serve as guide for operating an effective boot camp program (see Carole Knapel's chapter in this volume). In addition, two training films, *Boot Camps in Corrections* and *Boot Camps in Juvenile Corrections* are also available from the American Correctional Association. This planning guide responds to questions policy makers and planners have about how to establish and maintain an effective boot camp program and to assist them with developing goals, strategies and methods. A body of literature now is available from many sources, including: the National Institute of Justice, the states which have adult and juvenile boot camp programs, and research. A bibliography of related research, materials, and readings are appended to many chapters. A listing of states with ACA accredited boot camp programs as of this publication date is included as Appendix A at the end of this volume. The contact people are happy to answer your questions and assist you.

This planning guide is designed as a workbook, so that you may consider what form your boot camp might take or how best to evaluate the success of a currently operating program. Planners will be able to work directly in the manual, making notes and recording ideas. You may want to review the planning guide before beginning to work through the steps in this chapter, and to familiarize yourself with some of the ways others have approached the development of boot camps. Others have suggested working through this chapter after reading all the essays relevant to your concerns. Several models are presented in the guide, along with background information on effective programs, evaluation, training, and treatment designs and issues to consider in aftercare programs.

Preview this guide and identify topics that may be of particular use and interest to your task force or planning group. Then, see what questions you have that need to be answered before you begin the planning or evaluation process. This chapter will help the planning group to expand and focus on the planning process. Gather additional information from the models presented in this guide. Once the plan is underway, study the literature on the program, and visit model programs if time permits.

Cheryl L. Clark

Grants

The Office of Justice Programs, Corrections Program Office offers Correctional Boot Camp Technical Assistance grants to planners through the National Institute of Corrections. Applications may be made to: The Office of Justice Programs, Corrections Program Office, 633 Indiana Avenue, NW, Washington, D.C. 20531. Phone (800) 848-6325 or Fax (202) 307-2019.

Tips For Using This Planning Guide*

Preview this manual. Look it over to learn how it is set up and identify resources for your planning process.

Ask questions among the planning group. What do you need to know to develop an effective program?

Gather information from this manual in response to those questions. Begin to collect material from other sources listed in the bibliographies and from operating programs.

Expand your ideas by reviewing the research and literature. Use this manual to stimulate ideas and generate possibilities within the planning group. Reach out to other programs for materials they can send you.

Study the literature. Visit model programs and talk to practitioners. Review and read available research.

* source: Quantum Learning
Bobbi DePorter with Mike Hernacki
©1992 Bantam Doubleday, Dell Publishing Group, Inc., NY
(Printed with permission)

Proper Planning Prevents Poor Performance

Designing an effective boot camp program is both an opportunity and a challenge. There are as many models as there are programs, and each has its own unique spin. Designs are influenced by perceived need, correctional philosophy, legislation, population focus, size, agency and public policy, political influences and agency leadership impacting on the process. This guide suggests a system for addressing some basic questions you need to answer as you develop your boot camp initiative. The guide also can serve for ongoing evaluation efforts, monitoring, reviewing, making modifications and aftercare planning. Whatever model you choose to operate from, a well-designed plan is critical to ensure that you reach the goals set for the program. Investing time and energy in planning will pay major dividends in the end.

The guidelines presented here do not dictate a specific model; rather, they are a framework for organizing your plan. All corrections professionals know the basics of good report writing. To be effective, a report has to answer the questions: who, what, when, where, why, and how. A good program plan must also answer these basic questions. When planning, each of the six categories has two dimensions: internal and external. The implementing agency needs to be clear about their internal goals and also must account for the external influences which impact on them.

The mind map on the next page is a visual overview of the planning process presented here. Details on each section are provided later. For now, review the dimensions quickly to familiarize yourself with them.

Why does the agency want a boot camp? Why does the public, legislature or other external influence want this program? Why are you choosing a boot camp model as opposed to another?

Who is the program for? Adults/juveniles, men/women? Sentenced/pre-sentenced? With whom will you do it? Existing agency staff? Private group? Former military?

What is the content of the program? What are its goals? What will be included in it? Exercise? Academics? Substance abuse treatment? What is the context? What form will it take? Military style? Therapeutic community? Outdoor challenge? Combination?

When will it begin? When will it end? This is where you will make a timeline and decide on the length of the program. Aftercare is important.

Where will the program be located? Will it be co-located within or near another facility or free standing? From where will the clients come? Where will they return after release?

How will the program operate? Consider what methods will get the results you want. How will the program be structured? Consider the logistics of the operation.

If you are working on a team, reproduce the mind map on the next page on a chalkboard or a white board. Include all your ideas in a free-flowing brainstorming session. Remember, the only useless idea is one not expressed. Sometimes an idea that sounds ridiculous can trigger one that will work.

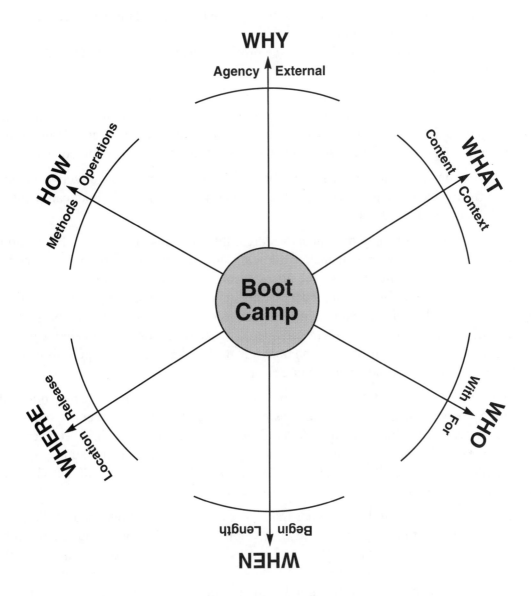

"The road to success is always under construction."

Why Implement A Boot Camp?

The first question that needs to be answered as you begin the planning process is: Why does the agency want a boot camp? What is the purpose for the boot camp? Why do you want to undertake this initiative? What is the problem you want to solve? Complete your answers on the worksheet on page 7.

Does the agency want to undertake this initiative, or are external factors creating the demand? What is motivating the decision to implement a boot camp in your area? Why does the public, legislature, or other external influence want this program? How do the external influences perceive the need? What are the goals and intended outcomes?

Why are you choosing a boot camp model? There are many other effective models available from which to choose. What is the motivation for choosing a boot camp at this time? Why not another model?

Most states use boot camp programs to address the problems of crowding. Boot camps are generally early-release mechanisms, allowing nonviolent offenders to serve shorter terms of incarceration, and allow scarce prison resources to be used to incarcerate violent offenders longer. With increasing concern about violence and drugs, scarce prison resources are challengeneral equivalency degree to deal with escalating prison populations. One way to ensure that violent offenders are confined longer is to find a way to incarcerate low-level drug offenders and nonviolent offenders for shorter periods of time, or provide effective alternatives to incarceration.

Between 1980 and 1993, the prison population in the United States more than doubled. In 1980, 57 percent of the offenders in prison were incarcerated for violent felonies. By 1993, with over twice the population, 55 percent of those incarcerated had been convicted of nonviolent felonies. The juvenile justice system has experienced a similar growth pattern; however, the violent population, associated with increasing gang activity, has exacerbated the problems in some juvenile systems.

Take some time now to list the ideas that occur to you as you think about these questions. If you have a planning task force with whom to work, use newsprint charts to be sure to include everyone's ideas. Have at least two scribes to record your ideas on the charts so you can move quickly. Keep everything in front of you as you work through this process. Suspend judgment as you begin. It is more important to get all of the ideas down. Evaluate them later. At this point, get your ideas on paper so you can see them. List assumptions. List whatever facts you have that are influencing the decision.

Make sure you block out enough time to work through this process. The more you invest up front, the fewer surprises you will have in the end. Another note of caution—do not expect this to be a one-time only process. In New York, we do this at least once a year, to be sure to keep ourselves on track. And, we have been operating the Shock Incarcertion program since 1987. In 1995, we used this process to develop another variation of the Shock Incarceration program to help us design a 90 day drug treatment program for offenders who are either sentenced by the courts or are returned parole violators. This program is presently the only licensed correctional drug treatment program in the state.

Why Do This?

Why do we want a boot camp? | Why do they want a boot camp?

_____

"One who lacks the courage to start has already finished."
—Road to Success

For Whom Is the Program Intended? Who Will Implement It?

For whom is the program intended? Are they adults or juveniles? Are they male, female, both? Of what types of crimes will the target population be convicted? Are they violent, nonviolent? How old? Is there an age limit? Is this group sentenced or pre-sentenced? Is your intent to divert a probation population or is the target group prison bound? Are they convicted felons? Adjudicated juveniles? The methods you choose need to be selected based on the needs of the group being addressed.

What types of physical, emotional and other presenting problems are you prepared to address? Many of the people who enter our systems have very low self esteem. They are often school dropouts or failures, without high school diplomas. Some do not read and write; thus, their opportunities for employment are limited. Research also indicates that many young offenders, most typically the population addressed by this type of program, have a history of child abuse or neglect. They enter the corrections or juvenile justice system with adjustment problems. Emotional, sexual and physical abuse is not uncommon with this population, both male and female. In a discussion about relationships with a group of young women in Shock Incarceration, one young woman offered as her reason that so many of them accepted bad treatment, the chilling response, "Oh ma'am, they all be child molested."

Who will select the population? Will judges, probation or parole, corrections, legislators or another group determine who the participants will be? How will you screen the population? Who will determine their suitability for the program?

Who will staff the boot camp? Existing agency staff? Private group? Former military? Consider staff selection very carefully; this will have a major impact on the operations of the program. Choosing the wrong staff for even the best program will cripple the program. Is your system a unionized one? If so, how will that affect staff selection? What leeway will you have in staff selection with choosing the right people for the right jobs? If your system is not affected by union-bidding practices and negotiations, what are your options in staff selection? If you choose ex-military staff, do you know what to look for and what information to review about their military service?

Most people who have been involved in this initiative for any period of time recommend that correctional boot camp staff have at least two-to-three years of corrections' experience, to be sure that they are familiar with corrections' policies and practices and know how to deal with offenders. Some agencies require a military background for drill instructors in this program; others do not feel that this is necessary. Before you make final decisions on staff selection, review the chapters on staff selection and training.

Who will evaluate the boot camp program? Evaluation is a critical tool for feedback about all aspects of the program. It is important to have a clear picture about what you are doing and whether it works. Will you use an in-house evaluation team, contract with an outside organization or do a combination of both? A good evaluation is also an effective tool for marketing your program and letting funding sources know how effective the program is. Read the chapters on evaluation in this book, which offer concrete guidance.

Who Is Involved?

For whom is the program intended?

Who will be the staff?

_____

_____

_____

_____

_____

_____

_____

Who will select participants?

Who will evaluate the program?

_____

_____

_____

_____

_____

_____

_____

_____

What Are The Goals Of The Boot Camp?
What Results Do You Hope To Achieve?

Having identified your target population, now ask: What are the goals of the program? What do you hope to accomplish with the boot camp? The content and context flow from what you have identified as the presenting problems of your target population. To reach your goals and achieve results, program methods need to be selected that are responsive to the needs of your target population and the agency establishing the program.

Use the S.M.A.R.T. rule for setting your goals. Simply stated, goals should be Specific, Measurable, Attainable, Realistic, and Timely. You will identify goals for the boot camp in detail later in this chapter, for now keep the S.M.A.R.T. rule in mind. For example, the Shock Incarceration program in New York has two, very simply stated goals. They are, first, to treat and release specially selected offenders earlier than their court-mandated minimum period of incarceration, and to do so without increasing the risk to the community and second, to reduce the demand for bed space. These are offered as examples only, of goals that are Specific, can be Measured objectively, and are both Attainable and Realistic given the Time constraints of the program.

By no means are they the only possible goals. Note, that there is no promise to "reduce recidivism" as one example of an unrealistic goal some programs have been forced to set. There are no guarantees in even the best planned programs. Offenders are at risk for parole or probation violations, and some will commit crimes again. Relapse is a fact of substance abuse. Plan to address the problem as best you can, but do not pin your hopes on the population you are releasing to the community. You will have no control over their decisions and actions once they leave your system.

What will the content of the program be? What are the identified problems and needs? Will participants need academic education to prepare them for jobs? Do they have high school diplomas? Are they dropouts? Did they have trouble in school? If they are juveniles, what school problems do you plan to address for this group? Study the presenting problems of the target population to be sure you are addressing why they have come to your attention. Are they substance abusers? If they are largely substance abusers or convicted of drug and alcohol related crimes, then substance abuse treatment is a critical component to include in the program. Many of the population, both adults and juveniles, have children. This is generally a more difficult issue for women than men, because women are more likely to be the primary caretakers of children. How will you address parenting issues and other lifeskills? This is no less important for men who are fathers; they need to learn to be responsible parents too. What about the issue of AIDS and other health issues related to substance abuse and neglect? What about vocational training? Is that a need you can address?

What is the context? What form will the program take? Will it be an alternative to incarceration or an alternative incarceration program? Will it be a correctional facility, a private facility, a probation program? Will it be residential or day treatment, or some combination of both? Are you planning for a juvenile or adult institution? Do you/they want a military style program, a drug treatment program, a therapeutic community, an outward bound, adventure or challenge program, a combination of these? Will you use a military model or not? If so, why? If not, why not? Make sure you list all of your assumptions, facts and feelings, both pro and con.

Content—what do we want in it?	For whom is the program intended?

"When I know what I want, I'm halfway there."

When Will You Begin? How Long Will the Program Be?

This is where you will make a timeline and decide on the length of the program. The literature suggests that to be effective, programs should be four-to-six months in length during the institutional phase and followed by at least an equivalent length aftercare program. In cases where the offender population only would be serving a one-year term, a six-month institutional phase is not practical, especially if one of the primary goals of the program is to reduce crowding and lower costs of incarceration.

Where programs can be no longer than ninety days in length, the need for an intensive aftercare program is even more critical. One cannot expect to impact on young, substance abusing offenders in ninety days with no follow-up. Critics of boot camp programs have repeatedly cited the short-term nature of boot camp programs as one of the reasons for their ineffectiveness. Initially, when planning the timeline, build in aftercare.

When will the program begin? When will offenders enter the program? Is the program for offenders entering the system or on their way out? Is there a bed-savings factor? Is a time cut part of the motivation for offenders to volunteer? Can they volunteer? What are the mechanisms for removing inappropriate candidates?

When will the program end? How long will the residential phase be? Given the demands for bed savings, how long can the institutional phase last and still be both cost effective to the agency and attractive to potential participants? Once participants are released to the community, how long will the aftercare phase last? If cost is a factor in the length of the program, aftercare is not the place to cut. There are many ways to involve the community in an effective aftercare program without incurring huge costs to small jurisdictions. Programs such as Alcoholics Anonymous and Narcotics Anonymous are free and open to everyone. Church groups and some business groups are also potential supporters of program graduates. See the chapter on Aftercare in this volume.

How long will the program day be? While this will be governed by program activities, the length of the day is raised here because there have been boot camp programs that have gotten participants up early, at 4:00 or 4:30 A.M. simply because administrators believed that early rising was essential to a boot camp. Participants were not going to bed until 10:00 P.M. Tired participants do not learn well.

Juveniles' and young adults' bodies are still developing; they need rest to function effectively. At least eight hours sleep needs to be part of the schedule. Academic or treatment classes requiring higher order thinking and reasoning should not occur until after 8:00 A.M., say learning theorists. Thus, even if participants are awakened at 5:30 A.M., there is plenty of time to have a physical conditioning class, a drill or run, have breakfast and prepare for classes or work details by 8:30 A.M. After a full day's activities, participants are more than ready to go to bed by 9:30 P.M. Treatment and education programs and group process activities should end by 9:00 P.M. to allow participants time to wind down. This also creates less strain on staff who are working with offenders at the end of long days. These practical considerations are important in planning the time schedule.

Timing Is Everything

When will the program begin?	When will it end?
_____	_____
_____	_____
_____	_____
_____	_____

How long will the institutional phase be?	Length of aftercare?
_____	_____
_____	_____
_____	_____

Daily Schedule

Time	Weekday Events Mon - Fri	Weekend Events
_____	_wake up, count_ _____	_____
_____	_____	_____
_____	_____	_____
_____	_____	_____
_____	_____	_____
_____	_____	_____
_____	_____	_____
_____	_____	_____
_____	_____	_____
_____	_____	_____
_____	_lights out_	_____

Where To Locate the Boot Camp and Aftercare

Where will the program be located? Will the boot camp be a free-standing facility with its own separate services? Will it be within, or adjacent to a larger facility and share services with that larger facility? What types of services will be shared? What about medical, dental, food service, support and other services? How will those services be accessed?

Where is the closest hospital or clinic? Where are physicians, dentists, hospitals and other health care services located? Are there easily accessible health care and other services within or near the facility? How will the boot camp access any necessary services and resources? If services are not available within the facility, how close are they?

Is the boot camp located in an urban or rural setting? Is the boot camp within or near the community where the participants live? Is it separated from home communities by long distances? How will you build rapport in the community where the program is located? Are there volunteer service groups that can support the educational or treatment services within the boot camp? What about Alcoholics Anonymous and/or Narcotics Anonymous groups? Are there Literacy Volunteers in the area who can work with participants? What about college intern programs to assist with educational programs? Might church or business groups be willing to provide support to the program and participants?

If offenders are going to work in the local community, how close are work sites? Are the work sites rural or urban? How will they get to the work sites? How will decisions be made about where community services are to be provided? Are there other government or local agencies for which program participants might provide services? Community service programs are a major way to enroll local community groups to support the program and earn a positive reputation for the program. They also provide participants with work skills and experience, which can help them obtain employment after release.

From where will the boot camp participants come? How close are their families and children? Will families and children be able to visit? Is the program in an area where family ties can be maintained? For indigent families, are there support services to assist families to visit?

While both male and female participants, including juveniles, are frequently parents, the women and girls are more likely to be primary caretakers of the children. Where and in whose care will the children of participants be? If the children are in foster care, will they be able to visit? How will the children get to the boot camp? If distance precludes visits, are there other ways parents can maintain ties with their children?

Where will the participants return after release? Will they return to one particular area or be located throughout a region, the state or county? Are transitional services available for program participants in the areas to which they will return? Are halfway houses and support services available? Are Alcoholics Anonymous and/or Narcotics Anonymous groups in home communities?

Map the Territory

| Where is the boot camp? | Where do they go after release? |

| Where are health care services? | Where are support services? |

| Where will they work? | Where are their children? |

| Where are aftercare jobs and services? |

How Will You Achieve Your Intended Results?

Therapeutic community experts believed that once participants had learned the language of change, they then had to take action, to demonstrate that they could do the right thing. Learning theorists say that muscle memory results in the strongest and most lasting learning. Learning becomes automatic when it is integrated in body, mind and spirit. The best models of training and education reinforce learners to see it, say it, and do it. What will the staff in the program be modeling and teaching? What will participants in the boot camp be learning and doing?

How will the program operate? Will it be a military model, a therapeutic community, treatment or educational model, or some combination? What educational or vocational programs will be included? What methods will achieve the results intended? Many excellent models of boot camp programs are described in this guide.

Here is a partial listing of program methods used in boot camp programs:

- Alcoholics Anonymous
- Narcotics Anonymous
- Cognitive Restructuring
- Transactional Analysis
- Decision Making and Life Skills
- The Magic Within
- Building Self-Esteem
- Social Control Theory
- Social Learning Techniques
- Meditation
- Physical Training

- Confidence Building
- Obstacle Courses
- Reality Therapy
- Family Relationships and Parenting
- Neuro Linguistic Programming
- Accelerated Learning Techniques
- Body-Mind Integration Techniques
- Military Drills and Ceremonies
- Aerobics
- Work Ethics
- Pre-Release Programming

How will the program be structured? How will the logistics of the operation work? Will offenders enter and leave together? Will intake be individual? The size of the program will dictate intake and release procedures. How will activities reinforce learning?

How will the flow of the program operate? Will there be formal movement to and from program activities, meals, work and school? Will drill instructors move participants? Will treatment teams working with offenders include a balance of security, treatment, education, and support staff? How will they be sure they are staying on track with program purpose, methods, and intended results? How will the program be supervised? Will outside service providers or volunteers be required to participate in staff training? How will they learn about expectations, program philosophy, methods and procedures? How will they be integrated into the team?

How will staff be trained? Will specialists have intensive training in particular areas of responsibility? Will drill instructors have specialized training in military bearing, drill and ceremony and physical training? Will treatment specialists have training in alcohol and substance abuse treatment? Will there be cross training, so that each group understands and appreciates the other's specialty? How will training be integrated?

Program Methods

Security	Treatment	Administration

Program Operations

Security	Treatment	Administration

Staff Training

Developing A Mission Statement

Review the work accomplished so far. The who, what, when, where, why and how of the boot camp have been identified. The internal needs of the agency and the external requirements of key stakeholders, officials, and the public have been explored. The reason for the program and the results the program intends to achieve are clear. Finally, methods to help achieve those results are identified. The process has been time consuming and challenging. Take some time acknowledge and celebrate this accomplishment. Celebrations are as important as the rest of the planning process.

Now that the basic framework of the program is sketched out, begin to pull everything together. Recognize what you have learned from this process. Quickly summarize, in the spaces provided on the next page, the essence of the work completed so far. The space is small to encourage a quick summary. Avoid the temptation to add things here. If more ideas occur, go back to the relevant page and add them to that worksheet.

After you have completed the summary, clarify the purpose of the boot camp program in a simple, direct statement. This will form the basis of the mission statement for the program and will be the guiding philosophy of the boot camp.

- Why have you chosen to operate a boot camp?
- Who is the target population?
- What are the goals of the program? What form will the boot camp take?
- When will it begin and end? Specify the timeline, including aftercare.
- Where will the boot camp and the aftercare program be located?
- How will the program operate? How will it be structured?

A mission statement is a clear statement of purpose. It lets others know the intent of the program. A mission statement answers the question, "Why are we doing this?" It tells staff what the expectations for their performance are, and reminds participants why they are in the program. A mission statement sets the course and direction for the program. It is the standard to be achieved, the guiding philosophy of the program. It helps to reinforce the purpose of the program to the public, to visitors, and legislators or funding sources.

The chapter on Shock Incarceration in New York (by Aziz and Clark) later in this guide includes an example of a mission statement. A mission statement can be expressed in a paragraph, a page or a sentence. Frequently, slogans summarize the mission statement of an organization. For example, "Be all that you can be. The few, the brave, the proud. Who dares, wins! Gateway to Excellence. Aim high. We make the things that make things work better. Shock is a positive environment for human development in a caring community." Take time now to think through the mission statement for your boot camp program.

Thank you for taking the time to go through this process. The quality of your program will reflect your commitment to this planning. The work corrections professionals do is important and contributes to the quality of life for everyone in society. Your commitment to excellence adds measurably to the image of the corrections professional worldwide.

Mission Possible

Why a boot camp? _____

_____

_____

_____

Who is it for? _____

_____

What context? _____

When? Timeline? _____

Where? _____

Aftercare where? _____

How will it operate? _____

_____

_____

_____

Mission Statement

_____

_____

_____

_____

_____

"Without a vision, a people perish."

Bibliography

Argyris, Chris. 1991. Teaching Smart People How to Learn. *Harvard Business Review*. May-June.

Clark, Cheryl L. 1978. Network Program Plan. Unpublished document of the New York State Commission of Correction. Albany, New York.

———. 1979. Network Program Procedural Manual. Revised and updated 1981, 1983, 1985. Unpublished document of the New York State Department of Correctional Services. Albany, New York.

———. 1987, 1988. Shock Incarceration, Program Procedural Manual. Updates with R. W. Moscicki, 1989, 1991, 1994. Unpublished document of the New York State Department of Correctional Services. Albany, New York.

Clark, Cheryl L., David Aziz, and Doris MacKenzie. 1994. *Shock Incarceration in New York: Focus on Treatment*. Washington, D. C.: National Institute of Justice.

DePorter, Bobbi and Mike Hernacki. 1992. *Quantum Learning: Unleashing the Genius in You*. New York: Bantam Doubleday Dell Publishing Group, Inc.

Edmundson, Amy. 1987. *A Fuller Explanation: the Synergetic Geometry of R. Buckminster Fuller*. Boston: Birkhauser.

Fisher, Roger and William Ury, with Bruce Patton, ed. 1981. *Getting to YES! Negotiating Agreement Without Giving In*. Boston: Houghton Mifflin Company.

Fuller, R. Buckminster with Kiyoshi Kuromiya. 1981. *Critical Path*. New York: St. Martin's Press.

Glasser, William M., M.D. 1965. *Reality Therapy*. New York: Harper and Row Publishers.

———. 1969. *Schools Without Failure*. New York: Harper and Row Publishers.

———. 1984. *Control Theory*. New York: Harper and Row Publishers.

———. 1986. *Control Theory in the Classroom*. New York: Harper and Row Publishers.

———. 1995. *The Control Theory Manager*. New York: Harper Business.

Hallowell, Edward M., M.D., and John J. Rately, M.D. 1994. *Driven to Distraction*. New York: Pantheon Books, Random House.

Harvey, Jerry B. 1988. *The Abilene Paradox and Other Meditations on Management*. Boston: D. C. Heath and Company, in association with University Associates, San Diego.

Holt, John. 1964. *How Children Fail*, with an introduction by Allan Fromme, Ph.D. New York: Pitman Publishing Corporation.

―――. 1967. *How Children Learn*. New York: Pitman Publishing Corporation.

Jensen, Eric P. 1988. *Super-Teaching*. Del Mar, California: Turning Point for Teachers.

―――. 1989. *Student Success Secrets*. Hauppauge, New York: Barron's Educational Series, Inc.

MacKenzie, D. L. 1990. Boot Camps Grow in Number and Scope. Washington, D.C.: National Institute of Justice. November-December, 6-8.

MacKenzie, D. L., and D. B. Ballow. 1989. *Shock Incarceration Programs in State Correctional Jurisdictions—An Update*. Washington, D.C.: National Institute of Justice.

MacKenzie, D. L., L. A. Gould, L. M. Reichers, and J. W. Shaw. 1989. Shock Incarceration: Rehabilitation or Retribution? *Journal of Counseling, Services and Rehabilitation*. 14(2), 25-40.

MacKenzie, D. L., and Eugene E. Hebert, eds. 1996. *Correctional Boot Camps: A Tough Intermediate Sanction*. Washington, D.C.: National Institute of Justice.

MacKenzie, D. L., and Claire C. Souryal. 1991. Boot Camp Survey: Rehabilitation, Recidivism Reduction Outrank Punishment as Main Goals. *Corrections Today*. October, pp. 90-96.

New York State Department of Correctional Services. 1988. First Platoon Graduates from Shock Incarceration. *D.O.C.S. Today*. April. 1:12.

―――. 1988. Shock Incarceration Not For Men Only. *D.O.C.S. Today*. 2:7.

―――. 1992. Shock Incarceration Five Years Later. *D.O.C.S. Today*. 4:3.

New York State Department of Correctional Services and New York State Division of Parole. The Annual Report to the Legislature: Shock Incarceration in New York State (1989-1996). Albany, New York: Unpublished report by the Division of Program Planning, Research, and Evaluation and the Office of Policy Analysis and Information.

Parent, D. G. 1989. Shock Incarceration: An Overview of Existing Programs: Issues and Practices Report. Washington, D.C.: National Institute of Justice.

Peck, Scott, M.D. 1978. *The Road Less Traveled*. New York: Simon and Schuster.

————. 1987. *The Different Drum*. New York: Simon and Schuster.

Senge, Peter. 1991. *The Fifth Discipline: The Art and Practice of the Learning Organization*. New York: Doubleday Currency.

Sensenbrenner, Joseph. 1991. Quality Comes to City Hall. *Harvard Business Review*. March-April.

Sullivan, Dennis. 1980. *The Mask of Love*. Port Washington, New York: Kennikat Press.

Tobias, Cynthia Ulrich and John Zachariah. 1994. *The Way They Learn*. Colorado Springs: Focus on the Family.

Wheatley, Margaret J. 1992. *Leadership and the New Science, Learning About Organization from an Orderly Universe*. San Francisco: Berrett-Koehler Publishers, Inc.

Shock Incarceration in New York

David W. Aziz, Ph.D.

Program Research Specialist III
New York State Department of Correctional Services
Albany, New York

Cheryl L. Clark

Director of Shock Incarceration
New York State Department of Correctional Services
Albany, New York

Shock Incarceration in New York

Overview

The Shock Incarceration Program in New York is a six-month discipline and treatment oriented activity. Eligible inmates, both men and women, are provided the opportunity to develop life skills, which have proven to be important for success in society. The program includes rigorous physical activity, work, intensive regimentation and discipline, instruction in military bearing, courtesy, drills, physical exercise, Network community living skills, a structured work program, intensified substance abuse and alcohol counseling, and structured educational programming to the high school equivalency level.

There are eleven states with active Shock programs (Parent 1989). In that survey, there were clear differences between these Shock programs relating to size, length of incarceration, placement authority, program volume (both entering and exiting), facility location, and level of release supervision. Additionally, the National Institute of Justice-sponsored survey of Shock programs nationally (Parent 1989) indicated that these Shock programs differ a great deal in their stated goals and in the amount of emphasis they place on rehabilitation, education, and treatment, in general.

Based on the Department's review of the national survey, the major program components which distinguish the New York State Shock Incarceration Program from similar programs around the country appear to be its foundation in a therapeutic community approach, known as Network, and its strong emphasis on substance abuse treatment.

New York's Shock Incarceration Facilities offer more than military discipline. Inmates are provided the opportunity to develop life skills which are commonly viewed as being important for successful reintegration into society. Shock Incarceration is a therapeutic environment which is designed to address many of the problems which inmates may have.

> [It] is not simply a boot camp. (We) do not believe we can turn someone's life around simply by making them do push-ups, march in formation, or take orders. The strict physical regimen is a pivotal tool in teaching discipline and respect for individuals as well as teaching them about teamwork and getting along with others. But, of equal importance and weight in our program are the components that deal with education, professional and peer counseling plus drug and alcohol therapy. It is the combination of programs that we believe offers young offenders the chance to get their heads on straight and their lives in order. And, as part of the Shock program, (legislation) mandated that Parole follow inmates closely upon release to see how they perform (Philip Coombe to ACA Congress of Correction, August 1988).

The Shock Incarceration Program consists of numerous programs that have been used individually in the past and have provided some success. In fact, multitreatment programs like New York's Shock Incarceration Program have been viewed as the most successful means of achieving positive changes in inmate behavior. (See Gendreau and Ross 1979, p. 485).

In addition to voluntary participation, some of the components of these successful correctional rehabilitation programs include "formal rules, anti-criminal modeling and reinforcement, problem solving, use of community resources, quality of interpersonal relationships, relapse prevention and self-efficacy, and therapeutic integrity." (MacKenzie 1988, p.4). Shock Incarceration in New York State has all of these elements, within the framework of the military structure to help inmate participants learn to be productive citizens.

Shock Incarceration is based on the therapeutic community model known as Network. Network was designed, in 1977-1978, by Cheryl Clark and implemented in 1979, to establish living/learning units within correctional facilities that are supervised and operated by specially trained correction officers and supervisors.

An underlying basis for the Network philosophy is the theoretical model of the causes of delinquency known as "control theory." As part of the group of social and cultural support theories of criminality, "control theory" proposes that "nonconformity is a product of the failure of the social bond. Through the attachment of individuals to others, conformity is assured. When such attachments fail to develop or when they are disrupted, the internalization of legitimate norms becomes problematic" (Farrell and Swigert 1975, p. 211). Control theory is designed to explain conformity in individuals and implies that deviation from conformity (or criminal behavior) can be explained by variations in an individual's ties to the conventional social order.

When Shock Incarceration was being developed in New York, the Commissioner of Correctional Services, directed that the Network Program be an integral part of this initiative. He stated:

> Network has been operating in New York State Correctional Facilities since 1979 and has strengthened our resolve to identify and deal with the special needs of our staff and inmates. It has proved successful in providing an opportunity for positive growth and change. That's what Shock is all about, bridging the external discipline of the military model with an internalized system of positive values.
>
> A sense of self worth and personal pride are the foundation for living a responsible lifestyle. Network environments are structured to foster respect for self and others and to focus on developing positive self-images. Standards of behavior expected from all community members have been developed, tested and refined by staff and participants since Network's inception in January 1979. Orientation to Network includes a review of these standards and a discussion on how they support individuals and the life of the community. Upon admission to Shock, each participant is required to make a commitment to his/her personal goals and to live up to community standards. These standards are reviewed and evaluated regularly in community meetings.

All staff of Shock Facilities are trained in the principles of Network, which help to make Shock Facilities function in a way which is very similar to the therapeutic community model. As one British author noted, "The basic idea of the Therapeutic Community is to utilize the interactions which arise between people living closely together as the means of focusing on their behavioral difficulties and emotional problems and to harness the social forces of the group as the medium through which changes can be initiated" (Whitley 1973).

Control theory is a key component of the Shock philosophy in New York. It is assumed that inmates entering the Department of Correctional Services are individuals whose bonds to society are either weakened or broken, and exposure to the philosophies and practices of this program should help restore this bond. The Shock program emphasizes the need for individuals to strengthen their indirect controls, their internalized controls, and their controls over opportunities for conventional activities by emphasizing their responsibility for choices and the consequences of their behavior. Inmates who show no evidence of this restoration process and who fail to live up to their responsibilities while in the program are destined to fail in Shock and will be returned to a regular prison to finish serving their sentence.

The main proponent of the control theory of delinquency, Travis Hirschi asserted, is that "delinquent acts result when an individual's bond to society is weak or broken" (Hirschi 1969, p.16). This bond consists of attachment to others, commitment, involvement in conventional activities, and belief in a positive value system. The assumption made by control theorists is that people who are at risk of engaging in criminal behavior are individuals whose bond to society has been weakened or broken. We believe that exposure to programs such as Shock Incarceration can help strengthen or restore this bond.

Under the Network model, there are confrontation groups that are designed to deal with negative attitudes of participants. These groups provide clear perspectives on the consequences of dysfunctional behavior, while suggesting positive alternatives to that behavior. Yet, we are cautioned, this only works in the context of a caring community.

Learning experiences are also used in Shock Incarceration to remind both individuals and the large community of the need to change bad habits to useful ones. These experiences consist of physical tasks or processes which serve as a reminder of the consequences associated with negative behavior.

An evaluation of the Network program by our research staff found that "satisfactory participation in the Network program is positively related to successful post-release adjustment as measured by return to the Department" (New York State Department of Correctional Services 1987). The report found the actual return rate (24.5 percent) of the satisfactory program participants was notably less than the projected rate (39.5 percent) based on the Department's overall return rates.

In light of the theoretical and practical value of Network, it was selected to be a major component of Shock Incarceration in New York State. As adapted for Shock Incarceration, Network creates a therapeutic community which can address many of the needs and problems of Shock inmates, especially drug dependency.

Emphasis on Substance Abuse Services

Within this Network therapeutic community model of the Department's Shock Incarceration Correctional Facilities (SICFs), the practitioners emphasize substance abuse treatment due to the documented drug or alcohol abuse histories of the majority of program participants. This strong emphasis on alcohol and substance abuse treatment provided within the context of a therapeutic community is unique to New York State.

Shock programs in six states have some form of drug and alcohol treatment, most often based on principles of Alcoholics Anonymous. New York has a more extensive Alcohol and Substance Abuse Treatment (ASAT) program which all inmates must attend. It combines elements of behavioral modification, drug education, and Alcoholics Anonymous/Narcotics Anonymous (AA/NA) philosophies. It includes individual and group counseling and development of individualized treatment plans (Parent 1989).

Shock in New York State is a two-part program involving both institutional treatment and intensive parole supervision for graduates. This intensive parole supervision and aftercare treatment for Shock graduates is still another key distinction which makes the New York program unique. With the most intensive supervision caseloads in the state, parole officers working in Shock have used community service providers to help in job placement, relapse prevention, and educational achievement for these inmates. During the first six months after an inmate graduates, parole staff continue to help maintain the decision-making and conflict resolution counseling which was begun at the facilities.

Goals in Shock Incarceration

Experts generally believe that the "careful definition of program goals is essential to effective program design. It must precede initial planning, and must inform all stages of decision making as the program progresses" (Parent 1989).

New York State's Shock Incarceration Program was established by enabling legislation in July 1987 (Chapter 262 of the Laws of New York 1987). In total, New York State operates the largest Shock Incarceration Program in the nation at this time with an annual maximum capacity of 3,000 individuals, involving two six-month cycles of 1,500 inmates. There were 100 female beds, designated in December 1988 at Summit and later moved to Lakeview in May of 1992, to increase capacity to 160 shock beds for females and 20 female beds dedicated to orientation and screening.

The expressed purpose of the Omnibus bill that included this program was "to enable the State to protect the public safety by combining the surety of imprisonment with opportunities for timely return to society." With respect to the Shock Incarceration Program, the legislative bill specifically stated:

Certain young inmates will benefit from a special six-month program of intensive incarceration. Such incarceration should be provided to carefully selected inmates committed to the State Department of Correctional Services who are in need of substance abuse treatment and rehabilitation. An alternative form of incarceration stressing a highly structured and regimented routine, which will include extensive discipline, considerable physical work and exercise and intensive drug therapy, is needed to build character, instill a sense of maturity and responsibility, and promote a positive self-image for these offenders so that they will be able to return to society as law-abiding citizens. (New York State Senate, Bill 6116, 1987-1988 Regular Session, June 2, 1987).

As first stated in the 1988 report to the legislature, the goals of New York's Shock program are twofold. The first goal is to reduce the demand for bedspace. The second goal is to treat and release specially selected state prisoners earlier than their court-mandated minimum periods of incarceration without compromising the community protection rights of the citizenry.

For Shock to reduce the demand on prison bedspace, the program targets offenders who would definitely be incarcerated. Thus, in New York, the only inmates in the program are those who are sentenced to serve time in a state prison. Any long-term reductions in bedspace demand are dependent on inmates successfully completing the program and keeping their rates of return to the Department of Correctional Servives custody consistent with the overall return rate for the Department. New York has responded to these issues by:

- limiting judicial involvement in the decision-making process of who goes to Shock, thus assuring that Shock participants would have gone to prison anyway

- creating the program as a back-end based operation which is not an alternative to probation but rather a program for incarcerated felons

- creating a treatment oriented program which emphasizes the development of skills designed to lead inmates to successful parole outcomes

- creating a strong intensive parole supervision program for Shock graduates that enlists the aid of independent service providers

Philosophy

In keeping with its foundation in the Network program, the Shock philosophy is the same as the Network program philosophy.

Shock Philosophy

Shock is . . .

A positive environment for human development in a caring community where members can help themselves and each other. Staff and participants work together to establish and maintain positive, growth-filled environments within prisons. Community members focus on behavioral change and confront attitudes which are destructive to members and the life of the program.

A place to set goals and to practice behaviors which lead to successful living.

A disciplined lifestyle bringing a process for examining attitudes and values and for learning to deal with stress.

Staff

Staff are the primary role models in Shock Incarceration. We believe that staff attitudes and behavior influence inmates' attitudes towards change, growth and the development of positive social norms. In New York, the staff do the program with the inmates. We expect staff to model the program philosophy at all times. This is not a "do as I say, not as I do" program. A drill instructor with gravy stains on his uniform and a day old growth of beard cannot effectively instruct inmates on grooming standards. The supervisor, counselor, or teacher who does not model the effectiveness of what we want to teach, undermines what committed staff do.

Since staff in the program so strongly influence the results, they must be clear about the examples they set. Their values are reflected in their behavior. The values that they are reinforcing among the inmates are influenced by the congruency of their words and actions. For example, our first general order for inmates is "I will follow all orders given by all staff at all times." As such, it is incumbent upon the staff to ensure that their orders are lawful, ethical and moral. We emphasize the SMART rule in every aspect of the program. Orders given must be Specific, Measurable, Attainable, Realistic, and Timely. An officer who is out of shape and could not do ten pushups on a good day should not be ordering an inmate to "drop and give me 100."

To this end, we expect staff to model what we are teaching in the Shock program. They are expected to "walk the talk," to demonstrate congruency, to show that the model works. We also emphasize an interdisciplinary approach to the program with consistency among the security, treatment and administrative staff. If inmates can play one discipline against another, the whole foundation of the program is undermined.

Methods

Shock in New York enables participants to internalize a positive, prosocial system of values designed to raise their self esteem. One emphasis is how their old values and choices resulted in their being excluded from society and their freedom being restricted. While inmates are in Shock, we want them to experience that positive values can produce positive results, and that a positive system of values is the key to changing behavior. Inmates participate in structured activities designed to prepare them for successful reintegration into society.

A sense of self-worth and personal pride are the foundation of living a responsible lifestyle. Shock environments are structured to foster respect for self and others and to focus on supportive community living methods. These methods have been developed, tested and refined by staff and participants over time and have been codified into a set of community standards.

William Glasser, a proponent of control theory, said " . . . to be worthwhile we must maintain a satisfactory standard of behavior" (Glasser 1965, p. 10). In the forward to Glasser's book, O. Hobart Mower reemphasized " . . . human beings get into emotional binds, not because their standards are too high, but because their performance has been, and is, too low." It flows from this premise that when we raise our standards of behavior, we raise our self-esteem. This is the core of our approach to change emphasized in every aspect of Shock from physical training in the morning through drill and ceremony, community service work, academic education, decision making skills and substance abuse treatment. From 5:30 A.M. to 9:30 P.M. we want every experience of the day to support inmates to build life skills that lead to success. All program activities are mandatory and are focused in the following areas.

Military Bearing

Inmates receive intensive instruction in military bearing, courtesy, drill, and physical exercise. Participants are initially oriented into the activities by drill instructors who are corrections officers. The drill instructors and other corrections officers work with inmate platoons, teaching and reinforcing military bearing throughout the entire six-month program. All correction employees reinforce military bearing in every activity throughout the program day.

Drill and Ceremony

Inmates move to and from every activity in Shock in formation. The purpose of drill and ceremony is to teach inmates pride in the way they carry themselves and to learn to move as a coordinated unit, emphasis in pride and dignity permeates everything we do in the program.

Physical Training

Each day at 5:45 A.M., the Shock program begins with forty-five minutes of calisthenics and a half hour run. The physical training is based on the United States Army Field Manual 21-20 with exercises modified to emphasize the importance of group support. We do no "ability" training or individualized exercises. The purpose of physical training in Shock is to enhance the inmate's physical fitness and well-being and to support them in a healthy lifestyle. By starting each day with physical training, the inmates are better prepared for the demands of the sixteen-hour Shock day. We have seen that inmate's academic scores, their attention spans, their physical and mental health and well being are enhanced by this phase in the program.

Treatment Program

Inmates participate in structured activities designed to prepare them for successful reintegration into society. Program activities are mandatory and are focused in the following areas.

Network

The foundation of the treatment program in Shock, emphasizes community living and socialization skills. Each platoon lives as a unit, meeting daily in community meetings to resolve problems and reflect on their progress in the program. The core curriculum of Network is a course emphasizing 5 steps to Decision Making, and a life skills program in which inmates practice behaviors which will help them to develop a responsible life style. They practice the discipline to seek realistic goals through honest effort.

Network therapeutic community living is an opportunity to live and practice the concepts taught in the Choices curriculum. Network promotes the positive involvement of inmate participants in an environment which has as its focus their successful reintegration into society. Network encourages inmates to seek out other positive groups in their home community to continue this reinforcement.

The Choices curriculum is taught in tandem with the 12 Steps to Recovery as espoused in Alcoholics Anonymous (AA) and Narcotics Anonymous (NA). As participants go through the twenty-six weeks of Shock Incarceration, they study each step of choices and the 12 Step program. Every aspect of the week, community meetings, groups, prerelease and some academic classes, are tied into the theme of the week.

The theme of the decision making curriculum taught in Network is "Choose Your Life, Live Your Choice." The curriculum is designed to teach inmates how to get their needs met appropriately. William Glasser's approach to control theory emphasizes the impact of internal controls and how they stem from basic needs. Glasser's theory says that the innate drive to meet ones needs is so strong that if these needs are not met in positive and constructive ways, they will be met in negative and destructive ways. We want inmates to learn how to get their needs met in responsible ways, that is, by not interfering with others getting their needs met (See Glasser 1965, 1986, 1987).

Under the Network design, peer confrontation groups are used to deal with the negative attitudes of participants. The strength of peer groups is the lack of authority-based coercive feedback to inmates. These peer groups provide clear perspectives on the consequences of dysfunctional behavior, while suggesting positive alternatives to that behavior. Yet, this only works in the context of a caring community. As with all communities, there are rules and standards for behavior to which members must adhere. If rule breaking is detected, the community will react.

> The pressure of the group, accepting, yet confronting, interpreting, pointing out, suggesting modifications, understanding and facilitation problem solving will be a different reaction from the authoritarian suppression he has hitherto provoked, and he may come to see that for him also there can be the possibility of a shift of behavior roles in this different type of society. If he continues to act out, then the community imposed sanctions mount in parallel with his misdemeanors until it becomes clear that he must change his pattern if he wants to stay or if he wants to continue in his old ways (and he is welcome to do so)—he must leave (Whitley 1973, p. 56).

Alcohol and Substance Abuse Treatment

Alcohol and Substance Abuse Treatment includes substance abuse education and group counseling. Nearly all of the offenders who participate in Shock have committed drug offenses or have committed crimes related to drug or alcohol abuse, or are from dysfunctional families or community environments where drug and alcohol abuse is prevalent. Inmates participate in classroom and treatment sessions several times each week throughout their participation in the Shock program for a total of 260 hours during the six-month program. Sessions are related to changing attitudes and habits of substance abuse. This program is based on the Alcoholics Anonymous and Narcotics Anonymous philosophy of abstinence and recovery.

The combined choices and alcohol and substance abuse treatment curriculum has been designed to involve inmates in experiential exercises, journaling, group discussions, and activities to allow them to practice the skills they are learning and plan for their future, post release. Our approach to learning is that the most long-lasting benefits result from practice.

Education

A structured educational program is developed for each inmate including remedial education, basic high school equivalency classes, and preparation for the general equivalency diploma. Inmates participate in a minimum of twelve hours per week in the academic school program, for a total of 300 hours of academic classes in six months. Those inmates in Shock who already have high school diplomas assist others as peer tutors.

"Muscle Memory" learning techniques insure that the program concepts which are taught to inmates are anchored in their experience. Cadences, sung as they march or run, reinforce the message of the sessions. Throughout their time in Shock, inmates are reminded that AA and NA meetings are everywhere in the world and that they are taking the first step in a program of lifelong recovery and choices about freedom. They are daily reminded that limits exist in everyone's life and that limits are not limitations. Choices teaches that limits are facts of life, while limitations are feelings and attitudes that can be changed.

Counseling

On arrival at the Shock facility, inmates meet with guidance counseling staff to develop an individualized treatment plan and to discuss any special needs that they have. Subsequently and for the remainder of the program, individual counseling sessions are scheduled on an as-needed basis by guidance, alcohol and substance abuse treatment, Network and parole staff. This includes an exit counseling session held just prior to a graduation. Guidance counselors also provide family outreach and reintegration planning, and run prerelease classes.

Group counseling sessions occur on a regular basis throughout the six-month program to help the platoons adjust to each phase of the program. These are held in conjunction with alcohol and substance abuse treatment and Network sessions for a total of 150 group counseling hours in six months. PreRelease programs are supervised by the senior corrections counselor. Guidance staff, in conjunction with parole staff, provide thirty-six hours of prerelease sessions to the inmates throughout their six-month stay.

Evaluation

Inmates are closely supervised and rated on a daily and weekly basis by drill instructors, crew officers, network officers, teachers, Alcohol and Substance Abuse Treatment staff, kitchen workers, and all staff with inmate contact, in five areas of participation. In addition, individual interviews and staff meetings are conducted regularly to review inmates' progress.

Earned Eligiblity

A six-month earned eligibility form is completed by the corrections counselor prior to the inmate's graduation from the program. An inmate who successfully completes the program is awarded a certificate of earned eligibility, which is forwarded to the parole board for their consideration.

Parole

Inmates are involved with parole staff from the beginning of their participation in Shock Incarceration and are closely supervised by parole on release. Parole staff develop a needs assessment and assist in the prerelease training provided to inmates during the six-month program. On release, parolees are supervised individually and in groups, continuing the decision making program begun in Shock Incarceration and applying the skills during their reintegration to society.

In alcohol and substance abuse treatment and in Network, we emphasize the need to change people, places and things and "90 meetings in 90 days" as well as the importance of having a sponsor to mentor and support them in their continuing sobriety. We recognize the need to belong as a powerful driving force in human beings and encourage them to seek support from post-release groups that will continue to reinforce their positive growth.

Shock in New York State is a two-part program involving both institutional treatment and intensive parole supervision for graduates. This intensive parole supervision and aftercare treatment for Shock graduates is still another key distinction, which makes the New York program unique. With the most intensive supervision caseloads in the state, parole officers working with Shock graduates have used community service providers to help enhance job placement, relapse prevention, and educational achievement. During the first six months after an inmate graduates, parole staff continue to help maintain the decision making and conflict resolution counseling which was begun at the facilities.

Many Shock graduates have done so well in post release that several have been hired by service provider agencies as employees. Graduates work with those newly released to help them reintegrate into the community. They facilitate Network in the community groups, provide life skills training, vocational training, services in the Alcohol Council and Fellowship Center in New York City and a range of other services. A team of Shock graduates is working with the New York City Probation Department teaching Network concepts to probationers. Periodically, successful graduates also return to Shock facilities to meet with inmates in the program to tell their stories and help prepare the inmates for the second phase of Shock.

Summary

We believe that Shock is a better way of doing prison. We keep inmates constantly engaged and programmed in what can be described as a shorter, more intense incarceration experience. We can build self esteem, detoxify addicts, and teach a modicum of responsibility to all who complete the program. In sum, we provide a prescription and the tools for inmates to succeed. There are many community resources for these offenders to follow-up on the prescription but failure to follow the prescription, as in the medical arena, can lead to relapse and recommitment.

New York State Shock Incarceration Program

W E E K	Alcohol and Substance Abuse Treatment Program	Network Decision Making Course	Pre-Release
1	ZERO WEEKS	OVERVIEW	
2	12 STEPS TO RECOVERY	INTRODUCTION TO NETWORK	
3	DENIAL	CONTROL THEORY	Unit 1 Introduction to Pre-Release Personal Shock Budget Short Term Goal Setting
4			
5	SELF	OPERATING IMAGE	
6	HISTORY		Unit 2 Social Security Cards Birth Certificates
7	1. We admitted that we were powerless over our addiction, that our lives had become unmanageable.	1. See the Situation Clearly	Unit 3 Self Awareness and Self Esteem Motivation Communication Skills
8			
9	2. Came to believe that a Power greater than ourselves could restore us to sanity.	2. I Am Accepted	Unit 4 Stress Management Anger Management
10			
11	3. Made a decision to turn our will and lives over to the care of God as we understood Him.	3. Know What You Want	Unit 5 Domestic Violence
12			
13	4. Made a searching and fearless moral inventory of ourselves.	4. Expanding Possibilities	Unit 6 Family Planning Sexually Transmitted Diseases Parenting
14	5. Admitted to God, to ourselves, and to another human being the exact nature of our wrongs.	5. Evaluating and Deciding	
15	6. Were entirely ready to have God remove all these defects of character.	6. Acting on Decisions	Unit 7 Family Counseling Relationships
16	7. Humbly ask Him to remove our shortcomings.	7. Freedom to Choose Your Attitude	
17	8. Made a list of all persons we had harmed and became willing to make amends to them all.	8. Choosing Responsibility	Unit 8 Career Planning Employment Search Job Applications Job Interviews Resumes
18	9. Made direct amends to such people wherever possible, except when to do so would injure them or others.	9. Economic Style	

New York State Shock Incarceration Program (continued)

19	10. Continued to take personal inventory and when we were wrong, promptly admitted it.	10. Social Style	Unit 9 Targeted Job Tax Credits Vocational Development Programs Economic Opportunity Center Education and Training Opportunities
20	11. Sought through prayer and meditation to improve our conscious contact with God as we understand Him, praying only for knowledge of His will for us and the power to carry that out.	11. Personal Style	
21	REVIEW: The first 4 steps and RELAPSE	- REVIEW CHOICES -	Unit 10 Conditions of Parole After Shock Budget
22		INMATES	
23	Prevention Strategies	LEAD SEMINARS	Unit 11 Nutrition and Health Recovery After Shock Fellowship Center Intake
24			
25			
26	12. Having had a spiritual awakening as a result of these steps, we tried to carry this message to others and to practice these principles in all our affairs.	12. Affirmation Gift Workshop	Unit 12 Community Preparation Long Term Goals Graduation Preparation

Shock Incarceration Correctional Facilities

Pursuant to Article 26-A and Section 70 of the Correction Law, the Departmental of Correctional Services designated the following correctional facilities to be Shock Incarceration Facilities:

Facility	Effective Date	Original Capacity	Capacity in 1993
Monterey	September 1, 1987	250 Inmates	300 Inmates
Summit	April 11, 1988	250 Inmates	250 Inmates
Moriah	March 27, 1989	250 Inmates	300 Inmates
Lakeview	September 11, 1989	750 Inmates	1,080 Inmates

Initially, inmates were between the ages of sixteen and twenty-four. In July of 1989 the law was amended to include participants between the ages of twenty-six and twenty-nine. Effective April 14, 1992, all inmates between the ages of sixteen and thirty-five, who are sentenced to their first term of state incarceration for a nonviolent felony, and who are within three years of parole eligibility, may complete six months of Shock Incarceration to be eligible for early release consideration.

Bibliography

Clark, Cheryl L. 1978. Network Program Plan. Unpublished document of the New York State Commission Of Correction. Albany, New York.

———. 1979. Network Program Procedural Manual. Revised and updated 1981, 1983, 1985. Unpublished document of the New York State Department of Correctional Services. Albany, New York.

———. 1987, 1988. Updates with R. W. Moscicki, 1989, 1991, 1994. Shock Incarceration, Program Procedural Manual. Unpublished document of the New York State Department of Correctional Services. Albany, New York.

Clark, Cheryl L., David Aziz, and Doris MacKenzie. 1994. *Shock Incarceration in New York: Focus on Treatment*. Washington, D. C.: National Institute of Justice.

Farrell, Ron and Lynn Swigert. 1979. Social Deviance. Philadelphia: Lippencott.

Gendreau, Paul and Robert Ross. 1979. Effective Correctional Treatment: Bibliotherapy for Cynics. *Crime and Delinquency*. (25):463-489. October 1979.

Glasser, William, M.D. 1984. *Control Theory*. New York: Harper and Row Publishers.

———. 1986. *Control Theory in the Classroom*. New York: Harper and Row Publishers.

———. 1965. *Reality Therapy*. New York: Harper and Row Publishers.

Hirschi, Travis. 1969. *Causes of Delinquency*. Berkeley and Los Angeles: University of California Press.

MacKenzie, D. L. 1988. Evaluating Shock Incarceration in Louisiana: A Review of the first year. Unpublished report by the Louisiana Department of Corrections.

———. 1990. Boot Camps Grow in Number and Scope. Washington, D.C.: National Institute of Justice.

MacKenzie, D. L., and D. B. Ballow. 1989. *Shock Incarceration Programs in State Correctional Jurisdictions—An Update*. Washington, D.C.: National Institute of Justice.

MacKenzie, D. L., L. A. Gould, L. M. Reichers, and J. W. Shaw. 1989. Shock Incarceration: Rehabilitation or Retribution? *Journal of Offender Counseling, Services and Rehabilitation*. 14(2), 25-40.

MacKenzie, D. L., and Eugene E. Hebert, eds. 1996. *Correctional Boot Camps: A Tough Intermediate Sanction*. Washington, D.C.: National Institute of Justice.

MacKenzie, D. L., and Claire C. Souryal. 1991. Boot Camp Survey: Rehabilitation, Recidivism Reduction Outrank Punishment as Main Goals. *Corrections Today*. October, pp. 90-96.

New York State Department of Correctional Services. 1987. Follow Up Study of a Sample of Participants in the Network Program, August.

———. 1988. First Platoon Graduates from Shock Incarceration. *D.O.C.S. Today*. April. 1:12.

———. 1988. Shock Incarceration Not For Men Only. *D.O.C.S. Today*. 2:7.

———. 1992. Shock Incarceration Five Years Later. *D.O.C.S. Today*. 4:3.

New York State Department of Correctional Services and New York State Division of Parole. The Annual Report to the Legislature: Shock Incarceration in New York State (1989-1996). Albany, New York: Unpublished report by the Division of Program Planning, Research, and Evaluation and the Office of Policy Analysis and Information.

New York State of Division of Program Planning, Research, and Evaluation. 1993. Characteristics of Inmates Under Custody 1985 - 1992. Albany, New York: New York State Department of Correctional Services.

Parent, D. G. 1989. Shock Incarceration: An Overview of Existing Programs: Issues and Practices Report. Washington, D.C.: National Institute of Justice.

Whitley, Stuart. 1973. Dealing With Deviants: The Treatment of Antisocial Behavior. New York: Shocken Books.

The Oregon Summit Program

Bill Beers

Superintendent, Shutter Creek Correctional Institution
Oregon Department of Corrections
North Bend, Oregon

Chris Duval

Program Manager, Shutter Creek Correctional Institution and SUMMIT Program
Oregon Department of Corrections
North Bend, Oregon

The Oregon Department of Corrections' boot camp for adult male and female incarcerated felony offenders is located at Shutter Creek Correctional Institution (SCCI) in North Bend, Oregon. It was established in March, 1994, and designed to ease prison overcrowding and have an impact on criminal recidivism.

SUMMIT is an acronym for "Success Using Motivation, Morale, Intensity, and Treatment." The program emphasizes cognitive change, basic education and work skills in a military framework, teaching discipline, teamwork, and responsibility.

The SUMMIT logo was created to emphasize the cooperative relationship between staff and offenders, as they work together to reach the common goal of change.

Implementation

The Oregon SUMMIT Program was mandated by the 1993 Oregon Legislature in House Bill 2481, sponsored by Representative Peter Courtney. Oregon Department of Corrections Director Frank Hall initiated the program, choosing to model it after the successful New York Shock Incarceration Program. Superintendent Ron Moscicki and Program Manager Cheryl Clark of the New York Department of Correctional Services provided the initial immersion style training for the staff of the SUMMIT Program just prior to the boot camp opening in March of 1994.

Change Is Possible

Shutter Creek Correctional Institution was a minimum security work camp prior to the implementation of the boot camp, and continues to house approximately 100 general population inmate workers as well as 166 boot camp participants. The general population workers provide fire protection for Shutter Creek Correctional Institution, as well as maintenance, laundry and food service duties on site, and are employed off site on public service projects in the forests, parks, highways, beaches and waterways in the area.

For staff to make the transition to being "change agents" as well as "keepers," Shutter Creek Correctional Institution management staff realized that a culture change would have to occur. Nearly one year before the boot camp actually opened, critical training was delivered to 100 percent of the staff, in the form of Gordon Graham's "Framework for Change." This training changed the culture at Shutter Creek Correctional Institution to one of a change program. To be successful, staff in a change program must believe that change is possible, that inmates are worthy of dignity and respect, and be invested in role modeling the prosocial qualities they are promoting in the inmates.

By the time of the immersion training, just prior to receiving the boot camp's first platoon of inmates, a significant number of staff had relocated to other facilities, and the majority of the staff remaining truly believed in the concept of a change program. Part of the SUMMIT Philosophy, printed below, states the program's direction clearly: "A place where what we believe and say, is what we do."

The Oregon Summit is:

A positive community, valuing each member as capable of change and worthy of dignity and respect.

An opportunity for staff and offenders to work together as a team to build mature, responsible citizens.

An intense time for community members to focus on behavioral change and to confront attitudes which are destructive to members and to society.

A place to set goals and practice new behaviors which lead to successful living.

A challenge; demanding individual effort and determination, and requiring teamwork, commitment and participation from all community members.

A disciplined life style, leading to accomplishments which raise individual self-esteem and community pride.

A place where what we believe and say is what we do.

A chance to change, to confront mistakes and to accept responsibility for our lives.

To achieve congruence and integrity as a change program, staff at SUMMIT are held to high standards of dress, attitude and behavior.

Motivation to Participate

Inmates volunteer for the six-month program and are motivated to do so, in that upon successful completion of both the institutional 180-day phase and the 30-day transitional leave in the community, they are released to a term of post-prison supervision ordered by the sentencing judge. Inmates typically receive from two-to-thirty months off of their original sentences. This "carrot" is essential in motivating the inmates to begin the program.

Without some meaningful initial motivation, inmates more likely would quit rather than endure long days of focused activity and the uncomfortable change process.

However, the time cut becomes a secondary motivator as the inmates begin to experience the program and their potential for change. When the inmates realize that they can change who they have been and live more productive and satisfying lives, they gradually rely less on external motivators and more on their changing internal values.

Participant Restrictions

The legislative bill which created the Oregon SUMMIT placed certain restrictions on participants. The program includes males and females from the age of juvenile remand through age forty. It excludes those convicted of sex offenses, most first-degree crimes, and mandatory minimum sentences. Also excluded are those with recent escape histories and unresolved detainers. Americans with Disabilities Act guidelines are followed in the health screening process prior to acceptance into the program. Eligibility screening is done on site, with an office specialist II maintaining computer records of applicants and completing background searches.

Platoon Formation

Inmates who qualify are accepted into a platoon and brought to the Shutter Creek Correctional Institution in platoons of approximately sixty inmates. Male inmates are housed in fifty-bed dormitories (overbooked by means of cots to manage bed space efficiently), and female inmates are housed in a sixteen-bed women's dormitory. Three platoons are in progress at any given time, each approximately two months behind the other. One platoon graduates every two months, and the following week, a new platoon arrives.

Arrival

Drama and tension play a large role as the new boot camp inmates arrive on site in Department of Corrections' Blue Bird buses. The minute the inmates come off the buses, drill instructors are delivering instructions and the inmates are taught the rudiments of military bearing. Dignity and respect are foremost, as the drill instructors coach, direct, assist, and insist on appropriate form and behavior. Staff use the titles "Mr." or "Ms." to address inmates. Inmates address staff by their title and last name. No smoking nor use of tobacco products is allowed.

Inmates are given a hot meal as soon as they arrive because it relieves some of the natural tension of arrival. Meals at SUMMIT are eaten in silence, with the inmates side-stepping through the chow line, and eating without distraction. The inmates must eat all that they take. The diet includes the availability of extra carbohydrates and adequate liquids to ensure good health for the high level of physical activity at SUMMIT.

After their initial hot meal, the inmates are then searched. Their property is inventoried, and they receive military-style hair cuts from the security staff. To meet the needs of the female inmates for whom shaved heads would be unacceptable socially, women's haircuts are two inches long, and done by a barber. The reason for the haircuts for both males

and females is not for humiliation, but to demonstrate military-style commitment to the program and cohesiveness as a platoon.

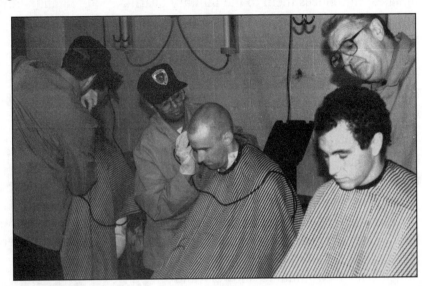

The inmates' transport clothing is exchanged for a set of gray sweats, blue watch cap and tennis shoes. This will be their garb for the next two weeks: Zero Weeks, named for the concept of starting at "ground zero."

Program Schedule

During Zero Weeks, inmates are oriented to the boot camp program concepts and schedule, and participate in daily double sessions of physical training (PT). After Zero Weeks, physical training is only once a day at 5:30 A.M., but there is also a confidence course and athletics each weekend. The purpose of physical training at SUMMIT is to teach teamwork, precision, and motivation, with a bonus of enhanced physical fitness. The inmates are not pushed to reach endurance goals, but they perform exercises and run together at a pace suitable for all platoon members.

On the morning of the second day at SUMMIT, the superintendent speaks to the platoon about his hopes for the platoon, and informs them of the three issues which will not be tolerated: romance, racism, and violence.

However, because the inmates have limited ability to control their impulses early in the program, staff are trained to help protect the inmates from violating these restrictions. In essence, the staff help the inmates have the chance to change by ensuring that they adhere to strict rules regarding male/female interaction, and by providing direct supervision at all times, and by preventing outbursts of violence or racism.

The program manager follows the superintendent's speech with an orientation to expected classroom behavior and program concepts. At SUMMIT, it is important for the administrative staff to have direct contact with the inmates in the program. It assists in convincing them that all SUMMIT staff, from the superintendent on, take this program seriously and are here to assist the inmates in the change process.

The remainder of Zero Weeks provides an orientation to the SUMMIT program for the inmates, introduces them to the military bearing required and allows them time to adjust to the new regimen, prior to the delivery of actual program materials. Classes are held which teach the inmates the basics of all program elements. At the end of Zero Weeks, a two-hour "captain's drill" is held. This brings the platoon together as a team through intense physical exercise and motivation. After the captain's drill, the inmates receive khaki pants, white shirts and ties, and black boots. This will be their classroom attire for the remainder of the program.

The inmates are given their classroom clothing at the end of Zero Weeks as a mark of their progress. In SUMMIT, everything is earned, and everything has a purpose that supports the process of change. Incentives are important in personal growth, and they motivate the inmates to keep up their effort.

Each sixteen-hour day at SUMMIT begins with reveille at 5:30 A.M., followed by an hour of physical training, breakfast, flag call, and then day-long work squads or program classes until 3:30 P.M. At that time, inmates take two-minute showers and dress for community meeting. The daily community meetings are held from 4:00-5:00 P.M., followed by evening flag call, dinner, and then more classes from 6:00-9:00 P.M. After a half hour in the dormitories to prepare for the next day, shine boots, make one phone call per week, and assist peers, the lights are out at 9:30 P.M. This schedule is followed seven days a week, for twenty-six weeks. Additionally, sandwiched into every moment, is drill and ceremony, and extensive memory work. "Intense" describes the program well.

Military Framework

Since the inception of the Oregon SUMMIT Program, staff have observed other boot camps, and they discovered that the term "boot camp" describes a wide variety of programs that sometimes have little in common.

The military framework of the Oregon SUMMIT Program is designed to teach self-control, self-discipline, teamwork, and pride in community. Interdependence among the peers in the platoon is fostered by the military framework, which leads to the practice of other-centered behaviors, the basis for community involvement when the inmates leave the program.

Cognitive Change

Within the military framework, the heart of the program is a modified therapeutic community, centered on the concept of cognitive change: the idea that changing thinking results in a change in behavior.

The change agents in the Oregon SUMMIT Program are not only staff members, but they are also the inmate peers in each platoon. This community approach places the burden of individual change on the group, leading to a change of heart, rather than a change due to demand from an authority figure or role model. True heartfelt, lasting change is born out of self-choice which is then internalized. Change that occurs from compliance often returns to the undesirable former behavior once the authority figure or coercion is absent.

The cognitive change basis of the Oregon SUMMIT Program is the pioneering work of Dr. Yochelson and Dr. Samenow in *The Criminal Personality*, which identified patterns of thinking called Thinking Errors common in the thinking of criminals. The curriculum used at SUMMIT was developed by Jack Bush, through the National Institute of Correction (NIC). Rather than relying on just one means to teach cognitive change, the Oregon SUMMIT Program brings together several cognitive approaches for maximum effectiveness.

Gordon Graham's "Breaking Barriers" is a video and activity model that promotes the concept that change is possible. Mr. Graham, an ex-convict, turned his life around and is a very effective role model for the inmates. In the videos, he captures their attention for hands-on exercises which assist the inmates in seeing their own situation more clearly, and gaining an understanding that change is truly possible for each of them.

The Franklin Reality Model video, created by the Franklin Quest Company (creators of the Franklin Day Planners and Time Management Seminars), features Chief Executive Officer Hyrum Smith in a video presentation which is an easily understood means to identify beliefs which do not work for individuals in the long term. Inmates who find that their beliefs are blocking their ability to change their behavior are able to use this "model" to discover alternate beliefs to implement, which will meet their needs over time.

To further enhance the cognitive restructuring process at SUMMIT, the inmates participate in Dr. Merry Hansen's Pathfinders, a cognitive skills-cognitive restructuring, hands-on program of self-change. This life-skills course covers such topics as team building, communication, job readiness, anger management, time management, and problem solving. In addition, we give the Keirsey Temperament Sorter along with classroom instruction in personality types, helping the inmates to know themselves better, as well as to understand others.

The goals of cognitive change at the Oregon SUMMIT are to hold inmates accountable by identifying and addressing their thinking errors and teaching them the skills needed to intervene and overcome these unhealthy thinking patterns which have resulted in socially unacceptable behaviors.

Inmates learn personal accountability for their behavior—that their criminal behavior is a result of the choices they have made, rather than due to outside influences, abuse, or chance. They learn that they have the ability to change if they desire to do so. In short, they learn to see themselves as others see them and to take responsibility for who they are and what they have done.

In addition to attending eight and a half hour classes in cognitive change and Pathfinders each week, cognitive change elements permeate the entire program at SUMMIT, integrating the concepts into the daily lives of the inmates from reveille until lights out for six months: a good beginning for a new habit.

By using a continuum of cognitive restructuring (understanding and overcoming errors in thinking) and cognitive skills (learning new ways to deal with problems and emotions, and new communication skills), the Oregon SUMMIT Program brings intensity to the change process and enhances the inmates' abilities to internalize new attitudes and behaviors, which meet their needs and the needs of others, over time.

Program Elements

In addition to the military framework, therapeutic community and cognitive change parts of the program, other program elements are delivered to the inmates to provide them with the life skills and information they need to become productive members of their communities on release.

Alcohol and Drug Services

Alcohol and drug services at SUMMIT consist of an hour and a half per week of alcohol and drug education, an hour and a half per week of discussion groups and three hours per week of 12 Step meetings. These services are "pretreatment" in that they are designed to prepare inmates to benefit from alcohol and drug treatment in their communities following successful completion of SUMMIT.

Emphasis is placed on the key concepts of addiction, the physical and social effects of alcohol and drug abuse, identifying denial and other defenses, the 12 Steps of Alcoholics Anonymous, Narcotics Anonymous, and recovery planning. Each inmate prepares a detailed and individualized relapse prevention and recovery plan which is shared with the counselor and the parole officer, and incorporated into the inmate's release plan.

Work Squads

Inmates work off-site three days a week, performing community service work and physical labor for nonprofit agencies, under the direction of the correctional work crew supervisors. The skills gained in cooperative work experience and improving community resources, such as beach clean up, stream enhancement, forest preservation, and playground repair, assist the inmates in learning pride in accomplishments, time management, decision making, and teamwork.

Education

Education classes at SUMMIT consist of approximately thirteen hours a week of adult basic education, work towards general education development certificates, and learning computer skills and resume writing.

Each inmate is also given Dr. Mary Meeker's Structure of Intellect (SOI) test, which is a practical application of J. P. Guilford's theory, the Structure of Intellect. This test measures abilities for learning, and includes follow-up modules which develop and enhance abilities for learning.

One goal of the Oregon SUMMIT program is to take advantage of the unique nature of our intense six-month program, to use this setting to give the inmates more skills in how to learn, not just more education, which they can obtain in a variety of settings. The Structure of Intellect test and modules achieve this goal. Four of the thirteen hours of education time each week are devoted to Structure of Intellect modules.

We also plan to implement the associated Integrated Practice Protocol (IPP), a diagnostic system, which looks behind cognitive problems to see if there are perceptual dysfunctions that underlie learning difficulties. The goal is to provide physical exercise protocols which remedy a broad range of these perceptual dysfunctions.

Color Vision Screening

Another innovative element of the Oregon SUMMIT Program, is color vision screening, which evaluates each inmate's need for visual color remediation. People with this particular deficiency suffer from lack of comprehension and difficulty in reading written material, due to apparent movement of written characters. We remediate this problem by using a personalized series of mylar color sheets to bring the written characters into sharp focus for individuals with this problem. The Oregon SUMMIT is committed to continuing to reach for the possible causes of lack of academic and social accomplishment and to offer means to overcome these obstacles.

Parole Readiness

Parole planning classes, held once each week, prepare the inmates for the positive relationship they will have with their parole officer after they are graduated from SUMMIT. The inmates memorize the general conditions of parole, as well as work with the counselor to create an appropriate parole plan, which will enhance their ability to remain in the community, crime free. The inmates' positive relationships with their parole officers are emphasized. In the fourth month of the SUMMIT program, a conference call is held with the parole officer, the SUMMIT alcohol and drug counselor, the SUMMIT platoon counselor, and the inmate, to discuss the parole plan and conditions. Prior to the conference call, each inmate has written a letter to his or her parole officer which includes a statement of accountability, clearly articulating what the inmate has done in the community and how he or she expects that to be different, as well as committing to five goals to be achieved after leaving SUMMIT.

This positive relationship with the parole officers is a critical bond to forge, and is unusual, in that most parolees from prisons view their parole officers as authority figures out to catch them doing something wrong, and to be feared, not as coaches who are assisting them in staying crime free.

Personal Wellness

Personal wellness classes are held weekly and are delivered by the health services staff on site. Inmates are taught how to evaluate their need to seek health care, identification of lifestyle choices which affect their health, and new skills to integrate positive health practices into their lives. Fitness evaluations are performed at intervals during the program to measure inmates' progress.

Spiritual Wellness

Spiritual wellness combines denominational worship for those inmates who choose the services offered, with comparative religion classes for those inmates who do not choose denominational worship. A part-time chaplain and many community volunteers assist in the effort to provide religious services.

Visitor Counseling

Inmates are allowed to have visitors every other weekend. The visiting period is three and a half hours long, due to the infrequency of the visits. Another value of a lengthy visiting period, is the ability to offer visitor counseling. The platoon counselor works one weekend day to be available to provide this element of the program. The purpose is to keep the visitors, friends, and loved ones of the inmates up to date on the changes taking place in the inmates.

The platoon counselor meets briefly with each inmate and his or her visitors, letting the inmate share some of what he or she is learning, and answering questions about the process. Once during each platoon's program, inmates and their visitors see the Franklin Reality Model video. The inmates demonstrate the concept that our beliefs often lead to actions which do not always meet our needs over time. The response from the visitor counseling program has been positive and has resulted in a smoother transition for the inmates and their families and friends when they return home.

Tools for Change

The Oregon SUMMIT Program offers a wide variety of support for personal change to maximize effectiveness and make every moment count. Three styles of learning are used in all program elements: visual, auditory, and kinesthetic—see it, say it, do it. Using the kinesthetic or "muscle" memory enhances the inmates' ability to retain information and concepts.

Memory Anchors

Inmates memorize the philosophy, community standards, general orders, 12 Steps to Recovery, general conditions of parole, evaluation categories, and community meeting elements. Memory work keeps the criminal mind busy and focused on productive matters, rather than focused on the manipulative machinations commonly found in their thought patterns.

Memory anchors, taught to SUMMIT staff by Cheryl Clark of the New York Shock Incarceration Facility, are used to facilitate the inmates' ability to memorize, by relating items to be memorized to a list of everyday items, which anchor them visually, auditorally, and kinesthetically, in the inmates' memories. Teaching the memory anchors on day three of the program gives the inmates a new skill early in the program and proves to them that they have the ability to learn far beyond their perceived limitations.

5 Steps of Decision Making

Also borrowed from Cheryl Clark are the 5 Steps of Decision Making, which give the inmates a handle on the means to make better decisions on a daily basis in any situation. The 5 steps are anchored to the five fingers on a hand, allowing them to "get a grip" on their choices, and are easily memorized and used in daily decision making in the program and in the community.

Community Meetings

As an integral part of the therapeutic community of the Oregon SUMMIT Program, daily community meetings are held, in which inmates admit their regressions, pull up the community to more productive behaviors and attitudes and teach each other, using a "what works for me" format which is nonaccusatory and nondirective. Issues are resolved within the community, benefitting the inmates as they learn interdependence and other-centered behaviors.

Individuals also report on the progress they are making and then report on progress noted in a peer. Learning to recognize improvements in self and others, and to articulate them, is a skill which will benefit the inmates lifelong.

Community meetings are highly structured in order to provide a comfortable and safe setting within which to admit wrongs and work on change. A staff member facilitates each meeting, with inmates taking turns leading meetings under the staff member's direction.

Clearings

Inmates commonly have little ability to identify specific feelings, or to express their feelings responsibly. Anger is usually one of the few feelings which they can readily identify, but the underlying reasons for the anger often are unknown.

Clearings are a means to practice identifying feelings, and to learn to appropriately express them in a caring community. As inmates spend more time in the program, their clearings become more meaningful and more specific. Again, these are skills which will benefit them with supervisors and co-workers on the job, and with friends and families.

Confrontations

When the inmates reach the third month of the program, confrontations are held once a week. This forum is highly structured and provides a means for peers to confront each other with care, regarding behaviors and attitudes which are detrimental to the individual and to the community.

Confrontations are not introduced until the third month of the program, because the inmates do not have the impulse control nor social skills needed before that time to confront with care. The platoon counselor facilitates the confrontations to ensure that they are done with care. The outcome from confrontations is a gradual turning of the mirror around so that inmates can see themselves as others see them.

Cadences

During the day, as inmates move about the facility, they do so in formation, either as a platoon, or in squads. As motivation, cadences are used, which are created largely by the inmates themselves, with approval from the program manager and drill sergeant. Cadences with prosocial messages are beneficial in keeping the inmates' minds on the change process and motivating them as a group.

Words as Tools

At SUMMIT, the message is that words are tools. They can be constructive or destructive. Inmates and staff ask themselves before speaking: "Will it help or will it hurt?" Because the goal is to create prosocial citizens, no jail slang or profanity is used or allowed. Jail slang is the comfort zone of inmates. We want to promote the comfort zone of nonoffending citizens. This is often a challenge to corrections personnel who have long-term habits of viewing jail slang as appropriate for their profession.

Teachable Moments

One of the values of having 100 percent of staff trained in program concepts is that there are no islands. All staff are able to seize the "teachable moment" and make a positive impact on inmates. Inmates cannot find a staff member on site who is unfamiliar with criminal thinking and tactics of manipulation.

Gordon Graham teaches that many internalized changes occur after a "significant emotional event." The experience of the SUMMIT Program confirms this. Staff at SUMMIT are trained to take advantage of the teachable moment after an inmate has experienced a significant emotional event, whether it be the loss of a loved one, threat of loss of the program, or seeing their own sickening behavior clearly for the first time. With Dr. Samenow's "persistence in probing" concept, staff assist the inmate in seeing his or her own behaviors clearly, and implementing interventions to change their future behaviors.

The Point of Power

New York Shock Incarceration facilities stress that the point of power is in the present. Program Manager Cheryl Clark states that "self-pity is all about the past. Fear is all about the future. If I stay stuck in False Expectations Appearing Real (FEAR), all I am doing is anticipating." Thus, modeling after New York, the inmates at SUMMIT practice keeping themselves firmly in the present moment. If they can act differently for the present moment, then gradually and incrementally, change will become habit.

Comfort Zones

People who are comfortable where they are, are unlikely to change. The SUMMIT Program uses the "Nine Dots" concept of getting outside comfort zones to illustrate this idea. Inmates who find themselves comfortable in the program are pushed to dig deeper into their issues, relating their current behavior to their crime and to their past, to uncover motivations, criminal thinking errors and tactics, and criminal masks which prevent them from operating in an "honest, open and willing" manner.

Acronyms and Mottos

Inmates respond favorably to the use of catch phrases, acronyms, and mottos. It enhances their ability to remember concepts as well as gives them a sense of belonging and common understanding in the program. Thus, the SUMMIT Program makes use of numerous acronyms and mottos.

Feedback is given which is SMART: Specific, Measurable, Attainable, Realistic, and Time-limited. To remain FREE, inmates are cautioned to: Focus on your thoughts and find each error, Remember where it leads, Eliminate the error before you act, and Explore the options for responsible action.

Mottos such as "Attitude Determines Altitude" help the inmates adopt program concepts. The concept of "Act As If" teaches the inmates to begin to act differently and let the understanding and emotions follow in due course.

New York Shock Superintendent Ron Moscicki's statement is true for SUMMIT also: "If you don't take responsibility, you take orders." Drill instructors tell the inmates on their first day in SUMMIT that the two hardest things about this program are to "keep your mouth shut and your ears open." These are the foundations of self-control.

Motivation

As part of the military framework, and to show motivation, inmates "sound off" when leaving dorms and classrooms. Roads on the Shutter Creek Correctional Institution site are clearly marked with signs indicating: "Attitude Alley," "Responsibility Road," and "Participation Parkway." In the inmate dormitories, the last thing each inmate sees before going to bed each night is a colorfully lettered motto, drawn on the wall over the length of the dorm which states: "If you keep on doing what you've always done, you'll keep on getting what you've always gotten." A large SUMMIT logo is prominently displayed on the outside of the Administration Building.

From the moment the inmates arrive on site, it is clear that this is not a typical prison. Keeping motivation high results in a more positive program for both inmates and staff.

Mapping Inmate Progress

To ensure that the SUMMIT program changes inmates' behaviors and attitudes for the long term, and does not become just a means to get out of prison early, a number of different tools are used to gauge inmate progress in the program and resulting internalized change.

Inmates are evaluated daily in a series of fifteen different categories, by staff in six program areas: alcohol and drug, drill instructors (both day and evening), education, Pathfinders, and work squads. Each day, inmates receive either a plus or a minus from each of these program sections, in the categories of respect, positive effort, cooperation, following instructions, accepting criticism, program progress, time management, neatness and cleanliness, military bearing, physical training, positive attitude, safety practices, study habits, treatment comprehension, and personal growth.

Every time a staff member gives an inmate a minus in any category, they also write down a comment on the form, indicating the specific desired behavior which would result in the inmate receiving a plus in that category. At the end of each week, the inmates review and sign the evaluation forms and read all feedback given them.

Each minus received is worth a designated number of points which is subtracted from the total numerical score an inmate can receive for the day. That designated number of "points per minus" increases during the program to raise the standards of behavior and attitude during the program.

In addition, the minimum expected daily score increases during the program. Inmates whose weekly scores fall below the expected standard for more than two weeks are given marginal letters, advising them to bring their scores up by focusing on details and adjusting their attitudes. Inmates who do not do so are given visible reminders, wearing blue watch caps, until their scores are brought up. Platoon members are held accountable for their peers and must assist them in bringing their scores up to standard.

Learning Experiences

Providing a means to address negative behaviors, and replace them with positive ones, is the learning experience process. Staff may refer inmates, or inmates may refer themselves to the Learning Experience Committee. On the referral form, they list the tools they have used without success to address the issue.

Learning Experience Committees, consisting of two staff and one inmate peer from the referred inmate's platoon, review the referral, interview the inmate, and give an assignment to the inmate which is designed to focus and resolve the issue. The Committee works to find an assignment, which will best suit the needs of the inmate, not as punishment for the problem, but something which will help to forge a new, more productive habit or attitude.

Staff from all departments at SUMMIT serve on the Learning Experience Committee, including clerical, maintenance, health services, food services, security, and program staff. This element of the program brings staff together, along with their expertise as human beings, to work for change in the inmates. The life experience of all staff is valuable in discovering what works to forge new habits for the inmates.

Superintendent's Committee

When inmates continue to demonstrate negative behaviors despite counseling, learning experiences, and peer assistance, they may be referred to the superintendent's committee. Referrals to the superintendent's committee also will be made for inmates with consistently poor evaluation scores, those who fail to abide by rules prohibiting racism, romance, and violence, those who receive misconduct reports for failure to abide by department of corrections rules of prohibited conduct, and for those who demonstrate behaviors which are detrimental to the platoon.

The superintendent's committee consists of two or more staff, who review the referral, interview the inmate, and make a recommendation to the superintendent about whether the inmate should be removed from the program, retained, or recycled to another platoon. The department of corrections' rule on the SUMMIT program gives the superintendent considerable authority to make a determination on an inmate's suitability to remain in the program, to be restarted in a new platoon, to be recycled back a platoon, or be returned to general population as a SUMMIT failure.

The goal of the superintendent's committee is behavioral change. It is evident that most of the inmates in the program justifiably could be removed at some time during the six months for behaviors and attitudes which are unsuitable. However, the challenge for staff is not to find reasons to remove the inmates, but to find reasons to keep them, and to build on the evidence of incremental change, through counseling, evaluations, and learning experiences, until the inmate demonstrates internalization.

Staff are trained in keeping their expectations of inmates in line with a gradient which ensures that too much pressure is not applied too soon, causing the inmates to voluntarily quit the program. Likewise, staff must expect more of inmates in the fifth month of the program than inmates in the second month of the program. One size definitely does not fit all at SUMMIT.

Hat Colors

As a visible sign of program progress, inmates are awarded colored hats at each stage of the program. During Zero Weeks, the inmates wear blue watch caps. Later in the program, these watch caps also are worn by those inmates with continual marginal evaluation scores.

During the first two months of the program, inmates wear green SUMMIT ball caps, demonstrating their status as "green" or new to the program, and a time for learning compliance. The next two months, the ball caps are red. The red symbolizes that time of the program when "heart work" is being done: inmates are becoming aware of their issues and change is beginning to be internalized. The final two months of the program, the inmates wear gold hats, symbolizing "digging for gold:" a time of looking deep into one's issues, being honest, open, and willing, and practicing new behaviors.

These visible reminders of progress not only provide a means for staff to remember what expectations to have of the inmates at any given time, but they also are important to the inmates as measures of progress. If the only program progress markers are criticism, lasting positive change is less likely to occur. A balance must be struck between positive reinforcement and constructive criticism.

Graduation

Graduation at SUMMIT is a joyful, yet somber occasion. Inmates are given credit for their accomplishments, yet cautioned to use their new skills to avoid problems in the communities to which they are returning. The graduating inmates begin the graduation ceremony with a cadence they created. Often parole officers, department officials, and former

SUMMIT graduates attend graduation. Those inmates who demonstrated outstanding effort and heart during the program receive awards.

Transitional Leave

After gradua-tion, the inmates leave with their families after grad-uation and return to their communi-ties on a thirty-day transitional leave. This transitional period allows the inmates to practice their new behav-iors and attitudes in their communi-

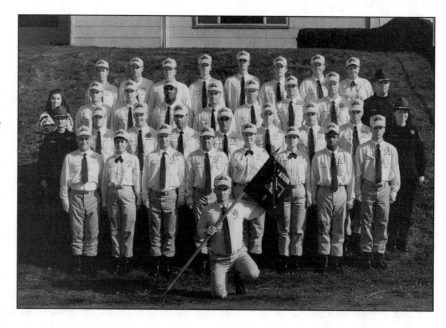

ties, under the supervision of parole officers, while still technically being inmates and the responsibility of the SUMMIT program.

If the inmates do not abide by 100 percent of their transitional leave conditions, including attending all required parole officer meetings and any mandated treatment, maintaining appropriate housing, and obtaining full time jobs, they are returned to the SUMMIT Program and reviewed by the superintendent's committee, which makes a rec-ommendation to the superintendent on their program status. Inmates who complete the thirty-day transitional leave are then placed on post-prison supervision for the period ordered by the sentencing judge.

A strong link between the SUMMIT program and the parole officers is necessary for the success of the inmates during the transitional leave period, as well as during post-prison supervision. Like many other residential programs, follow up is critical to long-term success. Cognitive change groups are available in many communities. Other parole offices make use of their day reporting centers to supervise SUMMIT graduates initially. Parole officers attended the initial immersion training with SUMMIT staff, and quarterly meetings have been held to network with parole officers assigned to SUMMIT graduates.

A defined "after SUMMIT" program involving the parole officers would be ideal, and would include a high level of supportive supervision and cognitive aftercare. However, large caseloads and limited funding have limited Oregon's ability to meet this challenge. Flexibility has been a key to working with the local parole offices to ensure focus on pro-gram goals in the supervision of SUMMIT graduates.

Staff as Role Models

Drill instructors at SUMMIT are correctional officers who have volunteered for the duty. The initial drill instructors were trained at the rehabilitation training instructor course, a program of the U. S. Army, at Ft. McClellan, Alabama, directed by Command Sergeant Major Joshua Perry (Retired)(See his chapter in this work). Those initial drill instructors now assist the drill sergeant in providing the on-the-job training for new drill instructors.

Although drill instructors are with the inmates the majority of the day, all staff must be trained in the program concepts to achieve the therapeutic community desired to support change. Role-modeling is essential to demonstrate to the inmates that staff believe in the concepts being taught. If inmates must have good bearing, so must staff. Thus, staff walk with purpose, wear well-maintained military style dress, and demonstrate good bearing, keeping hands out of pockets, not leaning on walls nor carrying coffee cups or cigarettes around the site.

To achieve congruence in the SUMMIT program, security and program functions are meshed by means of a drill sergeant who supervises the drill instructors, but reports to the program manager, rather than to the security manager. This drill sergeant provides training to new drill instructors as well as manages the superintendent's committee schedule and supervises the drill instructors.

Staffing Levels

Due to the intense nature of the program, with delivery of program elements sixteen hours a day, SUMMIT is staff intensive. Approximately ninety full- and part-time staff serve the combined 100 general population inmates and 166 SUMMIT participants. Some staff are employed by the department of corrections, and some are contractors who provide services, such as education, Pathfinders, and alcohol and drug services. Also, on "staff" are two canine members: Katie, a bloodhound trained in search and tracking, and Doc Holiday, a Labrador retriever trained in drug detection. These canines assist in community policing as well as on-site supervision of inmates and control of illicit drugs.

Staff Schedules

To meet the needs of the program, staff schedules at SUMMIT are varied and flexible. The ten drill instructors work either a day shift beginning at 5:30 A.M. and work four ten-hour days, or an evening shift beginning at 3:00 P.M. and work five eight-hour days. One counselor is assigned to general population and works a modified swing shift. The other four counselors work the day shift and are scheduled for one weekend day each.

The contractors who work in education, alcohol and drug, and the Pathfinders staff, include both full- and part-time staff members working a variety of shifts to cover classes which are scheduled from 8:00 A.M. until 9:00 P.M. seven days a week. Flexibility is essential.

Staff Training

Staff development training is held eight times a year for three hours each and serves to keep the program focused. Given the intensity of the program, combined with the hard work of change, the staff need to sharpen their skills and receive fresh insight on a regular basis to support their work.

SUMMIT Academy, a forty-hour reprise of the initial immersion training for new staff, was held when SUMMIT was two-years old. We anticipate that it will be offered once every year. This training provides an understanding of program concepts and of the personal commitment required to work in a change program.

Staff are the "inmates" in this training, and are required to dress for and participate in physical training, classes, and activities, under the direction of a drill instructor. Staff from all parts of the program participate together in this training. After completion of this training, all staff can say that they have truly experienced the program. They have learned how to hold inmates accountable, yet allow the chance to change.

For instance, staff are less likely to leave inmates at attention for more than a few minutes because they have been there and know what it feels like. Staff are less likely to feel the need to "push inmates' buttons" to get them out of their comfort zones, because after immersion training, the staff know that the program itself is outside most people's comfort zones, and provides a challenge for the inmates to practice self-control.

Preliminary Results

The preliminary outcome statistics of the SUMMIT program are impressive. The percentage of successful participants who failed on post-prison supervision and were returned to prison in Oregon is 11 percent. Of this 11 percent, 6 percent represented technical violations of post-prison supervision, and 5 percent represented new crimes.

Admittedly, two years is a short time period, and a small sample, with only 237 inmates having completed the program. Statistics will continue to be monitored as the program ages.

The money savings during the two years SUMMIT has been operational are significant also, with approximately $4.3 million saved, due to saving 89,000 bed days, as a result of the time cuts received. The cost of the program is approximately $60.00 per inmate per day, which is an increase of about ten dollars over the cost of general population inmates. Although the cost per day for SUMMIT is higher due to intense program delivery, the long-term cost is less, due to the fixed six-month duration and the time cuts earned by the graduates.

Program Support

The success of the SUMMIT program is due to many factors coming together to function well. Program direction is provided from the very top of the organization with support from the director of the Oregon Department of Corrections. The superintendent of the SUMMIT program provides the "backbone" of the program, assuring accountability. The SUMMIT program manager provides the "heart" of the program in keeping the program focused and staff trained in skills needed to facilitate change, as well as checking the tendency for staff to revert to "doing jail" rather than SUMMIT.

Conclusion

The SUMMIT program is a demanding and rigorous program physically, mentally, and emotionally. For every inmate who has graduated thus far, there has been another who has failed to meet the challenge to change and was returned to a regular prison to complete the original sentence. Those who have graduated, for the most part, have shown evidence of change. Those who were removed from the program were removed for lack of change, lack of effort, and lack of program progress.

The Oregon SUMMIT is a chance to make a difference—to change lives, and thereby to enhance the safety and security of Oregon's communities. The staff at SUMMIT believe that the work they do is evidenced in the positive lives of SUMMIT graduates, and is reflected in their families and in their communities. SUMMIT staff are committed to protecting the public and changing lives.

More information on the SUMMIT Program may be obtained by contacting the superintendent's office at Shutter Creek Correctional Institution, 2000 Shutters Landing Road, North Bend, OR 97459, (541) 756-6666 ext. 225.

The Vermont Model—Boot Camp Without the Boot

John G. Perry

Director of Planning
Vermont Department of Corrections
Waterbury, Vermont

Vermont is a small state, with only 570,000 in total population, and very rural; only a few towns are larger than 5,000, and most communities are less than 700 or 800. We are smaller in total than many medium-sized cities elsewhere, and most counties.

We are racially homogeneous (97 percent white), and ethnically about 25 percent of French-Canadian extraction. About 55 percent of the residents were born in other states. The violent crime rate is 16 percent of the United States' average, while the property crime rate is about 66 percent of the average.

We do not have urban blight. We do not have racial strife, and we do not have gangs (yet). We do have rural poverty and a per capita income well below average. We have Ben & Jerry's, maple syrup, snow, and fall foliage.

So, some people say that what is developed in Vermont corrections cannot have applicability to the rest of the country. On the other hand, we do have human beings here. We still have crime. We have courts, and justice, and prisons.

Because we are small (there are only 1,200 correctional beds in the entire state), we have another advantage over larger jurisdictions. We can implement new programs and see the results of our experiments fairly quickly.

Our corrections system is unitary. We integrate probation, detention, jail, prison, furlough, and parole in a single department of corrections. Every single defendant and offender, misdemeanor or felony, from arrest to parole expiration, is in our correction's jurisdiction.

Vermont also has a long history of being progressive with regard to crime and punishment. We were the fifth state, in 1809, to adopt the first good idea in punishment, building a prison as an alternative to "sanguinary punishment." We were the third state (1893) to implement the next good idea, probation, and the second state to adopt parole (1900). In 1975, we closed our only maximum-security prison, and created a community corrections system.

Despite this history of embracing reform, Vermont did not jump immediately on the boot camp bandwagon. We had been reading Doris Layton MacKenzie's work and recognized that the preliminary results were not very promising, but we began an internal discussion. Within the department, there was little interest in a pure military-style facility. While the demand for minimum-security bedspace far exceeded the supply, there was reluctance to expand the use of incarceration without significant treatment. The department's statutory mission defined the primary goal of corrections as providing for the "disciplined preparation of offenders to return to the community as productive citizens," but the statute also recognized that "traditional prisons do not work."

One proposal in early 1990 for an "intensive intervention program" for youthful offenders made use of the key features of traditional shock incarceration programs, but we recognized that correctional boot camp inmates "do not graduate into an established, respected and structured social status"[1] and, therefore, require not only aftercare but also intensive extended programming. If the program were to be an effective intervention, the intensity would be high, focussed on cognitive skill development and vocational and academic skill building, as well as on individual treatment.

The initial design of the program included a first phase of three months of military-style discipline, physical training, and team participation, followed by three months of intensive need/deficit reduction programming augmenting the discipline. This was capped by a wilderness survival exercise. This six-month incarcerated program was to be followed by an additional three-month community orientation phase, with day reporting, weekly outpatient group, work, and academic support. This, in turn, was to be followed by a one-year aftercare program with weekly reporting, and work, education, and vocational training in the community.

One problem with this model, of course, was the cost. This was a high-intensity, resource rich program, designed to implement the findings of the research, and targeted to work with high-risk offenders. The only way to make such a program cost effective would be to insure that the offenders selected for the program were bound for prison and were destined for long sentences. Given the indeterminate sentencing structure of the Vermont criminal court, there was no way to assure this. It was also clear that a program this rich would be a magnet, and might dramatically widen the net, attracting offenders to it who might otherwise be placed on probation.

Another problem was the internal department reaction to military-style discipline. While there were proponents, the concept encountered much criticism. One counterproposal was concerned with the potential of the program to create large numbers of well-trained, physically fit "urban guerrillas" who were reinforced in their belief that strength and intimidation equal power.

The Politics

In the external environment, there was little political pressure for corrections to build a boot camp; in fact, through 1989, the major political issue with corrections was where to site a new facility that nobody wanted.

Vermont, like all of the rest of the states, by 1990 was struggling to keep up with the explosive growth in the demand for incarceration. The population had burst the capacities of the prisons, and 20 percent of the incarcerated demand was on furlough, serving time in "house arrest." The legislature was passing new laws demanding tougher penalties, and judges were handing down stiffer sentences to more offenders, but no one wanted to build or operate new prisons.

In 1991, Vermont elected a new governor. Richard Snelling had been governor before, serving four terms from 1977–1984, and had returned from private life at the urging of his party. In his campaign, Snelling had urged a crackdown on crime, but had not focussed on corrections. However, his transition team identified prison crowding as a significant problem facing the state.

One of the solutions he "suggested" to the commissioner was a boot camp. The governor's idea of a boot camp was a picture of the one he remembered—wooden barracks heated by a coal stove, lots of marching and drill and ceremony, physical exercise, and hard work. On taking office in January 1991, the governor's "suggestion" became more explicit.

The governor's goals were clear. The new prison was to be cheap to build, cheap to operate, and accelerate the time an offender served. The target population would be young, first-time nonviolent offenders, and the program would involve intense interpersonal confrontation, with military drill, hard labor, uniforms, and drill instructors. The prison was to cost less than $20,000 per bed to build, and less than $16,000 a year to operate.

While the department began work on the design of the program that the governor proposed, in April 1991 the legislature funded $2 million for a 100-bed work camp facility, "to be heated with wood."[2] Several communities openly competed to be the site of the facility, a significant change from the previous decade of trying to site a real prison. This was clearly due to the nature of the population described for the new boot camp—young, first-timers.

The legislature also weighed in with program design ideas. One legislator introduced a bill calling for a "weekend work camp for parolees" that would require all offenders on parole to return to jail one weekend a month to work. Another bill, drafted by Senator John Carroll of Windsor County, was what the governor had in mind. Modeled directly after the "first generation" boot camps, it focused on drilling, marching, physical training, and exercising, targeted to young (under twenty-six, first-time nonviolent felony offenders with no prior violence and no prior incarceration for felonies, and no prior shock incarceration. Burglary was considered a violent offense, and burglars were precluded from participation.

The governor asked corrections to respond to the Carroll draft. The preliminary analysis of the existing populations on probation, on furlough, and in jail revealed that the following profiles met the criteria described in the bill:

- Of 800 inmates in jail or prison, 4-5 qualified

- Of 200 offenders on furlough, 25-30 qualified

- Of 5,500 on probation, 3,047 qualified.

Excluding first offenders reduced the number of qualifying probationers to 1,200; and including burglary increased the number of eligible prisoners to about 75. This clearly indicated that any boot camp with this set of criteria would widen the net, incarcerating numbers of offenders who would have been on probation otherwise. This clearly showed that we would not save money. The governor then directed the department to investigate models different from the strict military design.

The Next Battle—Goal Incompatibility

The political goals—cheaper operation, faster construction, shorter stay, first-time offenders—were in conflict with the literature on corrections effectiveness. The literature strongly suggested that intensive intervention with low-risk offenders made them more likely, not less, to reoffend.[3] The literature on boot camps suggested that they were more expensive to operate, just as expensive to build, did not divert prison-bound offenders, and had little, if any, positive effect on recidivism.[4]

In addition, the program goals of the department did not seem to lend credence to a program to intervene with nonviolent offenders. The idea of a 100-bed facility was extremely attractive to a department that only possessed 647 beds in the entire state. The department was extremely crowded. There was definitely a demand for minimum-security housing, although not composed of nonviolent first-time offenders.

Designing a Restructured Set of Goals

In 1991, the department embarked on a new design for corrections. The work camp was not merely to be added onto the existing prison system, to divert offenders from it or, more likely, to provide simple overflow bedspace or prerelease housing. The work camp was to be part of a separate system, to redirect corrections from a traditional, offender-centered system where the inmate was the client, not the product, to a victim- and community-centered system, where the public was the customer of corrections, and the services provided were for the victims and the community. This shift in thinking led to the development of a two-track approach to corrections.

We recognized that prisons were too expensive and too destructive to be used for other than the incapacitation and intensive treatment of predatory felons. To use prison space simply for the purposes of punishment or accountability was wasteful. What became clear was that the expectations of the criminal justice system, the public, the legislature, and the victims were not aligned. In fact, it was increasingly clear that the various interests of the stakeholders were often in conflict. The traditional purposes of sentencing simply do not fit with the needs of the stakeholders, and they do not fit with the traditional polar capacities of corrections: prison and probation.

Incarceration has been seen as a valid response to any or all of the purposes of sentencing: different judges use incarceration for different purposes, and different laws require it for different offenses. This means that prison must meet the demand for the multitude of purposes for which it is not only poorly designed, but often counterdesigned. In practice, however, this means that different offenders of totally different character and need are in the same place (prison) undergoing the same punishment for wildly disparate behaviors. The only variable offered by the justice system is the duration of that punishment. This is, it seemed to us, the root of the need to experiment with boot camps as a different kind of "disciplined preparation" to quote the Vermont corrections' statute (28 V.S.A. Sec. 1). Varying the intensity, quality, and experiential substance of the intervention might bring about more positive results. Clearly, it would be difficult to create worse results.

To break out of the impasse, we decided to create a model new to us. We recognized that it was critical to meet the needs of the various stakeholders, and that these needs were different from one another, and often incompatible. There are major differences in the expectations for outcomes from different participants in the justice process. There are also fundamental differences between the expectations of the participants and the wants and expectations of the nonparticipants in the process: the victims, and the community.

We identified four sets of stakeholders with expectations that must be aligned:

- First, the public, as a community, is interested in being safe from crime, and interested in seeing some balancing of the scales between the crime and the criminal, between the victim and the damage done, and between the community and the loss of quality of living.

- Second, the victims generally want more than simple revenge, which often derives more from being misused by the process than by the criminal. Victims want, in addition to and often instead of punishment, an apology, timely and total repair of the physical and emotional damage, assurance that the crime will not happen again, and, most important, the feeling that some meaningful good come from the event.

- Third is the criminal justice system, which wants to process all of the cases expeditiously, fairly, and equitably, yet individually.

- Fourth is the state, which needs to hold down costs, protect the citizenry, and enforce the laws.

There is a fifth party in the process—the offenders—but they are not stakeholders. The offender is the object, and the product, of the process, not the customer and not the client. In the past, the expectations of the offender (or surrogates) often drove the system. This is consistent with the American form of adversarial justice and protection of the individual from the state, but it does not address the other needs of human systems for commutative justice.

We recognized that the traditional purposes of sentencing were not enough, and traditional responses to crime were not effective. We decided to employ what does work, and to define a system to target offenders to the interventions that are most effective. The first step is to recognize that the current modes of implementing the traditional four purposes of sentencing do not address the needs of victims, nor do they, in large measure, address the needs of the public, for the vast majority of crime.

To meet those needs, it is necessary to add a new (not really new—see *Deuteronomy*) purpose for sentencing: reparation, or restoration. It is critical to the credibility and effectiveness of the criminal justice system that it is seen as sentencing offenders to repair the damage they have done, to restore the victim, and to add real value to the community in compensation for the values they have damaged. This fifth purpose, like the traditional four, is not, in and of itself, the single answer. However, it is the component of sentencing most blatantly missing from the others, and for which they most often attempt to overcompensate. Restorative justice may be an exclusive response to property crime; it may only be a partial response to violent crime. Offenders may have paid their debt to the law by doing time in prison, but they have not paid their debt to the victim until the victim is restored to wholeness, nor have they repaid their debt to the community until they have added some value to it and made amends to the community and the victim.

With this fifth purpose in mind, and perhaps uppermost in mind, the structure of correctional response to crime changes dramatically. It is possible to create new responses, and to target the existing system responses more effectively. This in turn creates more options for the criminal justice system to use, increasing discretion and the matching of offender needs and characteristics to victim and community needs and abilities. Ultimately, a restructuring of correctional responses can provide for increased public safety, timely victim restitution, and the adding of value to the community, as well as the rehabilitation of the offender.

This restructuring of goals allowed the department to choose a mission for the camp. It was to focus on work and on adding value to the community. It was to function as an alternative to traditional incarceration, but it was not a stand-alone. It was to be part of a new structure and a new set of opportunities for offenders and the criminal justice system.

Acceptance of the Strategic Design

In the spring of 1991, the design for restructuring corrections by expanding the options for the criminal justice system was ready to be presented to the governor. The new structure involved the implementation of two tracks for correctional services. The first, a reparative track, was to be exclusively for nonviolent offenders and initially only for misdemeanants. Offenders convicted of these crimes were not to be eligible for traditional jail or prison. At the lowest level of severity and risk, offenders were to be sentenced to reparative probation, a form of probation determined by boards of local community citizens who created agreements with the offender engage in activities to learn about the impact of his crime, to make amends to the victims, to learn ways to avoid criminal behavior, and to perform specified acts of community service that added value to the community.

Offenders who failed at this level of intervention, or continued to commit nonviolent crimes, would be sentenced to intermediate sanctions and perform community service on supervised work crews. Offenders who continued to violate the law, or who committed more serious nonviolent offenses, could be sentenced to the work camp. The work camp was to have a singular focus: work.

The presentation to the governor of this plan for corrections was scheduled for August 15, 1991. On August, 14, 1991, Governor Snelling died. He was succeeded by the lieutenant governor, Dr. Howard Dean. At a meeting held three days after he took office, Governor Dean approved the strategic vision and stayed the course.

Designing the Program with Single Focus

The key to designing the program for the work camp was the recognition that it had to be short term if it were to have any hope of diverting the prison-bound population, and if it were to have any cost-avoidance capacity. The pragmatics of a short-term program led to a clear focus: to give offenders the opportunity to return value to the community in a structured setting.

Clarity of purpose is critical to design. It is vital to define what the program would not do as well as what it would do. The work camp program was not to be a rehabilitative program in the traditional "treatment" sense, with offender change as the goal. It was not to be incapacitative, in that the facility was minimum security, and the offenders were not in it most of the day. It was not to be punitive, in that there was no degradation or reduction in status. And it was not to be a deterrent, in that reduction in recidivism was not a required outcome for success. The focus was clearly and consistently to be reparative. Accomplishment of other sentencing goals would be gravy.

The work camp was targeted at "offenders who commit relatively minor crimes and are sentenced to short sentences or probation and continue to commit criminal acts." These offenders have not committed serious crimes; nevertheless, they must be held accountable for their crimes. The only choice available to the court for these offenders had been either a sentence to traditional jail or prison, where they were housed in crowded facilities with more serious, violent criminals, or traditional probation, which demonstrably had not worked.

Not only was traditional incarceration inappropriate and ineffective (if not counterproductive, in terms of recidivism) for many nonviolent offenders, it often resulted in the offender being released early as a relief to crowded facilities. Early release does not serve the offender from a treatment perspective, nor does it serve the sentencing intent of the court. Most important, the community is not served, in that the offenders learn a lesson, but a rather different lesson than one would wish—the offenders learn that the community does not follow through with its punishments and that their behavior "isn't serious enough" to be taken seriously. Many offenders conclude, not unexpectedly, that they "got away with it."

The work camp was to take a different approach—the goal was to make a difference in the lives of offenders by teaching them to make a difference in the community.

The Theory: Adding Value to the Community Allows the Community to Value the Inmate

The Vermont public is not stupid. They think that inmates spending their time watching TV and playing cards in jail cells is a waste—that they should be adding value. How to force inmates to work productively has been a correctional conundrum for two hundred years. The Vermont Constitution, in its only language regarding punishment[5] says:

> To deter more effectually from the commission of crimes, by continued visible punishments of long duration, and to make sanguinary punishments less necessary, means ought to be provided for punishing by hard labor, those who shall be convicted of crimes not capital, where by the criminal shall be employed for the benefit of the public, or for the reparation of injuries done to private persons: and all persons at proper times ought to be permitted to see them at their labor.

How to force inmates to work is the wrong question. The better question is, "Why work?" We work because we gain benefit from working. We work because adding value to the community returns value to us. Forcing inmates to work does not provide any reciprocal gain even if they are paid, for there is no sense of exchange with the community. If the exchange is not visible, mutual, face-to-face, and valued, it does not engender reciprocal altruism on the part of the recipient.

The fundamental force in civilizing essentially selfish human beings (males in particular) is the understanding of reciprocity. We are selfish. We do nearly everything to gratify a short or long term self-interest (as we perceive it, and we are self-deceptive). What works with offenders is the same thing that works with all of us—doing favors for others results in others feeling like doing favors for us. When we do something for someone else, it creates a social obligation in our favor. They owe us. They are more willing to do something in return when we need it. If I buy you a drink, you will get the next round. If I coach your son in Little League, you will be more likely to invite my daughter to your Sunday school class. Doing favors for one another is what makes the social "contract" work. The problem with the contract is that it is not written. It is totally informal. We remember the favors people do for us. We remember the people who do them. The problem with offenders is that this system works in reverse, too. If you do something bad to me, I will not only do something back to you, I will remember it.

Allowing inmates to participate in the positive social reciprocity system changes everything. Traditional prison prevents the inmate from participating in that system, because in order for reciprocal exchange of favors to work, the opportunities must be frequent, the exchanges must be of greater value to the recipient than they cost the donor, the exchanges must be visible, and there must be a face-to-face mechanism to detect cheating. Putting prisoners out of sight reduces the possibilities for the exchange to mere fiscal accounting—that is too abstract for most people to care about, while putting the working offenders on chain gangs reduces the exchange to mere symbolism. It is not until the work is productive and meaningful and adds visible and tangible value to the community that offender work will be valued by the community.

Market Segmentation

The next step was the determination of the market strategy. Corrections traditionally thinks of itself as the last bastion of the public sector, doing a job that no one wants to do, that no one could conceive of making a profit doing. Consequently, until recently, corrections has not perceived a need to understand its market. It was not until the demand exceeded the supply that competition arose, and we began to recognize market forces.

The corrections customer is not simply the offender. Corrections has a variety of customers, each of whom wants a different product or service. The primary customer is the public. "The public" is an inclusive term, and because it includes a number of customers, often the public becomes a carry-all for the description of the market. However, understanding the market is the key to success in the private sector, and unitary market descriptions lead to many companies going belly-up. Understanding what business we are in requires understanding the markets. Most of that understanding is common sense.

Corrections provides a set of services to the criminal justice system. Courts, prosecutors, defenders, and police are customers. The services each demands are different from the others. The courts are served by the implementation of sentencing intent, translated as duration. The prosecutors are served by the implementation of accountability, which is contingent upon the availability of bed space, to provide the credibility of sentence implementation necessary for plea bargaining to work. The defenders are served by the availability of treatment programs, community release options, and, perversely, crowding, which allows pleading to a sentence they can be assured will not be implemented.

Corrections also provides services to victims of crime (though not nearly enough, according to many) by incarceration of offenders who pose serious threat and risk management of offenders in the community of those who are less risky. Corrections provides symbolic services to victims, implementing the restrictions of freedom imposed by the court. We also collect and distribute the restitution the offender owes the victim.

However, there are other segments of the market within which corrections exists that we traditionally do not see ourselves as serving. In fact, we do not usually see those segments as customers of corrections: certainly not the taxpayer, who sees us as a drain on resources expended on nondesireables, nor other government agencies, who see us as stronger competition for declining social service dollars. We are a tax burden to business and industry, and labor sees us as unfair competition, at best.

Most local governments see corrections as a drain on community services, and as over-users of emergency services. We also take property off the tax rolls. Most legislators see corrections as an unwelcome reality, which detracts support from otherwise politically sexy new crime laws by continually insisting on projecting the need for expensive new facilities that nobody wants in their backyard.

Finally, another market segment that corrections traditionally ignores is our own staff. Opening a new kind of correctional facility is not simply a matter of hiring new staff for a new program. A new facility means promotions, relocation, and new members for the union.

Market Research

To get a better handle on the public acceptance of our correctional strategy, we decided to employ another common business practice. We contracted with Doble Associates of Englewood Cliffs, New Jersey to conduct a series of focus groups with Vermont citizens. Unlike typical government "focus groups" where people bring together groups of bureaucrats or individuals with vested interests and advocates for a "public hearing," we used the technology of corporate America—a randomly selected representative sampling of small (eight-to-ten person) groups who were paid a small sum to participate in "discussions of new products."

From these focus groups and the random telephone survey which followed, we learned that the Vermont public did not think much of us. In fact, they told us they hated us. They did not think much of the judiciary, and they did not think much about probation. They knew jail did not work, and they knew we let people go too early. More than 75 percent of them thought the whole criminal justice system needed fundamental reform and a stem-to-stern overhaul.

But when they were told about the concept of a work camp, they said "about time" and "What took you so long?" Of course, some states have had public work camps for more than fifty years, and each day they send several thousand inmates out to work.

We learned that our public strongly favored allowing inmates to work on public projects, like the Civilian Conservation Corps during the depression. They strongly favored offenders who were not dangerous working and living in the community. They strongly favored nonviolent offenders appearing before community boards for determination of the form of their community restitution.

They were very clear that prisons should be reserved for dangerous violent offenders. They also were convinced that putting nonviolent criminals in prison was not a good idea. They thought that locking up a kid at $25,000 year for stealing a TV worth $500 was unbearably stupid. The market research showed us in John Doble's apt phrase, "the boundaries of political permission."[6] It showed a real readiness for the concept of a community service camp.

The Next Battle—Program Design

In designing the work camp, there were a number of competing interests. First was the internal department need to respond to the crisis in crowding. The six correctional facilities in Vermont were severely crowded. Like most other states, Vermont's sentencing demand far exceeded its bedspace supply. Vermont's solution was a little unique, out of necessity. While most other states chose to direct crowding from state facilities into local and county jails, Vermont was unable to do so. It closed most of its county jails in the 1960s. The few that were operational were used, but this only amounted to a couple of dozen beds.

Consequently, Vermont created a release mechanism. From 1988 on, with help from federal government funding, Vermont created the "Community Control" program, which provided a house arrest model furlough supervision. By 1993, more than 28 percent of the incarcerated population was not in jail, but on house arrest. This meant, from the perspective of the work camp target population, the camp would "compete" in sentencing with alternatives to incarceration. No public defenders in their right mind would trade a short term of jail that he knew would result in early release to house arrest for a longer term at the work camp. No offenders in their right mind, especially those who were targeted for the camp, repeat offenders who "knew the system," would trade a short stint in jail playing cards and watching television for a hard work accountability program without something to gain.

While we were doing the market research, we went ahead with the program design. We visited work camps in Idaho, boot camps in Oklahoma and elsewhere, and shock incarceration programs in New York. We "borrowed freely" (stole) from every program we saw. We made a number of critical design choices, based on the advice we heard, and the lessons learned.

We decided to start small. Even though the facility could accommodate a hundred beds, we decided to open it with only fifty. We then defined and answered the questions of fundamental criteria:

First, "Who is it for?" While this had been framed for us by the legislature, and negotiated with the host community as "nonviolent," we chose to limit the first participants to nonviolent misdemeanants only, excluding those with any history of violence or escape.

Second, "How do you get in?" Different programs had tried different gate-keeping mechanisms—court selection, court selection with corrections' veto, corrections' selection, and corrections' recommendation with court resentencing. Then, is it voluntary or mandatory? Each method has its theoretical drawbacks and advantages, but one thing we noticed they had in common: nearly all of the programs had difficulty finding a large enough population pool to fill the beds.

We decided to provide multiple avenues, in a priority ranking, so we did not hamstring ourselves. First priority was a reparative track population, offenders who had failed in less restrictive reparative sanctions, who were convicted of nonviolent misdemeanors, and who were classified minimum custody. Second priority were offenders who had failed on house arrest, and who were sentenced to less than a year. They were classified as minimum custody, and were approved by a judge. Finally, priority three was any minimum-custody offender who was nearing release. The three categories allowed us to respond to the competing interests of the courts, corrections, and community without compromising the program.

Initially, we had thought that offenders would enter the program in "platoons," but very early on it became clear that the courts do not sentence offenders in groups of thirty-six. More important, it became clear that most work is not done in groups that large, but that work is done in teams of five or six, and is flexible, not rigid. We realized that inmates would not graduate from the program into real life to work in platoons; real life entails teamwork. So, we decided on a program with open entry and open exit.

Third, "What is in it for the offenders?" We knew that for the program to work, the key had to be the willingness of the offenders to participate, to work hard, and to refrain from engaging in the type of behavior that got them there in the first place. Other programs had used sentence reduction to encourage inmates to volunteer for the program, so we recommended legislation. In April 1993, just before the camp opened, the legislature amended the good time statute to allow inmates at the work camp to earn double the amount of good time available. With the new incentive, inmates would earn a day of credit for each day served, and reduce their sentence by half. This provided the carrot to get offenders into the program.

Fourth, "How do you succeed?" We created a complex structure of incentives and reinforcers, but very early on, the inmates told us to "use the good time, it's what we want. Make it our responsibility." As a result, good time is the fundamental structure of success and failure. Getting up on time (5:00 A.M.) is the inmate's responsibility. There is no drill instructor to tell them what to do. Getting ready, showered, shaved, dressed, and to breakfast with their area cleaned up is their responsibility. They succeed by progressing through levels, keeping their noses clean, and completing their sentence. If they fail twice in a week, they go back a level. If they fail four times in a month, they also go back a level. At a reverted level, they get no extra good time. The good time is the incentive at first; as the offender progresses, the work itself becomes the incentive. Finally, "What do you do?" What you do is learn how to work on a crew, led by a correctional foreman (or a forewoman; most crew's chiefs are female). The work comes in different levels of difficulty:

Level One—Weeks One and Two

We realized the facility would always need maintenance, and we would always have offenders beginning their sentences. So, at level one, they are trained in basic safety education—every inmate is certified in first aid and cardiopulmonary resuscitation (CPR). Every inmate is trained in the proper procedures for cleaning a facility. They are all trained on tool use and maintenance, and tool safety.

In week two, they are issued their chain saw and trained in its operation and maintenance. Chain saws? Inmates? Yes, it is difficult to cut 1,000 cords of firewood without one. The work camp is adjacent to a medium-security facility, and both are heated with wood, which takes 500 cords a winter. The other wood is cut and split and delivered to welfare families who heat with wood.

The chain saw belongs to the offender. It is his. He is responsible that both he and the saw are ready for work each morning.

Level Two—Outside the Fence

The next level of responsibility is outside the fence, on the grounds of the facility. This work is mostly cutting, splitting, moving, and stacking wood. If inmates are judged ready for advancement to this level, they are allowed to interview for openings at the next level. The interview is conducted formally, and the offenders usually fail the first time. Then, they are helped to get a social security card, a work history, recommendations, and a resume.

At this level, the offenders are assessed for readiness to go off the grounds. Led by a correctional foreman or forewoman, they are assessed for their willingness to work, their competencies, and their attitude. When the caseworkers and foremen or forewomen decide they are ready, they can apply for level three jobs.

Level Three—Community Service

Level three is community service work of moderate skill. The work may occur on the grounds, in the greenhouse growing flowers to plant in the parks or on the road dividers, or they may work in the gardens, growing vegetables for use in the facilities and in many senior meal sites. We also grow pumpkins, and every school child in the county gets a pumpkin from the garden for Halloween.

In the community, the work is for local communities and local nonprofit agencies. Projects include sweeping the winter sand from sidewalks and roads in town; clearing skating rinks for elementary schools; cutting brush on interstates; maintaining cemeteries, parks, fishing accesses, beaches, and other facilities; providing assistance to community care homes for the elderly (shoveling snow, maintaining grounds); delivering firewood to needy and disabled; maintaining interstate rest areas and community parks and lawns; harvesting and raking leaves in the fall; cleaning grounds and planting in the spring; and weeding and tilling in the summer.

Level Four—Community Service Projects

Level four is for community service projects, involving higher skill levels, which create tangible projects of lasting value. This work includes the rehabilitation and major maintenance of buildings and structures, the construction of bike paths, scraping and painting of churches and town buildings, reclamation of cemeteries, construction of playground equipment and recreation facilities, such as Little League dugouts, hockey arenas, and obstacle courses, and preparation, planting, and maintenance of community parks and gardens.

How Well Is it Working?

The data are straightforward. As of January 1996, inmates of the camp have expended more than 200,000 hours of work, of which nearly 100,000 hours are community service work. Valuing the community service work at minimum wage works out to more than $400,000 of savings to local communities and agencies.

To go beyond the data, however, it is necessary to narrate an anecdote. When the work camp first began to send out community crews in 1993, we stuck to safe projects. We picked up trash on the interstate. We mowed lawns at the rest areas. We cut brush and cleaned up fishing access areas. As we developed confidence, we branched out. We began doing work for the town of St. Johnsbury, where the camp is sited. This included roadside brush cutting to prepare for winter snow plowing. We took on more public projects, sweeping up the winter sand from main streets, shoveling out senior citizen housing, cleaning up illegal dump sites from roadsides. We began to market our services, and some nonprofit agencies picked us up. We got a contract for the Food Bank, which repackages damaged foodstuffs donated by grocers for redistribution to the poor, and in the first year, we doubled the amount handled. We landscaped some public parks and highway dividers. We painted some cemetery fences. We made a deal with the Department of Forests and Parks that if they would buy the router, we would make the signs.

Word began to spread. People from the Congregational Church in the tiny town of Newbury asked if we could paint their church. We said we could, without thinking of the scope of the job, the scaffolding, or the time involved. Luckily, we had a painter. We had recruited work crew supervisors from existing staff, but we were not necessarily looking for "security types." We wanted people who knew trades—using sheetrock, wallpapering, doing carpentry and small engine repair or maintenance.

After we had been on the job for a week, some of the ladies of the church came to inspect the work. They were impressed. They also noticed that the crews were bringing their lunch in coolers, packed by the facility. At 88 cents per meal, they were not too appetizing. One of the ladies said, "That's not enough of a meal to work on!" So, they decided to provide lunch. Every day after this, different ladies from the community took turns bringing lunch, and sitting with the boys and talking. Since then, the crews have painted the Second Congregational Church in West Newbury, painted the Town Hall, The Grange, the Parsonage, and the Fire Station. When they painted the West Newbury Historical Society, the crew supervisor noted that the building was about to collapse and needed shoring up before the crew could paint. The building, more than a hundred years old, was a one-room school that housed a day care on the main floor, and in the basement, contained all the artifacts of the town's history. The crew jacked up the building, topped off the foundation, set new sills, built new posts and installed new joists, and built forms for a new concrete floor. When the floor was poured, they built interior walls in the cellar, leveled the deck, and then scraped and painted.

Then, they painted the senior center, and the Atkinson Retreat Center, and the Methodist Church's retreat headquarters. When they looked at the interior of the center, they built shelving for the kitchen, sanded floors upstairs to strip the paint off the wide pine boards, painted and wallpapered, put in new ceilings, textured the plaster, and regilded the raised carving on the fireplace mantel.

Last fall, Newbury held its annual Fireman's Picnic to thank the volunteer fire department members. This year was the 100th anniversary of the picnic, and the crews, the foremen, the forewomen, and the staff of the camp were invited as guests of honor.

This summer, one of the "boys" is getting out. He plans to be married in the church he painted. Most of the congregation will be there.

The Synthesis—Reparative Justice

The ladies of Newbury will tell you, if you visit, that they "used to be terrified of convicts." Now, they have decided to "adopt" the work camp. They are not afraid anymore.

The work camp was not designed as a restorative justice endeavor. Restorative justice has to do with "making the victim whole." The work camp offenders have little or nothing to do with the victims of their crimes. The work camp is focussed on repairing the damage done to the community, as a means of making amends in general. The community is a different type of victim, nonetheless. And it is the community that is demanding tougher sentences and harsher penalties.

The work camp is just the beginning. We have taken reparative justice another few steps, with reparative boards dispensing face-to-face community sentencing, and our community restitution program providing work crews across the state as a pure alternative to short terms of incarceration, for probation violation, and as a graduated sanction. The next step is to integrate restorative justice principles and practices.

Notes

1. Bush, Jack. Vermont Intensive Intervention Program. Unpublished concept paper. Waterbury, Vermont. February 1990.

2. Vermont General Assembly. Acts and Resolves, 1991 Session. Montpelier, Vermont.

3. Gendreau, Paul and Mario A. Paparozzi. 1995. Examining What Works in Community Corrections. *Corrections Today.* February, pp. 28-31; Andrews, D. A. et al. 1990. Does Correctional Treatment Work? A Psychologically Informed Meta-Analysis. *Criminology.* Vol. 28, pp. 369-404.

4. Parent, Dale. *Shock Incarceration: An Overview of Existing Programs.* National Institute of Justice, June 1989; MacKenzie, D. L. and J. Shaw. 1990. Inmate Adjustment and Change During Shock Incarceration. *Justice Quarterly*, Vol. 7, No. 1, March 1990; MacKenzie, D. L. 1990. Boot Camp Prisons: Components, Evaluations, and Empirical Issues. *Federal Probation.* September, pp. 44-52.

5. Vermont State Constitution. Chapter II, Article 64. Windsor, Vermont, 17777.

6. Doble, John. Crime and Corrections: The Views of the People of Vermont. Vermont Department of Corrections. 1993, 1994.

A Jail Boot Camp Program: Broward Sheriff's Office

Susan W. McCampbell

Director, Department of Corrections and Rehabilitation
Broward County Sheriff's Office
Fort Lauderdale, Florida

Boot camps for adult offenders, if nothing else, are controversial. It is often difficult to determine, in the light of the rhetoric, if boot camps are a wise, viable, economically feasible, effective option for a local corrections system, or just a fad. While it is the clear prerogative of each local corrections administrator, or a local government, to arrive at the decision to establish an offender boot camp, there are many factors which might influence the decision to add a boot camp to the options available in a local jail/corrections system. This chapter explores the Broward County Sheriff's Office Military Training Unit, as well as provides information for use by decisionmakers at the local level who may be considering a boot camp.

For the purposes of this discussion, we define "boot camp" as a very structured, intensive, correctional program, of short duration, employing military-style physical training and discipline. The desirable outcomes of the boot camp may vary by program (such as lowering recidivism, shortening sentences for less serious offenders or getting the attention of first-time offenders). During the offenders' incarceration, their regimen, schedule, privileges, speech, and total environment are under the control of corrections staff. In this definition, boot camps also incorporate education programs, vocational assessments, and other specialized services to meet the needs of this population. This definition is of a "first generation" boot camp; however, as many newer boot camp programs are evolving, we learn more about what works and what does not.

There is not perfect a model for a jail boot camp program. Each program, to be effective, must incorporate the expectations and goals of the local criminal justice system and the community. A boot camp program, because of its highly public nature, can only succeed if the local community and the justice system share the values incorporated into the program and participate in the program's operation.

The differences between the state-run adult boot camps as part of the state corrections system and jail-based boot camps are significant and impact the decision on whether to proceed with a local boot camp.

- First, most local jails/corrections systems do not have individuals serving long sentences in their system. Although boot camp sentences are relatively short, three to six months, this population is not often in a local jail.

- Second, the reality of sentencing is that there are few first-, second-, or even third-time offenders serving any jail or prison time. By the time an individual is sentenced to actually serve time, whether in jail or in prison, they may not be suitable candidates for a boot camp. Offenders may be too violent, have too serious a criminal history, have health or mental health problems due to ongoing substance abuse, be less amenable to strict discipline, and the sentencing judge may be unwilling to give the offender "one more chance." Consider the "qualifications" of the top boot camp candidates in Broward County, Florida which are discussed later.

- Third, there are limited fiscal resources available at the local level. Most agencies are struggling to do the basic job of running a local jail. Qualified staff is often difficult to recruit and retain, and specialized training is limited. Although these same issues confront state corrections operations, their burden is shifted statewide, rather than countywide.

- Fourth, local corrections is plagued by general lack of public support. Many citizens see "rehabilitation"—if they believe in it at all—as the state's job, not that of the local jail system. There are few places where there is any public interest in providing an effective continuum of corrections—from pretrial services, diversion activities, in-custody education and training programs, and postrelease aftercare programs as part of a local system.

Each of these issues weighs in a decision to establish a local boot camp.

The Broward Sheriff's Office Military Training Unit (Boot Camp) was established by Sheriff Ron Cochran in 1993, and accepted the first platoon of cadets in August 1993. Between that date and April 1996, almost 500 cadets have completed the program. Broward County, Florida, which includes the Fort Lauderdale metropolitan area, has a population of 1.2 million to 1.6 million, depending on the time of the year. The average daily population of the Broward County jail system is between 3,500 and 3,600 inmates, with plans to add 500 more beds in the immediate future. Approximately 700 inmates are serving felony sentences of a year or less in the county jail, and another 225 inmates are serving a sentence for a misdemeanor offense. The remaining inmate population is in pre-trial status.

The Broward Boot Camp

The Military Training Unit was initially designed to simultaneously serve 108 cadets, divided into two platoons, each beginning approximately six to eight weeks apart. The program lasts for 90 days. Individuals are sentenced to the program by the trial judge. All referrals from the courts are reviewed against the program's eligibility requirements, and each individual has a health assessment to assure they have no health problems which would preclude participation.

Program eligibility criteria include:

- a sentence to the county jail as an adult offender for 364 days or less
- less than thirty-three years of age
- medically, physically, and psychologically fit to participate in the program
- no open felony (nonadjudicated) charges pending
- no convictions for serious violent felonies

These criteria result in offenders as young as sixteen years of age being placed in the program.

The program was implemented without spending funds on new buildings or additional facilities, or hiring new staff, but was accomplished through reallocating existing resources. The current fiscal year budget is approximately $1.4 million. The program is located on the site of a medium-security facility which had cell areas available to accommodate the anticipated number of cadets. Staffing was set at twenty-three, including a lieutenant, three sergeants, one corrections counselor, and eighteen corrections deputies. The job of the correctional counselor is to assist the security staff with managing any special needs, and assisting with job-finding skills as well as housing. Deputies assigned to the unit completed the correctional drill instructor training course at Ft. McClellan, Alabama (see the chapter on this course in this volume).

The minimal start-up costs required for the program went toward uniforms for staff and inmates, foot lockers, obstacle course equipment, certificates and medals for graduation ceremonies, food and refreshments for family day, alumni meetings, and graduation ceremonies. The Military Training Unit is coed, with female participants sleeping in separate quarters, but both sexes working together during the day.

Programming in the Boot Camp consists of general equivalency diploma preparation, military drill and ceremony, physical fitness, drug and alcohol interventions, and religious programming. During their stay in the unit, cadets are not permitted to receive visits from family or friends. One week prior to graduation, the families are invited to be reintroduced to their cadet, who quite often has changed dramatically as a result of the program's fitness regimen and emphasis on respect and discipline. Most often, cadets are released directly from custody following notification to the sentencing judge that they have successfully completed the program; while others stay in custody to serve out the remainder of a local sentence (less than 364 days).

A typical day for a cadet begins at 4:45 A.M. with wake-up, breakfast served at 5:00 A.M., cleaning until 6:15 A.M., physical training until 7:40 (about which time other inmates may just be served breakfast). School begins at 8:00 A.M., followed by an afternoon of drill and ceremony, drug and alcohol counseling, community service, and there are religious services on Sunday, or life skills classes. Evenings include Alcoholics Anonymous, Narcotics Anonymous, and Cocaine Anonymous meetings, some earned quiet time, paperwork, and lights out at 11:00 P.M. This schedule is as rigorous for the staff as the participants, as staff must participate alongside those they supervise.

The staff must also use pre-approved lesson plans, handout materials, and video materials in a structured setting. The delivery of the class materials is shared among the deputies, teachers assigned from the school board, volunteers, Spectrum staff (substance abuse contractor), and other sheriff's office staff who are specially trained. Corporal punishment is prohibited. The staff may use a moderate level of "motivational" exercises to gain participants' compliance with rules, but not to such a level as to endanger the health of a cadet.

Cadets sentenced to the boot camp may be recycled to the "junior" platoon if their performance, attitude, or skill level does not keep pace with the remainder of the platoon. In all cases, the sentencing judge is notified. Cadets who are not healthy enough to complete the program are referred to the sentencing judge for imposition of a new sentence. If a "recycle" cadet cannot make it in the next platoon, the sentencing judge is notified and a new sentence is imposed. Cadets are discouraged from self-selecting out of the program as they know they will be faced with a longer sentence in the county jail, or state prison if they must reappear before their sentencing judge. The credibility developed between the sentencing judges and the unit staff enables the program staff to make a recommendation about the future of a participant who has not made the grade in boot camp. The dropout rate of the program is less than 20 percent.

One innovation in the Military Training Unit is the inclusion in the program staff of a probation officer from the state department of corrections. This full-time officer provides the link to the probation system into which most program participants will be released. Tours of the unit are provided to other probation officers whose caseloads will include program graduates. A goal for the future is to have specifically designated probation officers in the various regional offices serve the county whose caseload will include the Military Training Unit's successful graduates. This is another example of seeking wider support from members of the county's criminal justice system.

A formal graduation ceremony is conducted at the end of the ninety-day program for each platoon. These events have attracted a growing audience at each graduation as members of the community and criminal justice officials, along with the cadets' family members, join the real celebration. Certificates and medals are presented along with the awarding of general equivalency degrees and other special recognitions. The program includes the cadets' demonstration of an usually impressive grasp of military drill and ceremony. This "graduation" is often the first celebration of anything positive in the cadet's life, and is a significant event for the cadets and their family. The critical link in all this good will is having an aftercare program in place that will take the positive energy and good intentions of graduation day and transform them into resources, training, and education to prevent the cadets from returning to the activities that resulted in their entry into the criminal justice system.

Aftercare

The planning for the implementation of the Military Training Unit did not include specific aftercare services. The Military Training Unit staff, at its own initiative, began "alumni" meetings on one designated day each month so that graduates could return and visit the deputies and their fellow graduates. Staff attempt to keep track of the addresses and telephone numbers of all graduates and will make efforts to contact all graduates to remind them of the alumni meeting. Usual monthly gatherings bring fifty former cadets to the site of the unit. This gathering also presents opportunities for future programming involving issues facing the former inmates.

It became immediately evident that an aftercare program was essential to the program as the deputies were personally intervening to help graduates who needed housing, jobs, and guidance. Although no quantifiable goals were set at program implementation, there was increasing concern that graduates were beginning to be rearrested most often for violation of the terms of their probation, rather than for new crimes. While there was no lack of businesses volunteering to take graduates as employees, these were often low-wage jobs for the mostly unskilled graduates.

In response to this concern, planning efforts were undertaken to build the coalition necessary to put an aftercare program in place. The Spectrum staff began working in the Military Training Unit in October 1994, the program operating under the name of ABC—After Boot Camp. The mission of the ABC project is to provide treatment for and coordinate aftercare services for program participants who have drug and alcohol problems. ABC provides a comprehensive psychosocial assessment of all individuals' needs when they enter the Boot Camp; skill building and reintegration groups to help the inmates make the transition back to the community on release; a comprehensive aftercare plan to delineate the services the participants will need after boot camp; and the case management to insure that services are being accessed in the community. Funding for the staff was received from the local substance abuse commission.

ABC's psychosocial evaluations and assessments are conducted by trained substance abuse staff to identify, delineate, evaluate, and determine problems and needs of prospective program clients including a case history. The procedure includes a preliminary DSM IV diagnosis. Individual therapy is a one-on-one individualized treatment session between the program client and clinical staff. Each session is to help the client to improve functioning or prevent further deterioration, minimize consequences of substance abuse, and reduce the potential for future abuse. Sessions are provided weekly, however, there may be nonscheduled visits during times of increased crisis. Individual sessions usually take one hour—time necessary for documenting client files is also included in the unit cost.

Case management activities in ABC are provided by clinical staff and include offender tracking and reporting, making contacts (calls, letters, personal contacts) and scheduling appointments for medical, public social services, vocational, court/legal, and other services on behalf of the client as well as arranging for transportation and child care, as needed. Treatment plan development is goal oriented, designed to address client issues and problems that had led to the need for treatment. It is developed jointly by the client and clinical staff and contains written objectives that address the recipient's individualized treatment goals. Intervention services in ABC reflect calls, personal contact, correspondence, or other assistance on behalf of the client. The correctional counselor assigned to the unit assists in maintaining records and in addressing needs not included within Spectrum's scope of work.

The ABC program by no means represents the end of the attempt to strengthen aftercare. Among the options being considered are formal arrangements with community churches to provide individual mentors for graduates, more intensely involving family members in the program, working with groups of retired military in Broward County to provide role models and advocates for the graduates, and contracting for future services based on grant-fund availability and specific needs of the graduates. Increased consideration by judges of specific aftercare plans as part of the sentencing order is also being pursued. Such specific direction includes not only the completion of a period of probation, but also the completion of educational, vocational, substance abuse, or other treatment programs.

In selecting the contractor to provide the services in ABC, there was an assumption made that substance abuse would be the single largest problem shared by the cadets. We anticipated that focused efforts to address substance abuse would be necessary before addressing other issues. What the profiles of the cadets revealed, however, was astounding. Those sentenced to the Military Training Unit are the "best" young criminals in Broward County. These individuals appear to the judge, the state's attorney, and the public defender as having the best chance of a strict military-style program making a positive impact on their lives. The profile of this group of young people, however, points at how much energy and resources are needed to even begin to have an impact on this population. Here is a brief overview of profiles of the first 183 cadets.

1. <u>Unstable Living Environment</u>—Seventeen percent of cadets have an unstable living environment reporting they move in and out of their parent's home, homes of friends, or others. Those cadets who are really homeless often gave an address just to satisfy probation or community control officers. This circumstance may result in some cadets being found in violation of their probation agreements when they are not at the location noted in their agreement when visited by their probation officer.

2. <u>Medical Needs</u>—While medical needs are not prevalent for this youthful population, 30 percent of the cadets reported head injuries during their childhood; many report a previous diagnosis of Attention Deficit Hyperactivity Disorder.

3. <u>Educational Needs</u>—Sixty-one percent of cadets reported dropping out of school. Most cadets reported a significant history of truancy, fighting, and suspensions. Initial testing by the school board shows academic achievement two-to-three grades below the last grade reported completed. Approximately 33 percent of the cadets have been previously enrolled in special classes for the learning disabled, or those with behavioral and/or emotional problems. (Note: 13 percent reported dropping out in sixth grade; 1 percent in sevenh grade; 16 percent in eighth grade; 33 percent in ninth grade; 35 percent in tenth grade; 23 percent in eleventh grade; and 4 percent in twelfth grade.)

4. <u>Vocational Needs</u>—Sixty-five percent of the cadets report they lack sufficient skills to compete with nonoffenders in the workplace. The most frequently listed occupations are landscapers, roofers, or laborers. Most cadets are frustrated in obtaining or maintaining legal employment above the minimum wage, which contributed to their decision to engage in criminal behavior.

5. <u>Alcohol and Drug Involvement</u>—All cadets report a history of substance abuse with 74 percent reporting abuse of alcohol; 68 percent reporting abuse of marijuana; 27 percent powdered cocaine; 11 percent crack cocaine; 18 percent hallucinogens; 9 percent inhalants, 15 percent barbiturates, and 11 percent opiate abuse. Two different groups of abusers emerge—one group of offenders primarily selling drugs who are not users; the second group engaged in high levels of drug use and are drug dependent. Cadets reported their alcohol use, on average, began between ages twelve and thirteen; marijuana use typically began between ages fourteen and sixteen. Most cadets report no prior substance abuse treatment.

6. <u>Criminal Justice System Involvement</u>—The majority of cadets (54 percent) report a significant arrest history, both adult and juvenile, for shoplifting, petty theft, grand theft, burglary, and robbery. Approximately 40 percent of the cadets reported a significant history of violent charges. The majority of cadets have a history of violations of probation due to technical violations or new charges.

7. <u>Family Needs</u>—Cadets report a significant family history of alcoholism (43 percent), drug addiction (44 percent), or criminality (16 percent). Most cadets report that their parents are separated or divorced. Most cadets report that they were targets of family violence, but many viewed the "beatings" they received from their parents as "normal." A significant history of sexual abuse was reported among female cadets.

8. <u>Psychological Needs</u>—At least one-third of the cadets have experienced significant depression or suicidal thoughts. Suicide attempts and gestures have been done

through the use of potentially lethal means (guns, hanging). Approximately 15 percent report previous psychiatric hospitalization. Cadets with violent histories are more likely to be court referred for psychological evaluations; however, cadets typically do not comply with evaluation recommendations. The vast majority of clients report difficulty managing anger appropriately. Histories often include property destruction and assault.

A summary of the needs identified by the psychosocial assessment include:

Assessment Need Area	% of Total
Housing	17
Medical	30
Legal	52
Education	61
Vocation	65
Substance Abuse	67

The results of the assessments identify with great clarity the huge scope of needs of these youthful offenders. It is difficult to imagine a corrections, or even a traditional community environment, that could begin to address these overwhelming needs to reeducate and resocialize these offenders. The drug and alcohol needs identified by the initial informal surveys of the cadets are shown as only one of a great many needs. These offenders are probably the "best" in the system in terms of their past criminality and current offenses.

Of the 183 cadets screened in ABC's first year, all have been referred to aftercare services; eighty-nine have been referred to Spectrum-run services (drug/alcohol in/out patient) which allows for tracking of the individuals to determine if they completed the course of treatment prescribed. A summary of all program referrals is as follows:

Type of Program	# of Referrals	% of Referrals
Outpatient Drug/Alcohol	78	42.62
Family Therapy/Outpatient	37	20.22
Boot Camp Alumni Meetings Only	22	12.02
Residential Drug/Alcohol	21	11.48
Drug/Alcohol Prevention Education	14	7.65
Battered Women Program/Outpatient	3	1.64
Intensive Outpatient Drug/Alcohol	2	1.09
Private Mental Health Outpatient	2	1.09
Alanon	2	1.09
Further Psychological Assessment	1	0.55
Mental Health Outpatient	1	0.55
Total	183	100

An additional expected outcome of ABC will be a profile of what type of offender does best in the boot camp program. This information will be given to the sentencing judges, as well as used by the jail classification system, in program referrals. This information will help refine the planning for beds for the program into the next decade.

For the future, funding has been received from the county, state, and sheriff's office trust fund to relocate the adult boot camp to the edge of the Everglades, a remote area at the western edge of the county. Also, on this site will be a juvenile boot camp and a conservation corps type of program for juveniles. The average number of adult boot camp referrals is expected to increase as the county's inmate population increases and as the number of youthful offenders grows.

A Local Coalition—Boot Camp or Not?

A local government considering establishment of an offender boot camp needs to involve decisionmakers from the local criminal justice system and the community in the process. The support of the sentencing judges, the prosecutor, the public defender, the private defense bar, and the community is essential if a program is to be implemented and succeed. If sentencing judges are not interested, if prosecutors will not recommend a boot camp sentence, and if defense attorneys are uninterested in this option for their clients, the boot camp is not viable.

At the state level, boot camps are often added to a state corrections system through an act of the state legislature, sometimes with little or no input from corrections professionals. At the local level, there is more chance that a deliberative process will occur of weighing how a boot camp could be an asset to the local criminal justice system. The local process is different as the money to operate a boot camp in a local corrections setting most likely will be local money—which must be allocated by the local governing body.

An ad hoc committee of influential criminal justice officials and community leaders to assist in evaluating the feasibility of a boot camp option also will be vital to the next step in the process—defining what it is the community wants a boot camp to accomplish.

Goals, Objectives, and Setting Reasonable Expectations

The criticisms of offender boot camps are based on the program's not meeting expected outcomes. Often these outcomes are unstated, or confused, allowing program critics wide latitude in evaluating the program. The local government should ask "What do we want to get out of a boot camp?" What are we trying to do?

- provide another sentencing option for frustrated judges?
- operate a strict program to get the attention of first-time offenders?
- reduce the future recidivism of offenders who complete the program?

- reduce the jail time served for selected, eligible offenders?
- respond to the citizens' needs to see offenders "punished?"

The boot camp's goal then will be determined by what yardstick the program's success will ultimately be measured. Each possible goal has ramifications which could go far beyond the local jail. For example, if the goal is to provide a strict program to get the attention of first-time offenders, the program may well add to the jail's budget as many of these first time offenders would never have been sentenced to jail without a boot camp option. If the goal is to reduce future recidivism, then a comprehensive tracking and aftercare program must be in place to provide intensive services to the program's graduates as well as to measure the results.

The first step in establishing a boot camp is to clearly define and agree on its goals, objectives, and expectations. The next step is to use a coalition to assure that the program is organized, managed, and coordinated to meet the mutually agreed upon goals. In most cases, the community and local government will require a strong partnership to achieve their mutual goals. As those who get involved with effective crime control know, little positive will happen without this partnership.

In Broward County's case, the evaluation of the program's success for the sheriff's office is centered around the cost avoidance of the program, rather than promising change in a youthful offender population after only ninety days of program exposure and with limited aftercare services. Because of the high visibility of the program, and the public's frustration over what is seen as a failed corrections philosophy in the United States, more was expected of the program's graduates. Efforts are now underway with a coalition of community and criminal justice officials to set outcome measures for the future.

Knowing the Offender Population

What are the eligibility criteria for offenders who enter boot camp? Although differing among boot camps, eligibility should focus on individuals who are viewed as amenable to the environment because they have a less lengthy criminal record, are youthful, are physically fit enough to participate in the program, and have not been arrested or convicted for crimes involving violence. The dilemma, as seen by the data gathered in Broward County and elsewhere, is that the absence of an arrest for a crime involving violence does not mean that the individual has a violence-free background. An "in your face" boot camp program for individuals with limited anger management skills can be a threat to the safety of staff and other inmates. The experience in Broward has been the interim reduction of bed space for the program from the initial 108 beds to the current 64 beds. Better management of the program and increased support of the judiciary will help reach the 1996 projection for 100 beds for the program in a system holding more than 700 sentenced felons. Perhaps for smaller local jail systems, a regional approach to implementing a boot camp may be a viable option.

The same local coalition involved with determining the boot camp's feasibility also might be involved with shaping eligibility criteria. This will reflect the coalition's endorsement and support for the program's target population.

As with any new corrections program with some promising potential, offender boot camps in a local jail setting are at risk for "widening the net." Judges may see a boot camp option as viable for some offenders who, prior to the boot camp's opening, the judge would have placed on probation. If judges are permitted to specifically sentence to boot camp, this net widening will be aggravated. If the jail classification system is the process by which sentenced offenders are identified and referred, then the net widening might be mitigated. Most inmates will not volunteer to be part of boot camp when the alternative may be to do nothing all day; so the manner in which referrals and sentences are made is critical to identifying the population and assuring their "commitment" to completion.

When the eligibility criteria are established, the next task is to determine if there are any candidates for a local boot camp in the jail's population. As most local jails face crowding, an analysis of the population will lead to this answer. If the population is predominately pretrial, boot camp may not be an effective sentencing option. If the jail holds individuals serving short sentences, this is the target population. Of this inmate group, how many are less serious offenders, with less of a history of violence? How many are in a physical condition to get through military-style physical training? Of this population, how many do not have high school diplomas, have a history of substance abuse, or have needs that can be met as part of a boot camp program?

Staff Selection and Training

Staff selection, training, and performance evaluation are critical to the program's success and the avoidance of liability. Most staff who volunteered to become part of the unit's initial staffing had military backgrounds. Above all else, corrections boot camps are corrections programs, not the military. This is often a difficult concept to grasp for staff who believe that their own military experience was a major turning point in their lives. It is important to acknowledge that the staff's goal is not to turn out citizen-soldiers, but to engage in activities to redirect the inmate to return into society without resorting to crime.

We recommend that part of the staff selection process include psychological assessments, interviews, and review of current performance to assure the safety of staff and inmates. This is especially recommended if juveniles are to be involved. Supervision of staff is important to assure that the program's integrity is maintained, problems identified early, and corrective action taken.

Staff training must focus on more than replicating military basic training. While this element may be essential to some program designs, training needs to be given to staff in how to help the cadets change their lives. Staff must have strong interpersonal communications skills and be able to provide effective supervision models. Some cadets find that the deputies assigned to them as drill instructors become the family they never had. The staff genuinely care about the cadets, and the staff becomes very frustrated when they do not see the cadets succeeding after graduation due to forces beyond their control. Another area to address is the frustrations of the staff who are working very closely with a very difficult client group.

Written Policies and Procedures

As with all corrections programs, boot camps require written statements of policy and procedures for both staff and program participants. The Broward County Military Training Unit borrowed their initial procedures from existing programs across the United States, and the directives have been evolving ever since. The written directives would have been improved had clearer and more quantifiable goal statements been part of the initial planning process. Written policies and procedures also are provided to program participants for them to understand the program's objectives during their incarceration.

Program Structure

A primary difference between a jail boot camp and the rest of the jail's sentenced population is that most of the boot camp participant's time is highly structured. This requires appropriate resources. In designing the program's everyday schedule, the program's goals will guide the development. Resources can be solicited from the public schools, public and private social service agencies, local universities and colleges, and community volunteers to assure that the right mix of programming is developed to achieve the stated goals and objectives.

A significant part of the Broward Military Training Unit program involves community service. Each cadet works at least four hours a week, under the supervision of deputies, on community projects such as neighborhood cleanups, graffiti painting, work at Habitat for Humanity home sites, cleaning up the county's public ball park after games, beach cleanup, and any other activities in support of public agencies, or private not-for-profit organizations. The Miliary Training Unit cadets, as well as other inmate workers, support the Broward Sheriff's Office community policing initiatives by providing a work force that has an impact on community policing efforts across the county.

Other considerations in program design include: the extent to which the program will award "good" time or "gain" time to participants, time off their sentence, and whether program completion can mitigate the inmate's sentence.

Aftercare Services

It is clear that boot camps, to have any impact at all, must include aftercare. This is one instance in which the available research matches practitioner's experience. Aftercare services must meet the needs of the offenders that have been identified. The aftercare services can rely on existing community services for which many of the boot camp participants are already eligible, or for which they are already part of the caseload. All participants should leave the program with a written plan which has been discussed with them, including time deadlines for reporting and ways to measure participation. One way to "encourage" participation is to have the sentencing judge mandate the specific aftercare plan as part of the probation plan.

Program Evaluation

In addition to increasing aftercare services, the next priority for the current Broward County program is creating a meaningful, program relevant, and simple evaluation system. Clearly the agreed on set of objectives will be the first phase in this effort. Grant funds were sought from the U. S. Department of Justice, but were not awarded. Much of the National Institute of Justice and Bureau of Justice Assistance research into boot camps is difficult to translate into practical application by those of us at the local level.

The dilemma frequently facing local criminal justice practitioners is creating a program evaluation model outside of the funding consideration that provides useful information for evolving the program. Developing a comparison group within the sentenced offender population and tracking the outcomes for those inmates may be one way to proceed with determining if boot camps are shortening the stay of offenders and decreasing their chance of rearrest or violation of probation. Most local governments, however, do not have the resources or, more important, the expertise to engage in that level of research. Often local public and private universities are interested only if dollars are available for them for devoting resources to the evaluation effort.

In the end, the recommendation is to keep evaluation measures simple, related to agreed on objectives, and to use measurable indicators, easily gleaned from the local criminal justice information system. Each local boot camp will be different as it reflects the community. Those considering boot camps should be less concerned about meeting some poorly defined national standard, and more concerned with meeting the needs of the local citizens, and running a cost-effective program.

Advantages and Disadvantages of Jail-based Boot Camps

Advantages:

- **Expand Sentencing Options.** In most states, due to severe crowding within the state corrections system, various legislative initiatives are passed. These result in fewer sentenced inmates serving time in state facilities but pass on the problem to local jails that struggle over what to do with this offender population. Boot camps may provide a sentencing option for the community. The program must be thoughtfully constructed so that "net widening" does not occur. A careful review of the sentenced inmate population will answer whether a boot camp is the sentencing option which is the most cost effective.

- **Integration of the Community into the Jail.** The process of determining if a boot camp is a viable option, as well as the process of establishing a boot camp, are effective processes for getting the local citizens involved in the jail's operation. Critical public support is missing from most local correctional activities; jails just are not very sexy. Public involvement in a new idea which has already received wide public interest will result in a positive partnership. Public support will lead to funding, volunteers, aftercare services, and a better understanding of corrections.

- **Provide for Staff Development.** The presence of corrections sentencing options is also a healthy staff development tool. Too frequently, we have few innovative programs to excite and challenge corrections staff. A properly planned and operated boot camp will provide options for quality staff to expand their horizons in corrections while performing a critical community-based function.

- **Coalesce the Local Criminal Justice System and the Community.** There are too few opportunities for a coordinated approach to effective local corrections. A deliberative planning process toward evaluating options and establishing a boot camp can be one of those experiences. This program will not succeed without the support of the entire local criminal justice system and the community.

- **Aftercare Success.** A valid criticism of boot camps at state correctional facilities are that once offenders return to their community, they are often far away from the staff and support of the program. Probation and parole officers handle enormous caseloads and often are unable to handle the boot camp returnees any differently from that of their other caseload. A local jail-based boot camp sentencing option has the great luxury of linking all required community and social services to the program participants before they leave the boot camp.

Disadvantages:

- **Motives and Goals.** The criminal justice system has a history of programming which has proven to be nothing more than fads. This is often in response to the frustration of trying to address the public's concerns about what really works in crime control. Boot camps have been the subject of political motives which do not necessarily mirror good correctional programming. This is why it is essential to clearly establish the program's goals and objectives before beginning implementation planning.

- **Defining Success.** It may be difficult to reach a consensus on the measures of success which are acceptable to all political and corrections parties involved. If future local funding relies on a promise that no boot camp graduate will commit a crime for years after graduation, the program already has failed. High expectations must be tempered with reality.

- **Allocation of Scarce Local Corrections Dollars.** If sentencing options or jail crowding options are necessary, boot camps may not be the most cost effective answer. Boot camps will require more intensive staffing than a "normal" correctional environment. A more intensive staff selection process is needed, as well as specialized training and good supervision. More counselors, aftercare workers, and volunteers will be needed to support a boot camp program than for other inmate programming. The price may be worth paying, but the price should be known. Given the status of most local corrections systems, there are not the extra financial resources to stray too far from provision of basic services to the maximum number of inmates.

- **Net Widening.** Most new correction programs, like most new corrections beds, are filled faster than ever anticipated. It would be very difficult for a conscientious judge not to sentence a youthful offender to a new boot camp program, rather than probation, if the judge really believed that program might turn the offender's life around. As such, planning for boot camp implementation should conclude that the program will bring in more youthful offenders than would have entered the local system without the boot camp.

Conclusion

The example of how the Broward Sheriff's Office Military Training Unit operates is provided for the consideration by those local governments thinking about establishing a boot camp. Boot camps alone are not the answer to any one set of crime problems facing a community. Boot camps may be a part of a more comprehensive local corrections system in a system designed to target specific types of offenders.

Boot camps are a more costly alternative in terms of staff-to-inmate ratios, staff selection processes, and staff training. Reallocation of existing resources may not be an option for local jail systems facing fiscal crises in managing the everyday environment. Finally, boot camps require a partnership between all parties in the criminal justice system and the community to be successful. If these elements are understood by all parties, then jail boot camps may provide an effective correctional option for your community.

Correctional Boot Camps for Juveniles

Doris Layton MacKenzie, Ph.D.

Associate Professor, Department of Criminology and Criminal Justice
University of Maryland
College Park, Maryland

Andre B. Rosay

Graduate Student, Department of Criminology and Criminal Justice
University of Maryland
College Park, Maryland

Burgeoning prison populations have led states to search for innovative alternatives to address correctional problems (Morris and Tonry 1990). Many of the alternatives proposed, however, place the offender in the community and may be viewed by the public as being "soft" on crime. Not wanting to appear to be soft on criminals, politicians hesitate to support many of these alternatives. Boot camp prisons are one alternative that can be touted as tough on crime. Supporting this perspective are the media reports of boot camps, where drill instructors are shown yelling at young offenders. Perhaps this is what has most influenced the rapid growth of the boot camps. Since their beginning in Oklahoma and Georgia in adult prisons in 1983, more than thirty-two states, the Federal Bureau of Prisons, ten local jurisdictions, and an increasing number of juvenile detention centers have opened correctional boot camps (Cronin 1994).

Originally, boot camps programs were distinguished from other correctional programs by their emphasis on physical labor, exercise, and a military-style atmosphere (Cronin 1994, United States General Accounting Office 1993, MacKenzie and Souryal 1994, MacKenzie and Parent 1992). Although most of the boot camp programs used military basic training to some extent, they differed considerably in other respects (Cronin 1994, United States General Accounting Office 1993, MacKenzie and Souryal 1994, Clark and Aziz 1996, Cowles and Castellano 1995).

More recently, the camps are referred to as second-, third- or even fourth-generation boot camps indicating a series of changes that placed an increased emphasis on rehabilitation, aftercare, or work skills and a diminished emphasis on the tough, confrontational, military components (Gransky et al. 1995). These new camps take names such the Work Ethic Camp in Washington's Department of Corrections, or the Youth Leadership Academy in New York's Division for Youth. The new camps have moved away from the old-fashioned view of military boot camps with aggressive confrontation, tough physical training, and hard labor towards the newer view of boot camps as leadership training opportunities. However, there are still a wide variety of correctional boot camps. Some continue to emphasize aspects of the old-style military boot camps while others emphasize individual programming, positive behavioral change, or work skills. Obviously, these differences among programs will result in wide variations in the effectiveness of the programs in achieving specific goals.

While the boot camp programs originally developed in adult prisons, an increasing number of programs are currently being designed for local jails and juvenile populations. As the boot camps become popular for juveniles, new issues have arisen (Cronin 1994, Austin et al. 1993). For example, while adult programs could target nonviolent offenders in prison, nonviolent juveniles were much less apt to be incarcerated. Thus, net widening and the associated costs have become critical issues for juvenile programs. This is particularly relevant given the history of concern with the destructive environment of detention centers for nonviolent juveniles or status offenders.

The deceptively seductive idea of providing discipline and structure for disruptive juveniles means there is a real threat that increasingly large numbers of juveniles will be placed in boot camps, whether or not it is a suitable alternative sanction. Furthermore, in contrast to adult boot camps, academic and therapeutic programming and aftercare are viewed as necessary components in juvenile programs. In fact, there are questions about how much the boot camp programs actually differ from other residential facilities for juveniles. Questions revolve around the specific conditions of confinement or the environment of the boot camps. How do the boot camp conditions differ from traditional detention or training centers? What are the impacts of these conditions on those involved? If they do indeed differ, there are questions about the effectiveness of the camps for certain types of juveniles (such as higher risk, older, those with more past detention experiences). Furthermore, some are fearful that aspects of the camps may be particularly damaging for some juveniles such as those who were physically or sexually abused in the past or those who are first-time offenders.

Survey of Juvenile Boot Camps

Starting in June 1995, we surveyed state and local juvenile correctional administrators to identify all juvenile boot camps currently operating. In all, we located thirty-eight different boot camps (see Table 1). We obtained descriptive information on thirty-seven of the boot camps in twenty-two different states. One of these programs, The First Arizona Youth Academy in Arizona, will not begin operations until later this year. All administrators were asked to return a survey addressing key characteristics of their programs. The results are summarized below and shown in Tables 1-11, which begin on page 103.

The emergence of juvenile boot camps has indeed been a recent but explosive trend (see Table 2). Out of the thirty-eight boot camps we surveyed, we only found one boot camp, the Challenge Program in Texas, which started operating before the 1990s (one other boot camp, called About Face, near Memphis, Tennessee that existed in the 1980s has been closed). The next program to develop was the Los Angeles County Drug Treatment Program in 1990 in two different camps. Two programs were implemented in 1991 and an additional four in 1992. All others started operating during or after 1993. Currently, we estimate that about 10,500 juveniles participate in boot camps each year. In 1995, the Office of Justice Programs (OJP) in the United States Department of Justice with funding from the Crime Act provided funds to twelve jurisdiction to renovate or construct facilities for juvenile boot camps; another twelve jurisdictions were given funds for the purpose of planning juvenile boot camps. Given these numbers, juvenile boot camps most likely will continue to increase in the next few years.

The existing juvenile boot camps vary dramatically. For example, while the Challenge program in Texas has a capacity of twelve juveniles, the Tallulah Correctional Center for Youth in Louisiana has a capacity of 396 youth. The duration of the programs show as much variation as the capacity (see Table 2). One program, the specialized Treatment and Rehabilitation in Texas, can be a one-day program for juveniles whose parents and school believe a one-day participation in drill will be effective. The longest program we surveyed was the Thurgood Marshall Boot Camp in the District of Columbia, where juveniles stay for 540 days.

The types of juveniles who participate in boot camp programs tend to be fairly similar (see Tables 3 and 4). However, unlike adult boot camps, juvenile programs are rarely limited to individuals convicted of or committed for their first serious offense, nor are juveniles apt to be required to volunteer. The typical juvenile in boot camp is a nonviolent male between the ages of fourteen and eighteen. These juveniles are placed in the boot camp by a juvenile judge. Only about 60 percent of the boot camps are limited to nonviolent offenders; the other 40 percent will accept offenders convicted of violent offenses.

Because of a heavy emphasis on education and counseling (see Table 6), it is no surprise that juvenile boot camp administrators rate rehabilitation as a very important goal of their programs (see Table 5). On a scale of 0 (not a goal) to 4 (a very important goal), administrators, on average, rated rehabilitation as a 3.7. Reducing recidivism also was rated as very important. The ratings for reducing crowding and costs, punishing, and deterring were varied. Nevertheless, it appears that reducing crowding and costs are more important goals than punishment. Note, the ratings we received are very dependent upon the raters. Because different administrators have different goals and because goals tend to change over time, these results lack reliability. However, we can safely conclude that while rehabilitation and lowering recidivism are important goals, punishment is not.

Almost all of the boot camps that these juveniles go to emphasize a military atmosphere with military drill, platoon grouping, discipline, physical labor, military titles and uniforms (see Table 6). Only three of the boot camps surveyed do not use military drill (the Alabama Department of Youth Services Chalkville HIT Program, the Highly Structured Program for Juveniles in Iowa, and the Genesis Youth Center in Utah). The Chalkville HIT Program and the Genesis Youth Center were also two of the four that do not have platoon grouping. All surveyed programs use discipline. We were concerned because there has been some debate about whether either group punishments or summary punishments are appropriate for juveniles. Some group punishments entail punishing the whole group for the poor performance of one individual while summary punishments involve immediate sanctions such as doing push-ups or running laps by the individual.

Nine of the boot camps use neither group rewards and punishments nor summary punishments. On the other hand, about fourteen of the programs use either group rewards and punishments or summary punishments and about twelve use both methods. The Green River Boys' Camp in Kentucky, the Columbia and Oakley Training Schools in Mississippi, and the Regimental Wilderness Program in Florida use both group rewards and summary punishments but do not use group punishments (see Table 6). About 75 percent use military titles and uniforms for staff and juveniles (see Table 7).

In addition to the military atmosphere, the majority of the programs include physical labor in the daily activities (see Table 6). All but one of the boot camps engage youth in physical fitness and sports activity, and the majority also have some type of challenge or adventure programming for the juveniles. Overall, juveniles spend between one-to-ten hours per day in physical training, military drill, and work. For example, while youth in the Boot Camp in Doncaster, Maryland only spend one hour per day in these activities, youth in the Martin County Sheriff's Office Juvenile Boot Camp in Florida spend ten hours per day in these activities. On the average, juveniles spend about three and a half hours on physical training, military drill, and work, depending on the boot camp.

In comparison, they will spend, on average, about six and a half to seven hours in educational classes or counseling (see Table 6). No juvenile boot camp program spends less than three and a half hours per day on education and counseling. In some programs, such as the Junior Reserve Officer's Training Corps in South Carolina and the Leon County Sheriff's Office Boot Camp in Florida, youth respectively spend thirteen and twelve hours per day on these activities. More specifically, juvenile boot camp programs offer drug and alcohol counseling, education programs, and vocational training. Youth in all but three of the programs spend some time in drug and alcohol counseling. All programs surveyed had educational programs, and about half of the surveyed programs offered vocational training.

The boot camps also vary in their dropout and expulsion policies and rates (see Table 8). Our survey reveals that most boot camp programs do not allow voluntary dropout. When voluntary dropout is permitted, very few juveniles actually decide to drop out of the program. Indeed, dropping out of the boot camp programs is very much discouraged. For example, while both the Twin Pines Ranch in California and the Junior Reserve Officers' Training Corps in South Carolina permit the youth to drop out, only 2 and 1 percent, respectively, do so. Almost all boot camps have a procedure to expel juveniles who have not met the program requirements. The percentages of those expelled are usually fairly low (about 10 percent). Some programs, such as L.E.A.D. in California tend to have higher expulsion rates. L.E.A.D. has an expulsion rate of about 30 percent. On the other hand, several boot camps report that although expulsions are possible, no juveniles are expelled (the Abraxas Leadership Development Program in Pennsylvania and the S.T.A.R. Day Boot Camp in Texas). Juveniles who drop out or who are expelled are usually returned to either juvenile court or to their institution of origin for longer sentences.

The boot camps surveyed also report high graduation rates (see Table 9). The majority of the boot camps report rates of above 90 percent, and several have graduation rates of 100 percent (the average rate is 95 percent). The Juvenile Boot Camp at Doncaster, Maryland, the Youth Leadership Academy in New York, and Camp Washington in Virginia allow neither dropouts nor expulsions; all participants must graduate from the program. Most of the programs have public graduation ceremonies for the graduates.

On release, boot camp graduates most often participate in aftercare programs with varying levels of supervision (see Table 10). While participating in aftercare, the graduates stay at home with their families. These aftercare programs vary as much as the boot camps themselves do. The capacity of the programs tends to be fairly large as many have over 100 juveniles. Several aftercare programs report an unlimited capacity. There are several, however, which are kept small. For example, the Abraxas Youth Leadership Development Program reports a capacity of twenty-four delinquents. On average, boot camp graduates stay in these aftercare programs for about a year, but again this varies greatly. The three boot camps in Alabama keep graduates in their aftercare programs for three months. On the other hand, graduates from the Tallulah Correctional Center for Youth in Florida can participate in their aftercare programs for up to three years.

While in the aftercare programs, boot camp graduates participate in a wide array of activities (see Table 11). Most programs include treatment, education, family counseling, and intensive supervision as components of the aftercare. About half of the programs also include employment and/or vocational training. Beyond these basic components, aftercare programs emphasize a variety of other elements such as, among others, anti-gang programs, community service projects, mentorships, independent living training, recreation programs, and financial resources and assistance.

This short survey of the juvenile boot camps indicates substantial differences among the programs, both during the incarceration phase and the aftercare phase. While there are some consistencies (for example, a military atmosphere and physical training), there are many differences that we expect have varying impacts on the participating youth.

Examining the Effectiveness of Boot Camp Programs

Most of the research examining correctional boot camps comes from studies of adult programs. Some research indicates that boot camps can reduce prison crowding if they are designed as early release mechanisms (MacKenzie and Piquero 1994). While the programs may have the potential to reduce prison crowding, in actuality they seldom do. For example, in the multisite evaluation, two of the five boot camp programs appeared to save prison beds (MacKenzie and Piquero 1994, MacKenzie and Souryal 1994). In the remaining three states, the boot camp program appeared to cost the state jurisdiction prison beds. Thus, the evidence that boot camp prisons reduce crowding is not extremely persuasive to date.

Given the rapid proliferation of boot camp prisons across the nation and the fact that reducing recidivism is one of the major objectives of many of the programs, it is somewhat surprising that there have been few empirical studies of the impact of these programs on recidivism. Much of the existing literature has been produced by state correctional officials themselves (Florida Department of Corrections 1990, Flowers et al. 1991, State of Texas 1989, New York State Department of Correctional Services 1992). However, after reviewing some of these studies, Cullen et al. (1993) warned that the results should be viewed with caution due to methodological problems. A particularly important criticism centered on the failure of these efforts to rely on experimental designs in their group comparisons. Compounding this problem, argued Cullen and his colleagues, was the lack of statistical controls for potentially important variables (such as community supervision intensity) whose levels differ among comparison groups.

Although not a random assignment study, MacKenzie et al. (1995) did control for differences among groups in a multisite study of boot camps in eight states. The analysis suggested that those who completed boot camp performed about the same as their comparison group counterparts. The researchers found some evidence that suggested a reduction in recidivism for boot camp participants in programs where participants received three or more hours of treatment or education, volunteered, and had follow-up aftercare. They ended with the question: "Does the military atmosphere add anything above and beyond a short-term, quality prison treatment program?" In another study, MacKenzie and Brame (1995) found that boot camp releasees adjusted more positively than comparison samples during community supervision in only one of five sites. Thus, both the recidivism studies and the positive adjustment studies suggest that there may be some programs that have positive impacts on participants. However, the specific components that lead to the positive effects are unclear.

To date, research examining boot camps has shown very little negative impact from the programs. Offenders report being drug free and physically healthy when they leave the boot camps (MacKenzie and Souryal 1992). They also believed the program helped them, and they were optimistic about the future. This was true of the "enhanced" boot camp programs that emphasized treatment as well as programs that focused predominantly on military training, hard labor, and discipline. However, when MacKenzie and Souryal (1995) examined changes in antisocial attitudes, they found that those in the boot camps as well as the comparison samples of prisoners became less antisocial. Again, results on the effectiveness of the boot camps are mixed, and we are left with questions about the specific components of the camps that led to positive change. In some exploratory analyses, MacKenzie and Souryal (1995) did find some evidence that participants became less antisocial in boot camps that devoted more time to rehabilitation, had higher dismissal rates, and were voluntary.

Research on Juvenile Boot Camp Programs

Few studies of juvenile boot camp programs have been completed. The Office of Juvenile Justice and Delinquency Prevention of the United States Department of Justice funded three juvenile boot camps in Cleveland, Ohio, Denver, Colorado, and Mobile, Alabama. The intention was to demonstrate and test juvenile boot camps for nonviolent offenders.

The boot camps, opened in April 1992, combined military regimentation and conditioning with rehabilitation and aftercare services. The study used random assignment to the programs (versus comparison facilities) so that differences in recidivism rates could be compared within each state. Early analyses of the data indicate no difference between the boot camp graduates and comparison samples in two sites, and in the third, the boot camp graduates actually had higher recidivism rates than the control group. In all the sites, there were problems related to the development and implementation of the boot camps, and the researchers speculate that these difficulties are most likely the reason for the failure to see a positive impact of the boot camps.

In 1992, the California Youth Authority (CYA) established a boot camp called L.E.A.D. (Leadership, Esteem, Ability, and Discipline) designed to serve the state's nonviolent and least serious offenders (Bottcher et al. 1996). Its expressed goals were to reduce recidivism and to provide a cost-effective sentencing option for these juveniles. The California Youth Authority research branch has initiated a study of the program including a random assignment comparing participants to controls. The researchers provide valuable yearly evaluation reports describing interim information on the implementation and impact of the program. While the full results of the recidivism portion of the study are not yet available, preliminary analyses of recidivism comparing the boot camp juveniles with the comparison sample do not show any significant differences in recidivism during the first thirty days after release. However, the researchers caution that the data is very limited at this time.

As was found with adults, the boot camp participants in L.E.A.D. report being physically healthy and safer in the boot camp in comparison to the control group. Also, similar to the adult programs, the data examining cost savings indicated that the program has the potential to reduce costs. However, the researchers cautioned that there are many factors at play that could rapidly decrease any savings realized by the program. For example, an examination of judicial recommendations indicated that some judges may be committing youth to detention for the boot camp; youth who would not otherwise be sent to a facility. Between 29 and 33 percent of the entrants do not complete the boot camp programs. Most of the time this is because of gang-related conflicts, general disciplinary problems related to lack of motivation, and/or assaultiveness.

Florida operates more juvenile boot camps than any other state in the nation (Cass and Kaltenecker 1996). An unusual aspect of the programs is the partnership between local and state governments. The camps are run by the county sheriff's departments with oversight by the Florida Department of Juvenile Justice. General guidelines are established by statute and defined by administrative rules; otherwise, each locality has the flexibility to develop a program that makes use of local resources and involves the community. All of the camps are required to last at least six months and to provide intensive education, physical training, and rehabilitative programs appropriate for children. According to early reports, most of those who enter the programs eventually graduate (87 percent or more) and 75 percent do so in the expected four months.

Preliminary information on recidivism from one of the boot camps shows that 74 percent of the youths who finished the program in 1993 were arrested in 1994 (*Miami Tribune*, March 21, 1995), a number the program administrators found to be disappointingly large. In contrast to the adult programs, the Florida boot camps target juveniles committed for serious offenses or who have a record of past felony adjudications. Preliminary data from the programs indicates that juveniles placed in Florida's boot camps have extensive histories of delinquency.

This short review of the literature on boot camp programs for juveniles and adults demonstrates that most research has focused on individual programs and the impact of these programs on later criminal activities. The problem is that the programs differ dramatically in goals and components. Thus, knowledge about the effectiveness of one program may be dependent upon very atypical aspects of the program or even a charismatic leader, and not necessarily be related to boot-camp-type characteristics of the program. The research results may show us a program that works but not why it works. To understand why the program works, we need to know more about the relationship between the specific components of the program and the impacts on the individuals involved.

The Debate About Correctional Boot Camps for Juveniles

Boot camps are controversial for a variety of reasons (MacKenzie and Hebert 1996, MacKenzie and Souryal 1995a, MacKenzie and Parent 1992, Meachum 1990, Morash and Rucker 1990). Much of it has to do with a kind of instinctive reaction toward the military atmosphere. It is important, however, to separate this instinctive reaction from the debates that occur among people who are knowledgeable about juvenile programming and corrections in general. Here, there is a much more interesting debate. One perspective exhibited by many knowledgeable correctional experts is what might be called a "Machiavellian point of view" (MacKenzie and Souryal 1995). These individuals expect little direct benefit from the military atmosphere of the boot camp programs, but they are willing to use it to achieve two ends: early release for nonviolent offenders and additional funds for treatment programs (both within and outside prison). In their opinion, the popularity of the boot camps with policy makers and the public allows corrections to obtain early release, separate less serious offenders from others, and provide treatment that otherwise would not be available to these offenders.

From 1984 until 1990, the admission rate for juveniles in public facilities rose from just over 400,000 in 1984 to 570,000 in 1990 (Parent et al. 1994). A large percent of the juveniles in secure confinement are committed for nonviolent offenses (Krisberg and Austin 1993). In these facilities, they are mixed with more serious violent offenders. The resulting crowding means that the time and resources devoted to rehabilitation, education, and other constructive activities become increasingly limited (Altschuler 1994). Boot camps provide a method of separating the less serious juveniles from others and a way to develop a daily schedule of constructive and therapeutic activities appropriate for these juveniles. The "get tough" appearance of the camps answers the policy makers need to emphasize punishment, public safety, and offender accountability. However, as was shown in the survey we did of juvenile programs, those responsible for developing the boot camps are interested in rehabilitation as well as recidivism reduction. They are much less interested in the punishment aspects of the camps.

In contrast with those who use the boot camps to surreptitiously achieve their correctional goals, others fear the dangers of boot camps. Despite the potential benefits, many psychologists with experience in both corrections and behavioral change strongly argue against the boot camp programs. They believe that the potential dangers of the military models are too great to compromise for early release or funds for treatment. Furthermore, they argue that boot camps cannot provide a mechanism for treatment because many of the characteristics of the programs (confrontation, punishment instead of reward) are antithetical to treatment. The confrontational interactions may be particularly damaging for some individuals such as those who have been abused in the past or others who have problems with dependency in relationships. Morash and Rucker (1990) contend that aspects of the boot camps actually may inflict damage on participants.

Additionally, the boot camp opponents fear that, even though some programs may be used as early-release mechanisms, most have a serious potential for widening the net. This point is particularly critical for the newly developing juvenile programs. The boot camps appear to be a deceptively simple way of managing the disruptive juvenile who is a status offender or who has been involved in relatively minor criminal activities. There is a real danger that after working so hard for the past twenty-five years to deinstitutionalize status offenders, the boot camps will increasingly be used for status offenders (Holden and Kapler 1995). The fear is that the programs will greatly increase the numbers of juveniles incarcerated because the programs appear to many to be the perfect solution for unruly and undisciplined juveniles.

There are some additional concerns about using these programs for juveniles. Juveniles are in a different stage of development than adults. It may be difficult for juveniles to obey authority figures if they do not believe that such obedience is in their own best interest. They may rail against the injustice of group punishment. Some juveniles, such as those who have been victimized in the past, may have additional problems that make the boot camps a harmful experience for them. Furthermore, the programs may not address the risk factors that are important precursors of delinquency (Gottfredson et al. 1996). For example, by removing the children from the community, the boot camps may not provide family counseling or help the youth develop new and positive social activities with nondelinquent peers.

Practitioners also express concern about the need for individualized programming and whether the boot camps with group punishments and rewards will be able to address the variety of needs of these youth. Lipsey's (1992) meta-analysis of treatment programs found that interventions of longer duration involving more structured and focused treatment that were behavioral and skill-oriented, as well as those incorporating multimodal treatments were more effective than less structured and unfocused approaches. While the boot camps may have the required structure, they may lack other principles of successful treatment programs such emphasizing rewarding good behavior much more frequently than punishing bad behavior, individualized programming, and skill-oriented education.

Yet, a third perspective argues that the military atmosphere is an effective model for changing offenders. Persons who have worked in drug treatment programs—where strict rules, discipline, and confrontational interactions are common—seem to be more comfortable with the military model. Military personnel assert that the leadership model of basic training provides new and appropriate techniques for correctional programming. Of course, many of those responsible for the development and implementation of individual boot camp programs are committed to and believe in the viability of this approach. They argue that the stress created in boot camp may shake up the inmates and make them ready to change and take advantage of the treatment and aftercare programs offered. Further, the military atmosphere of boot camp actually may enhance the effect of this treatment by keeping the offenders physically and mentally healthy and enabling them to focus on their education, treatment, and therapy.

So, the debate continues. What is clear is that these boot camps are proliferating across the nation, yet we do not know much about them—their effects on the individuals involved nor the impact on correctional systems. The main point may be that we need to learn exactly what are the beneficial aspects of the camps and what are the negative aspects. Certainly, we can assume that the effect of the camps will differ depending on the needs of the individuals involved. We need detailed information on the specific components of the programs and how these components affect those involved. We need to learn what type of boot camp is (or is not) effective for specific types of offenders.

Table 1: Juvenile Boot Camps: Who Operates Them and Their Placement Authority

State	Name of Program	Who Operates	Placement Authority
AL	A.D.Y.S. Autauga Campus	Alabama Dept. of Juvenile Services	Dept. of Youth Services and Juvenile Court Judges
AL	A.D.Y.S. Chalkville HIT Program	Alabama Dept. of Juvenile Services	Dept. of Youth Services and Juvenile Court Judges
AL	A.D.Y.S. Thomasville Campus	Alabama Dept. of Juvenile Services	Dept. of Youth Services and Juvenile Court Judges
AR	First Arizona Youth Academy[1]	First Corrections Corporation of America	Dept. Youth Treatment & Rehabilitation
CA	L.E.A.D. [2]	California Youth Authority	California Youth Authority
CA	LA County Drug Treatment[2]	LA County Probation Department	LA County Superior Juvenile Court
CA	Twin Pines Ranch	Riverside County Probation Dept.	Juvenile Court
CA	Rehabilitation Oriented Training Center	San Bernardino County Probation	Juvenile Court
CO	Camp Falcon	Rebound Corporation	Juvenile Court Judges [3]
DC	Thurgood Marshall Boot Camp	L.S.W.A.	Courts; OHYC Treatment Team Coordinators
FL	Martin County Sheriff's Office Juvenile Boot Camp	Martin County Sheriff's Office	Juvenile Court
FL	Pinellas County Boot Camp	Pinellas County Sheriff's Department	Juvenile Justice
FL	Leon County Sheriff's Off. Boot Camp	Leon County Sheriff's Department	Florida Department of Juvenile Justice
FL	Regimental Wilderness Program	North American Family Institute	State Department of Juvenile Justice
GA	Irwin Youth Development Campus	Bobby Ross Group	Juvenile Judges
IN	Camp Summit	Dept. of Corrections, Juvenile Division	Juvenile Division Intake
IA	Highly Structured Program for Juveniles	Clarinda Youth Corp./ Family Resources, Inc.	Juvenile Court
KY	Green River Boys' Camp	Dept. for Social Services, Div. of Youth Services	Department for Social Services
LA	Tallulah Correctional Center for Youth	Trans American Development Assoc., Inc.	State Diagnostic Center
MD	Juvenile Boot Camp at Doncaster	North American Family Institute	Juvenile Justice
MS	Columbia Training School	Division of Youth Services	Juvenile Courts
MS	Oakley Training School	Division of Youth Services	Juvenile Courts
NJ	Wharton Tract Juvenile Boot Camp	State of NJ; Dept. of Law and Public Safety	Juv. Reception Classification Committee
NY	Youth Leadership Academy	Division for Youth	Division for Youth
OH	Camp Roulston	North American Family Institute	Cuyahoga County
PA	Abraxas Leadership Development Prog.	Abraxas Foundation Inc.	Juvenile Courts
PA	Fort Charles Young Boot and Hat Camp	VisionQuest	Juvenile Courts
SC	Junior Reserve Officer's Training Corps	Department of Juvenile Justice	None, voluntary placement
TX	Challenge Program	Juvenile Probation	Juvenile Judge
TX	Community Corrections Inc. (C.C.I.) Boot Camp	Community Corrections Inc.	Probation Department
TX	Specialized Treatment and Rehabilitation	Dept. of Community Supervision and Cor.	Juvenile Court and Probation
TX	S.T.A.R. Day Boot Camp	Juvenile Probation	Juvenile Judge
UT	Genesis Youth Center	Division of Youth Corrections	Juv. Court Bench/Youth Parole Authority
VA	Camp Washington	Youth Services International, Inc.	Commonwealth of VA; City of Richmond
WA	Basic Training Boot Camp	Juvenile Rehabilitation Administration	Juvenile Rehabilitation Administration

[1] Scheduled to start July 1, 1996. [2] Operates in two locations–data has been combined. [3] Judges act on probation officer recommendations.

Table 2: Juvenile Boot Camps: Year Started, Capacity, and Length of Stay

State	Name of Program	Year Began	Capacity	Usual Stay in Days	Stay Can Be Extended (Length)
AL	Autauga	1994	78	28	Yes, for 7 days
AL	Chalkville	1991	24	28	Yes, for 17 days
AL	Thomasville	1992	37	28	Yes, for 17 days
AR	First Academy	1996	24	90	Yes, for 30 days
CA	L.E.A.D.	1992 / 1993	120	120	Yes, for 30 days
CA	Drug Treatment	1990	210	168	Yes, for 60 days
CA	Twin Pines	1993	70	180	Yes, for indefinite period
CA	R.O.T.C.	1995	40	150	Yes, for 30 days
CO	Camp Falcon	1994	80	60	No
DC	Thurgood Marshall	1991	30	540	Yes
FL	Martin County	1994	30	125 – 130	Yes, for 30 days
FL	Pinellas County	1993	30	120	Yes, for indefinite period
FL	Leon County	1994	60	240	Yes
FL	Regimental Wilderness	1994	30	120	Yes, for 30 days
GA	Irwin Youth	1995	316	90	No
IN	Camp Summit	1995	42	90	Yes
IA	Highly Structured	1995	50	90	No
KY	Green River	1994	40	90	No
LA	Tallulah	1994	396	90 – 180	Yes, for 90 days
MD	Doncaster	1994	30	84	Yes
MS	Columbia	1993	175	105	Yes, for indefinite period
MS	Oakley	1992	200	105	Yes, for indefinite period
NJ	Wharton Tract	1996	60 - 70	120	Yes
NY	Leadership Academy	1992	30	180	Yes, for 60 days
OH	Camp Roulston	1993	30	90	Yes, for 30 days
PA	Abraxas	1994	105	105	Yes, for 35 days
PA	Boot and Hat	1994	90	90	Yes, for 30 days
SC	J.R.O.T.C.	1993	150	240	No
TX	Challenge	1988	12	180	Yes, for 180 days
TX	C.C.I.	1995	54	180	Yes, for 30 days
TX	Treatment & Rehabilitation	1993		1 – 180	
TX	S.T.A.R.	1995	24	168	Yes
UT	Genesis	1994	72	54	Yes, for indeterminate period
VA	Washington	1996	45	150	Yes, for 30 days
WA	Basic Training	1996	48	120	No

State	Name of Program	Age Limits	Gender
	Table 3: Age and Gender of Juvenile Boot Camp Enrollees		
AL	Autauga	12 – 18	Males
AL	Chalkville	12 – 18	Females
AL	Thomasville	12 – 18	Males
AR	First Academy	14 – 17	Males
CA	L.E.A.D.	14 – 24	Males
CA	Drug Treatment	16 – 18	Males
CA	Twin Pines	15 – 19	Males
CA	R.O.T.C.	13 – 16	Males
CO	Camp Falcon	12 – 18	Males
DC	Thurgood Marshall	14 – 18	Males
FL	Martin County	14 – 18	Males
FL	Pinellas County	14 – 18	Males
FL	Leon County	14 – 18	Males
FL	Regimental Wilderness	14 – 17	Males
GA	Irwin Youth	11 – 17	Males
IN	Camp Summit	13 – 17	Males
IA	Highly Structured	14 – 17	Males
KY	Green River	14 – 17	Males
LA	Tallulah	13 – 20	Males
MD	Doncaster	15 – 18	Males
MS	Columbia	10 – 17	Both
MS	Oakley	10 – 17	Males
NJ	Wharton Tract	14 – 19	Males
NY	Leadership Academy	13 – 17	Males
OH	Camp Roulston	13 – 18	Males
PA	Abraxas	14 – 18	Males
PA	Boot and Hat	13 – 18	Males
SC	J.R.O.T.C.	9th – 12th grade	Both
TX	Challenge	14 – 16	Males
TX	C.C.I.	11 – 16	Both
TX	Treatment & Rehabilitation	10 – 16	Both
TX	S.T.A.R.	10 – 14	Both
UT	Genesis	14 – 21	Males
VA	Washington	14 – 18	Males
WA	Basic Training	13 – 18	Both

State	Name of Program	Non-violent	First Offense	First Serious	First Com-mitment	Volun-teers	Other Target Groups
AL	Autauga	No	No	No	No	No	Low risk
AL	Chalkville	No	No	No	No	No	Low risk
AL	Thomasville	No	No	No	No	No	Low risk
AR	First Academy	Yes	No	No	Yes	Yes	
CA	L.E.A.D.	Yes		No	Yes (to CYA)	Yes	
CA	Drug Treatment	No	No	No	No	No	Drug / Alcohol abuse history
CA	Twin Pines	Yes	No	No	No	No	Serious offenders
CA	R.O.T.C.	Yes	No	No	No	Yes	Failed in alternative programs
CO	Camp Falcon	No	No	No	No	No	
DC	Thurgood Marshall	No	Yes	Yes	Yes	Yes	Detained and committed youths
FL	Martin County	No	No	No	No	No	
FL	Pinellas County	No	No	No	No	No	Committed for life/capital/1st degree felony or 3rd degree felony with 2+ prior felonies
FL	Leon County						
FL	Regimental Wilderness	No	No	No	No	No	
GA	Irwin Youth	No	No	No	No	No	
IN	Camp Summit	Yes	No	No	No	No	
IA	Highly Structured	Yes	No	No	No	Yes	Out-of-home placements
KY	Green River	No	Yes	No	No	No	
LA	Tallulah	Yes	Yes	Yes	Yes	No	Property crime offenders
MD	Doncaster	No	No	No	No	No	
MS	Columbia	Yes*	Yes	Yes	Yes	No	All training school youths
MS	Oakley	Yes*	Yes	Yes	Yes	No	All training school youths
NJ	Wharton Tract	Yes	No	No	No	Yes	Committed to NJ Training School
NY	Leadership Academy	No	No	No	No	Yes	
OH	Camp Roulston	No	No	No	No	No	
PA	Abraxas	No	No	No	No	No	
PA	Boot and Hat	No	No	Yes	No	No	Probation violations
SC	J.R.O.T.C.	No	No	No	No	Yes	
TX	Challenge	Yes*	No	Yes	No	No	
TX	C.C.I.	No	No	No	No	No	
TX	Treatment & Rehabilitation	No	No	No	No	No	Youths disruptive at school
TX	S.T.A.R.	Yes	Yes			Yes	Middle school
UT	Genesis	No	No	No	No	No	
VA	Washington	Yes*	Yes	No	Yes	No	
WA	Basic Training	Yes	No	No	No	Yes	

Table 4: Enrollment Limits for Juvenile Boot Camp Enrollees

* Also includes violent offenders.

		(Not a Goal = 0 to Very Important = 4)						
State	Name of Program	Reduce Crowding	Reduce Costs	Punishment	Protect Public	Deterrence	Rehabil- itation	Lower Recidivism
AL	Autauga	3	2	2	4	2	4	4
AL	Chalkville	3	3	0	3	3	3	4
AL	Thomasville	3	2	0	4	3	4	4
AR	First Academy		3			4	4	
CA	L.E.A.D.	4	4	0	3	0	4	4
CA	Drug Treatment	1	1	1	4	4	4	4
CA	Twin Pines	4	4	3	4	4	4	4
CA	R.O.T.C.	4	2	0	4	1	4	4
CO	Camp Falcon	2	4	1	3	0	2	4
DC	Thurgood Marshall	2	1	3	3	3	4	3
FL	Martin County	3	3	2	4	4	4	4
FL	Pinellas County	0	0	1	4	4	4	3
FL	Leon County							
FL	Regimental Wilderness	4	1	3	3	2	2	3
GA	Irwin Youth	4	2	2	3	3	3	2
IN	Camp Summit	4	2	2	4	3	3	3
IA	Highly Structured	2	2	3	2	4	4	4
KY	Green River	0	2	0	1	4	3	4
LA	Tallulah	0	1	0	3	3	4	4
MD	Doncaster	2	2	0	4	4	4	4
MS	Columbia	4	4	N/A	4	4	4	4
MS	Oakley	4	4	N/A	4	4	4	4
NJ	Wharton Tract	4	4	3	3	3	4	4
NY	Leadership Academy	3	3	0	3	2	4	4
OH	Camp Roulston	4	4	0	3	1	4	4
PA	Abraxas	2	2	0	2	0	4	3
PA	Boot and Hat	3	4	0	4	2	4	4
SC	J.R.O.T.C.	0	0	0	0	4	4	4
TX	Challenge	3	3	3	4	4	4	4
TX	C.C.I.	0	0	0	3	3	4	4
TX	Treatment & Rehabilitation	1	3	1	2	4	4	4
TX	S.T.A.R.	4	4	4	4	4	4	4
UT	Genesis	4	3	3	3	2	2	2
VA	Washington	2	2	2	4	4	4	4
WA	Basic Training	4	3	1	4	1	3	3

Table 5: Goals of Juvenile Boot Camp Programs

Table 6: Activities and Hours of Juvenile Boot Camp Programs

State	Name of Program	Military Drill	Discipline	Physical Labor	Physical Fitness / Sports	Challenge Adventure	Drug & Alcohol	Education	Vocational Training	Platoon Grouping	Summary Punish-ment	Group Rewards / Punishment	P.T./ Drill / Work	Education Counseling
													Hours/Day	
AL	Autauga	Yes	Yes	No	Yes	Yes	No	Yes	No	Yes	No	No	3	3.5
AL	Chalkville	No	Yes	No	Yes	Yes	Yes	Yes	No	No	No	No	2	6
AL	Thomasville	Yes	Yes	Yes	Yes	Yes	Yes	Yes	No	No	No	No	3	6.5
AR	First Academy	Yes	Yes	Yes	Yes	Yes	Yes	Yes	Yes	Yes	No	Yes		
CA	L.E.A.D.	Yes	Yes	No	Yes	No	Yes	Yes	No	Yes	Yes	Yes	3	6
CA	Twin Pines	Yes	Yes	Yes	Yes	Yes	Yes	Yes	Yes	Yes	No	Yes	4.0	3.5
CA	Drug Treatment	Yes	Yes	Yes	Yes	No	Yes	Yes	Yes	Yes	Yes	Yes	2	8
CA	R.O.T.C.	Yes	Yes	Yes	Yes	No	Yes	Yes	Yes	Yes	Yes	Yes		
CO	Camp Falcon	Yes	Yes	No	Yes	No	No	Yes	No	Yes	Yes	Yes	8	4
DC	Thurgood Marshall	Yes	Yes	No	Yes	Yes	Yes	Yes	Yes	Yes	Yes	Yes	2	5
FL	Martin County	Yes	Yes	Yes	Yes	Yes	Yes	Yes	Yes	Yes	Yes	No	10	6
FL	Pinellas County	Yes	Yes	Yes	Yes	Yes	Yes	Yes	No	Yes	Yes	Yes	2	8
FL	Leon County	Yes	Yes	No	Yes	No	Yes	Yes	Yes	Yes	No	No	3	12
FL	Regimental Wilderness	Yes	Yes	Yes	Yes	Yes	Yes	Yes	Yes	Yes	No	Group reward only	2 – 3	8 – 10
GA	Irwin Youth	Yes	Yes	Yes	Yes	No	Yes	Yes	No	Yes	No	Yes	6	5
IN	Camp Summit	Yes	Yes	No	Yes		Yes	Yes			Yes	Yes	5	4
IA	Highly Structured	No	Yes	Yes	Yes	No	Yes	Yes	Yes	Yes	No	Yes	2 – 3	6 – 8

Table 6 continues on following page

Table 6: Activities and Hours of Juvenile Boot Camp Programs continued

State	Name of Program	Activities											Hours/Day	
		Military Drill	Discipline	Physical Labor	Physical Fitness / Sports	Challenge Adventure	Drug & Alcohol	Education	Vocational Training	Platoon Grouping	Summary Punishment	Group Rewards / Punishment	P.T. / Drill / Work	Education Counseling
KY	Green River	Yes	Yes	Yes	Yes	Yes	Yes	Yes	Yes	Yes	Yes	Group reward only	5	7.5
LA	Tallulah	Yes	Yes	Yes	Yes	No	Yes	Yes	No	Yes	No	No	3	6
MD	Doncaster	Yes	Yes	Yes	Yes	Yes	Yes	Yes	Yes	Yes	No	No	1	6
MS	Columbia	Yes	Yes	Yes	Yes	Yes	Yes	Yes	Yes	Yes	N/A	Group reward only	3	5
MS	Oakley	Yes	Yes	Yes	Yes	Yes	Yes	Yes	Yes	Yes	N/A	Group reward only	3	5
NJ	Wharton Tract	Yes	Yes	Yes	Yes	Yes	Yes	Yes	Yes	Yes		Yes	7.5	6.5
NY	Leadership Academy	Yes	Yes	Yes	Yes	Yes	Yes	Yes	Yes	Yes	No	No	1.5 – 4	6 – 6.5
OH	Camp Roulston	Yes	Yes	No	Yes	Yes	Yes	Yes	Yes	Yes	No	No	4	8
PA	Abraxas	Yes	Yes	Yes	Yes	Yes	Yes	Yes	No	Yes	No	No	1.5	8 – 9
PA	Boot and Hat	Yes	Yes	Yes	No	No	Yes	Yes	No	Yes	No	Yes	4	7
SC	J.R.O.T.C.	Yes	Yes	Yes	Yes	Yes	Yes	Yes	Yes	Yes	Yes	Yes	3	13
TX	Challenge Program	Yes	Yes	Yes	Yes	Yes	Yes	Yes	No	No	No	No	3	6
TX	C.C.I.	Yes	Yes	Yes	Yes	Yes	Yes	Yes	No	Yes	No	No	3	8
TX	Treatment & Rehabilitation	Yes	Yes	Yes	No	No	No	Yes	No	Yes	No	No	3	9
TX	S.T.A.R.	Yes	Yes	Yes	Yes	Yes	Yes	Yes	No	Yes	Yes	Yes	4	8
UT	Genesis	No	Yes	Yes	Yes	No	Yes	Yes	No	No	No	Yes	5.5	4
VA	Washington	Yes	Yes	Yes	Yes	Yes	Yes	Yes	Yes	Yes	No	Yes	2	7
WA	Basic Training	Yes	Yes	Yes	Yes	Yes	Yes	Yes	Yes	Yes	No	Yes	5	7

Table 7: Degree of Military Involvement in Juvenile Boot Camp Programs

State	Name of Program	Staff		Juvenile Military Uniforms
		Military Titles	Military Uniforms	
AL	Autauga	No	No	No
AL	Chalkville	No	No	No
AL	Thomasville	No	No	No
AR	First Academy	Yes	Yes	No
CA	L.E.A.D.	Yes	Yes	Yes
CA	Drug Treatment	Yes	Yes	Yes
CA	Twin Pines	Yes	Yes	Yes
CA	R.O.T.C.	Yes	Yes	Yes
CO	Camp Falcon	Yes	Yes	Yes
DC	Thurgood Marshall	Yes	Yes	Yes
FL	Martin County	Yes	No, Police Uniforms	Yes
FL	Pinellas County	Yes	No	Yes
FL	Leon County	Yes	Yes	No
FL	Regimental Wilderness	Yes	Yes	Yes
GA	Irwin Youth	Yes	Yes	Yes
IN	Camp Summit	Yes	Yes	Yes
IA	Highly Structured	No	No	No
KY	Green River	No	No	No
LA	Tallulah	Yes	Yes	No
MD	Doncaster	Yes	Yes	Yes
MS	Columbia	Yes	Yes	Yes
MS	Oakley	Yes	Yes	Yes
NJ	Wharton Tract	Yes	Yes	Yes
NY	Leadership Academy	Yes	Yes	Yes
OH	Camp Roulston	Yes	Yes	Yes
PA	Abraxas	Yes	Yes	Yes
PA	Boot and Hat	Yes	Yes	Yes
SC	J.R.O.T.C.	No	Yes	Yes
TX	Challenge	No	No	No
TX	C.C.I.	Yes	Yes	Yes
TX	Treatment & Rehabilitation*	Yes	Yes	No
TX	S.T.A.R.*	Yes	Yes	Yes
UT	Genesis	No	No	No
VA	Washington	Yes	Yes	Yes
WA	Basic Training	Yes	Yes	Yes

* Do not live at facility.

Table 8: Dropout and Expulsion from Juvenile Boot Camp Programs

State	Name of Program	Vountary Dropout			Expulsion		
		Yes/No	%	Consequence	Yes/No	%	Consequence
AL	Autauga	No	0		Yes	10	Returned to court
AL	Chalkville	No	0		Yes	5	Returned to court
AL	Thomasville	No	0		Yes	14	Returned to court
AR	First Academy	Yes					
CA	L.E.A.D.	No	0		Yes	30	Returned to standard correctional programs
CA	Drug Treatment	No	0		Yes	5	Returned to court, placed in more secure camp
CA	Twin Pines	Yes	2	Returned to court	Yes	3	Returned to court
CA	R.O.T.C.	Yes		Returned to juvenile hall	Yes		Returned to juvenile hall
CO	Camp Falcon	No	0		Yes	3	Probation revocation and commitment
DC	Thurgood Marshall	Yes	2	Transferred to another unit	Yes	3	Transferred to another unit
FL	Martin County	No	0		No	0	
FL	Pinellas County	No	0		Yes	2	Transferred to other program
FL	Leon County	No	0		Yes1	5	
FL	Regimental Wilderness	No	0		Yes	< 10	Transferred to other facility
GA	Irwin Youth	No	0			0	
IN	Camp Summit	No	0			0	
IA	Highly Structured	No	0				
KY	Green River	No	0		Yes	8	Transferred to other facility
LA	Tallulah	No	0		Yes	2	Transferred to more secure facility
MD	Doncaster	No	0		No	0	
MS	Columbia	No	0		Yes	1	Referred back to court
MS	Oakley	No	0		Yes	1	Referred back to court
NJ	Wharton Tract	Yes					
NY	Leadership Academy	No	0		No	0	
OH	Camp Roulston	No	0		Yes	1	Returned to juvenile court
PA	Abraxas	No	0		Yes	0	Referred back to court
PA	Boot and Hat	No	0		Yes	10	Sent to court or to year long VisionQuest Impact Program
SC	J.R.O.T.C.	Yes	1	Returned to non-JROTC dorm	Yes	20	Returned to non-JROTC dorm
TX	Challenge Program	No	0		Yes	1	Returned to institution/court
TX	C.C.I.	No	0		No	0	
TX	Treatment & Rehabilitation	Yes		Returned to court	No	0	
TX	S.T.A.R.	No	0		Yes	0	Sent to youth commission or placement
UT	Genesis	No	0		Yes	3	Returned to detention
VA	Washington	No	0		No	0	
WA	Basic Training	Yes		transferred to institution	Yes		Transferred to institution

1 Released only for medical reasons.

Table 9: Graduation from Juvenile Boot Camp Programs

State	Name of Program	%	Public Ceremony
AL	Autauga	90	Yes
AL	Chalkville	95	No
AL	Thomasville	86	Yes
AR	First Academy		Yes
CA	L.E.A.D.	70	Yes
CA	Drug Treatment	95	No
CA	Twin Pines	95	No
CA	R.O.T.C.		Yes
CO	Camp Falcon	94	Yes
DC	Thurgood Marshall	95	Yes
FL	Martin County	95	Yes
FL	Pinellas County	98	Yes
FL	Leon County	95	No
FL	Regimental Wilderness	> 90	Yes
GA	Irwin Youth	100	No
IN	Camp Summit	100	No
IA	Highly Structured		
KY	Green River	92	Yes
LA	Tallulah	98	No
MD	Doncaster	100	Yes
MS	Columbia	99	Yes
MS	Oakley	99	Yes
NJ	Wharton Tract		Yes
NY	Leadership Academy	100	No
OH	Camp Roulston	99	Yes
PA	Abraxas	100	Yes
PA	Boot and Hat	90	Yes
SC	J.R.O.T.C.	80	No
TX	Challenge Program	99	No
TX	C.C.I.	90	Yes
TX	Treatment & Rehabilitation	100	Yes
TX	S.T.A.R.	99	Yes
UT	Genesis	0 [1]	N/A
VA	Washington	100	Yes
WA	Basic Training		Yes

[1] The Genesis Youth Center does not graduate youths.

Table 10: Supervision and Aftercare in Juvenile Boot Camp Programs

State	Name of Program	For Whom	Days	Capacity	Setting
AL	Autauga	Some	90		Home with family
AL	Chalkville	Some	90		Home with family
AL	Thomasville	Some	90		Home with family
AR	First Academy	All	180	96	Home with family; community transition center; crisis center
CA	L.E.A.D.	All	180	120	Home with family; halfway house; group home; other
CA	Drug Treatment	All	180	250	Home with family
CA	Twin Pines	Some	180	35	Home with family; halfway house; Conservation Corps.
CA	R.O.T.C.	All	240	60 – 80	Home with family
CO	Camp Falcon[1]				
DC	Thurgood Marshall	Some	180 – 360		Home with family; group home
FL	Martin County	All	240	90	Home with family
FL	Pinellas County	Some	120 – 240	30	Home with family
FL	Leon County	All	120	30	Home with family
FL	Regimental Wilderness[2]	All	90	25	Halfway house; day treatment
GA	Irwin Youth	Some	Varies		
IN	Camp Summit	All	180 – 270	100	Correctional facility
IA	Highly Structured	All	180	400+	Home with family
KY	Green River	All	90	Unlimited	Home with family; group/foster home; private child care facility
LA	Tallulah	Some	360 – 990		Home with family; group home
MD	Doncaster	All	270 – 360	105/yr	Home with family
MS	Columbia	All	360	Unlimited	Home with family; transitional living centers
MS	Oakley	All	360	Unlimited	Home with family; transitional living centers
NJ	Wharton Tract	All	240	100	Home with family; group home; residential program
NY	Leadership Academy	All	150	30	Home with family
OH	Camp Roulston	All	270	120/yr	Home with family
PA	Abraxas	All	Varies	24	Home with family; group home; residential placements
PA	Boot and Hat	Some	1 weekend per month for 3 months	Unlimited	Platoon
SC	J.R.O.T.C.	Some	180 – 360		Home with family; halfway house; group home
TX	Challenge	All	90	Unlimited	Home with family
TX	C.C.I.	Some	Remainder of probation	0	
TX	Treatment & Rehabilitation	All	Indefinite		Home with family
TX	S.T.A.R.	All	180 – 360		Home with family
UT	Genesis	Some	Varies		Home with family; group home; foster care
VA	Washington	All	180	100	Home with family
WA	Basic Training	All	Remainder of disposition		Home with family; group home; foster care

[1] Information on aftercare program has not yet been gathered. [2] This is a day treatment program.

Table 11: Aftercare Components of Juvenile Boot Camp Programs

State	Name of Program	Treatment	Employment	Education	Vocational Training	Family Counseling	Intensive Supervision
AL	Autauga	No	No	No	No	No	Yes
AL	Chalkville	No	No	No	No	No	Yes
AL	Thomasville	No	No	No	No	No	Yes
AR	First Academy[1]	Yes	Yes	Yes	Yes	Yes	
CA	L.E.A.D.		Yes	Yes			Yes
CA	Drug Treatment[1]	Yes	Yes	Yes	Yes	Yes	Yes
CA	Twin Pines[1]	Yes	Yes	Yes	No	Yes	Yes
CA	R.O.T.C.[1]	Yes	Yes	Yes	Yes	Yes	Yes
CO	Camp Falcon						
DC	Thurgood Marshall	Yes	Yes	Yes	Yes	Yes	Yes
FL	Martin County	Yes	Yes	Yes	Yes	Yes	Yes
FL	Pinellas County	Yes	Yes	Yes	No	Yes	Yes
FL	Leon County	Yes	Yes	Yes	No	Yes	Yes
FL	Regimental Wilderness[1]	Yes	Yes	Yes	Yes	Yes	No
GA	Irwin Youth						
IN	Camp Summit	Yes	No	Yes	No	Yes	Yes
IA	Highly Structured	Yes	No	Yes	Yes	Yes	Yes
KY	Green River[1]	Yes	Yes	Yes	Yes	Yes	Yes
LA	Tallulah[1]	Yes	No	Yes	No	Yes	Yes
MD	Doncaster[1]	Yes	Yes	Yes	Yes	Yes	Yes
MS	Columbia[1]	Yes	Yes	Yes	Yes	Yes	Yes
MS	Oakley[1]	Yes	Yes	Yes	Yes	Yes	Yes
NJ	Wharton Tract[1]	Yes	Yes	Yes	Yes	Yes	Yes
NY	Leadership Academy[1]	Yes	Yes	Yes	Yes	Yes	Yes
OH	Camp Roulston[1]	Yes	Yes	Yes	Yes	Yes	Yes
PA	Abraxas	Yes	Yes	Yes	No	Yes	Yes
PA	Boot and Hat[1]	Yes	No	No	No	Yes	Yes
SC	J.R.O.T.C.[1]	Yes	Yes	Yes	Yes	Yes	Yes
TX	Challenge[1]	Yes		Yes		Yes	Yes
TX	C.C.I.[1]					Yes	
TX	Treatment & Rehabilitation	Yes	Yes	Yes	No	Yes	Yes
TX	S.T.A.R.	Yes		Yes		Yes	Yes
UT	Genesis [2]						
VA	Washington	Yes	Yes	Yes	Yes	Yes	Yes
WA	Basic Training[1]	Yes	Yes	Yes	Yes	Yes	Yes

[1] Other services also offered. [2] Genesis offers a wide range of options. There is not a formal aftercare program.

References

Altschuler, D. M. 1994. Tough and Smart Juvenile Incarceration: Reintegrating Punishment, Deterrence and Rehabilitation. *St. Louis University Public Law Review.* 14:217-237.

Austin, J., M. Jones, and M. Bolyard. 1993. *The Growing Use of Jail Boot Camps: The Current State of the Art.* Research in Brief. Washington, D.C.: National Institute of Justice.

Bottcher, J., T. Isorena, J. Lara, and M. Belnas. 1995. LEAD: A Boot Camp and Intensive Parole Program: An Impact Evaluation. Unpublished report to the Legislature of the State of California, Department of the Youth Authority, Research Division. Sacramento, California.

Bottcher, J., and T. Isorena. 1996. First Year Evaluation of the California Youth Authority's Boot Camp. In D. L. MacKenzie and E. Hebert, eds. *Boot Camp Prisons: A Tough Intermediate Sanction.* Washington, D.C.: National Institute of Justice.

Cass, E. S. and N. Kaltenecker. 1996. The Development and Operation of Juvenile Boot Camps in Florida. In D. L. MacKenzie and E. Hebert, eds. *Boot Camp Prisons: A Tough Intermediate Sanction.* Washington, D.C.: National Institute of Justice.

Clark, Cheryl L., and David W. Aziz. 1996. Shock Incarceration in New York State: Philosophy, Results, and Limitations. In D. L. MacKenzie and E. Hebert, eds. *Boot Camp Prisons: A Tough Intermediate Sanction.* Washington, D.C.: National Institute of Justice.

Cowles, E. L., and T. C. Castellano, 1995. Boot Camp Drug Treatment and Aftercare Intervention: An Evaluation Review. A Final Summary Report to the National Institute of Justice. Washington, D.C.: National Institute of Justice.

Cronin, R. C. 1994. Boot Camps for Adult and Juvenile Offenders: Overview and Update. National Institute of Justice Research Report. Washington, D.C.: National Institute of Justice.

Cullen F. T., J. P. Wright, and B. K. Applegate. 1993. Control in the Community: The Limits of Reform? Paper presented at the International Association of Residential and Community Alternatives, Philadelphia, Pennsylvania.

Florida Department of Corrections, Bureau of Planning, Research, and Statistics. 1990. Research Report: Boot Camp Evaluation. Tallahassee, FL.

Flowers, G. T., T. S. Carr, and R. B. Ruback. 1991. *Special Alternative Incarceration Evaluation.* Atlanta, Georgia: Georgia Department of Corrections.

Gottfredson, D. C., M. D. Sealock, and C. S. Koper. 1996. Delinquency. In R. J. DiClemente, W. B. Hansen, and L. E. Ponton. *Handbook of Adolescent Health Risk Behavior.* New York: Plenum Press.

Gransky, L., T. C. Castellano, and E. L. Cowles. 1995. Is There a 'Next Generation' of Shock Incarceration Facilities? The Evolving Nature of Goals, Program Components and Drug Treatment Services. In J. Smykla and W. Selke, eds. *Intermediate Sanctions: Sentencing in the 90s.* Cincinnati: Anderson Publishing Co.

Holden, Gwen A., and R. A. Kapler. 1995. Deinstitutionalizing Status Offenders: A Record of Progress. *Juvenile Justice.* II(2):3-10.

Jablonski, J. R. 1991. *Implementing Total Quality Management: An Overview.* San Diego: Pfeiffer.

Krisberg, B. and J. F. Austin. 1993. *Reinventing Juvenile Justice.* Newbury Park, California: Sage Publications.

Lipsey, M. W. 1992. Juvenile Delinquency Treatment: A Meta-analytic Inquiry into the Variability of Effects. In T. D. Cook, H. Cooper, D. S. Cordray, H. Hartmann, L. V. Hedges, R. J. Light, T. A. Louis, and F. Mosteller, eds. *Meta-analysis for Explanation.* New York: Russell Sage Foundation.

MacKenzie, D. L., and D. G. Parent. 1992. Boot Camp Prisons for Young Offenders. In J. M. Byrne, A. J. Lurigio and J. Petersilia, eds. *Smart Sentencing: The Emergence of Intermediate Sanctions.* London: Sage Publications.

MacKenzie, D. L., J. W. Shaw, and C. Souryal. 1992. Characteristics Associated with Successful Adjustment to Supervision. *Criminal Justice and Behavior.* 19 (4): 437-454.

MacKenzie, D. L., and A. Piquero. 1994. The Impact of Shock Incarceration Programs on Prison Crowding. *Crime and Delinquency.* 40 (2): 222-249.

MacKenzie, D. L., and C. Souryal. 1994. *Multi-Site Study of Shock Incarceration.* Final Reports I-IV and Executive Summary to the National Institute of Justice. Washington, D.C.: National Institute of Justice.

MacKenzie, D. L., and R. Brame. 1995. Shock Incarceration and Positive Adjustment During Community Supervision. *Journal of Quantitative Criminology.* 11(2): 111-142.

MacKenzie, D. L., R. Brame, D. McDowall, and C. Souryal. 1995. Boot Camp Prisons and Recidivism in Eight States. *Criminology.* 33(3):401-430.

MacKenzie, D. L., and C. Souryal. 1995a. A Machiavellian Perspective on the Development of Boot Camp Prison: A Debate. University of Chicago Roundtable. Chicago: University of Chicago Press.

————. 1995b. Inmate Attitude Change During Incarceration: A Comparison of Boot Camp with Traditional Prison. *Justice Quarterly*. 12(2).

MacKenzie, D. L. and E. Hebert. 1996. Preface to *Correctional Boot Camps: A Tough Intermediate Sanction*. Washington, D.C.: National Institute of Justice.

Meachum, L. M. 1990. Boot Camp Prisons: Pros and Cons. Paper presented at Annual Meeting of American Society of Criminology, Baltimore, Maryland.

Morash, M. and L. Rucker. 1990. A Critical Look at the Ideal of Boot Camp as a Correctional Reform. *Crime and Delinquency*. 36: 204-222.

Morris, N., and M. Tonry. 1990. *Between Prison and Probation: Intermediate Punishments in a Rational Sentencing System*. New York: Oxford University Press.

New York State Department of Correctional Services and New York State Division of Parole. 1992. The Fourth Annual Report to the Legislature: Shock Incarceration - Shock Parole Supervision. Albany, New York.

Parent, D. G., V. Leiter, S. Kennedy, L. Livens, D. Wentworth, and S. Wilcox. 1994. *Conditions of Confinement: Juvenile Detention and Corrections Facilities*. Washington, D.C.: Office of Juvenile Justice and Delinquency Prevention, U. S. Department of Justice.

Texas Department of Corrections, Texas Adult Probation Commission, and Texas Criminal Justice Policy Council. 1989. Special Alternative Incarceration Program: Enhanced Substance Abuse Component. Austin, Texas.

United States General Accounting Office. 1993. *Prison Boot Camps: Short-term Prison Costs Reduced, but Long-term Impact Uncertain*. Washington, D.C.: U. S. Government Printing Office.

The Youth Leadership Academy Boot Camp: An Examination of a Military Model

Colonel Thomas H. Cornick, U. S. A. (Retired.)
Director
Sergeant Henry Johnson Youth Leadership Academy
South Kortright, New York

Boot camps historically have been associated with a military effort to get tough, establish discipline, and increase a positive response to authority. Assuming that these are the desired outcomes of a boot camp, if those outcomes are tied to a vision or higher purpose, and are achieved as intended, the boot camp can be an effective link in developing soldiers. Certainly these outcomes are the driving force behind the boot camp growth in both juvenile and adult corrections programs.

Before jumping on the bandwagon, however, one should consider the purpose of the boot camp as used in the Army within the broader context of training soldiers for combat (the end outcome or purpose). Boot camps generally achieve these outcomes. However, soldiers are subsequently provided advanced technical training and sent to a unit where their new-found skills are to be practiced and further developed under the tutelage of platoon sergeants who mentor, guide, train and motivate soldiers to be a part of an empowered and highly skilled small unit. If the reader is tempted to doubt this, one has only to reflect on the most recent conflicts involving the Army and other United States military forces and the high levels of effectiveness they have demonstrated under extremely varied circumstances. These soldiers are not robots following authority blindly. They are highly skilled and empowered people taking on missions with high motivation and initiative. The military boot camp, even if done perfectly, is only an opening foray in the development of a top notch soldier.

Given the decision to run a correctional boot camp, are these camps run in a true military model? The language used to describe these programs seems to associate the term "military" with a harsh, confrontation-based program model. The vernacular seems to indicate that the more "military" a program is, the more hard core it is. This approach may have existed many moons ago in the military; however, each of the services long ago went through deep cultural changes regarding how people are to be trained and treated. Certainly troops are confronted for norm violations, and drill sergeants are prone to enforce a violation with a few push-ups, but soldiers are trained to think on their own. They are not endlessly and angrily confronted for minor norm violations, and commanders insist on the highest standards of good, positive leadership from their drill sergeants.

Drill sergeants are selected for the job through a centralized process, and only the very best trainers and leaders are selected, in the first place, to be drill sergeants. A military boot camp is a positive, highly normed training environment where soldiers learn the basics of weapons training and individual survival.

The norms are necessary and reasonable because the soldier is engaged in training environments which require attention to safety. Soldiers must obey the norms associated with each training environment. For example: One does not walk down range, on a rifle range to check a target until cleared to do so by the range officer and one does not debate with the range officer. Each norm of behavior makes sense and is tied to a need whether that need be hygiene, safety, or any other outcome. Norms also are consistently enforceable.

Correctional boot camps get in trouble when norms and discipline take over a program. In the harshest of models, the program establishes intricate norms regarding movement and communication under the banner of discipline. Correctional officers are trained to confront, in an angry and loud manner, each observed violation of these various protocols. Failure to obey norms often equates to rejection of authority and the central theme is obedience to that authority. Conversely, soldiers know they have to be responsive because the norms are related to the training environment and the need to follow instructions carefully. The inmate may not be operating under the same assumptions and probably is not. The difference lies in whether the individual norms make sense and if the norms and an individual's acceptance of the norms and compliance with them is associated with some higher purpose than the norms themselves.

A boot camp program must have goals or outcomes and objectives being sought for its clientele beyond the rather simplistic expectation of order and control. An Army boot camp is orderly and controlled, but most importantly, a great many training objectives are covered, and the individual becomes a potentially useful member of the Army family at the end of the training process, only a small part of which is the boot camp. Anyone contemplating using the boot camp approach to change the lives of an offender clientele should have the same expectations and should use the disciplined environment of the boot camp only as a vehicle to achieve goals, outcomes, and objectives determined to be important by the jurisdiction paying the bills.

The boot camp should not become an end in itself, and the protocols associated with it should not take over for important treatment interventions. Moreover, the boot camp environment should complement treatment interventions and give synergy to them rather than inhibit them. When the boot camp staff spend hours demeaning and punishing its clientele, it is hard to imagine that this treatment could have any kind of synergy with educational and counseling treatments. The staff representing control and the staff representing treatment almost inexorably would drift apart in such a setting.

If the primary goal of the jurisdiction were to deter crime and future incarceration, which is the primary goal of any correctional program, it may be terribly simplistic to believe that by creating a punitive environment the program serves to deter future crimes. The evaluative literature strongly rejects this assumption, but let us look at it from a common sense point of view. First, most correctional boot camps are short-term alternatives to longer sentences and, by their very nature, are voluntary. The harsh programs experience high failure rates as the clientele reject the program, often knowing that the longer sentence will not occur in any event. Secondly, most of the clientele is accustomed to poor treatment from a number of different sources, and the boot camp environment, while intense, has minimal impact other than to control behavior. Thirdly, most young offenders have high anger levels and low impulse control. A program which creates anger toward authority and provides few outlets is not consistent with and certainly not synergistic with the goal to foster future positive and self-controlled behavior.

To build a correctional boot camp in the true and current military model, the following steps should be put in place:

- Clearly articulate the vision of what the program seeks to achieve in the client, in positive terms (not just to deter).

- Provide a leadership model which overtly establishes how the client is to be treated.

- Start with tight controls over behavior, but progressively empower and encourage decision making.

- Provide training and education for enrollees that is designed to achieve the intended outcomes.

- Offer constant feedback to clients of perceived progress or lack of it.

- Use confrontation to push for excellence rather than to demean.

- Create extensive new skills.

- Do not allow for failure—make clients into winners.

- Tie to future demand and environments—prepare people specifically.

A boot camp in the military model does all this by design. The product of a boot camp is a skilled person who has accepted a new set of values and has high pride and esteem that is associated with completing a program which was the most demanding thing in his or her life. Another outcome is an ability to work in teams where trust and mutual support are important. Most important is the ability to make decisions independently and to pick up a mission where others have left off. These outcomes can be achieved in correctional boot camp programs.

One such program is New York's juvenile boot camp, the Sergeant Henry Johnson Youth Leadership Academy (YLA). The academy is a juvenile program located in upstate New York servicing a population, age fourteen to seventeen, from New York City. The boot camp consists of two consecutive program phases. Basic Challenge is a very fundamental, highly normed entry-level program followed by Advanced Challenge, which is less highly normed and more involved in skill development. The aftercare program, City Challenge, is a five-month day placement program located in Brooklyn. The population entering the Youth Leadership program are "limited secure" juvenile delinquents who have committed felonies, generally violent ones. They are screened for limiting physical disabilities and for mental health limitations. They can be considered a chronic, inner city delinquent population.

The program model used is an empowerment model in the tradition of Total Quality Management applied to the needs and special challenge of the client population. The clients are taught four values; self-discipline (accountability), affiliation (trust giving and relationship forming), self-esteem (personal competence), and self-worth. In Basic Challenge, they cognitively learn what these values are. In the balance of the program, they relate these individual values to the program and redefine them individually in terms of the two external or exit values: family and education. Empowered clients build esteem related to their educational accomplishments, which are challenging yet designed to assure their success after requisite effort. If the effort is not provided, the individual loses status and privilege; however, no punishment ensues. Staff are taught to seek out people giving extra effort and to reward good news. There is no down time in a sixteen-hour duty day, seven days a week. Interface between staff and the clientele is guided by a well-articulated leadership model which prohibits demeaning, profanity, power trips, and stand off leadership styles. Staff must participate with the clients in everything. The result is a positive, reinforcing culture with few behavioral issues.

Listed below are proposed program standards for any boot camp together with a discussion of how the Youth Leadership Academy met each standard.

The program addresses outcomes, has a central guiding theme or clinical approach, and is clearly defined and articulated. This startup work should involve practitioners as well as planners. The jurisdiction should create a clear idea of what they expect to see when graduates come out of the boot camp. These outcomes can form evaluation criteria. The practitioner or leader should develop his or her vision of how these outcomes are to be accomplished in every graduate. This will generally be an evolutionary process, and the original vision probably will not hold firm, but there has to be a will to move the vision to accommodate the outcomes. In time, the vision becomes a written program with all the "bells and whistles," but even then there has to be built-in flexibility. The practitioner's vision of how things are to be done should not become the principle program outcome. Peter Drucker said that efficiency is doing things right while effectiveness is doing the right things. The practitioner must do the right things to accomplish the jurisdiction's outcomes and should be held accountable to those outcomes.

The Youth Leadership Academy developed a mission statement which incorporates the principle outcomes of the program. The mission of the Youth Leadership Academy is:

> to prepare youth for positive, successful lives by developing self discipline, affiliation, self-esteem, and self-worth as individuals, by developing the family as a viable support for goals, developing alternative placements where necessary, and establishing education as a source of esteem and worth.

This mission statement proposes a value set which is developed in the individual and is tied to the two most powerful forces in an adolescent's life: family and school. The outcome is a positive and successful life. This is the central focus of every program and subprogram in the academy. Having established this focus, it became a matter of developing the leadership, counseling, education, training, and fitness programs with the best chance of producing the outcome. The last task is to be sure that all these programs are tied to the central focus and that they work in consonance with each other. The result is a detailed picture of how things are supposed to work. We will call that product the program model.

The mission statement served to drive the program in several directions but provided a central theme or vision of what needed to be done with each client cadet. Values are hard to teach and even harder to measure. A counseling program was developed around these values, which over time became the core of the program. Cadets discover these values by discussing them every day in the context of their home environment. In the City Challenge aftercare program, they live the values and engage in mutually supportive counseling groups to discuss the impact of the values in fending off challenges and temptations to revert to the "old self." Family and education programs were developed, also over time, which served to also build the value structure in the child and to assure a solid base or starting point on the individual's return to the city.

Program Execution Follows the Model

The model is useless unless systems are put in place to assure that it is working the way it was designed. Nothing is more embarrassing than having the boss describe in glowing detail how the boot camp is supposed to work only to have subordinates explain how it "really works." This takes lots of communication and hard work, but most importantly, the top person and his or her management team must train, constantly articulate the model, and check its implementation through staff and clientele. If the model is developed by a higher authority and the practitioners either do not understand it or particularly adhere to it, there will be immediate separation from the model. If you have a model you like for the boot camp, be sure the person you hire to run it understands and believes in the model. Military folks tend to have strong beliefs about leadership and empowerment and, thus, generally would be likely to buy into a model which provides an environment similar to that to which they have become accustomed.

The Youth Leadership model is completely committed to written materials. Training programs cover each program component. These components, moreover, were developed largely by the staff operating in an empowered environment. The program concepts and general documentation were provided by the director, but the detail work of each program was handled by the direct care and treatment staff. Therefore, it would be difficult, but not impossible, for staff to adopt other approaches since they helped build the academy program. The most critical compliance issue is the leadership model and staff treatment of the clientele. The program's first sergeant monitors this consistently. He operates the model, mentors, guides, trains, and counsels employees. We solicit constant feedback from the clientele through an effective grievance system which is operated by the first sergeant and fully supported by the entire leadership of the program.

Clientele is Successful

The program model assumes that the clientele will change and develop in accordance with the mission statement. It does not assume the opposite and set about to find evidence of failure. It seeks evidence of progress in each individual. The program must deal with failures, but it does so in a manner which encourages turnarounds and success. Motivation is toward higher levels of status and privilege as opposed to avoidance of pain. The program staff find it extremely difficult to give up on people.

The Youth Leadership Academy has written this assumption into its leadership model. We expect each and every individual to complete the program. When it is necessary to hold a person in the boot camp for longer than the normal time, this is done rather than transfer the client into another facility which does not know him and has to start all over. The academy even goes to the extent of bringing people back who show clear signs of failure on the street—to fine tune them, give them a measure of respite, solve problems encountered in the home environment, and send them out to try again. Giving up is contagious, and the program can not model giving up.

The Program Provides an Excellent Learning Environment

A well-run boot camp becomes an organizational culture which enhances around-the-clock learning experiences. Everyone on the staff has something to offer the clients, and it is a matter of harnessing that knowledge and energy, then delivering it. The subcomponents that create an optimum learning environment are presented next:

- The clients feel safe and secure at all times. They need to know that they are safe from each other and safe from the practitioner. It is normal for them not to feel safe and to behave in a manner which deters aggression toward them. A well-normed facility operating with a positive leadership model will produce a safe environment.

- The schedule is packed with teaching, experiential education, and evaluation. The clientele generally is composed of dropouts and people who view themselves as academic failures to one extent or another. This must be reversed with demanding academic programs which do not allow them to fail and that support their achievements.

- The leadership model and the workforce allows direct care staff members to become primary mentors, trainers, and motivators. This role is complemented by training programs which provide them with the tools to fill this role.

The leadership model is a component of the program model which mandates exactly how staff are to lead, motivate, and confront the clientele. Given our austere times, direct care staff members must be more than guards; they must be coaches, mentors, teachers, and even proxy parents to the clientele. The delineation between security and treatment staff is almost imperceptible in a program where a positive leadership model is operational. Given the difficult and trying nature of correctional clientele, there will be a tendency to drift toward a more confrontational and even coercive operation and away from the model. Therefore, it is imperative that systems be in place to identify model failures and correct them. The ideal staff member confronts when necessary, but does so in a nonthreatening and constructive manner. Staff members are engaged in constructive activities with clients throughout the day and are well attuned to the mental state of each client in care.

Over a period of time, the Youth Leadership Academy has developed into a total learning environment where the clientele are constantly engaged in developing their knowledge and skill base. The leadership model is the most critical factor because it places the direct care staff in the role of a caring mentor who teaches and trains as well as enforces the rules consistently and fairly. The clients follow a sixteen-hour duty day which includes counseling, classroom education, experiential skill training, fitness, hygiene, and socialization. Cadets are evaluated each day and receive constant feedback on progress and always know where they stand within the program. These evaluations are corporate in nature and not subject to the vagaries of individual likes and dislikes.

When cadets are confronted, it is normally in the manner of expecting them to achieve at a higher level and to express values which are substantially different from those that took them away from their families and created victims. Time is valuable and every available minute is filled with learning activities. Each cadet prepares and presents papers every day, engages in structured debates, learns skills associated with various jobs which are realistically available to them in New York, and learns a wide variety of life skills. They learn how to study and conduct research. There is no television and recreation is as structured as any other part of the program.

The Program is Empowering to its Clients

The initial stages of the boot camp experience provide structure for people who are not able to consistently control their behaviors without assistance. The program must set standards or expectations for self-discipline which will allow the client to advance to a status which provides more freedom. The more they accept self-control, the more freedom and decision making is allowed until the gates are opened, and the client returns home. At that point, the client is either empowered and self-disciplined or failure is a high probability. Throughout the boot camp experience, the client is not a powerless person. Systems are in place whereby the client can express concerns, request reviews of incidents, provide feedback on programs, and give input which will be listened to and acted on consistently. In this manner, the client becomes a part of the organization as opposed to a powerless pawn. Communication links are maintained and staff are held to the high standards articulated in the leadership model. Failures of that model are reported and reviews are always conducted. Thus, both staff and clients are provided expectations regarding their behavior, and each hold the other accountable to that standard. The management team plays the role of facilitator and broker to assure that expectations on both sides are maintained.

The Youth Leadership Academy started with only the director acting to control the leadership model. This was an impossible task, and the leadership in the facility drifted inexorably toward a more harsh and confrontational model as opposed to the articulated model. A series of formal as well as informal positions were established with the primary purpose of pushing the leadership toward the intended model. A key part of this was the establishment of an noncommissioned officer (NCO) chain of command consisting of the most effective direct care staff members who were given the responsibility for the behavior management program and the leadership model. Links were strengthened with the clientele through an effective and high profile grievance program. The top leaders in the program are required to conduct group counseling sessions with clients on a daily basis thus giving them daily direct access to each client. Most importantly, staff consistently responds to and deals with complaints.

Staff failing to live up to leadership standards are counseled, retrained, or even dismissed from service. One very effective method is to conduct group sessions between staff members who clients viewed as angry and overly confrontational with those clients under controlled circumstances. In these sessions, which are relatively rare, both sides always have been able to iron out their differences. The staff members involved gained knowledge about the effect they were having, and their authority was not eroded, but strengthened by the respect they gained in the process.

Staff are Well Trained and Empowered Members of a Team

The model is a starting point; however, the staff is the force that makes the model work. The model is useful for the staff because it mitigates any tendencies to move toward more simplistic, dictatorial modes. All staff members are taught the entire model. The leaders of the program must explain the model, but also they must be open to complaints and concerns about it. This is not to say that because people complain about the model that it will adjust in that direction. Some parts of the model are the will of the director and are bottom line, non-negotiable components. The leadership model is the best example of a non-negotiable component. Other components are always open to change and development. The staff is provided with a means to make their concerns known and management acts objectively and quickly to address those concerns. Good performance is always recognized and bad performance is corrected followed by training and mentoring to be sure that the correction is a permanent one.

At the Youth Leadership Academy, staff training and development within the model occurs every day. The noncommissioned officer chain sees to it that the events of every day are discussed with the staff members. There is a constant dialog regarding better ways to handle situations together with updates on high-risk clients. If a new member of the staff is having difficulty motivating and containing clients, a mentor is assigned to that staff member to watch him or her in the conduct of duties. In some events, it even can be useful to conduct small groups with high performing clients to gain some understanding of the dynamic and see where the staff member is losing contact with the clientele. Formal sessions are conducted quarterly in a group setting where the director and the entire management team give their assessment of where the model is, what developments are in the future, and to openly discuss any current communication or training issues. The director and assistant director also have an open door policy, and any staff member has access to them throughout the day.

The Program Provides for Family Development (Particularly Juveniles)

The family is critical to the habilitation of each client, thus necessitating the inclusion of the family every step of the way. Most correctional clients have few positive personal relationships outside the family. Inner city environments are often brutal, offering few alternatives to having a supportive family. Moving outside the home involves moving into old negative relationships. If the home, itself is a battle ground, the client has no options. Damage done to family relationships prior to incarceration should be addressed while the client is incarcerated. Aftercare programs are important in working with families even while the client is incarcerated. Often, the real trouble starts when the client returns home and programs must be in place to help the already fragile family to get through the stress of taking the client back. It is important to start working with the family immediately and to continue the process through aftercare. When the family simply cannot or will not support the return of the client, systems must be in place to identify the situation early and to work out alternative placements, preferably in the extended family.

The Youth Leadership program visits the home of each client within thirty days of incarceration with a joint team of academy and aftercare staff members. The entire program is explained and commitments of support from the family are solicited. For the balance of the academy stay, a steady stream of written progress reports are provided and biweekly conference calls are made involving the client, the parent, and the counselor. Where alternative placements or additional family support are needed, the staff find and visit members of the extended family as backup placements or as sources of positive mentorship. During aftercare, an already established relationship between the staff and the family is further intensified as the client and the family are guided through an often difficult transition.

Clients are Treated as Individuals Rather Than as Members of a Cohort

Clients come to the boot camp with widely varying impulse control, psychological damage, family support, academic potential, and physical abilities. This is only a cursory list of variables. When they return home, they will succeed or fail as individuals—not as a cohort. Cohort programs should be closely examined with regard to desired outcomes and their ability to produce results. Given the wide swings we have in the variables among clients, inevitably cohort programs either hold clients back or push them too fast. Both the individual and the cohort suffer and often fail.

Youth Leadership started with a cohort program. On one day, every quarter, the senior cohort would graduate and leave the facility. The junior cohort would move into its space and a new cohort fresh from the reception center would fill behind the promoted and now senior cohort. There were big changes in the program culture. We now allow individuals to progress between cohort groups as individuals based on well-documented progress within the various program components which are group counseling, education, training, and behavior. In this way, an individual wishing to learn and behave spends a limited time in the entry-level cohort, progressing to a higher level with greater demands for independent action within the senior cohort. Conversely, the impulsive individual stays a longer time in the entry cohort which provides the highest level of external controls. In this fashion, the client is empowered to determine his own program.

Clients are Provided with Extensive Opportunities to Master Skills With Real Applicability to Successful Living

The boot camp provides an excellent learning opportunity; for the first time in years, the client is under control with time to learn and, usually, a will to learn. Programs must be in place which involve the entire staff, not just a segment of it. Most of the learning experience should be performance based and experiential. The list of tasks or skills should be tied to and synergistic with the program's philosophy or theme. Time is a critical resource and the clients' time must be accounted for in a demanding, sixteen-hour daily learning schedule. Hours of drill and ceremony combined with intricate, time consuming military-type protocols are not consistent with the development of such a skill base.

The Youth Leadership Academy had problems during the first six months of operation as skill-based training programs had not been developed. We never allowed the clients to watch TV or kill time, so we engaged in excessive drill and ceremony along with other simplistic, irrelevant, and time-consuming activities. As a result, the cadets were bored, restless, and difficult to handle. Subsequently, we developed several skill-based training programs aimed at providing the client with substantial life skills as well as academic prowess. This training is tied to the empowerment theme; self-esteem is enhanced by hard work and accomplishment as individuals. The existence of such a demanding as well as relevant program very substantially reduced behavioral issues. The programs placed the direct care and support staff in positions of teachers, mentors and role models.

A good boot camp not only has aftercare programming, but that program is woven into the entire program and is consistent within the boot camp. A boot camp is an intense, short alternative to longer periods of incarceration. The client must return to an environment that has not changed much, if at all. No matter how effective the boot camp is in attaining its outcomes, there must be a guided reentry to that environment where decision making is monitored and adjustments made. Failures should be retrieved and reoriented so that they may try again. Aftercare programming should provide a heavy focus on family and education. The philosophy and vision of the boot camp must carry into and be interwoven with the treatment approach in aftercare. Clients are not only expected to succeed, they are required to succeed even if this means going out and retrieving them physically as well as tailoring a program around their specific needs. All the good work done in the boot camp can be quickly undone in an aftercare program that does not pick up on the philosophy of the boot camp and is not carefully integrated with it.

The director of the boot camp is also creator, director, and supervisor of the aftercare program and City Challenge. All the clientele come from New York City and return there to the centrally located facility. The aftercare program always has been carefully integrated with the boot camp, but has been substantially more difficult to pull together operationally.

An early mistake was to vigorously enforce norms and standards in aftercare at the same level as in the boot camp, thus heightening the revocation levels. The standard of not allowing a client to fail needs to be dominant in the thinking of aftercare workers. City Challenge goes all out to pull every client through the reintegration to the community. It also continues the education and skill-based learning opportunities for clients. The program includes a board of education certified high school program as well as a nonprofit culinary arts program with out-placement services. Each graduate of the academy receives a detailed treatment and educational strategy, which is to be carried out under the supervision of City Challenge. This includes approaches to any substance abuse issues, family issues, and particularly any special traumas or distractions current or not dealt with of the individual.

The Program Provides a Moral Vision

Without a moral vision, the graduate of a boot camp can easily be a physically fit, disciplined criminal with no understanding of consequences or empathy for victims. It is essential that the principal outcome of the program be an individual who can make sound, positive decisions based in a moral code. This is a most difficult task in any short-term program; however, it is probably the most critical undertaking. Criminals produce victims and the client of the boot camp must be pressed to mentally look into the eye of that victim and understand the pain they have created.

If nothing else is sacred to these young people, their families are. The whole dimension of victims rights, restorative justice, violence against women, and other burning societal issues with this clientele must be addressed in the most powerful manner within a high speed, intense program such as a boot camp. The fulcrum for dealing in moral areas lies in the client's relationship to his or her family as that is the one place where emotion will be found and can be associated with the pain of others. Not approaching these critical moral issues in the most advantageous context places them in the category of other cognitive issues which are understood, but which raise no value or emotion-based cause for thought. It is necessary to completely rework family relationships around many clients.

The Youth Leadership Academy now has young clients who are third-generation prisoners. Many have extended family members who are heavily involved in drugs and violence. Crack and AIDS continue to plague the family. There is almost no sense of a national, American identity or association with our traditional national values. As a result, we have seen a tendency in these young people to have a very distorted view of what is normal and acceptable. They know that they do not want to be incarcerated again, and they know that they miss their freedom and their families. The counseling programs of the Youth Leadership Academy cause the clients to repeatedly affirm in written papers and in presentations that they have allegiance to their families as well as to themselves and their futures. This allegiance is verbalized in biweekly conference calls home.

In many high-risk cases, the family situation requires that the client return home as the principal care giver to be a decision maker and a mentor to young siblings. As this connection is strengthened, it is possible to discuss very openly the victims of crime and, specifically, the victims they have created. This is done by relating the plight of the victim to the family of the client. It does not always work; however, the love of family, no matter how damaged the family may be, is the most powerful emotional link for promotion of a moral point of view. There has to be a sense that wrong behavior is wrong because of the consequences to people other than self. Without that even tentative mental brake on behavior, the values and training provided by the boot camp will erode over time and result in a new offense.

In conclusion, correctional boot camps can be used very effectively to address the habilitation needs of juvenile or adult offender clientele. These programs should be held to a high standard and should be viewed as a part of a continuum of programs which progressively empower the individual to return to the community as a contributing citizen. The client who comes to the facility fresh from the community will need strict norms and controls as he or she is unable to self-impose those controls or feels a need to act out with impulsive behaviors as a self-protective mechanism. A boot camp environment with carefully selected, relevant norms will provide the controls and behavior modification required to start working effectively with each individual. The focus needs to shift rapidly from tight norming to decision making and skill development. The clients represent a valuable potential resource to our communities. If they become skilled, educated, and moral people, they can return to the communities they endangered and become a plus as opposed to a minus in those communities. The confrontation in the boot camp needs to be directed toward the program's expectation that this will happen. Expectation must be focused on achievement in a variety of highly relevant training, counseling, and educational programs designed to ready the client for reimmersion into the community.

Army basic training starts the process of preparing soldiers for intense and stressful environments. A correctional boot camp must have the same focus, but train its clients to become successful survivors in another, often lethal and demanding environment. If the boot camp empowers them and replaces strict controls with freedom to make decisions, and if there is a powerful and well-run aftercare program to help guide them back into their communities, then the comparison to the military way of doing things is most appropriate.

Remember, just about all of our correctional clients are parents or will become parents at a relatively early age. Many of our youngest juvenile clients are parents. The Youth Leadership Academy has had several fifteen- and sixteen-year-olds with as many as three children. The leadership used to motivate and guide these young people will go a long way toward determining how they will act as parents in the future. An angry, threatening approach may well produce a parent who acts that way, particularly if his or her background includes parents who were equally angry and confrontational. Conversely, developing a positive model, where the confrontations are used to develop high achievement but are not loud and angry, will go a long way toward developing effective and supportive parents in the future. Almost all clients return to homes where there are young siblings so the leadership will always have an immediate impact on that family. Treating people firmly but well in residential placements goes a long way toward delinquency prevention.

The Youth Leadership Academy Skill Development Program

The Youth Leadership Academy has developed a sixteen-hour per day program with varied learning activities, including a series of training programs based on their counterpart in military programs. We have borrowed from Army training technologies and replaced military skills with life skills, designed to prepare the young person to reenter his neighborhood and his school. In all cases, these programs place the direct care staff member in the position of teacher, mentor, and evaluator, thus bridging the gap between treatment staff and what other programs refer to as military staff. In the academy, all staff is treatment staff operating within the same model with the same intended outcomes. Direct care staff, teachers, and even administrators have a role in these critical training programs and approach the learning objectives of each as a team. Following are the important outcomes generally sought by these training programs:

- To develop the youth's living skill base
- To enhance individual self-esteem by providing a series of competencies
- To place the instructor in the role of teacher, mentor, and expert
- To provide a consistent evaluation mechanism in skill development, motivation, and adherence to program norms

The most heavily used significant training program is the "job book." It consists of a series of performance-based tasks, which have been developed based largely on expertise available in the program combined with the real needs of a young person in aftercare and beyond. There are 290 tasks contained in three job books, that coincide with the three phases of the program from entry through aftercare. The tasks are increasingly difficult.

The tasks are backed by a training manual, which explains the tasks fully to the staff member and stipulates performance criteria and standards to be met by the cadet in performing the task for evaluation. There are also lesson plans for each task. The tasks are scheduled for instruction two weeks in advance by specific members of the direct care staff. The staff member must teach the task, demonstrate it where appropriate and allow the cadets preparation time. The task is then performed for evaluation or a presentation is made for evaluation. The cadet receives a "Go" on the task if the standard is met and a "No Go" is the standard is not met. The evaluations are passed to the staff chain of command and are entered in the overall quantitative assessment of the cadet for that week or day. The norms associated with each program phase are taught, practiced, and evaluated as the first set of tasks in each phase job book. These norms have important life outcomes as well.

One of the tenets of the Youth Leadership Academy is that each youth knows exactly where he stands in relation to the program and in relation to his peers at every step of the program. Accordingly, scores are assigned on a twenty-five-point scale for the principal components of the program: training, counseling, school, and behavior. A weekly order of merit is established from the top cadet to the lowest and all privileges flow from that evaluation process. The job book is the most important evaluation in the training component. It lends itself to such a quantitative process because performance is effectively evaluated against stipulated and consistent criteria. The cadet's track record in this program is easily accessed and becomes a part of the cadet's performance record. The record is something that the cadet takes great pride in, particularly as he feels more accomplished and completed having passed a long line of important life skills, including first aid, cardiopulmonary resuscitation, adventure skills, job skills, environmental skills, and others.

A recent addition to the latest editions of the job books has been English and mathematics. The teachers, of course, cover these subject areas in the formal classroom. However, the job book covers a series of academic tasks central to daily life. While somewhat redundant in some cases, these subjects are taught and evaluated by the direct care staff thus demonstrating that people other than teachers can perform the tasks. These tasks serve to fully align the teachers with the direct care staff as they augment and compliment each other. They also share in the evaluation process.

When our cadets meet with outsiders or with their parents the "job book" almost immediately becomes a subject of discussion. The cadet can visually demonstrate that he is competent in a range of skills not available to many of their age group. The speed with which the tasks are mastered is an indication of potential as well as motivation and is factored into important academic recommendations to the aftercare managers. The job book in the Advanced Challenge phase of the program includes a series of vocational skills. Mastery of these skills is measured and becomes part of the vocational interests' assessment to be provided to the aftercare managers. Overall the "job book" is an important tool in the development of Youth Leadership Academy.

Juvenile Boot Camp: The Abraxas Model

Corby A. Myers, Ed.D.

Director
Abraxas Leadership Program
South Mountain, Pennsylvania

An Historical Note

Throughout history, examples of privatization of correctional systems can be recognized. During the 1700s, the use of transportation systems which moved offenders from England to the colonies of America and Australia became a marketable service for many ship owners. In colonial America, it was considered common practice to sell the services of felons to provide cheap labor to industry, and the superintendents of the Walnut Street Jail in Philadelphia and the Auburn Prison in New York integrated private investors into the operation of their facilities (Johnson 1996).

The idea of allowing private investors to aid in the management of public institutions has received more attention in recent years. Driven by the increasing costs of incarceration, overcrowding, and civil liability due to poor conditions of confinement, some jurisdictions are revisiting privatization as an alternative method of service delivery. Although less than 1 percent of the nation's total adult prison population is held in privately funded facilities, there exists four trends within the adult system which suggest that privatization may become more firmly rooted as a part of the mainstream. The first is the management of "special niche population needs," which is being done successfully in some adult institutions and is fairly common in juvenile facilities in some states. Second, the size of the privately operated facility is growing, suggesting that private companies may now be able to handle more complex operations than previously thought. Third, prisoner classification levels in some privately funded facilities have been upgraded from minimum to medium and maximum security, and finally, the private industry is becoming more aggressive in construction of facilities and marketing the lease options back to the government (Bowditch and Everett 1987).

Privately owned and operated facilities and programs are, and have been, much more prevalent in the juvenile justice system for some time. In Pennsylvania, for example, there are over 200 privately operated programs offering services to juveniles statewide. With an impressive track record of providing treatment and rehabilitation services to youth through residential and community-based programs, it should come as no surprise that as public sector monies became available in the form of planning, development, and construction grants, the private operation of boot camps would become an attractive market for the private sector. This chapter looks at one such juvenile boot camp from the initial planning process, through the development of the program, and into the implementation and operation of the facility as it currently exists.

The Abraxas Leadership Development Program

Program Planning

In 1993, the Abraxas Foundation Inc. applied to the Office of Justice Programs, Bureau of Justice Assistance for a grant to provide seed money to plan and develop a juvenile boot camp program. Abraxas Inc., a nonprofit foundation, has an extensive history in working with adjudicated juvenile offenders, operating thirty programs in five states, ranging from community-based treatment, mental health services, day treatment, and a sex offender program, to a 170-bed residential drug and alcohol rehabilitation facility. The development of the boot camp was in response to a desire by Abraxas executives to continue the diversification of services offered by Abraxas and to create a new model for boot camps based on what had been effective in the other areas of their system of services.

In procuring federal monies to start the camp, Abraxas had to establish a private/public partnership to be eligible for funds under Bureau of Justice Assistance guidelines. The partnership was established with Cumberland County, Pennsylvania, with their probation department acting as the grantee. A grant in the amount of $298,900 was used primarily to hire the administrative staff responsible for program implementation and to purchase some equipment essential for startup. In return for acting as the conduit for obtaining the Bureau of Justice Assistance funds, Cumberland County Juvenile Probation Department received two bed spaces per class for the first year of operation. The team assembled by Abraxas to implement the project was led by the Pennsylvania Executive Director and the Director of Education and Special Projects, who wrote the initial program description and provided the blueprint for the project.

The site selected for the program was determined partly on the basis of a desire to be centrally located in Pennsylvania, and partly due to the winds of fortune. The Pennsylvania Department of Public Welfare had made a decision to offer several vacant state buildings under their control for use by private service providers. Abraxas officials toured several available state buildings in central Pennsylvania, and finally selected a building on the grounds of the South Mountain Restoration Center in South Mountain, Pennsylvania. The Restoration Center was originally built as a tuberculosis hospital in the early 1900s. In the 1960s, it was converted to inpatient care for mentally ill patients committed to the state mental health system. The hospital eventually evolved to specialize in providing care for geriatric patients committed to the state, which remains its function today. Twenty-two buildings exist on the grounds of the Restoration Center, but only four are currently used by the hospital, making the remaining eighteen buildings potentially available for private use.

The Leadership Development Program facility is located in a building that formerly served as personal housing for the nursing staff who worked at the Restoration Center during the period when it was a tuberculosis hospital. Abraxas entered into a lease arrangement with the Department of Public Works to acquire the building for one dollar per year. The Restoration Center provides utilities to the facility and charges the Leadership Development Program based on a formula which may be reviewed and revised on an annual basis. The lease also provides for use of several areas on the grounds of the Restoration Center for recreational activities and construction of ropes courses.

Abraxas was responsible for renovation to the building, which amounted to approximately $700,000 in capital expense for the construction of classroom space, design and outfitting of food service areas, demolition of several walls, asbestos removal, replacement of floor tiles, and painting of the entire interior of the building. The Restoration Center maintains the grounds (including snow removal from parking areas and lawn maintenance) while Abraxas is responsible for maintenance of the physical plant. The building had been vacant for sixteen years and was used by the state for equipment storage purposes. Renovations to the building occurred literally one step ahead of cadets progressing through the program, construction and finish work were not completed until the program had been in operation for two months.

Program Development

The hiring of staff took place over four months and in three phases. Eight key administrative staff were hired first and began employment on August 15, 1994. These included: the facility director, the clinical director, the business manager, the educational director, the admissions coordinator, an administrative assistant, and two treatment supervisors, one of whom was to be responsible for the wilderness component of the program. One half of the remaining clinical and support staff were hired and began employment in the middle of September, and the remaining staff began in November.

For program implementation, the staff was allowed to take ownership of both the design and the operation of the program. The administrative team initially focused on the nuts and bolts aspects of the program, which included issues of hiring staff, ordering materials and supplies, achieving oversight of the renovation work to the building, and compiling information, resources, and materials that could be used to develop the clinical and educational programming and beginning the process of staff-orientation training. We emphasized cooperation and collaboration between administrative team members and the development of a sense of shared responsibility.

The members of the administrative team each brought a different perspective to the job based on their diverse backgrounds in terms of work, experience, and education. The common thread evident among team members was their overall lack of a military background. Team members had come primarily from careers in other social service agencies working with youth (such as drug and alcohol programs, juvenile detention facilities, and probation), and only one member of the team had an extensive military background. Sheer numbers dictated that the Leadership Development Program would adopt a traditional residential treatment philosophy within a military-style framework. With this thought in mind, hiring of staff also was focused on applicants who had experience and education in working with delinquent youth, and yet, who were open to learning the military model components of the program. No drill instructors were employed and only about 10 percent of the total staff had any form of formal military service.

Although a blueprint for the program existed in the form of the original program description written to meet the Bureau of Justice Assistance grant application requirements, the administrative team made a conscious decision to use only the major themes contained in the description and allow for flexibility of the program design based on the skills and abilities of the staff who would be responsible for the day-to-day operations. The process of hiring during the first months was simply to tell applicants that the program would be a boot camp design, give them a general overview of some of the major program elements that were mandated (such as education, counseling, physical training, wilderness experiences, and so on), and to allow them to express their ideas and perceptions of the program. Not only did these interviews yield some exceptionally talented people who were hired as staff, but it also provided a forum for people to express ideas, which were later incorporated into the final design of the program and development of the clinical programming.

The main focus of the administrative staff, aside from staff hiring, was to look at the resources needed to house, feed, clothe, and provide for the daily necessities of life for the first platoon of twenty-four cadets due to arrive in October and to coordinate the delivery and storage of materials in a facility still undergoing renovation. One day prior to admitting the first class, the administrative team was still working out of one makeshift office and only one wing where the cadets would be housed was completed. The staff had long since adopted the philosophy that cadets would undergo rehabilitation along with the building and that we could make a positive experience out of the inconvenience of not having the facility totally prepared.

New staff-orientation training began three weeks prior to the first client intake. The first week consisted of state-mandated training requirements including; fire safety, safe physical management, exposure control, first aid/cardiopulmonary resuscitation, child abuse reporting procedures, and instruction on the Department of Public Welfare's requirements for operation of a residential child-care facility. The program is licensed under the regulations of the Pennsylvania Department of Public Welfare as a residential child-care facility, and as such is not considered to be part of the correctional system in the state, but rather is a part of the juvenile justice/child-care system. Under this license, training of skills and competencies must be provided on an annual basis and are part of the annual review process by the state, which does on-site inspections.

The second two weeks of training consisted of a facilitation process in which staff were first briefed on the major program components, and then asked to participate in deciding how each area should be operationalized. The result of this type of training design was that staff developed very quickly into a cohesive team, and each member of the team was encouraged to take ownership in making decisions on how the program would operate. Evaluations completed at the end of each day consistently documented the staff expressing feelings of empowerment in being able to take part in the decision-making process. Staff was enthusiastic even in topic areas that most people would consider mundane, such as developing policies and procedures and the daily routine.

Funding

Although a start-up grant was obtained from the Bureau of Justice Assistance, this money accounted for only a small fraction of the initial cost in starting the program. Continuation funding for the program is provided through Pennsylvania Act 148, which means that each county in the state is responsible for making their own referrals to the program. Pennsylvania has sixty-seven counties, and the Leadership Development Program is contracted by sixty-five of those, to provide services (Philadelphia and Allegheny counties have other arrangements). If the referral is accepted for admission, the county pays a per diem rate to the program for services provided and the state in turn, reimburses the referring county for 80 percent of the cost.

The program also receives funding from the public school district in which the youth is enrolled for educational services provided while in the program. The program contracts with the local school district (Waynesboro) to collect the reimbursement for educational services from the client's home school district under the provisions of the Pennsylvania Public School Code and Act 1306, which are regulated by the Pennsylvania Department of Education. The Waynesboro School District collects a small administrative fee from the program to cover their cost for billing and funnels the remaining funds directly to the program.

Food costs are also partially reimbursed by the National School Breakfast/Lunch Program. Each of these funding sources are subject to inspection and audit by the administering agency, and the program must comply with all the regulations promulgated by the respective department.

Program Description

Overview

The Leadership Development Program is a short-term, cost-effective residential treatment program serving both delinquent and dependent youth. The vast majority of referrals are court adjudicated delinquents; however, a few referrals have been made for dependency clients who are deemed to be "incorrigible" youth. The program is considered a boot camp design; however, it is in fact much closer to a military school in focus. The fifteen-week (105 day) program consists of three distinct five-week phases, one of which is a five-week wilderness challenge similar to an Outward Bound experience. The program is designed to develop self-discipline, self-respect, self-esteem, life skills, education, and to challenge and change irresponsible attitudes and thinking. It also seeks to create an environment which is physically, academically, and morally challenging. At its core, the program has the regimentation and structure of military-style leadership training and ends with a high adventure wilderness experience. Physical training includes the basics of running, calisthenics, and fitness tests, as well as structured intramural recreation activities and off-grounds athletic competitions.

Education occurs on site in conformance with the Public School Code of 1949. The educational program is operated under the auspices of the local school district and complies with all the requirements of the Pennsylvania Department of Education for a privately licensed secondary school. Both educational and clinical staff are employees of Abraxas. If a student is a high school graduate or possesses a General Equivalency Diploma, provisions are made for career counseling or vocational education programming. The school, which is referred to as the "Learning Center," is in session Monday through Friday with academic subjects interspersed with cognitive development, life skills, independent living, and wilderness survival curriculum. Educational grouping occurs based on the educational records, educational assessment testing, and educational needs of the cadet. Group counseling, counseling in the experiential context and theme groups (such as values clarification and resocialization, moral dilemma, drug and alcohol education, criminal personality theory, and building refusal skills) occurs daily with an emphasis on self-examination.

The program accommodates 105 cadets. A platoon of thirty-three cadets is admitted every fifth Tuesday. Six beds are reserved for cadets who need additional work in meeting their treatment goals and who are recycled for an added five weeks. Cadets are between the ages of fourteen and eighteen, and are classified as first- and second-time offenders. The program is designed for nonviolent, mentally stable, physically capable males. All referrals undergo an interview process prior to formal admission to the program and must meet the criteria for acceptance which includes: no psychotropic medications, no history of arson, an IQ of at least 80, and the client's verbal commitment to the program. Abraxas court liaisons, who are community-based professional staff and responsible for specific geographic locations throughout the state, administer the Adolescent Problem Severity Index instrument to the client, and collect psychological and psychiatric information, prior placement reports, probation summaries, and health records. This information is sent to the program admissions coordinator, who makes a decision on acceptance into the program.

The last five weeks of the program is a high-intensity wilderness component which continues the goals of the program through extensive and vigorous adventure-based counseling, experiential learning, and physical fitness activities. Cadets are challenged with intense success-oriented trials which allow them to test the skills they have learned in the first ten weeks. Cadets rock climb, rappell, hike, camp, whitewater raft, and do a three-day solo in remote areas of various national and state parks. The cadets also use on-site high and low ropes courses to overcome fears and learn the value of teamwork. Cadets are encouraged to learn to respect and appreciate the world around them by achieving goals, solving problems, and overcoming adversity in an outdoor setting. The wilderness program is designed to also allow the cadet to experience and develop inner qualities such as self-control, self-esteem, and mutual respect, and to provide an opportunity to spend time alone to make a self-assessment of his progress in the program and to contemplate his return to the community.

Treatment Program

The treatment program at the Leadership Development Program is based on a combination of several models, including therapeutic communities, reality theory, and criminal personality theory. The primary goal of the treatment program is to engage cadets in process that will change their thinking, values, and behaviors. This is accomplished through an intensive three-phase program that challenges them as a team, overcomes obstacles, and has them consistently perform at a high level. The treatment goals of the specific phases are as follows:

Phase I

The goal of Phase I is to quickly gain the cadets' attention and engage them in the treatment process by using a modified military model. Most cadets will be very uncomfortable with the regimentation and military terminology, which creates a tension conducive to engaging the cadet in an experiential and cognitive treatment process.

Cadets are also unaccustomed to the team-oriented approach of the program. From the first day, they become part of a thirty-three member platoon and a six-member treatment team. Counselors are responsible for the individual treatment and the development of on-going small groups with their team of six cadets. All activities, other than individual counseling, occur within the parameters of either platoon or treatment team groups. Unlike most groups, which are transient or time bound, these teams function as a team continuously for fifteen weeks. Team success is stressed over individual success and virtually all activities are done from the perspective of members of the team.

Treatment activities during Phase I involve self-examination and the evaluation of values. Cadets are encouraged to consider their belief system and the impact of those beliefs on their lives and the lives of others. An emphasis on health and physical fitness is also considered along with the educational and cognitive components of the program. The physical training program is designed to build and gradually improve the cadets' level of fitness. After five weeks of running and calisthenics, combined with other program components, most cadets will have much improved self-esteem, self-awareness, and self-confidence. Throughout the program, inappropriate behaviors and ways of thinking are confronted and the cadets are held accountable at all times for their actions.

Phase II

Phase II continues many of the themes of Phase I but places increased emphasis on group problem solving and personal and group leadership skills development. By the time Phase I is completed, cadets will be functioning as a well-developed team ready to accept more difficult challenges. They will also be well disciplined in military drill and ceremony, allowing for less time spent on the military model and more on higher level clinical activities. Expectations are increased as staff direction is decreased in favor of more self-direction and opportunities to exhibit leadership skills.

In Phase I, staff are very directive; however, during Phase II, their role is expected to become more observant/consultive. Cadets assume revolving leadership roles as squad and platoon leaders, and as the company commander. Cadets are not given any authority over other cadets but assume more of a coordination role to assure the team is functioning smoothly. Mentorship relationships are also encouraged by having Phase II cadets work with Phase I cadets to role model program expectations and help the new cadet adjust to the program.

This phase also begins to introduce some of the concepts used in the wilderness phase of the program by using the low and high ropes course. These activities serve as both individual and group challenges, as well as preparation for the third phase. The goal of Phase II is to develop highly efficient, physically fit, self-confident teams that are prepared for the intense, high-adventure wilderness challenge in Phase III.

Phase III

This phase of the program, known as the WILD (Wilderness Interaction for Leadership Development) program, has two goals which, at times, may appear to be contradictory. This phase revolves around a very intense wilderness experience designed to challenge cadets and demonstrate their effectiveness as a team. The phase also addresses the issues of aftercare planning and the carryover into the community on release from the program.

Criticisms of the use of this type of adventure-based counseling traditionally have been centered around questions of its effectiveness with urban youth who are either unable to relate to the experience or unable to apply the lessons learned into their daily lives primarily due to the types of methods used to process the experience. The Leadership

Development Program recognizes these criticisms and has developed a model for wilderness activities which strives to address this problem. As a rule, the wilderness experience approach has not been used with a highly motivated, physically fit group of cadets. The Leadership Development Program has adopted the belief that the value of the experience is greatly enhanced by the readiness of the cadet group. The wilderness experience is undertaken after ten weeks of preparatory work, not as a standalone program in which there is little or no advance preparation. Given that more preparation time is spent on overcoming resistance and fear, there is more time available for processing, counseling, and goal planning. The wilderness experience mirrors, as much as possible, the intensive counseling and education that a cadet receives while in the first two phases of the program (Knapp 1990).

Cadets also must prepare for a return to their community in Phase III. For this reason, the program content is designed for its carryover value so that cadets can relate the here and now to the future. The concept of "future pacing" is stressed heavily throughout the phase, and this link between the experiential and cognitive learning process is essential to a cadet's future success. The final week of Phase III is devoted to making future plans and goals final and to contacting and solidifying the continuing care plan with the committing court. The final day of the program is devoted to a graduation ceremony attended by court personnel, and other persons significant in the life of the cadet. Graduates receive awards in clinical, educational, and wilderness areas, and graduation certificates. A keynote speaker and a cadet address also highlight the ceremony.

Phase IV

The overall success of the Leadership Development Program is dependent on an ability to provide substantial, quality, continuing care services to cadet graduates. Abraxas strongly supports the concept that continuing care is necessary to improve the cadet's successful transition back to the community. Community-based services to assist and support the returning cadet are recommended for a minimum of sixty days following release from the program. Follow-up services including counseling, job search assistance, and life skills training are an integral part of the overall service. Several options for continuing care services exist within the framework of the program.

Abraxas Community Treatment (ACT) programs presently combine intensive case management services, family intervention and counseling, community resources, and client monitoring and surveillance. Abraxas staff are available to the youth twenty-four hours a day, seven days a week. This model provides specialized training that reinforces the curriculum presented in the Leadership Development Program. Each cadet has a personalized service plan developed by his primary counselor and treatment team. Within that service plan is the recommendation for the types of service that a cadet needs to continue to receive in his follow-up care. In some jurisdictions, ACT services are not available and other Abraxas programs may be used to provide continuing care. These may include: day treatment, mental health services, and long-term drug and alcohol rehabilitation services.

Abraxas also is willing to enter into joint programming with existing county programs to ensure the continuing care of cadets. In this option, Abraxas will provide program specific information (special training) relevant to the treatment curriculum within the Leadership Development Program to ensure treatment continuity. The cost of this service is negotiable. In counties where Abraxas continuing care services are not available and the county has no existing providers, Abraxas will work with the county to identify resources and will train individuals to provide follow-up services.

Treatment Planning

A comprehensive treatment plan is developed for each cadet during the first phase of the program. Treatment planning occurs in the third week of the program and is prepared by a treatment team consisting of the primary counselor, the senior treatment supervisor, the treatment supervisor, the education supervisor, the probation officer, the family, and the cadet.

The program intake coordinator is responsible for an initial treatment plan on intake. Although the first phase of the program is very structured, the initial treatment plan indicates issues identified in the referral materials that may be relevant to the health and welfare of the cadet as well as provides information essential to all staff. This would include information on medical needs, history of AWOLs, emotional issues, drug and/or alcohol usage, outstanding treatment issues, or presenting family problems. The intake coordinator places such information into the form of a "red flag" document, which all staff assigned to the intake team are required to read, to be familiar with the cadet and his needs prior to admission.

The treatment plan is prepared as a formal document by the primary counselor, following the treatment planing conference and is reviewed, approved, and distributed to all involved parties. The general needs of the cadet are addressed through the clinical program schedule itself, as these will be needs shared by the majority of the cadets in the program. Specific needs are personalized and addressed through the individual counseling process and other aspects of the treatment plan.

During the tenth week of the program, a formal treatment plan review occurs. This serves to evaluate the cadet's progress in the program and to formally update the treatment plan in preparation for his discharge and community-based continuing care. The review also identifies those cadets who have not adequately addressed their treatment goals and who may need additional time in the program. These cadets will be reviewed by the treatment managers for a possible recycling through an additional five weeks in the program. The review is again prepared by the primary counselor with input from the treatment supervisor and other members of the treatment team. The review document is also prepared, reviewed, and distributed, prior to the cadet leaving on the wilderness field operation in week twelve of the program.

A discharge summary document is then prepared by the continuing care staff, with input from the cadets' wilderness counselor, and the other members of the treatment team. It is an evaluation of the cadets' overall performance in the program and a formal discussion of continuing care options and recommendations. This document is prepared and completed prior to graduation and is distributed on the date of graduation.

Treatment Philosophy

The Abraxas Leadership Development Program recognizes that using a military model in its purest form (boot camp) can be dehumanizing and insensitive to the needs of troubled youth. The treatment model of the program has been designed to purposely challenge youth without damaging their self-esteem. While the program is intensive and demanding, it couples experiential learning with education to help cadets develop self-discipline and critical thinking skills.

The program uses the concept of people security as a major component of the treatment philosophy. People security refers to not just being where the cadets are, but also being meaningfully involved with them. Physical proximity and direct supervision are essential; however, meaningful interaction with a cadet also involves participating in activities, discussing their thoughts and feelings, anticipating and intercepting problems, and teaching new skills and attitudes.

Program security is a critical element of any program. At the Leadership Development Program, this includes providing a detailed structure and setting high expectations throughout the program. All daily routines and activities take place within an established structure and clear expectations for cadet involvement are established, communicated and enforced. Staff is highly energetic in the application of the principles of people and program security. The Leadership Development Program does not allow noncompliance with program norms. The approach to compliance is based on being intense, directive, and confrontive of negative or delinquent behaviors, acting out or refusal. Staff is firm, consistent, and demanding of change at the behavioral level. This use of a direct confrontation of irresponsibility is also used as a vehicle for the cadet to gain an immediate sense of the consequences of his behavior. In addition to the personal consequences of his behavior, the cadet is also assisted in becoming more sensitive to how his behavior affects those around him.

Patience, persistence, perseverance, communication, and a high degree of teamwork are essential elements of the program. Staff are encouraged to role model and be aware of their role as agents of change. Although the program takes a confrontive approach in which accountability is the cornerstone, the primary goal of the treatment program is to help the cadet change and grow. Clients are treated fairly and with dignity and respect. Staff consistently confront negative behaviors but more importantly, affirm positive behaviors. Genuine care and concern are essential elements in encouraging the cadet to accept the guidance and support of the staff and in having the cadet accept the opportunities for positive growth that staff present.

The program combines elements of several accepted therapeutic models into the clinical curriculum. Conceptually, the Leadership Development Program uses concepts gleaned from criminal personality theory, adapting the concepts of accountability and taking responsibility for one's actions, and criminal thinking errors into the clinical curriculum in the form of theme groups and into the overall program philosophy (Samenow 1984, Yochelson and Samenow 1977). The program also borrows from the therapeutic communities' model in which there is a strong sense of community and peer support, elements of ritual (drill and ceremony, military dress, and haircuts), and a focus on behavioral change. Treatment also includes ideas taken from the schools of Reality Therapy, Aggression Replacement Training, and a variety of resources in the drug and alcohol field (Glasser 1965, Goldstein and Glick 1987).

Discipline

Discipline at the Leadership Development Program is viewed as corrective in nature. When disciplinary action becomes necessary, it is handled in a timely manner and within state-mandated guidelines. With the emphasis of the program on accentuating positive achievement, discipline is viewed as being restorative (in other words, fix what is broken). It is also seen as an opportunity for intensive counseling resulting in growth for the cadet.

As previously stated, the Leadership Development Program agency design is much closer to a military school than to basic training. Drill instructors are not used, and staff, though directive and confrontive of irresponsible behaviors, are respectful of cadets at all times. The normative culture of the program emphasizes effort, achievement, and the development of a positive peer culture. At no time are cadets demeaned or verbally or physically abused. They are challenged to test themselves and to achieve, but always with emphasis on the positive. The goal of the program is to build the cadets up, not tear them down.

Staff

The program seeks to employ staff that have a treatment-oriented background, and who may, or more often may not, have a form of military background. All staff are trained in military drill and ceremony, as well as experiential learning concepts. Upon employment, all staff, including support and administrative personnel, participate in a thorough orientation and training program. Although appropriate credentials are necessary, the more important qualities for a staff member are character, courage, and compassion, combined with a sincere desire to help young people change their lives.

Senior treatment and treatment supervisors are college graduates with master's degrees or relevant experience of no less than two years' work with a delinquent population. Ideally, these staff have a background that includes prior supervisory experience, drug and alcohol counseling, other counseling, and/or specialized work with delinquents.

Counselors are at least college graduates. Qualifications include social service experience, a criminal justice background, or teaching credentials. Life skills workers and house parents have a minimum of a high school diploma, college preferred, and are required to receive appropriate training. Additionally, the program employs teaching staff who are fully accredited in their subject areas, nursing staff who are also fully licensed, and a variety of support and administrative personnel.

Educational Program

The Leadership Development Program developed its educational curriculum with an emphasis on outcome-based education, to account for the variability of educational levels and academic skills among the cadets. Individual outcomes are set by the educational director and the teaching staff with a focus on active learning. Recognizing that many of these students have been unsuccessful in a traditional school setting, the teaching techniques used encompass a variety of instructional approaches. These include methods such as: giving mini-lectures; brainstorming; using role plays, games, small group work, and cooperative group work; employing student self-directed activities, reciprocal learning, situation and illustration analysis; using guest experts, case studies, simulations, self-assessment instruments, and community-involvement activities.

Formal and informal assessment occur daily. The instruction is designed to meet the needs of the whole person. This holistic approach includes, but is not limited to, intellectually, physically, morally, and behaviorally challenging the student. The program stresses that learning is a life-long process which continues to change the learner's perceptions and behavior. Experiential learning and exploration by teachers and support staff determine what is relevant curriculum. Students learn within a caring and structured environment that promotes dignity, honesty, values, and respect. Students are encouraged to learn to respect others and the law; they are guided toward increased self-initiative with the targeted outcome of becoming conscientious, contributive citizens.

The curriculum is focused on incorporating the object lesson while addressing specific educational needs of students. The object lesson is developed specifically for at-risk youth. The program recognizes that there is a significant difference in the method of instruction and type of educational program that is provided to delinquent youth. Learning success in the program is geared toward matching a student's activity level and learning style. Class size is small (eight students to one teacher) and consideration is given to learning and teaching styles, and curriculum, to improve educational outcomes. Instruction is provided by certified teachers in the basic skills areas as well as in areas of cognitive development, life skills, independent living skills, vocational education, and for general equivalency diploma preparation. The major focus remains on mathematics, language arts/reading, social studies, and science, even with this wide-ranging educational approach.

The educational curriculum also supports the clinical curriculum by offering components of drug and alcohol education designed to help the student develop a knowledge base, and decision making and coping skills to avoid use and/or abuse. The overall curriculum includes decision-making skills instruction to aid the student in making responsible choices. Each student receives five and a half hours of classroom instruction each day. The educational program supports and reflects the goals established by the Pennsylvania State Board of Education, providing for a quality education for all children living in the Commonwealth.

Special education students are also served by the educational program. Once it has been determined that a student qualifies for special education services, an Individualized

Educational Program (I.E.P.) is developed and approved for implementation. The educational program complies with all state and federal policies and regulations regarding exceptional students.

Family Involvement

The Leadership Development Program encourages family involvement and provides for family participation in family conferences at specific times throughout the program. Parents or guardians, siblings, grandparents, attorneys or legal representatives, volunteers and clergy are allowed to visit—subject to approval by the program director. There is no visitation during the first thirty days of the program, during which time the cadet is undergoing orientation to the program and the staff are working to overcome his initial resistance to program norms. Visitation is allowed on weekends following this initial orientation phase; however, visits occur in the context of a family planning conference and as such, are scheduled with the primary counselor. During these visits, family members are expected to work on establishing long- and short-range goals with the cadet and the counseling and continuing care staff in preparation for the cadets return to the home. Visits are treated as an integral piece of the treatment process.

Program staff will make all reasonable efforts to include the family in the overall treatment process and to solicit and encourage their support in aftercare planning. Phone calls and mail are used extensively to maintain family involvement. Additionally, counselors contact families bi-weekly to discuss in detail, the progress of the cadet and to initiate continuing care planning. Families also are strongly encouraged to attend and participate in the cadet's graduation ceremony. Families also may be broadly defined based on the needs of the cadet, as some cadets are parents or themselves may be married. In these types of instances, persons who have proven to be a significant influence in the life of the cadet also may be included into the treatment process and allowed to visit.

Religious Observances

While the Leadership Development Program does not employ a chaplain on staff, religious programming is offered by volunteer ministers from the community and by the South Mountain Restoration Center Chaplain. Abraxas provides staff support for this purpose and sufficient time is built into the weekly schedule to allow for the observance of religious activities. Moral development and spiritual enrichment are seen as important components of the program and religious materials, such as bibles and pamphlets, are considered to be appropriate literature for cadets to keep in their possession.

Cadets also participate in volunteer and community service activities which also exposes them to religious programming, including escorting patients from the Restoration Center to and from church services each Sunday, and participation with several church youth groups from the nearby community. Religious restrictions on diet are also considered and food service staff make accommodations for those cadets who are required to refrain from eating specific foods for religious reasons.

Wilderness Activities

In the final five week phase of the program, cadets are exposed to a high intensity wilderness challenge similar in style to Outward-Bound type programs. The wilderness phase continues the goals of the program, through intensive adventure-based counseling and experiential learning, in a setting that provides an element of adversity and which demands that they perform together as a team to overcome obstacles and fears. Cadets are encouraged to learn to respect and appreciate the outdoors while continuing to address their treatment goals.

The first week of the wilderness phase is devoted to preparation for departure. Supplies and materials are inventoried and packed for transport to the wilderness site. Cadets spend the week in educational seminars that provide information and instruction in a variety of wilderness concepts from how to pack a backpack to low-environmental impact camping. The first week also serves as a transitional week in which the primary counselor meets with his or her wilderness counterpart to discuss relevant issues about the cadets entering their caseloads.

One of the early concerns about the wilderness phase was this transition of cadets from a primary counselor with whom they had spent ten weeks discussing issues and developing a trusting relationship, to a new counselor with whom they had to begin a new relationship. These early fears that there would be a disruption in the clinical process have proven to be unfounded for several reasons: first, the counseling staff at the facility have focused on preparing the cadet in advance of the change and have worked closely with the wilderness counselors to make appropriate matches between wilderness counselor and the cadet and to improve the flow of information between the two teams; second, due to the highly intensive nature of the wilderness activities (such as rock climbing, rappelling, and solo experience) cadets are encouraged to build trust relationships very quickly with both the counselors and their peers; and third, the work done during the first two phases of the program has promoted the development of social skills that allow the cadet to create bonds between themselves and the wilderness counselor much more easily. In fact, the combination of preparatory work in house, and the need to develop a trusting relationship under very adverse wilderness conditions allows for some of the most significant clinical gains to be made during the wilderness phase of the program.

During the second, third, and fourth weeks of the wilderness phase, cadets are exposed to the wilderness field operation. Cadets are transported to a remote wilderness area of a state or national forest. Sites are selected according to several criteria including: availability of medical services, public access, availability of terrain conducive to wilderness activities, weather patterns, and cooperation of the local authorities. During the winter months, field operation are generally located in southern states to take advantage of warmer climates. Summer field operations normally take place in Pennsylvania and locations closer to the facility.

Cadets will hike during the first ten days of the field operation (five-to-seven miles per day) establishing a new campsite each evening. The hiking phase is followed by a three-day solo experience, and the final week is spent performing high-angle activities such as rock climbing and rappelling. In addition to these wilderness activities, the wilderness phase attempts to mirror, as much as possible, the clinical and educational components found in the program facility during the first two phases. Educational packets are prepared and used during field operations with the added element of using the environment to enhance the educational experience. Experiential education relies on the use of behavioral and social learning methods used in a nontraditional learning environment which will result in greater, more meaningful behavioral change, greater learning, and longer retention of information. For example, science class may consist of star charting at night or identifying and documenting of local flora and fauna during the hikes. History class may make use of a local area of historic interest to make the class more meaningful to the student (Kraft 1990).

The clinical program also is similarly adapted for use outdoors. Individual counseling may occur during a hike while theme groups or seminars will take place around the campfire at night. The emphasis on counseling shifts during the third phase to focus on issues of "future pacing," getting the cadet to look at how he will make the transition back to the community and how to stay successful when he returns home. Medical services are also provided in the wilderness by staff who are certified as wilderness first responders or wilderness EMTs (Knapp 1990).

The wilderness staff are broken into two ten-person teams, each with a treatment supervisor and a lead counselor in charge. While one team is in the field, basically working around the clock with cadets, the second team has time off. Staff do earn time off in the field and are allowed to use Abraxas vehicles, within a limited range, to attend to personal activities. Wilderness staff are selected on the basis of the same criteria as regular facility staff with the addition of demonstrating specific skills in wilderness types of activities and a commitment to the type of lifestyle that is required by the nature of the program.

During a field operation, cadets are self-contained in terms of the resources needed to survive in the outdoors. Each cadet carries a sixty-pound backpack containing food, water, clothing, and shelter. Equipment for all wilderness activities meets or exceeds the industry standards established by the Association for Experiential Education and there is a strong emphasis placed on the safety of both the cadet and staff. All staff are required to pass competency tests prior to being released to perform high-angle activities, and training and instruction of wilderness staff is ongoing and evaluated regularly.

Summary

Although the Leadership Development Plan has not been operational for a long period of time, early results in terms of recidivism rates is encouraging. Of the two classes that have been discharged from the program for at least one year, 80 percent of the program graduates continue to be successful and have not reoffended. To generate some meaningful information about the long-term effects of the program, a research study is being conducted under the auspices of the National Institute of Justice as part of an on-going evaluation process to identify and evaluate innovative program models. The focus of the study is to look beyond recidivism as the primary indicator of program success to examine the impact of the Leadership Development Program on a variety of offender attributes that are theoretically related to successful cadet community readjustment. These include offender problem-solving skills, self-esteem, and coping mechanisms. The results of the study should be completed by the fall of 1996.

The Abraxas Leadership Development Program is one example of the type of "special niche" program in which the private provider can be used best. The program is innovative and creative in its approach to the boot camp model in part because of the freedom to try experimental approaches which may not be as quickly embraced in a more conservative arena. Although originally designed to simply provide a short-term, cost-effective alternative to more long term residential placements, the approach taken by program planners allowed for considerable latitude in breaking out of the traditional concept of what a boot camp should resemble.

The blend of military model, residential style treatment programming, wilderness challenge, and outcome-based education components, was the result of an approach in which staff was encouraged to take ownership of the program. This ownership translated into a model in which people could create a safe, secure environment in which the focus is on the change process and in which all program elements are complimentary and supportive to one another in assuring that the cadet is able to realize positive changes in his life.

References

Bowditch, C. and R. Everett. 1987. Private Prisons: Problems Within the Solution. *Justice Quarterly*. 4:441-453.

Glasser, W. 1965. *Reality Therapy*. New York: Harper & Row.

Goldstein, A., and B. Glick. 1987. *Aggression Replacement Training*. Champaign, Illinois: Research Press.

Johnson, R. 1996. *Hard Time: Understanding and Reforming the Prison*. Belmont, California: Wadsworth Publishing.

Knapp, C. 1990. Processing the Adventure Experience. In Miles and Priest, eds. *Adventure Education*. State College, Pennsylvania: Venture Publishing.

Kraft, R. 1990. Experiential Learning. In Miles and Priest, eds. *Adventure Education*. State College, Pennsylvania: Venture Publishing.

Samenow, S. 1984. *Inside the Criminal Mind*. New York: Times Books.

Yochelson, S., and S. Samenow. 1977. *The Criminal Personality, Vols. I & II*. New York: Aronson.

To March or Not to March: Is That the Question?

Cheryl L. Clark

Director of Shock Development
New York State Department of Correctional Services
Albany, New York

Ronald Moscicki

Superintendent
Lakeview Shock Incarceration Facility
Brocton, New York

Command Sergeant Major Joshua Perry (Retired)

Training Specialist
United States Army Military Police School
Fort McClellan, Alabama

The Birth Of Boot Camps

Soon after the first modern boot camps were established in Georgia and Oklahoma in 1983, the military model of corrections was touted as the answer to the problems of systems bursting at the seams because of escalating prison populations. Mandatory drug sentencing laws of the 1970s resulted in prisons increasingly overcrowded with offenders committed for nonviolent offenses and drug-related crimes. In the ten year period between

1973 and 1983, with the "war on drugs" accelerating, the prison population doubled; in the next ten years, it doubled again. By October 1994, more than one million men and women were incarcerated in the United States. Six million others swelled the ranks of probation and parole.

Criminal justice officials, the public and legislators were desperately attempting to find solutions. Everyone was worried; criminal justice because overcrowding was straining scarce resources to the limit, fraying tempers and fanning the fears of the incarcerated and staff alike. Increasingly, gang activity, in and out of prisons, erupted in fights, tension, and deaths. The public was afraid to take a walk in neighborhoods where once they did not have to lock doors. Senior citizens, locking themselves into their homes at dusk, were afraid to answer their doors because of their fear of young predators, ready to steal welfare and social security checks for drug money. Legislators and government officials struggled, because the demand to punish even more offenders is a costly undertaking. How does one satisfy constituents by making them feel safe but keep taxes down? As a nation, the "drug wars" were on everyone's mind. What was the solution?

In 1983, two states simultaneously led the way into the future of corrections with correctional "boot camps." Oklahoma and Georgia were the first to experiment with this innovative idea. The belief was that a highly intensive, brief incarceration period might be a more effective means of dealing with this increasingly young, nonviolent population. Early intervention, a "scared straight" approach that lasted for longer than an afternoon, coupled with teaching self-discipline, became the leading edge of incarceration programs. Legislators saw boot camps as a means of having an impact on crime, while at the same time conserving scarce tax dollars, because of the shorter duration of the programs. Those who had served in the military remembered with fondness how the military "made a man" out of them. The public liked the "get tough on crime" message from media presentations featuring "in your face" drill instructors yelling at young offenders blamed for the lack of safety in their communities. Conservatives appreciated the "tough, no nonsense" approach to the problem of drugs in the community. Liberals liked the idea that young, nonviolent offenders were released early. Everyone breathed a collective sigh of relief. The boot camp phenomenon in prison was born.

By the beginning of 1987, there were eight states with "boot camp" programs. In August of 1987, the New York State Department of Correctional Services became the ninth state to implement the phenomenon, but with a new twist. Rather than solely emphasize military components, hard labor, physical training, drill and ceremony, the New York Shock Incarceration program focused on intensive substance abuse treatment, academic education, decision making and life skills, for a full six months, rather than the average 90 to 120 days for most boot camps, and it included an intensified aftercare program. A few other states, notably Louisiana, had included some optional education and treatment components by this time, but New York was the first to make "intensive substance abuse treatment and education" mandatory for all participants. Another key addition was a requirement for an intensive, one month period of training for all staff who worked in the program. Soon, this "second generation" of boot camps became a model for others to follow (Clark, Aziz, and MacKenzie 1994).

The very names "boot camp" or "shock incarceration" trigger reactions in everyone. Those who served their country in the military remember their boot camp experience and their drill instructors with a mixture of nostalgia, pride, stubbornness or regret, and either try to recreate it or rewrite it. Liberals worry over the harsh sound of "Shock," but nonetheless want offenders incarcerated for less time. The public wants to "get tough on criminals" and conservatives want to be sure that the streets are safe, with criminals behind bars, "where they belong." By the end of 1995, more than fifty-five states and jurisdictions had some type of boot camp for offenders, and the Office of Justice Programs had awarded $24 million dollars for planning and construction grants to another forty-four jurisdictions. The American Correctional Association (ACA) had published *Standards for Adult Correctional Boot Camp Programs* and *Standards for Juvenile Correctional Boot Camp Programs* and had produced two videos addressing the issues of adult and juvenile boot camp programs.

The "Joe Six-Pack" Phenomenon

In the last few years, some sentiment against boot camps has emerged. Some of this is deserved. Media features of boot camp programs focus on drill sergeants shouting, punishing and demeaning young, scared offenders to the delight of those who believe these offenders are to blame for robbing them of their freedom and safety. Some policy makers and/or staff of these programs genuinely believe that it is their job to punish and those programs reflect that philosophy. Critics, objecting to what is considered unnecessarily cruel treatment of young offenders, have blamed the military components for what they believe to be "harsh" and even "brutal" methods. "Military" has been equated with abuse. This paper attempts to clarify some of the issues and present some distinctions for planners and administrators of boot camps or other alternative correctional programs.

Some of the responsibility for the antimilitary sentiment can be placed with those who administer boot camp programs. Some programs have vaguely articulated goals and poorly executed methods. When boot camp programs do have stated goals, they often are presented and marketed poorly. In the rush to punishment, the programs are presented as tough, harsh and demanding. Some have responded to what Command Sergeant Major Joshua Perry refers to as the "Joe Six-Pack" mentality, and let those who are the least informed about what constitutes good correctional practice, dictate policy about the incarceration of young offenders. Boot Camps have a reputation for "getting tough" on crime and "Joe Six-Pack" believes that is how corrections ought to be. "Three strikes and you're out!" was the rallying cry of every state of the state message across the country in January 1994. Sound bites of the governors throughout the country showed virtually the same message. The public mandate had been clear during the elections that previous November, it was time to "get tough on crime."

"Joe Six-Pack" so enjoys a media presentation showing well-muscled drill sergeants throwing scared, young offenders off a bus, grabbing them by the collar, throwing them to the ground and up against a fence, calling them "scumbags, . . . punks" and harassing them until they cry, all within thirty minutes of arrival, that it aired, by popular request, three or four times a year in the state where that program operated. The judges and politicians interviewed about the program in the news series, endorsed this abusive behavior as "very effective." It is not. It is abuse. It is also not "military." It is abusive treatment like this that gives the "military model" a bad name. When evaluated, these types of programs show very poor results, leading to the conclusion that all of the programs based in a "military model" are ineffective and brutal.

"Joe Six-Pack" also thinks chain gangs are a great idea, ignoring the fact that the 1.5 percent of offenders in his state actually able to participate in a road work gang are earning fourteen days good time for every month they work and will be back in his neighborhood twice as fast as they would have been. Meanwhile, he never sees the 99.985 percent who really scare him. They are in maximum and medium security prisons, denied outside clearance. "Joe" likes the chain gangs so much that a referendum to allow caning, in the same state that has returned the gangs to current correctional practice, has an overwhelming majority of popular support in straw polls. Two other states are planning to re-establish chain gangs in the near future.

But Do Boot Camps Work?

If boot camps are harsh, it may be because correctional policy responds to what society appears to want. The National Institute of Justice report on boot camps (MacKenzie and Hebert 1995) said, ". . . here is little evidence that the getting tough element of shock incarceration by itself, will lead to behavioral change." Most heard, "Boot camps don't work!", (A.P. headline) but still want inmates punished. In the race for federal funding, it appeared that the only programs with a chance of acquiring scarce resources were those which appeared to "get tough on crime" and assured that violent offenders would be locked up for longer and longer periods of time. The public however, does not always distinguish between violent and nonviolent criminals. Purse snatching feels violent to the person who has been violated.

The general public equates prison with murderers, rapists, and child molesters. When the nightly news opens with five stories of gang violence, drive-by shootings, and alarming features of increasing violence in cities, it is obvious that "they" belong behind bars. Elected officials who get votes are those who vow to "lock them up and throw away the key." They are bowing to the mandate of their constituents. For all the different perspective and experience, the corrections professional is still a member of a community, influenced by the larger society and cultural norms. It is up to correctional professionals to set the tone and articulate standards and goals of effective corrections practice. It is up to those who endorse the concept of boot camp programs to ensure that the programs are founded in principles of integrity and support the success of all involved, both staff and inmates. Punishment does not reduce violence, evidence suggests it increases it.

The demand for discipline and adherence to rules characterized by the military model is seen by critics as rigid, dehumanizing, humiliating, and as breaking the spirit. They ask,

"Why can't they talk at meals? Shouldn't they be learning how to have dinner conversation?" When trying to keep the mess hall running on time, this is the last question the sergeant wants to hear. However, it is a valid question for which a reasoned response clearly is necessary. To those who have had to quell fights in prison mess halls, the question may appear ridiculous and the answer obvious. However, as a poster showing a huge rhinoceros diving off a high circus platform into a tiny bucket of water declares, "Nothing is obvious to the uninformed." It is the responsibility of those with experience in correctional institutions to respond to these questions appropriately.

Meals are one of the few times in a day when offenders in these highly structured programs do not have to actively perform. Once they get used to eating in silence, inmates experience the quiet at meals as an opportunity to reflect on their day. When the mess hall is full and those seated at the tables can be members of rival gangs from the old neighborhood, silence helps maintain order. The last thing a correctional officer needs is a problem erupting between Crips, Bloods, Latin Kings, Néta or other rival gang members seated at the same table. There is little opportunity for privacy in prison. The luxury of a private thought relieves tension. A task force of senior correctional professionals who recently visited the Shock Incarceration program in New York, marveled at something they observed in the mess hall. It was lunch time and approximately 250 inmates were seated at tables eating or moving quietly through the line, waiting for food. A power surge caused the lights to go off. The lieutenant, a seasoned employee, said, "I've never seen anything like it, the lights went off and nothing happened! Nobody got excited, upset or reacted in anyway. No fights broke out, they just kept eating." He shook his head and said, "What a great way to do business."

Form Follows Function

Those who come for tours from outside the correctional experience frequently raise questions about why boot camps operate the way they do. It is important for administrators and staff of programs to know the reasons for their methods and present the rationale in a way that makes sense to those unfamiliar with correctional practice. Even more important, administrators and staff have to understand and clearly articulate the reasons for policies and practice. In one program that Ms. Clark and Mr. Moscicki visited, inmates were awakened at 4:30 A.M., but the first event of the day was breakfast at 7:30 A.M. When asked why the early wake-up time, administrators responded, "It's boot camp." Inmates were left standing around, making beds, getting dressed and filling idle time learning military commands. The staff spent most of the three hours until breakfast shouting at the inmates, trying to achieve order.

When the consultants suggested that physical training be scheduled before breakfast, they were told that it would disturb other inmates in the compound. Since the boot camp was in the center of general confinement dormitories, inmates in the next dormitory were complaining loudly about the noise from boot camp staff and inmates arguing. The consultants next advised that since there was no planned early morning activity, perhaps participants should sleep until 7:00 A.M. That suggestion was rejected because "It would-n't be boot camp." This attitude and other similar problems resulted in the program closing in less than a year, one more boot camp failure. The form a program takes has to support the function of the program. The reason for early wake-up in a boot camp program is to ensure that there is enough time for physical fitness, breakfast and to get participants to work or school on time. Getting people up early for no purpose creates problems.

When designing programs, the content of the program has to serve the purpose and goals. Methods that may work for one program may not translate to another setting. Programs for adults and juveniles differ in population served, demographics of partici-pants, offense type included, cultural differences, age and sophistication of the clients and goals. It follows that methods that may be effective for adults may not work for juveniles. Methods selected have to serve a purpose.

For example, an administrator of a small, thirty-bed juvenile program does not see the need for an emphasis on drill and ceremony. There is not much space in the facility and the dormitories are in the same building with the school, program areas, and mess hall. There is not a need for much formal movement in that facility. On the other hand, admin-istrators who operate 100-, 200-bed or larger facilities have to get inmates to the mess hall and programs on time. Orderly movement in platoon formation supports the smooth operation of those programs, reinforcing cooperation and teamwork. In New York, the smallest of four Shock Incarceration facilities has 250 beds; the largest programs have 700 inmates in Shock, 160 of whom are women, within a facility of more than 1,000 inmates. All inmates move in formation; they go everywhere in a platoon. Drill and ceremony promotes order and has a practical function in addition to the learning goals previously stated. It is counterproductive to include strategies that have no purposeful function.

"Why do they have to say 'Ma'am and Sir?' Why can't they say 'I, me, my?' Why do you cut the women's hair? Aren't learning experiences harsh? Why do you need the mil-itary piece? Why not just do treatment? Why do they have to stand so rigidly at attention? What is the point of drill and ceremony?" These questions worry the sensitive, compas-sionate, and inexperienced who come for two- or three-hour tours. We have been told by visitors that they have been brushed off by some to whom they posed these questions, or told, "Because that's how we do it." Responses like that do not help those who support a military model in these programs. The following is offered as a response to the questions posed above from the authors' perspective, to stimulate discussion and ideas. They are not intended to be perceived as the answers.

Graduates of Shock Incarceration, working for aftercare service providers, know how hard it is for those with criminal records to get decent jobs. Their advice: "Sir" and "Ma'am" go a long way to getting you a job. Politeness and respect count. You are competing in a tough job market, stand out from the crowd. Mothers, fathers, and other relatives are touched by the respect from children over whom they had despaired. "I didn't recognize him/her. S/he called me 'Ma'am.' That never happened before. . . . I had to wait to come to prison to go to my child's graduation," they say with tears in their eyes. Those who are younger and will be returning to school after graduation from Shock frequently have been excluded from schools as behavior problems. They were considered troublemakers by teachers in the past and need to convince them that they deserve another chance. How they speak, act, and handle their feelings is critical to overcoming their past.

It is easy to say "I, me," or "mine" without thinking. A key reason many young offenders end up in prison is because acting without thinking is a bad habit of theirs. While this may be true for other than those who go to prison, offenders have not had the resources to avoid a prison sentence when they have legal problems. They need as many tools they can get to help them overcome obstacles to employment or educational opportunities. Good programs teach offenders how to make autonomous choices by increasing expectations for personal responsibility. One simple way to help them to learn to control impulsive behavior is to have them consciously hesitate the two-to-four seconds it takes the brain to integrate feelings and thoughts. That is why they are expected to stop, state their name, then, make their request. When participants refer to themselves by name, this slows them down and gives them time to think. In large programs, it also helps staff to learn their names faster. On the other hand, detaching from one's feelings is not appropriate in group processes designed to have them fully experience a wide range of feelings, so referring to themselves in the third person is not a functional strategy for those sessions.

Women's hair is cut short for many reasons in Shock Incarceration. First and most importantly, for ease of cleanliness and convenience. The day moves quickly from 5:30 A.M. until 9:30 P.M. It is packed with events. There are as many as ninety women in a single dormitory, sharing sinks, showers, living space and trying to get to program activities on time. They do not have time for hair styling. Another reason for this practice is because both the men and women have been so attached to their negative "operating image" that they are challenged to let go of their limiting beliefs about who they are and what makes them unique, to shed the old, negative image, and give themselves six months to redefine who they are and where they are going with their lives.

The women have frequently defined themselves and their self-worth in the past by their power to attract a man. (See the separate chapters on women in this volume.) Many, often because of abusive relationships, alcohol and drugs, are co-dependent, giving up their sense of self to others who use and abuse them. Their past relationships have failed. The goal of Shock Incarceration in New York is to have them focus on themselves and on what they need. They also learn skills to help them be good mothers to their children when they return home. The last thing they need to worry about is how attractive they look to the guy, another convicted felon, in their platoon. Co-dependency is one of the principal contributing factors to criminal behavior and addiction in women. The women's hair is not cut to degrade or humiliate them, nor is that appropriate. It has a function in a program with large numbers of women. It may not be as necessary or functional in programs where there are very few women. They may need the advantage of people remembering that they are women and not "one of the boys."

Learning experiences should be designed to interrupt a pattern of repeated negative behavior when people continue to take the same self-defeating actions over and over again. One state, which has since closed down its program, used the term "thrashing" to describe corrective actions and interventions. Terms like that are asking for trouble. Inmates who are learning to replace negative behaviors with positive ones need to be supported in their learning, not punished. One of the slogans on the walls in Shock Incarceration says "Most people change, not because they see the light, but because they feel the heat." This is vitally important with a population where "the heat" has been guns, police, pressure from "friends," crack, cocaine, and other addictive drugs. With this group, the desire to change has to outweigh the attraction of the "old life" and because of the short duration of these programs, it has to happen quickly. Learning experiences turn up "the heat," making them uncomfortable with self-defeating habits and receptive to new behaviors.

Military bearing teaches people to listen, to control their bodies, and to pay attention. This is critical for a population raised on Ritalin, with Attention Deficit Disorder (ADD), and other learning dysfunctions, who are addicted to crack cocaine and other drugs which change the chemistry of their brains and impair their healthy functioning. In both the six-month Shock Incarceration program and the new ninety-day Drug Treatment Center modeled after Shock, average academic grade level improvements are two-to-three years for all participants. Many achieve as much as five-to-seven or eight-grade level improvements.

Inmates in Shock attend academic classes twelve hours a week and treatment sessions twenty-eight hours a week. In the drug treatment program, participants attend academic classes twelve hours each week and are in treatment an additional thirty-four hours weekly. Staff who have worked in other correctional settings are impressed with the responsiveness of Shock participants, their commitment to and active involvement in recovery-oriented treatment sessions. Teachers (who also work in public schools) remark about the eagerness to learn of the students in these programs. They enjoy teaching and are relieved at not having to function as security guards, hall monitors, and police. Service providers who continue substance abuse treatment with this population after release are pleased with the "treatment readiness" of program graduates. Follow-up research indicates that while limited employment opportunities for offenders may not result in any greater employment for Shock graduates than for other parolees, they are much more likely to be involved in personal growth and recovery-related activities. They are far less likely to violate parole or return to new crimes than comparison groups (annual reports).

Research in accelerated learning and "whole brain" learning techniques cite the body-mind connection in learning. The rhythm and movement of drill and ceremony in time with cadences has a direct, positive effect on the brain and learning. The movements duplicate "cross-crawling" methods developed to improve hand-eye coordination, reading and thinking skills in those with learning disabilities or emotional disorders. Most of those who enter the program have learning or emotional difficulties. Brain research encourages rhythmic movement and breathing techniques as important interventions for emotional and psychological difficulties, and for improving general learning ability in anyone (DePorter 1992, Jensen 1988, 1989). Brain chemistry is positively affected by the physical movement of drill and ceremony. It is severely damaged by addiction. Structured environments, with clearly established rules, controls and expectations are highly recommended by therapists working with those who suffer from attention deficit disorder (Hallowell and Ratey 1994).

The "New Generation"

In an attempt to soften the "harsh" approach of boot camps, critics of the "military model" have begun to promote "new generation" boot camps, which can be any combination of pseudomilitary, Outward Bound, or Vision Quest types of programs, to programs which emphasize group treatment of a population incarcerated for drug offenses, with no military component at all. Those who recently have come to support the "new generation" boot camp assert that there is no reason for a military model as the basis for a boot camp program, still believing that "military" equals "abuse." Their commitment to correcting a problem is obvious. The authors here also abhor violence and brutality in the name of the "military" and urge those who endorse military components to ensure that programs stop cruelty disguised as treatment and insist on appropriate performance standards and goals for programs and staff.

New York is identified with the "new generation" of boot camps because of the emphasis on substance abuse treatment, academics, life skills, and the Network therapeutic community in the Shock Incarceration program. However, Shock Incarceration is also subject to the same criticisms as other military models. This holistic, integrated model was the basis of the program design in 1987 and continues to the present.

Program goals emphasize strengthening body, mind, and spirit. There is a strong emphasis on military methods in Shock Incarceration. Discipline in Shock is integrated within the overall structure of the program. Effective discipline avoids problems and drama. Visitors often remark on the quiet tone in the four facilities where Shock operates. Indeed, the media often ask if it is possible to stage an inmate being "disciplined" so they can get footage of an inmate being upbraided. When the difference between discipline and punishment is explained to them and they learn that we will not "set up" an inmate, they sigh regretfully, hoping to catch some of what Superintendent Moscicki calls the "flash and dash" that makes for a dramatic sound bite, but does little or nothing to support learning among participants. The facilities look like well-cared for campuses, and inmates act like well-mannered military school students. Many visitors forget they are looking at convicted felons and fall into the trap of referring to the inmates, sixteen to thirty-five years old, as "kids." Infantilization is no better than humiliation.

Boot Camps: Purpose and Goals

The term "boot camp" was coined by the military, to identify a six-to-eight week period of intensive training designed to turn young recruits into disciplined, effective soldiers. The "boot" is the newest member of the armed forces. Like the boots they wear, they are on the lowest rung of the ladder. They spend their time in boot camp learning how to be "all that you can be," "one of the few," "the brave, the proud," and "to aim high." Basic training is designed to teach "boots" military bearing and discipline, how to take care of body and mind, personal hygiene, to learn problem solving skills, teamwork, and respect for authority. In addition, it teaches recruits how to march in step in formation, pay attention to those around them, and to develop pride, esprit de corps, physical fitness, knowledge, skills and abilities. In brief, boot camps were designed to teach new soldiers how to survive in combat conditions. After the initial period of instruction, advanced training focuses on skill development including leadership skills, and other specialized training.

The "war on drugs" was a natural for borrowing the terminology and methods of a boot camp program, originally designed to help young, raw recruits survive in combat, by incorporating the methods into a similar program for offenders. The inner cities, from where most of these young offenders come, are referred to as "combat zones" where weapons abound. The guilty and the innocent, children and senior citizens alike, are killed along with young people engaged in the "turf wars" in the struggle for power the drug trade feeds.

Corrections, like the military, is an authority-based, hierarchical model. Jobs are designated by the same terms as those of the military. Rank, structure, and chain of command are all from a military model. As Vietnam War era veterans have come of age and begun to influence public policy, it is a logical outgrowth to look back at one's own experience for solutions to problems. What was it that helped that callow, naive, young high school graduate or dropout learn how to "be a man"? For that matter, some of those who will admit it say that the military was what saved them from going to prison themselves. Since the end of the draft in 1972, the prison population has quadrupled in the United States. Many cite the end of the draft as the beginning of the escalation of crime and prison crowding. Boot camps for offenders are a logical response to this paradigm.

Critics and supporters alike use the term "boot camp" to describe a wide variety of program offerings, perhaps because of the nostalgia around the term, perhaps simply because the name has become an identifier for funding sources. In the recently published National Institute of Justice Research Report, *Correctional Boot Camps: A Tough Intermediate Sanction*, (MacKenzie and Hebert 1996) John Zachariah reports:

The Armed Forces manual explicitly states several key issues that are essential to military boot camp training goals:

- Organization. The program must be organized with formal intermediate goals or progressive phases so that the conversion process can be properly structured and both the trainer and new soldier are clear on progress.

- The dignity of the new soldier . . . Every effort must be made to instill a sense of identification with . . . the training unit, and the leaders of that unit. This cannot be accomplished in an atmosphere of "we/they." From the start of the training cycle, the new soldier must be presented an atmosphere that says "leader/soldier," where the drill sergeant, . . . group trainer, and officers are seen as role models to emulate rather than people to be feared and avoided.

- Degree of control. The leaders of training units must continue to develop self-discipline in their soldiers. Self-discipline begins early in boot camp by ensuring . . . total control over . . . activities. This control is relaxed over time as soldiers demonstrate their willingness to accept responsibility for their actions.

- Responsibility. If new soldiers are to be successful and productive members in (the) future . . . they must learn responsibility for others as well as themselves. Every work detail, every period of instruction, and every opportunity to reinforce leadership should emphasize the necessity for cooperation and teamwork.

- Training cadre role. The . . . operative philosophy is to train soldiers by building on their strengths and shoring up their weaknesses. It is not to "tear them down and build them up again"(Department of the Army, *Basic Combat Training Program of Instruction*, 1991).

The authors of this paper consider those goals the essence of any good correctional boot camp program. They encourage self-discipline and respect, physical, mental, and spiritual development. Critics and proponents of the "military model" are urged to ensure that correctional boot camp programs strictly adhere to these goals, regardless of specific program methods. Those who operate punishing, brutal programs must rethink their goals, objectives, and methods or they will continue to fail in having an impact on offenders and crime. The National Institute of Justice Research Report is an excellent collection of some of the best thinking and research on these programs (MacKenzie and Hebert 1996).

The authors of this paper applaud the many excellent programs around the country, boot camps and others. It is their position that if a program is called a "boot camp," then the military component is fundamental to its design. There are any number of excellent treatment programs around the country that use no military methods at all. When Cheryl Clark started Network in 1979, it had no military components because that was not part of her experience. However, the living units were disciplined, total learning environments.

When planning a boot camp, its leaders should take responsibility for the development of a program that is designed to teach offenders skills that will help them to be successful in society and reject criminal behavior as a lifestyle. Self-discipline is an essential component of success.

Discipline is not punishment. Discipline is setting standards, establishing clear expectations of behavior, and living up to those standards. Discipline leads to strength, to the development of personal integrity. Command Sergeant Major Josh Perry's definition of discipline is, "Being at the appointed place at the appointed time, in the proper uniform, doing what you're told, when you're told and how you're told." He goes on to say that, "Unless you're Bill Gates, you're going to work for someone else. You aren't going to last long at McDonald's if you don't understand that basic fact." Most of the offenders in boot camps are going to be working for someone; even as they did in their street dealing days. They need to learn discipline to get and keep jobs, study and earn diplomas, pay the rent, buy groceries and raise their children.

Discipline is not abuse, nor is it humiliation. Director Clark and Superintendent Moscicki were asked to review a script for a training video on boot camps. It had been written by someone who never worked in a prison. One planned voice-over line read "Punishment and humiliation play an important role in the boot camp experience." They do not! There is no place for punishment or humiliation in these programs. Those behaviors are dangerous. The script included one scene in a mess hall where the drill instructor was supposed to throw water in an inmate's face, while the inmate, looking "upset," stood rigidly at attention. This was intended to show how boot camps instill discipline in inmates; certainly not in staff if this scene had played. At Lakeview, there are more than 250 inmates in each mess hall at one sitting. The two mess halls are only separated by an open kitchen. Imagine that! The writers of the video script obviously had never been in a mess hall when there was a fight, if they had ever been in one at all.

As Command Sergeant Major Joshua Perry says, "Violence begets violence." There is no excuse for abuse, or for harassing inmates in the name of the "military model." Superintendent Moscicki discussed the issue of the backlash of antimilitary sentiment from boot camp critics:

> I am concerned that critics of the boot camp program almost always associate screaming drill instructors, cursing, brutalizing and humiliating the inmate with military discipline, the "Full Metal Jacket" approach to corrections. . . . Bad boot camp programs . . . provide our critics with all the ammunition they need to shoot us down. [They] rely on compliance and teaching inmates to follow orders. Compliance alone is not enough. Compliance only works when you're being watched. The compliance model supports our critics' claims that boot camp programs produce robots who just know how to follow orders and do pushups. These programs rarely work and have no lasting effect on inmates. Push-ups will not make you smarter.

> Military discipline is not just following orders. Military discipline is not punishment. Military discipline is the ability to perform a task to specifications with exacting attention to detail. Military discipline teaches inmates to listen, controlling their minds and bodies. Once that is accomplished, the academic and treatment components of the program can take hold and inmates can learn pride and dignity. The combination of discipline and treatment is what works. This combined approach is what can make the difference in the lives of the inmates in boot camp programs.

The Importance of Consistency

The balance between treatment and discipline is important. Both are necessary in order to be effective. Staff must respect and reinforce each other's discipline. They must set appropriate limits. In the old therapeutic community days, such discipline was called "finger in the chest." At the same time, it is important to have the sensitivity to be able to "pat them on the back," to encourage and support them when that is necessary. Some inmates have been so deprived that they do not know how to tie their shoes or bathe properly. Calling them "stupid" does not teach them anything and is cruel and cowardly. There is no excuse for cruelty in any program, especially boot camps. As a leader, you are responsible for everything that happens in the boot camp program. If you see abuse, stop it. Insist on standards of performance and then monitor and supervise to ensure that staff are doing what is expected. Be clear about what you expect.

All staff have to be trained alike. They have to be "on the same sheet of music" for the program to be effective. An inmate cannot think that alcohol and substance abuse treatment is only important to the counselor and military bearing only the concern of the drill instructor. That kind of thinking drives wedges between staff and inmates. An African proverb says, "It takes a whole village to raise a child." Similarly, in the boot camp environment, everyone is responsible for every aspect of the program. It takes everyone in the program, working together, to produce a high quality program.

Command Sergeant Major Joshua Perry says, "A leader must be competent, consistently firm, fair and impartial, and practice honesty in word, deed and signature." Competent leaders command respect. They do not have to demand it. Firmness is commitment, not harsh or tyrannical behavior. If leaders demonstrate those principles of integrity, subordinates will respect them and follow them anywhere. They may not like "the boss," but they will respect him or her. When subordinates respect their leaders, they will do the job expected of them. Critics may not like the program, but they too will respect the job you do.

Command Sergeant Major Perry often talks about Miss Lucille, who lived in his neighborhood and watched out for the children. When she would catch them up in the tree, stealing apples, she would go out and send them home, saying "You little mannish boys better get down out of that tree! I'm going to tell your daddy!" No one even thought about disobeying Miss Lucille, certainly not sassing her back. They knew there would be trouble with "daddy" when they got home if they did. Today, Miss Lucille would probably be sued for interfering with the boys. It is a sad state of affairs that people have become so alienated from each other, that what was a normal, routine intervention a generation or two ago, has become the subject of court litigation today.

Do you remember when the ushers in the movie theaters on Saturday afternoon knew all of the children by name and would announce to the theater who was acting out and would make the same promise Miss Lucille made, to tell their parents? That this country has become the most litigious in the world is a sad commentary on the attitude toward discipline and community responsibility for the quality of life in neighborhoods. It is this erosion of community values that has helped to lead us to a place where discipline has become a negative word and is confused with punishment.

Dennis Sullivan, in the preface of his book, *The Mask of Love* (1980), cites the need for community responsibility for correcting the problems of crime so often pushed off on the corrections' system. His words also speak to those working in treatment programs in corrections when he talks about "shared responsibility." He says:

The history of evolution demonstrates that civilizations organize themselves in ways to produce their own internal energies to survive their failures or treasons. They give birth to people and artifacts who cleanse, who teach, who convince—in short, who do whatever is necessary to give us a chance. That's it—to give us a chance. Perhaps the ultimate criterion for assessing any work or art or sociology or physics or any human act is whether it gives us a chance, a chance to survive both as individuals and as a community. Any work that professes to be human must contain this latter element of collectivity, some sense of shared responsibility for life or mutual aid.

One of the goals of Shock Incarceration in New York is to teach the idea and practice of "shared responsibility" to the inmates in the program. This is the essence of the community living component of the program for which drill instructors, teachers, counselors, cooks, supervisors, and administrators are responsible. Inmates can learn this principle only from the staff who work with them. Staff learn how to teach these principles from their leaders. In setting the direction for a boot camp program, leaders have to be clear about the course they set "in word, deed and signature." Thankfully, this does not require that leaders always be at their best, just that they do the best they can. Murphy's Law says, "Only a mediocre person is always at his best." Leaders do have to demonstrate how to deal with failure, even their own, to admit their mistakes, correct them and move on. We learn from mistakes, our own and others. We need to teach inmates how to learn from their mistakes, as well. Staff learn how to be effective from leaders ". . . who cleanse, who teach, who convince—in short, who do whatever is necessary to give us a chance." To be such a leader, one has to be willing to set the pace, not just to follow the tide.

Dostoyevsky said in *Crime and Punishment*, "A society can be judged by entering its prisons." In the United States, one in three black men is either incarcerated or on parole. One and a half million children in the United States have a parent in prison; that is one out of fifty. More than two-thirds of all offenders are in prison for nonviolent crimes, usually related to drug and alcohol abuse. This is the collective failure of society. As a society, we must work together for solutions. As corrections professionals, we are responsible for the quality of treatment of offenders entrusted to our care. The question is then, do our programs "give us . . . a chance to survive both as individuals and as a community?" Whatever the correctional program, it must provide the opportunity for growth. If a boot camp model is what you choose, then it is even more important to focus on goals, because of the limited time offenders spend in these programs.

Boot Camps Are Not an Easy Answer

There are some people in boot camp programs who do not understand the responsibility of power. There are always people who will abuse power if they have it. Abuse of power has occurred at every level in every organization throughout history. That does not excuse abuses of power in any system. Being vigilant, monitoring, training, and supervising guard against that. Ensuring that clearly articulated goals and standards are followed is another way to maintain a quality program. Do not fall into the trap of believing that you will ever be "finished" once you start a program like this. This is a commitment. If you accept the responsibility, then you must follow through. It takes continual maintenance to ensure a quality program.

The results in New York have shown that consistent policy, training of all staff, monitoring and ensuring that policies are followed, with all staff working together toward the same goals, has produced impressive results. As of the end of November 1995, the Shock Incarceration program had graduated more than 13,500 inmates and had saved the State of New York more than $439.5 million dollars in cost of confinement and capital construction, since the first inmates began being released in March of 1988. The fact that there has been a strong aftercare program postrelease in most of the state is important as well. Just as the military does not put soldiers into war zones without followup and further training after boot camp, corrections cannot expect that a boot camp program will have a lasting effect without followup.

Aftercare is important in boot camp programs. Drug abuse is a life-threatening disease. Relapse prevention does not happen in a vacuum. It takes time and commitment of resources. Even with good aftercare programs though, it is still ultimately the offender who decides its success or failure, not the program. John Zachariah cautions that hospitals are not blamed if patients relapse after they are discharged when they no longer need hospital care. If a patient does not follow the recommendations of the doctor and refuses to take prescriptions, hospitals are not blamed if the patient gets sick again. Corrections is not forgiven in the same way if parolees refuse to follow the programs prescribed for them while they were in the system. In the course of educating society, legislators, and critics of the system, it is important to remind them that continuing treatment and resources in the community are as important as the institutional phase.

Boot camps can be very effective with the right people in charge, with committed, well trained staff, good supervision, and for a select population of inmates. These programs have powerful tools. They can be misused to become terrible weapons. Boot camps are not for the faint-hearted. These are "in your face" programs, there is no getting around it. If you are a gentle soul, with a tendency to fall for the "sad, sad tales" that are often real, then you need to be very clear that "tough love" is critical to the boot camp model. If you are uncomfortable with confrontation, do something else. Do not do this program. There are many excellent models for change. Boot camps are not for everyone, neither inmates nor staff. Boot camps may not be the answer, despite how much you may want them to be.

If you have problems with "in your face" confrontation, boot camps are the wrong program. If you do not agree with the philosophy of a boot camp model, then develop a program which is consistent with your own values and principles. Do something to which you can be committed, that is the key to success. In conclusion, Dennis Sullivan (1980) has expressed the sentiment of the authors quite eloquently:

You who do not agree that our human problems are . . . as I see them, I urge you to begin to express yourselves from the point of your own disagreement with, and confusion about what I have proposed. I urge you to carve out a vision for yourselves, with your own personal imprint and experience, using your own confusion and frustration as a starting point. If you too find no sympathetic or understanding listeners to what you have uncovered, at least you will have unmasked for yourselves some of your own confusion about what is humanly possible. You will not have forfeited your own identities or been treasonous to yourselves in your own work. You will have charted for yourselves a new direction, new maps, with new awareness about self, about community, about the struggle to be human. There will be more hope for quality of life for everyone . . . for one more will have struggled for all.

We wish you much success and offer you our support, whatever you decide.

Bibliography

Clark, Cheryl L. 1978. Network Program Plan. Unpublished document of the New York State Commission of Correction. Albany, New York.

————. 1979. Network Program Procedural Manual, revised and updated: 1981, 1983, 1985. Unpublished document of the New York State Commission of Correction and the Department of Correctional Services. Albany, New York.

————. 1987, 1988. Shock Incarceration, Program Procedural Manual, updates with R.W. Moscicki. 1989, 1991, 1994. Unpublished document of the New York State Department of Correctional Services. Albany, New York.

Clark, Cheryl L., David Aziz, and Doris MacKenzie. 1994. *Shock Incarceration in New York: Focus on Treatment*. Washington, D.C.: National Institute of Justice.

DePorter, Bobbi and Mike Hernacki. 1992. *Quantum Learning: Unleashing the Genius in You*. New York: Bantam Doubleday Dell Publishing Group, Inc.

Division of Program Planning, Research and Evaluation. 1993. Characteristics of Inmates Under Custody 1985-1992. New York State Department of Correctional Services. Albany, New York.

Flanagan, T., D. Clark, D. Aziz, B. Szelest. 1990. Compositional Changes in a Long-term Prisoner Population: 1956-1992. *The Prison Journal*. 80:1.

Glasser, William, M.D. 1965. *Reality Therapy.* New York: Harper and Row Publishers.

———. 1969. *Schools Without Failure.* New York: Harper and Row Publishers.

———. 1984. *Control Theory.* New York: Harper and Row Publishers.

———. 1986. *Control Theory in the Classroom.* New York: Harper and Row Publishers.

Hallowell, Edward, M., M.D., and John J. Ratey, M.D. 1994. *Driven to Distraction.* New York: Pantheon Books, Random House.

Holt, John. 1964. *How Children Fail*, with an introduction by Allan Fromme, Ph.D. New York: Pitman Publishing Corporation.

———. 1967. *How Children Learn.* New York: Pitman Publishing Corporation.

Jensen, Eric P. 1988. *Super-Teaching.* Del Mar, CA: Turning Point for Teachers.

———. 1989. *Student Success Secrets.* Barron's Educational Series, Inc.

MacKenzie, D. L., and D. B. Ballow. 1989. Shock Incarceration Programs in State Correctional Jurisdictions—An Update. Washington, D.C.: National Institute of Justice.

MacKenzie, D. L., L. A. Gould, L. M. Reichers, and J. W. Shaw. 1989. Shock Incarceration: Rehabilitation or Retribution? *Journal of Offender Counseling, Services and Rehabilitation.* 14 (2): 25-40.

MacKenzie, D. L., and Eugene E. Hebert, eds. 1996. *Correctional Boot Camps: A Tough Intermediate Sanction.* Washington, D.C.: National Institute of Justice.

MacKenzie, D. L. 1990. *Boot Camps Grow in Number and Scope.* Washington, D.C.: National Institute of Justice. November-December, 6-8.

MacKenzie, D. L., and Claire C. Soural. 1991. Boot Camp Survey: Rehabilitation, Recidivism Reduction Outrank Punishment as Main Goals. *Corrections Today.* October, pp. 90-96.

New York State Department of Correctional Services. 1988. First Platoon Graduates from Shock Incarceration. *D.O.C.S. Today.* 1:12.

———. 1988. Shock Incarceration Not For Men Only. *D.O.C.S. Today.* 2:7.

———. 1992. Shock Incarceration Five Years Later. *D.O.C.S. Today*. 4:3.

New York State Department of Correctional Services and New York State Division of Parole. 1996. Annual Report to the Legislature: Shock Incarceration in New York State. Albany, New York: Unpublished report by the Division of Program Planning, Research and Evaluation and the Office of Policy Analysis and Information.

Parent, D. G. 1989. Shock Incarceration: An Overview of Existing Programs: NIJ Issues and Practices Report. Washington, D.C.: National Institute of Justice

Peck, M. Scott, M.D. 1978. *The Road Less Traveled*. New York: Simon and Schuster.

———. 1987. *The Different Drum*. New York: Simon and Schuster.

Sullivan, Dennis. 1980. *The Mask of Love*. Port Washington, NY: Kennikat Press.

Tobias, Cynthia Ulrich and John Zachariah. 1994. *The Way They Learn*. Colorado Springs: Focus on the Family.

Substance Abuse Programming in Boot Camps

Ernest Cowles, Ph.D.
Center for Legal Studies
University of Illinois at Springfield
Springfield, Illinois

The glitter associated with all new things is beginning to wear off correctional boot camps. No longer is the press clamoring to get pictures of meek young convicts with their noses pressed against a wall at induction while a drill instructor berates them over the mess they have made of their lives. Correctional boot camps are coming of age, and, as with any maturation process, their character is gradually changing. Core elements such as the drill and ceremony, physical conditioning, and military-styled structure and discipline that gave these programs their distinctiveness still remain.

However, today's "second generation" (Gransky, Castellano, and Cowles 1995) boot camps are much more likely to emphasize program components such as education, life skills, and substance abuse programming than the early models. Given these changes, it is an appropriate time to examine the nature of boot camp programs, including their design and impact. This article focuses on one of the most commonly found program elements seen in boot camps throughout the nation, namely that of substance abuse education and treatment.[1] In this discussion, the emphasis will be on the practical considerations related to the content and implementation of substance abuse programming. In doing so, many of the larger issues associated with (re)habilitation in correctional boot camps hopefully will be illuminated, as well. We hope that such an approach will be of value to those in the practitioner community who are charged with the responsibility of developing and overseeing substance abuse programs as part of a correctional boot camp sanction.[2]

What basic questions should correctional policy makers, administrators, and program professionals consider in the development and implementation of substance abuse programs in boot camps?

Identifying the Program's Purpose

Before considering the structure or mechanics of setting up substance abuse programming in boot camps, those starting such programs should first consider a fundamental question. What is the purpose of having a substance abuse program? At first glance, this question seems almost rhetorical, and its answer simple common sense—because offenders need it. Yet, beneath its simplicity, the answer to this inquiry determines the goals, structure, and processes that shape the operation of the substance abuse program, and ultimately, governs whether the program will produce the desired results.

Two aspects need to be considered in addressing the purpose for a boot camp substance abuse program. The first aspect concerns the goals of the larger boot camp program. Research on boot camps has shown fairly consistent goals among boot camps for state correctional systems (see MacKenzie 1990). Some of these goals are at the system level, such as reducing prison crowding, establishing an alternative to longer-term incarceration, and lowering costs. Others are institutional/facility goals that concentrate on control and management, for example, instilling offender accountability; promoting positive offender/staff contact; ensuring a clean, healthy, secure environment; and creating an environment promoting rehabilitation. Finally, there are goals at the individual level. These goals, such as developing less negative and more positive behavior; promoting more positive attitudes, behavior and motivation; improving offender confidence, self-discipline and responsibility; increasing respect for authority and reducing drug use, all target offender change.

An important consideration for those developing boot camp substance abuse programs is the agreement between these goals, and the compatibility between these goals and the actual program elements provided within a boot camp facility. To illustrate the point, consider the following example. If a primary goal of the correctional system is to develop a boot camp program to channel offenders out of traditional secure bedspace, as a mechanism to alleviate overcrowding and save costs, then the facility should be designed to accommodate a high volume of offenders. This would require a facility able to hold a large population for a relatively short program length. Under these conditions, a substance abuse program model premised on individual interaction between a counselor and inmate that required an extensive period of program involvement most likely would be difficult to carry out and ultimately would produce poor results.

The second aspect concerns the alignment between philosophical and theoretical assumptions underpinning the boot camp program and the type of substance abuse program to be offered. Our basic beliefs about what shapes offender behavior will largely determine the programs we use to change that behavior. For example, in New York State's program (which authorities there adamantly maintain is a "shock incarceration" program rather than a "boot camp") the therapeutic model called "Network" is "based on control theory and seeks to restore inmates' bonds to society" (Clark and Aziz 1996, p. 43. See also their chapters in this volume). The New York Network program is based on the work of F. Ivan Nye that suggests the control of human behavior develops through a learning process of direct control, indirect control, internalized control, and control over opportunities (Wells and Rankin 1988).

In concert with this perspective, New York carries out a highly structured "boot camp" program. Its elements include compliance with rules and authority, identification with positive role models, internalization of positive behaviors and attitudes, and the development of autonomy involving the self-directed choice of appropriate lifestyles (Clark and Aziz 1996).

Whatever the effectiveness of this approach, it seems to reflect a high degree of congruity between the perceived causes of criminal behavior and the therapeutic approach taken to correct it. If, on the other hand, we hold that substance abuse is a disease with an identifiable pathology, particularly if this pathology has an underlying physical basis such as a neurochemical imbalance or genetic predisposition, then a treatment model based in control is not going to be sufficient to deal with abusing behavior. Program developers need to be attentive to this underlying relationship between the assumptions made about the genesis of criminal behavior and the (re)habilitative approaches used to deal with it. This caution is particularly important when programs are developed by copying other established program approaches such as those found in New York, Georgia, or Oklahoma as models.

Recommendation 1:

Before considering the structure or mechanics of implementing substance abuse programming in boot camps, those implementing such programs should: (1) identify the system, facility, and offender change goals the program will strive to achieve, and (2) specify the underlying theoretical perspective used to explain the offender's criminal and substance abuse behavior.

The program goals at all levels must agree with one another and the substance abuse program must be in harmony. The substance abuse program should fit logically with the accepted explanation for criminal behavior and the underlying reasons for the offender's substance abuse.

What program components should a well-designed substance abuse program include? No matter what specific theoretical approach is chosen, several program features are essential to all substance abuse programs. These key components would include: assessment, strong linkages between assessment and treatment, multimodal treatment approaches, appropriate staffing, and solid aftercare programs. Each of these areas is briefly reviewed in the following sections.

Assessment

Substance abuse treatment in the free world community generally is based on an assessment of the nature and extent of the individual's substance abuse problem(s). Such an assessment gives the clinician important information about the most appropriate treatment approach for a given individual, and provides a baseline from which to gauge the individual's progress in dealing with a substance abuse problem.

Five primary approaches are used to determine the level of drug use by an individual or the degree to which a person is addicted to drugs (including alcohol), and the impairment in the individual's functioning created by substance abuse. These five approaches include:

- face-to-face interviews
- the use of case histories
- psychological/behavioral tests
- biological markers
- the use of classification systems

In our study of substance abuse programs in boot camps, we found that face-to-face interviews were the most common tool used to assess substance abuse problems in correctional boot camps. About 94 percent of those conducting such assessment used some form of an interview. Assessment interviews may involve simple questions about the offender's perceptions of drug use/abuse or may use a structured format such as the Clinical Structured Interview based on established protocols found in the *Diagnostic and Statistical Manual* (DSM) that is put out by the American Psychiatric Association.

The second most common type of substance abuse evaluation, used by nearly 83 percent of the respondents conducting assessment, involved the use of case histories. Usually these case histories consisted of typical correctional case files that included initial classification instruments, prior assessments, presentence investigations, available prior treatment information, and offense information. Case histories may provide a good picture of the offender's past drug involvement and problems, but alone supply little insight into the individual's current status or present problem perceptions. Additionally, these case histories are only as complete or accurate as the information contained within them. Further, prior misperceptions or misinterpretations of an individual's substance use/abuse tend to be replicated in later entries if staff simply extract material from existing narratives for later reports.

The third most frequently employed assessment tools were psychological/behavioral tests. Over three-quarters of the facilities doing assessment indicated the use of such tests. Among the most commonly seen were the Michigan Alcohol Screen Test (MAST), the Inventory of Drinking Situations, the Alcohol Use Inventory, the MacAndrew Scale (an MMPI subscale), the Addiction Severity Index, the Alcohol Dependence Data Schedule, and the Self-Administered Alcoholism Screening Test (SAAST).

One advantage of screening instruments is that most have undergone rather rigorous validation to ensure they actually measure the problem behavior in question. Additionally, because of their general use, they have established data or norms to provide a basis for comparison with the boot camp offenders tested. Their disadvantages include the fact that many are proprietary, and may be costly when given in large numbers. Further, many require training in their administration and a level of clinical sophistication in the interpretation of their results.

The remaining two types of assessment procedures include the use of classification systems and biological markers. Classification systems use some type of objective criterion, often incorporating other instruments or subscales, to identify inmate treatment needs and specify appropriate interventions. Two popular clinical classification systems are the ICD9 developed by the World Health Organization and the *Diagnostic and Statistical Manual* fourth edition produced by the American Psychiatric Association. Many correctional systems have developed their own objective classification systems.

The problem with many of these correctional classification systems is that they were initially developed to address behavior risks, both public and institutional, and those areas remain the predominant foci. Identification of treatment needs such as substance abuse problems, is often added without true integration and provides only a cursory review of the area. If a correctional agency intends to use its own classification instrument to assess treatment needs for this offender population, we recommend that the instrument be specifically designed for the boot camp program and expressly address substance use/abuse.

Biological markers, primarily urine or blood tests, commonly are used in the criminal justice field as mechanisms to assess substance use. However, their use within the boot camp environment is quite limited both for initial assessment procedures and for ongoing participant monitoring. The limited use of these techniques at initial assessment is due primarily to the fact that most boot camp participants have been in confinement for a time before their placement at the facility, thus reducing the likelihood of finding physical evidence of drugs in their blood or urine. Regarding ongoing monitoring, the highly structured and closely supervised environment of most boot camps effectively reduces the potential use of prohibited substances during the incarceration phase of the program. Thus, the use of urine or blood tests can be reserved for rare situations or eliminated entirely.

Recommendation 2

Using a professional evaluation of the need for treatment is an important first step in the development of a drug treatment program.

Many psychological/behavioral tests specifically designed to identify individuals with substance abuse (including alcohol) problems and/or addictions exist. When coupled with other evaluation techniques, particularly the use of a clinically structured interview and review of a case history, this assessment provides the foundation for placement in appropriate treatment and serves as a baseline to gauge the offender's success in dealing with a substance abuse problem.

Assessment and Treatment Linkages

Despite a common use of substance abuse assessment in correctional boot camps, inadequate links exist between the substance abuse assessment and the subsequent treatment programming in many facilities. In our study of substance abuse programs, we found that only about 81 percent of those providing substance abuse treatment had corresponding assessment. Perhaps even more striking was the fact that of those programs conducting assessments, only half indicated using assessment data to classify inmates for treatment programs. We saw more evidence of weak ties between assessment and treatment placement in the number of facilities that had mandatory substance abuse treatment based on nonclinical decisions. Six responding boot camp facilities noted that substance abuse treatment was mandated by statute, two reported that the sentencing judge could mandate treatment, and two additional facilities stated that treatment was mandatory through other mechanisms. One boot camp official noted that any inmate sentenced to the boot camp also received substance abuse treatment—a situation apparently common to many boot camp programs.

Should correctional boot camps mandate substance abuse treatment? The answer to this question is both no and yes. The notion of mandatory treatment is not without controversy, but researchers have found that threat of criminal justice sanctions motivates offenders to enter and continue in treatment for longer periods, which heightens the permanence of behavior changes (Leukefeld and Tims 1988). Thus, the objection here is not so much to mandatory treatment, but to mandatory treatment without any evaluation of need.

Mandated treatment without assessment leads to a "one-size fits approach" that is likely to lead to reduced treatment effectiveness for some within the group and results in a waste of scarce correctional resources. For example, it is obvious that a casual user who smokes marijuana on the weekends has a different drug problem than the serious coke addict whose entire life is permeated with a quest to obtain and smoke crack cocaine. In the case of the first individual, an educational approach (discussed below) providing realistic information about the issues and problems associated with substance abuse, coupled with a behavioral management program, might be a suitable treatment approach. In the latter case, a much more intensive treatment regimen likely involving counseling to deal with the underlying psychological issues commonly associated with such drug use, a health program to counter the physical impacts of such a lifestyle, and a long-term behavioral management program to develop and maintain drug-free behaviors would be needed. Obviously, a drug education program would probably have little impact upon the lifestyle of the serious addict, and placing a casual marijuana smoker in the intensive treatment paradigm described for the serious cocaine user would be an inappropriate use of resources.

The inappropriate placement of offenders in treatment even may have a more serious, unintended consequence. In our survey of boot camp inmates at facilities reflecting three different program levels, we were surprised to find that inmates at facilities with the more intensive programs viewed both the general boot camp program and the substance abuse program as less helpful and beneficial than those in facilities with less developed programs. In exploring this puzzling finding further, however, we discovered that when we separated those offenders who saw themselves as having substance abuse problems and as needing to be involved in treatment from those who did not, those offenders acknowledging a problem were much more positive about their involvement in the substance abuse treatment and about the general benefits they were receiving from their involvement in the boot camp program. Thus, those without substance abuse problems who are force-fit into these programs not only do not see the treatment program as having benefits, but they also may view the entire boot camp experience in a less positive light.

Essentially, the linking of assessment with treatment establishes a treatment plan. This treatment plan identifies what the offender's problems are regarding substance abuse and lays out a strategy for overcoming these problems. Programming approaches then can be designed to fit offenders with various substance abuse treatment needs.

For example, Illinois uses a "level" system. Level I inmates are those designed as having no probable substance abuse. These individuals receive two weeks of drug education only. Level II inmates are those identified as probable substance abusers. They receive the same two weeks of substance abuse education as the Level I offenders, but additionally are involved in a four-week treatment program dealing with issues such as denial and family support. Level III inmates are those determined to have probable drug addictions. Their programs include the material covered by Level I and II participants, but also cover topics such as family addiction dynamics and substance abuse release during an extended ten-week period. Both Level II and III inmates also work with substance abuse counselors to arrange referrals for treatment on release (Karr and Jones 1996).

Many states also have pursued similar hierarchial treatment models in which those inmates with more serious treatment needs receive greater levels of programming. This approach is sound both as to treatment efficacy and from an economic perspective.

Recommendation 3

Placement of boot camp offenders into substance abuse treatment programs should be driven by clinical assessments, rather than by legal or policy mandates. Further, a treatment plan should be developed in which the type of treatment received by the offender is based on an assessment of the individual's substance abuse problem.

Multimodal Treatment

One of the most complex issues when considering a substance abuse treatment component in boot camps relates to the choice of therapy. As discussed previously, whatever therapeutic approach is selected, at the very least it should be compatible with the basic philosophical orientation and the primary goals of the boot camp. Additionally, it must be able to address the particular type of substance abuse problem found in the offender population sentenced to the boot camp.

Before continuing, two technical distinctions need to be highlighted concerning terms used to describe treatment. The first term is "modality," which as used here, refers to the general treatment delivery approach employed by the program. Group counseling, the Alcoholics Anonymous model (also reflected in the Narcotics Anonymous and Cocaine Anonymous models), individual counseling, milieu therapy, and therapeutic communities are those modalities most commonly used in boot camps in the order of the frequency of their use.

The second term frequently used is treatment "intervention." In this context, intervention denotes the specific type or style of treatment offered. Surprisingly, our study of substance abuse revealed that despite the type of modality or delivery approach used, a great similarity existed in the specific treatment interventions provided. All of the reporting programs except one used multiple modalities. Within these modalities, the Alcoholics Anonymous 12-step approach, Reality Therapy, and Stress Management were consistently ranked as the top three interventions employed (except for the therapeutic community approach which was only found in two facilities).

The widespread use of the same treatment interventions, despite the type of modality of delivery approach, suggests two important characteristics of boot camp substance abuse programming. First, there is an eclectic nature to abuse programming, which has both positive and negative aspects. On one hand, multimodal treatment services can cover a wide spectrum of problems underlying drug use and dependency. On the other, this mixed approach can create a lack of clarity and specificity as to the theoretical orientation or treatment approach being employed. Research generally has supported the use of multimodal approaches because of their greater breadth; however, the practitioner also should keep in mind that without a well-defined program base, the program can resemble a ship without a compass, erratically changing its course and never reaching its final destination.

The second feature about the therapeutic approaches commonly employed within correctional boot camps is that most appear to take a pragmatic, skill-building approach focused on assisting offenders in developing coping strategies to deal with the problems they will encounter on their reentry into the community. By contrast, we do not commonly see traditional psychotherapeutic approaches, designed to identify and eliminate underlying psychological and emotional problems precipitating substance abuse, in these facilities.

Functionally oriented, skill-building approaches seem to fit well with common boot camp program ideologies; however, correctional administrators and program developers should keep the limitations of these approaches in mind. They are not designed to deal with substance abusing behavior based in deeply seated psychological or emotional difficulties, such as a posttraumatic stress disorder. Further, accompanying limitations, such as time, do not support a capacity within the substance abuse treatment program to develop and reinforce major lifestyle changes needed by many offenders whose substance abuse is well integrated into their daily routines. Aftercare (discussed later) becomes particularly important in this situation.

> ## Recommendation 4
>
> Due to the variety of substance abuse problems that are likely to be encountered in boot camp offenders, we recommend multimodal program approaches. Pragmatic, skill-building approaches such as the 12-step model, Reality Therapy, and Stress Management are popular boot camp therapeutic interventions, but such interventions should be selected only after considering the nature of the substance abuse problems likely to be encountered and the conditions under which treatment will be provided.

Therapeutic Communities and Other Treatment Considerations

One particularly effective substance abuse treatment approach not commonly found in boot camp environments is the therapeutic community. This approach is well suited to the environment of most correctional boot camps since it is a residential program model—although somewhat longer (fifteen to twenty-four months) than most incarceration phases of boot camps. The model is premised on the ideas of mutual self-help and peer pressure. Community residents are immersed in a culture emphasizing positive behavior, motivation for change, and maintenance of a drug-free lifestyle. Further, while the therapeutic community approach stresses the role of the participants through reciprocal responsibility and the impact of individual action on the larger group, the staff serves to anchor the program as the rational authority. They serve as role models and parental surrogates who encourage the development of participants through social learning processes.

Similar to correctional boot camps, the therapeutic community uses the ideas of earned privileges and disciplinary sanctions as the mechanisms to control participant behaviors. Privileges are given as rewards that reinforce the value of earned achievement. Discipline is used to preserve the health and safety of the community, tacitly teaching residents both the mechanisms and value of acceptable behavior. The beauty and strength of incorporating the therapeutic community concept into the boot camp program is that the entire boot camp experience from entry to graduation becomes part of the substance abuse treatment program. New York and Wisconsin use this approach.

In summary, the issue for the correctional administrator or clinician is not what is the best therapy, but what is the most applicable therapeutic approach for the boot camp environment? The general nature of correctional boot camps sets distinct parameters that should be considered in this decision.

Boot camps are ideal substance abuse treatment environments in several ways. They are self-contained, highly structured, and generally isolated from outside influences. Moreover, they generally promote healthy lifestyles with physical labor, exercise, nutritious meals, and abstinence from cigarettes, alcohol, and illegal drugs. They also have considerable potential to help the individual develop a sense of self-worth, and to promote an esprit de corps in which the individual learns mutual respect, responsibility, consideration of others, and the value of teamwork. On the negative side, they are generally short in length (a negative treatment consideration) and may have limited time available for substance abuse programming. Further, offender participants, although identified as drug offenders, are likely to present a variety of substance abuse backgrounds and problems.

Recommendation 5

Those charged with developing boot camp substance abuse treatment programs are strongly urged to consider the use of therapeutic communities. This modality has shown considerable promise in correctional environments and seems very compatible with both boot camp ideologies and other program elements found in these facilities.

Where does substance abuse education fit as a treatment approach? Some confusion exists regarding the differences between substance abuse education and substance abuse treatment. Frequently, there is a blurred distinction between the two. Some substance abuse treatment experts (such as Lipton, Falkin, and Wexler 1992) argue that substance abuse education/information programs are not actually treatment modalities. Rather, they see such education programs as support for treatment. In our study of substance abuse programs, we found all existing programs provide substance abuse education in some form. About one-quarter of the responding boot camps said that they only provided substance abuse education, while half maintained separate and distinct substance abuse education and treatment components. The remaining 25 percent did not provide a distinct substance abuse education program, but incorporated such education into their treatment regimen.

The popularity of substance abuse education in part may be explained by the availability of this type of program and the fact that the delivery of education material generally requires staff members with less formal education and/or specialized training than those conducting treatment programs. Findings in our study suggested the delivery of substance abuse education was fairly standardized across programs, with all using some type of class presentation supplemented by videos and movies. About three-quarters of the programs provided written materials through some type of handouts, and about two-thirds used pamphlets and books. Only about a quarter of the programs used ex-addicts or guest speakers in their programs—an education technique that is very commonly used in education programs in the free world. Over half the facilities that provided education programs without any other treatment programs used in-house staff to provide these programs. Staff ratios for educators to inmates ranged from around 1 to 10 on the low end to around 1 to 250 at the high end. The most common ratios were 1 to 20 and 1 to 30. The majority of substance abuse educators in boot camp facilities were not certified, nor were they required to be.

Compared with the requirements for providing traditional substance abuse treatment, development and delivery of a substance abuse education program seems quicker, cheaper, and less staff intensive. In this regard, such substance abuse education programs may be a good starting point in the development of a more comprehensive substance abuse program. Education programs may meet the programming needs of those offenders coming to the boot camp with minimal or no prior substance abuse involvement; however, education programs by themselves do not fulfill the treatment requirements of those with identified substance abuse problems.

Recommendation 6

Substance abuse education problems are generally quicker, cheaper, and less staff intensive to implement, and they may serve as a good starting point in the development of a more comprehensive substance abuse program effort. However, they should not be considered a replacement for therapeutic interventions.

What is the most appropriate way to staff substance abuse programs in boot camp facilities? There are two basic issues to be considered when planning the staffing of substance abuse treatment: 1) the quality of the staff, and 2) the size of the staff in relation to the inmate population being served and the type of treatment being offered. In general, three common models or approaches exist for staffing substance abuse programs in boot camps.

In the first of these models, the program is provided by full or part-time agency staff. This "in-house" staffing model is, by far, the most common approach across the United States. A second or "mixed" approach employs contracted substance abuse providers to augment the services provided by the agency staff. The third model involves contracting all treatment services through individuals or an outside entity such as a community mental health provider or a private vendor such as Gateway. There are distinct differences among these approaches. Findings summarized from our study displayed in Table 1 show the differences among the three approaches in critical areas such as the staff-to-inmate ratios, the percentage of staff with formal training, and the percentage of staff who are certified.

Table 1: Substance Abuse Treatment Staff at Facilities Providing Treatment

Table 1: Substance Abuse Treatment Staff at Facilities Providing Treatment (n=22)					
Staff Type	Number of Facilities With (%)	Average # of Staff	Range of # of Inmates per Staff Member	% of Staff With Formal Training	% of Staff Certified
Full-time Contracted	6 (27)	3.2	4 - 41:1	83	75
Full-time Agency	20 (91)	2.7	10 - 90:1	70	40
Part-time Contracted	7 (32)	3.7	10 - 33:1	71	33
Part-time Agency	1 (4)	5.0	15:1	0	100

Source: E. L. Cowles, T. C. Castellano, and L. A. Gransky. 1995. *Boot Camp Drug Treatment and Aftercare Intervention: An Evaluation Review*. Washington, D.C.: United States Department of Justice, Office of Justice Programs, National Institute of Justice.

Our research suggests full-time contracted staff had much better credentials than either full-time or part-time contracted agency personnel and part-time contracted staff. Yet, even part-time contracted staff had more formal training than did either of the in-house staff groups. Facilities that used contracted staff also had better inmate-to-staff ratios than those relying on correctional agency personnel.

The fact that contracted personnel generally had better preparation in the substance abuse arena reflects a sad, but all too common occurrence in staffing correctional programs. This situation is created when staff is called on to provide services that are beyond their formal education, training, or job preparation. The "yesterday I was a correctional caseworker, today I'm a correctional substance abuse counselor" syndrome is repeated in many variations throughout corrections, and is presently exacerbated by the burgeoning number of facilities and programs.

The use of contracted personnel can be a good, if only short-term solution to this problem. Since the area of concern is the vendor's primary domain of expertise, it is likely that the individual or group will be qualified. Further, the contracted vendor must demonstrate an appropriate level of expertise, or it is unlikely that the agency will be willing to enter into a contract with this party. The use of such contracted vendors also permits the correctional agency/facility to respond rapidly to changing needs. A program can be developed and initiated quickly, and can be increased or decreased in size simply by changing the contract terms.

The use of contracted personnel is, of course, not without its drawbacks. Vendors' costs, particularly for speciality services, are typically high. Besides direct personnel and materials costs, most external vendors also will include some charges to support their overhead. In this regard, correctional administrators should be particularly vigilant in reviewing the vendors' administrative costs associated with these contracts. Also remember, contracts are binding, and use caution to ensure mechanisms are in place within the contract framework to remedy unsatisfactory services or solve staff problems quickly.

Particularly problematic for some correctional boot camps is the fact that the facilities may be found in remote areas where securing the services of qualified contractors is difficult. Finally, the reliance on vendors in the longer term can promote a failure by the correctional agency to develop its own treatment capacity. In new or expanding facilities, resources are frequently more available to hire and train staff. However, once this "window of opportunity" passes, getting new staff positions later may be very difficult. The facility that opts for a contracted vendor model without considering this potential pitfall may have little recourse but to continue using the vendors in the future, even if they are not performing satisfactorily.

At what point should postrelease programming be considered in boot camp substance abuse treatment? The incarceration phase of the boot camp sanction tends to be the image brought to mind when these programs are reviewed in the popular press and professional discussions. Yet, as most in the field recognize, the short duration of the prison portion of boot camps seriously limits their ability to develop sustainable long-term behavior patterns needed by offenders to live as acceptable members of the free community. If the positive changes initiated and maintained during the imprisonment portion of the boot camp are to become permanent, a framework must be established to reinforce them after release. In this regard, boot camp programming needs to be considered as a continuum, beginning with the imprisonment portion of the sanction, continuing through community reintegra-

In the area of substance abuse programming, the reintegration and maintenance areas are addressed through relapse prevention. Relapse prevention strategies are designed to give the abuser tools for maintaining the drug-free lifestyle initiated in the incarceration portion of the boot camp. The development of such strategies must begin while the offender is incarcerated, and should be incorporated as part of the overall treatment plan when it initially is developed. We recommend the offender's active participation in the development of the treatment plan as this involvement fosters ownership and prompts the offender to begin taking responsibility for his or her future.

Although it is likely that specific elements of the offender's postrelease/aftercare plan will change during the boot camp experience, its primary emphasis falls in two areas. The first involves developing the offender's ability for self-management rather than externally imposed control. The prison portion of the boot camp presents a highly structured environment in which external control over behavior is emphasized through scheduling and daily routine, close supervision, discipline (both summary punishment and the threat of expulsion), and loss of privileges. A postrelease/aftercare program that eases the control over the offender's behavior through gradual reductions in the restrictions placed on the individual's movements and activities and relaxation in the level of supervision will help the offender develop internal self-control as the external control structure is gradually removed.

The second area concerns the supports that are in the community to help the offender deal with the problems of community life and maintain a drug-free lifestyle. Again, remember that a correctional boot camp is an artificial environment, as are other prison settings. Many stresses of daily life such as responding to family responsibilities and financial considerations, getting and maintaining employment, and handling negative peer influences, are placed on "hold" during the incarceration.

On release, offenders are suddenly thrust back into a world filled with the pressures of daily life, and for many, escape into drugs may be a familiar path for avoiding problems. The identification and establishment of formal links with resources in the community should be in place before the offender is released from confinement. In this regard, it is important that the linkages between the incarceration portion of the program and the released part of the program are formalized. New York, for example, involves the community parole officers in this process by having them involved with the inmates prior to release.

Recommendation 7

Planning for release should be integrated into the boot camp early in the sentence. Three major components of the boot camp sanction: institutional programming, community reintegration, and maintenance of long-term positive behaviors, should be viewed as an integrated continuum.

In summary, substance abuse programming in correctional boot camps should be designed to integrate with the larger aims, philosophy, and structure of the boot camp sanction. To the extent possible, treatment approaches should be targeted toward the identified needs and problems of the individuals offender. Just as some offenders are not appropriate candidates for boot camp placement, the treatment needs of some offenders simply may not be compatible with the type of substance abuse programs that are practical within this environment. Due to the short duration of the imprisonment phase of most boot camp programs, formal treatment linkages for reintegration of offenders and their long-term maintenance of a drug-free lifestyle must be established if substance abuse treatment is to be successful.

Notes

1. Much of the information presented in this article come from our National Institute of Justice funded study on substance abuse programming in boot camp. I would like to acknowledge and thank my colleagues, Tom Castellano and Laura Gransky, for their insights in the development of this material. Those wishing to review a more technical presentation of this information should consult the research report, E. L. Cowles, T. C. Castellano, and L. A. Gransky. 1995. *Boot Camp Drug Treatment and Aftercare Intervention: An Evaluation Review.* Washington, D.C.: National Institute of Justice.

2. For those wishing more in-depth research on the these programs, there are several publications available. Among them, see D. L. MacKenzie and E. Herbert, eds. 1996. *Correctional Boot Camps: A Tough Intermediate Sanction.* Washington, D.C.: National Institute of Justice; D. L. MacKenzie. 1996. Shock Incarceration as an Alternative for Drug Offenders. In D. L. MacKenzie and C. Uchida, eds. *Drugs and the Criminal Justice System: Evaluating Public Policy Initiatives.* Newbury Park: Sage Publications; J. W. Shaw and D. L. MacKenzie. 1992. The One-Year Community Supervision Performance of Drug Offenders and Louisiana DOC-Identified Substance Abusers Graduating From Shock Incarceration. *Journal of Criminal Justice.* 20:501-516.

References

Clark, C. L., and D. W. Aziz. 1996. Shock Incarceration in New York State: Philosophy, Results and Limitations. In D. MacKenzie and E. Herbert, eds. *Correctional Boot Camps: A Tough Intermediate Sanction.* Washington, D.C.: National Institute of Justice.

Gransky, L., T. C. Castellano, and E. L. Cowles. 1995. Is There a 'Next Generation' of Shock Incarceration Facilities? The Evolving Nature of Goals, Program Components and Drug Treatment Services. In J. Smykla and W. Selke, eds. *Intermediate Sanctions: Sentencing in the 90s.* Cincinnati: Anderson Publishing Co.

Karr, S. P., and R. J. Jones. 1996. The Development and Implementation of Illinois' Impact Incarceration Program. In D. MacKenzie and E. Herbert, eds. *Correctional Boot Camps: A Tough Intermediate Sanction.* Washington, D.C.: National Institute of Justice.

Leukefeld, C. G., and F. M. Tims, eds. 1988. *Compulsory Treatment of Drug Abuse: Research and Clinical Practice.* National Institute of Drug Abuse Research Monograph Series, No. 86. Washington, D.C.: United States Government Printing Office.

Lipton, D. S., G. P. Falkin, and H. K. Wexler. 1992. Correctional Drug Abuse Treatment in the United States: An Overview. In C. Leukefeld and F. Tims, eds. *Drug Abuse Treatment in Prisons and Jails.* National Institute on Drug Abuse Research Monograph Series, No. 118. Washington, D.C.: United States Government Printing Office.

MacKenzie, D. L. 1990. Boot Camp Prisons: Components, Evaluations and Empirical Issues. *Federal Probation.* September, pp. 44-52.

————. 1996. Shock Incarceration as an Alternative for Drug Offenders. In D. L. MacKenzie and C. Uchida, eds. *Drugs and the Criminal Justice System: Evaluating Public Policy Initiatives.* Newbury Park: Sage Publications.

Shaw, J. W., and D. L. MacKenzie. 1992. The One-Year Community Supervision Performance of Drug Offenders and Louisiana DOC-Identified Substance Abusers Graduating From Shock Incarceration. *Journal of Criminal Justice.* 20:501-516.

Wells, Edward L., and J. H. Rankin. 1988. Direct Parental Controls and Delinquency. *Criminology.* Vol. 26, No. 2, pp. 263-285.

McNeil Island Work Ethic Camp: Innovations in Boot Camp Reform

Jackie Campbell

Superintendent
Work Ethic Camp
McNeil Island, Washington

Background

The Work Ethic Camp is an alternative sentencing option for adult offenders. The Work Ethic Camp is a four-month program at the McNeil Island Corrections Center, Minimum Security Annex in Washington State. The camp became operational November 1, 1993. The facility is open to both male and female offenders.

In the mid-1980s, elected officials began promoting the concept of "boot camps" for offenders. The reasoning behind these programs was that what worked for the military—transforming misdirected young persons into productive citizens—should also work for corrections. With strong roots in conservative Southeastern states, boot camps began to spread nationally. Public officials and policymakers, many of them graduates of military boot camps, were easily persuaded to support this new reform. The flaw in this rationale is that military basic training programs were designed to mold young civilians to the needs of the military, not to alter criminal attitudes or behaviors. In the absence of research showing successful outcomes from the "boot camp" approach, this military model dominated the approach to dealing with youthful offenders.

In the early 1990s, elected officials in Washington State began to express strong interest in funding a correctional boot camp. Correction's Secretary Chase Riveland was strongly opposed to this concept because of the lack of evidence that boot camps positively affected long-term behavior of inmates. He also was concerned that correctional boot camps do not have the ongoing support system that military basic training programs have upon completion. Finally, he was concerned about the potential abuses of boot camps where the philosophy is to "break people down, and then build them up."

During 1993, when it became clear that there was bipartisan support for a correctional boot camp, Secretary Riveland looked for compromise. He worked to develop a program that could be packaged to meet the public's interests in reducing the cost of incarceration and provide an intensive, regimented program for youthful offenders. He also retained his strong professional belief that the program should address more long-term needs by focusing on inmate responsibility through intensive training in the work ethic. The "Work Ethic Camp" was unanimously supported by the legislature. Because it was packaged as an intensive, disciplined program, it was not challenged by conservative law enforcement.

Secretary Riveland was also successful in limiting this program to those who were already bound for prison. In many states, boot camp programs target youth who normally would not be sentenced to prison. This "widens the net" of those under criminal justice control and increases costs.

The Washington State House and Senate Corrections Committees are actively involved in the design and subsequent expansion of the Work Ethic Camp. These committees are composed of eleven legislators each. Their role is to legislate which offenders may be eligible for the Work Ethic Camp based on crime, age, and length of the sentence, as well as determine judicial sentencing guidelines, program length, and community supervision requirements. The Department of Corrections provides testimony to the legislature, upon request, on the status of the program and arranges on-site legislative visits. In the development and modification of the Work Ethic Camp legislation, judges, prosecutors, and defense attorneys also provided input and testimony.

Within the framework of the legislation, the Department of Corrections is responsible for policy, administrative rules, program design and operation. There is no additional board or committee directly involved.

Women

Since Washington had a relatively small population of females eligible for the program, it would not have been cost effective to operate the program at two sites. To ensure parity of sentencing options for women, it was decided that the Work Ethic Camp would be co-ed. McNeil Island Corrections Center, a state prison for twelve years, had never had female offenders. Assistance was sought from Department staff who had experience with co-ed facilities and women offenders. Those staff, including the management of Washington's women's facility, volunteered to provide training to the McNeil staff who would be working with women. Several areas required immediate attention prior to program implementation:

- developing policies addressing co-ed issues
- providing sexual harassment training to male inmates

Additionally, staff contacted the National Institute of Corrections, which provided one week of training to a Work Ethic Camp team on "Managing Women Offenders" and is following up with a technical assistance grant.

Location

The McNeil Island Minimum Custody facility cannot accommodate only Work Ethic Camp inmates because of its unique location. The McNeil Island Corrections Center is located on a 4,400-acre island reachable only by boat. The island, which also has a 1,500-bed medium correctional facility, is almost entirely self-sustaining. Minimum-custody inmates, supervised by department employees, operate the power station, sewage plant, water filtration plant, motor pool, passenger ferries, and barges. They also provide the labor pool for road repair, construction, facility maintenance, and food preparation. This wide range of real world work opportunities is one reason McNeil Island was selected as the site for the Work Ethic Camp. However, due to the training time for some jobs, at least one hundred long-term inmates are needed to keep the island functioning. Thus, mixing of the two groups of inmates, to some degree, especially on work sites, is unavoidable.

Because the Work Ethic Camp is not a standalone facility, male and female Work Ethic Camp inmates are co-housed with regular inmates in a three-story, six-dormitory building. The Work Ethic Camp currently uses four of the six dormitories (185 beds in the 285-bed facility). This results in inmates who are serving their full sentences, many of whom have been incarcerated for years, who contaminate the teachings of Work Ethic Camp staff. Dining, classroom, recreation, and medical services are largely separated now. A construction grant from the Department of Justice also will enable the Work Ethic Camp to have a separate housing facility by 1997. However, some mixing of the two populations still will occur.

Initial Challenges

The initial challenges were designing the program, bringing the program from plan to operational status in only ninety days, and developing staff training. Other challenges included "selling" a concept to legislators and line staff that was a major departure from traditional prison practices, including overcoming the national trend to replicate prison boot camps in lieu of exploring more contemporary alternatives. These challenges were overcome by soliciting legislative concurrence during the concept stage and allowing front line staff to design the program. The hiring of staff with diverse skills, backgrounds, and strong work ethics along with absolute support from Department of Corrections administrators and the executive team of McNeil Island Corrections Center (the Work Ethic Camp site) provided a powerful team effort to overcome the obstacles and challenges.

The true innovation of the Work Ethic Camp, however, is the programming provided to offenders. Secretary Riveland set the stage for this process by creating an internal implementation committee and providing "guiding principles" for how the program would be designed and operated. Because of the program's success, the 1995 legislature expanded the criteria for those eligible to include offenders of any age.

Overview

The philosophy of the Work Ethic Camp is that the behaviors and attitudes that reflect work ethics can be learned and transferred to all areas of an offender's life. The camp experience is based on an intensive intervention model that provides discipline and structure. Opportunities are provided for offenders to succeed in the workplace, the classroom, and daily life.

The purpose of the Work Ethic Camp is to provide a practical, cost-effective alternative to traditional prison sentences and boot camps. The Work Ethic Camp converts an adult offender's sixteen- to thirty-six-month prison sentence into a four-month intensive employment experience within a prison environment. Adult offenders with no history of violence or sex crimes are eligible. The Work Ethic Camp is designed to address the following issues:

- Creating a contemporary alternative to prison boot camps and traditional prison sentences
- Addressing the shortage of prison beds for violent offenders
- Reducing the high cost of incarceration
- Impacting criminal thinking and behavior

The Work Ethic Camp adopts the alternative sentence structure of boot camps (four highly structured months in lieu of a longer unstructured prison sentence) and incorporates traditional security practices of the prison system. However, it departs from other prison programs by converting the prison environment to an employer environment.

The purposes of the The Work Ethic Camp include the following:

- Provide offenders the opportunity to develop a positive work ethic and crime-free lifestyle through a regimented program
- Provide a cost-effective, sound alternative to traditional incarceration without compromising public safety
- Provide a unique environment with programs that enhance the likelihood of long-term diversion from incarceration
- Provide structured programs including work ethic training, workplace education, life/work skills, drug/alcohol education and treatment, rigorous physical training, and transition planning
- Provide offenders a unique opportunity to be successful, make significant changes, and leave the Work Ethic Camp with the following attributes and skills:

  - Self-discipline
  - Self-respect
  - Transferable work skills
  - Respect for others
  - Appropriate work habits
  - Math, reading, and writing skills that are needed in the workplace
  - The ability to get along with different types of co-workers and supervisors

(continued on the next page)

- ❑ The ability to set and achieve goals
- ❑ Knowing ways to manage stress and anger
- ❑ Control over any chemical dependencies
- ❑ The ability to get and keep a job after release
- ❑ Knowledge of community resources that can help in times of crisis
- ❑ Ways to deal with family problems to keep relationships positive
- ❑ Acceptable activities to do in their free time

A judge now may recommend the Work Ethic Camp if the offender is sentenced to a term of total confinement of between sixteen and thirty-six months, has no current or prior convictions for any offenses for violence or sex (other than drug offenses), is at least eighteen years old at the time of sentencing, has the physical and mental capability to participate in the program, and if the offender qualifies for minimum custody. A recent escape, or a serious infraction while in Department of Corrections' reception, are examples of incidents that would affect custody eligibility.

For eligible offenders, judges must recommend the Work Ethic Camp in the judgement and sentence. The Department of Corrections then accepts the offender into the program with priority for those without detainers (a warrant or deportation order) from another jurisdiction. The offender also must volunteer for the program.

Approximately 1,700 offenders a year are now eligible for the Work Ethic Camp. Of those, judges recommend the Work Ethic Camp for about 60 percent (835 inmates). Of those, 600 will be accepted for the Work Ethic Camp. The remaining 235 are those with detainers and those who choose not to participate. Of the 600 who enter the program each year, approximately 25 percent are terminated for failure to appropriately participate or for serious behavior violations. Those offenders are transferred to other facilities to serve their full sentence.

After the screening for eligibility, the offender is offered the opportunity to decline or agree to Work Ethic Camp participation. The agreement form includes an overview of the program and highlights restrictions—such as a thirty-day blackout on visiting and smoking.

If the sentencing judge determines that the offender is eligible for the Work Ethic Camp program and is likely to qualify, the judge shall impose a sentence within the standard range and may recommend that the offender serve the sentence at a work ethic camp. The sentence provides that if the offender successfully completes the program, the department shall convert the period of Work Ethic Camp confinement at the rate of one day of Work Ethic Camp confinement to three days of total standard confinement.

In sentencing an offender to the Work Ethic Camp, the court specifies:

- that on completion of the Work Ethic Camp the offender be released on community custody for any remaining time of total confinement

- that violation of the conditions may result in a return to total confinement for the balance of the offender's remaining time of confinement

Program Scope

The Work Ethic Camp's two-phased program starts with a highly structured prison sentence, which is based entirely on employer's expectations. The second phase of the program involves transition into the community and aftercare. This phase is supervised by the community corrections staff. The Work Ethic Camp philosophy is that behaviors employers look for in good workers—reliability, willingness to learn, effective communication, and ability to get along with others—apply to all aspects of life. The Work Ethic Camp staff, including custody officers, teach and model workplace maturity and appropriate workplace behavior in all program components and offender interactions.

The Work Ethic Camp program builds on the concepts of work ethics, self-esteem, self-respect, respect for others, self-confidence, and teamwork. This is an intensive, high stress program. Expectations are set high and are continuously monitored by staff, supervisors and the individual participants themselves. The class curriculum focuses on helping each individual to review and reevaluate values, morals, decision making, interpersonal skills, and life skills.

Some of the program restrictions include the following:

- no tobacco products are allowed

- an initial thirty-day restriction on family visits, telephone use, and commissary

- barrack-style living

- long days, from 4:20 A.M. "lights on" until 10:00 P.M. "lights out"

Participants must continuously reduce negative behavior and adopt positive, socially acceptable behaviors. Each day includes a full day of work experiences and classes in employment-related behaviors or skills, such as anger/stress management, conflict resolution, general equivalency diploma preparation, job readiness, chemical dependency treatment, and wellness. Thus, work, education, employment readiness, classes in chemical dependency and physical fitness are required Work Ethic Camp activities. Full participation is required.

Classroom Activities

All participants are assessed for educational level, chemical dependency, and physical fitness. They also are screened for job interests, aptitudes, and skills. Classroom activities then are geared towards these areas.

The conventional educational goal is that all participants will improve their existing level of education. Many participants will do this through adult basic education classes. Many others are able to obtain their general equivalency diploma prior to completion of the confinement portion of the program. Other education areas addressed are learning workplace math, reading, and writing skills.

Chemical dependency education is a process that starts when potential participants are at the state reception center in Shelton, Washington. Each individual is assessed for chemical dependency via the Substance Abuse Subtle Screening Inventory (SASSI). On entering the program, each participant receives a two-week chemical dependency orientation. Those identified by the SASSI as chemically dependent then go on to complete a four-month intensive outpatient program, which includes additional chemical dependency education, group counseling, individual counseling, and transition into aftercare on completion of the program. Cognitive thinking is offered to intensive outpatient program participants and to selected individuals who have not been identified as chemically dependent. It is a cognitive-behavioral treatment intervention that attempts to alter how one thinks, while at the same time shapes desired behavior. As in all of the programming, the desired objective is to address and alter criminal thinking and behavior.

Chemical dependency education is the primary educational thread that permeates all other classes. Because chemical dependency is an issue for such a large percentage of the participants, all instructors relate their education pieces back into the chemical dependency focus. Other areas addressed under the chemical dependency umbrella include training in life skills, anger and stress management; identifying individual potential and skills; developing employment readiness (including taking interviews and writing resumes); and maximizing health and fitness. Specific learning includes the following.

The Integrated Curriculum for Achieving Necessary Skills (ICANS) is a skills-based instructional system to assist learners in achieving the necessary basic skills to function on the job and in society, and in developing their knowledge and potential. These skills include learning to learn, workplace reading, writing, computing, communicating, preparing for employment, thinking skills, and improving group effectiveness.

The first emphasis in Adult Basic Education is on general education diploma preparation. The second emphasis addresses additional basic and/or remedial skills in mathematics, reading, and writing, which are tied directly to workplace competencies. Additionally, an English as a Second Language (ESL) program is offered to the population who demonstrate such a need.

In the anger/stress management skills-based curriculum, participants learn appropriate techniques for reducing personal stress in their environment. Students learn the domino effect of crime on their victims (there are no "victimless" crimes). Students learn citizenship skills for successful living in the community. Topics covered include negotiation skills, violence in the community, and community service.

Through the Dependable Strengths Articulation Process (DSAP), students benefit by gaining a significant increase in self-esteem, motivation to achieve, and sense of responsibility. The process helps people study their good experiences, identify their dependable strengths, and adjust their activities so that those strengths are applied more frequently at work and in their personal lives. Participants practice how to communicate that reliability, how to use their knowledge of their dependable strengths to build teamwork, and how to cope with parts of a job or task they dislike.

Students explore interpersonal and family relationships, including the family disease concept of addiction, functional versus dysfunctional family interaction, and issues of adult children of dysfunctional families.

The unlocking your potential course focuses on self-esteem, personal potential, self-taught affirmations, self-management, motivation, and winning lifestyles. This program serves as the foundation for the continuum of treatment care model.

All recreation is structured. The emphasis is on developing teamwork and building fitness for a wide range of work activities. Participants receive approximately three hours of recreational activity per week. There is no television. Movies are provided twice per week.

Work

During the first thirty days, offenders are assigned to island clean-up crews. They are supervised by correctional officers who teach basic work habits: following instructions, planning tasks, developing teamwork, using interpersonal skills, caring for tools, and developing supervisor-employee relationships. During this first month, the specific job, such as pulling tansy, scrubbing boats, constructing projects, and cleaning up, changes at least every three days to expose program participants to a wide range of job learning experiences.

During the second, third, and fourth months, Work Ethic Camp inmates are assigned to one of thirty-eight regular island work crews. These crew jobs support all the operations of McNeil Island, including repairing of roads; constructing buildings; repairing automobiles; painting structures; working in the meat plant, boat operations; handling maintenance; and grounds keeping. These positions are very similar to jobs that exist in the community and include supervision by crew leaders with extensive work experience in their field. During this phase, work ethic expectations are reinforced, and basic job skill training is provided. Individual work assignments are based on interest, aptitude, or skills that need to be learned and the needs of the institution.

Standards

High standards are set for the way inmates groom, manners, cleanliness, and behavior. Self-respect and respect for others are required at all times. Participant behavior continuously must reflect an effort to drop negative behavior and adopt positive, socially acceptable, behaviors.

Discipline

All discipline is directly related to acceptable work behaviors. For example, a participant who makes an insulting remark about another racial group may be required to use leisure time to write a paper on the cultural contributions of the ethnic group involved. Someone who cannot get along with others may do a presentation on teamwork. Serious behavior problems, such as fighting, refusing to work, or cumulative negative behavior, generally result in termination from the program. Restarting the program is also a possible sanction if no behavior improvement is apparent in the first thirty days.

Termination

Offenders who fail to complete the Work Ethic Camp program who are administratively terminated from the confinement portion of the program, or who otherwise violate any conditions of community supervision, are reclassified and serve the unexpired term of their sentence as ordered by the sentencing judge, and are subject to all rules relating to earned early release time. If offenders fail to complete the program successfully, they are reclassified to another institution to serve the original sentence, with credit for time served.

Aftercare

The second phase of the Work Ethic Camp is transitioning. This involves placement and aftercare in the community. Staff for the division of community corrections are "out stationed" at the camp to assist with the transition and placement process. Placement plans are investigated, approved, and then sent to the community for final confirmation. Transition issues are repeatedly addressed during the last three months of incarceration. Prior to release, the offenders are evaluated, and referrals are developed for employment and continued counseling/treatment. On release, the remainder of the offenders' sentence is served under a high level of supervision in the community.

Current research on boot camps and similar programs indicate that a strong postrelease supervision component is essential to reduce recidivism. Further, studies indicate that transition planning for community release must begin during the incarceration phase. Since implementation, Work Ethic Camp graduates have been required to be on intensive supervision in the community for one year after completion of the program. However, they were not receiving the type of integrated transition, or postrelease service, that the research indicated was needed. As a result, the Work Ethic Camp and Community Custody staff completely redesigned the transition components provided in the camp, and the supervision and services provided in the community. This enhancement, just now being implemented, is considered to be the most significant achievement of the program.

During Incarceration

The offender works with an assigned counselor to develop an individualized case plan, including plans for housing, employment or school, treatment, if needed, and ways to change criminal thinking and behavior. The offender signs an agreement to continue programming after release; failure to comply is a violation. Community Supervision staff are out stationed at the Work Ethic Camp to provide a prerelease orientation to community supervision and individualized transition plans.

A Work Ethic Camp employment specialist provides information on job-specific employer expectations, techniques for interviewing, resumes, federal bonding information, and preparation of transition packets including community resources and employment opportunities. The employment specialist registers offenders in the Employment Security JobNet system. JobNet is an automated system of current and available job openings from local and statewide employers.

Transition planning is led by the community transition specialist and the Work Ethic Camp employment specialist. They work together to provide a combination of group and individual activities that "wrap up" all preceding education, counseling, and work experience into a release plan. On the last day in the Work Ethic Camp, offenders are provided with job referrals in their community of release.

In the community, the community custody officer requires that all Work Ethic Camp offenders participate in a daily reporting regimen for a period of between seven and thirty days. This may be at a formal day reporting center or at the local field office. The community custody officer ensures that during the first two weeks after release, offenders will work at a program at least fifty hours a week. This includes some community service hours. After that time, the program can include a combination of school/training, work, community service, treatment groups, or any activity approved by the community custody officer. If offenders are employed full time on release, they complete ten hours per week of community service for a period of two weeks. This reinforces Work Ethic Camp concepts that ensure continuing behavior change in the community.

Programs initiated as part of the Work Ethic Camp case plan, such as chemical dependency, are continued. The community custody officer does field, home, work, and school visits and monitors court-ordered conditions, as well as monitors employment. If the participants are unemployed, they are required to perform community service and develop a job-seeking plan. The community custody officer monitors behavior through urinalysis, home and site visits, and searches, if appropriate. This individual provides offenders disciplinary interventions, as needed. He or she follows up on sanctions. Sanctions are based on the seriousness grid and may include day reporting, electronic monitoring, team partnering with local police, volunteer work, community service, home detention, counseling, drug and alcohol testing, and/or support groups.

Program Assessment

Effectiveness: Bed Savings

The program was implemented in November 1993 and serves to free up bed space that will be better served for housing the violent offenders. As of December 31, 1995, 436 offenders were graduated from the Work Ethic Camp; 178 in calendar year 1994 and 258 in calendar year 1995. The average length of a stay was six months, two months in reception and four months at the Work Ethic Camp. Without the Work Ethic Camp, the average length of a stay would have been sixteen months for each offender. The bed savings, which enable the Department to house more violent offenders, equate to 148 beds in 1994, and 214 beds in 1995. The total of 362 beds represents the number of additional offenders who could be housed for one year without building additional prison space.

Additionally, cost savings are an important factor. For simplicity, fiscal year 1995 costs were used for both years of graduates to calculate savings. The average cost per month at a minimum facility during fiscal year 1995 was $1,446. The average cost per month at the Work Ethic Camp during fiscal year 1995, over and above the minimum facility cost, was $549 per month.

By releasing each Work Ethic Camp graduate ten months early, the Department saves $12,264 per offender (after subtracting the additional cost of the Work Ethic Camp). The cost savings for the 178 graduates in 1994 was $2,182,992. The cost savings for the 258 graduates in 1995 was $3,164,112. Total savings for two years is $5,374,104.

While recidivism is not yet considered a relevant measurement because of the low number of graduates who have been in the community for a least one year, a preliminary analysis was done. All of the 178 Work Ethic Camp graduates in 1994 were tracked for a year after their release to the community. Those returned to prison for violating a condition of community custody or new crimes were identified. Of the 1994 Work Ethic Camp graduates, 17.4 percent returned for a violation and 7.98 percent returned for a new sentence (some of these offenders included those previously returned for violations). These return rates were not significantly different from the rates of a comparison group of offenders who were released in 1994 after having served their full prison terms. Of the comparison group, 17.6 percent returned for a violation and 5.5 percent returned for a new sentence.

Work Ethic Camp graduates appear to return to prison at a rate no greater than like offenders who served out their traditional sentences in prison. With the recently enhanced chemical dependency program and postrelease supervision changes, the return to prison rates should be lowered.

Behavior Change: Offender Quotes

The most important factor in figuring effectiveness comes from the offenders themselves. These are reactions we have received from the offenders on completing the confinement portion of the Work Ethic Camp:

- "This camp gives you a second chance to realize your worth and gain social skills."

- "Being accepted and able to participate in this program has changed me a lot."

- "I have gotten a lot more from this program than I ever expected."

- "I learned how to get the best results on a job hunt, from interviews to changing jobs."

- "They have helped me regain my self-confidence, self-esteem, and honor. They treated me with the same type of manners they would like to be treated with."

- "I have more skills to be a better employee, and this will be helpful when I get out."

- "I learned that work wasn't a bad place. I look forward to going to work, and like it so much I even go to work when they ask for volunteers, pay or no pay."

Outside Sources

To better manage inmate services, the Work Ethic Camp has contractual relations with: Pierce County Alliance, a nonprofit organization that provides certified chemical dependency staff to the Work Ethic Camp; Pierce Community College that provides instructors for the Work Ethic Camp education program; Employment Security - JobNet Services; and local communities for the Work Ethic Camp inmate crews to provide labor for local betterment projects such as planting, painting, and cleaning up.

Evaluation

The Work Ethic Camp currently is being evaluated through a grant from the National Institute of Justice. The Work Ethic Camp was selected as an evaluation site because of its innovative approach. This initial study involves an assessment of the Work Ethic Camp's short-term impact on a variety of offender attitudinal and decision-making attributes (self-esteem, coping strategies, problem solving, and work ethic values). The process involves surveying offenders before admission and at release to community supervision. Preliminary results will not be available until late in 1996. The study is being conducted by Dr. Thomas Castellano of The Center for the Study of Crime, Delinquency and Correction, at Southern Illinois University.

Additionally, the Work Ethic Camp was recently selected by the National Council on Crime and Delinquency, again through a grant from National Institute of Justice, for a long-term process and outcome evaluation, which has not yet begun.

Future Projection

In five years we expect, both in Washington and nationally, that there will be a continuing demand for more prison space and simultaneously, that ways to reduce the cost of corrections will be needed. Significant changes in the field of corrections tend to occur in time periods longer than five years. For example, the shift from a rehabilitation and education emphasis to "hard time for hard crime" and resurrection of chain gangs represents a twenty-year span. With the need to address crimes of mindless violence, such as drive-by shootings, there is minimal emphasis or allocation of resources to address what works for lesser offenders. Yet, it is these lesser offenders who occupy bed space, at high cost, that is needed for more violent offenders.

In five years, approximately 2,400 additional offenders will have been through the Work Ethic Camp; of those, 75 percent, or 1,800, will have completed the program and will have been in the community for at least one year. From that larger statistical base, offender and staff input, evaluations, and continual refinements of the program, we should have some clear sense of "for whom the Work Ethic Camp works."

Because of the need to reduce the cost of corrections and create space for additional offenders, expansion of the program may be considered by legislative policy makers for other types of offenders or longer-term offenders. Because of the Work Ethic Camp seven-day week and fourteen-hour days, Work Ethic Camp is designed to be effective in conjunction with a sentencing incentive. To invoke such a regimen without incentives invites participant failure. Conversely, to expand the scope of eligibility to include offenders with longer sentences or violent offenders invites public opposition.

Questions identified for future research and possible program design changes include the following:

- Would a shorter period of time in the program get the same results?
- Is a longer period of time needed?
- Does the postrelease supervision component have the highest possible impact?
- Are there offenders with shorter or longer sentences who might be appropriate for the Work Ethic Camp?
- Are there certain types of offenders, such as those convicted of drug or property crimes, who do better or worse in this type of program?
- Is age a factor in success?

Replication

Program replication would not be difficult for the following reasons:

- Almost all states, and most cities and counties, have existing facilities that now house minimum-custody inmates. Additionally, federal statutes provide for the transfer of unused federal facilities, such as military bases, to state and local correctional entities at no cost.

- The program uses existing correctional job classifications, such as officers, counselors, and teachers. The hiring system does need to ensure that staff volunteer for the program. It is critical to the program's success that staff buy into the work ethic concept.

- While operational costs are higher per day than for other minimum types of incarceration, the cost savings from reducing sentences of sixteen to thirty-six months to four months is almost immediate. Those savings enable funding of the program at the level needed to have an impact on behavior in four months.

The availability of real work is critical to the program design. With nonviolent, nonsex offenders, both institution jobs and work for nearby communities are options. By combining both, inmates also acquire the concepts of community service and restitution. Additionally, community service projects bring the inmates recognition and praise from citizens, a powerful tool in changing inmates' perceptions about work rewards. The recent availability of research on why traditional boot camps do not work well with inmates can assist correctional efforts to secure policy maker support for alternative approaches.

Since the program foundation is based on a wide range of existing correctional functions, such as work, education, and community service, it does not require a major shift from traditional activities. Disseminating and integrating the work ethic concept into staff approaches and all activities in lieu of traditional custody approaches is the most difficult task.

Substance Abuse Treatment in Boot Camps: The Doing Life! Program

Lisa Matheson

Cofounder and Managing Director
Doing Life International Inc.
Sunderland, Ontario, Canada

Introduction

In this chapter, you will . . .

❏ Learn about a holistic approach to substance abuse treatment.

❏ Preview Doing Life!, a substance abuse treatment program designed specifically for use in boot camps.

> *"A journey of a thousand miles begins with one step."*
> —Lao Tzu

What is substance abuse treatment?

- A program for treatment and correction of the misuse of a substance
- The acquisition of new life skills for sobriety
- A structured environment and opportunity for recovery

In the new generation of boot camps, emphasis is placed on substance abuse treatment, academics, life skills, and a therapeutic community. These boot camps hold a holistic approach to incarceration where no factor of the inmate's life is separate from the others, but all influence each other.

Dostoyevsky said in *Crime and Punishment*, "A society can be judged by entering its prisons." In the United States, more than two-thirds of all offenders are incarcerated for nonviolent crimes, usually related to drug and alcohol abuse. This represents a failure that is reflective of more than the inmate; it is reflective of our society as a whole. Turning a blind eye to the reality of substance abuse will not make the problem go away, nor will it lower the rates of incarceration or reduce recidivism.

The problem of substance abuse can be addressed outside of the correctional system. However, the current numbers of offenders within the prison system who are addicted to alcohol or narcotics mandates us to address the problem inside, as well. And, as corrections professionals, we are responsible for the quality of treatment of offenders entrusted to our care. Drug abuse is a life-threatening disease. Treatment takes time, commitment, and resources. Treatment also requires empathy, an understanding of the addicts' life, where they have come from, and what has influenced their actions. If people are lost, you need to find out where they are before you can give them directions to their final destination.

In this chapter, you will be given a brief introduction to *Doing Life!*, a substance abuse treatment program designed specifically for use with offenders. It is a challenging program that ultimately requires participants to take responsibility for their past and for their future. Many of the concepts presented are new to the participants, as, in fact, they are to the the educational field in general. The goal of the program is to lead participants down the road of recovery, providing them with skills they need to navigate the new territory they encounter.

The mandala on the next page is a representation of the *Doing Life!* approach to the 12 Steps. The dictionary describes a mandala as "a continuous circular design, containing geometric forms which symbolize the totality or wholeness of the universe." Our mandala represents the ongoing cycle of the 12 Steps. Take a moment right now to think about why substance abuse treatment should be part of your program. Write your thoughts down on the next page.

The Doing Life! Approach

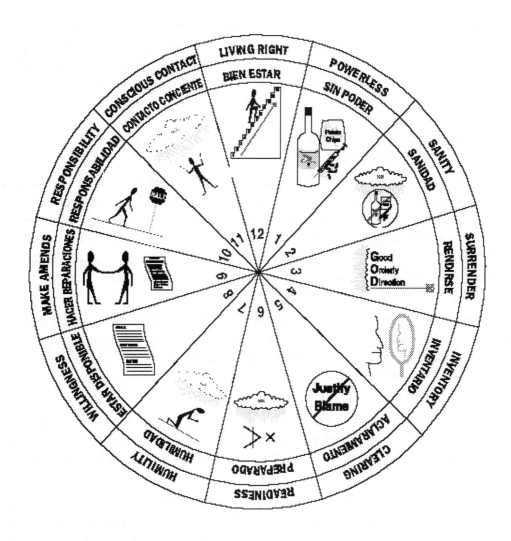

Substance Abuse Treatment is Important Because:

❑ _____

_____

❑ _____

_____

"When I hear I forget, when I see I remember, when I teach, I learn."

—Ben Franklin

What Is 'Doing Life!'?

Doing Life! is a program for recovery designed for people who are addicted to drugs, alcohol or other mood altering substances. For most of them, drinking or drugging has caused many problems, including, for many, problems with the law. Because those problems with the law often result in doing time in jail or prison, the workbooks we employ were initially designed for use with drug treatment programs for offenders. Versions are also available for adolescents who are committed to juvenile justice programs or in school intervention/awareness programs, and for alcoholics or addicts who are private citizens, who as yet have not encountered problems with the law.

Doing Life! is a series of thirteen workbooks. The first of these is an Overview. Each of the twelve subsequent workbooks focuses on one of the 12 Steps to Recovery and one aspect of the 5 Steps to Decisions. *Doing Life!* uses the structure of these two concepts to provide the participant an opportunity to acquire a new perspective on life and the skills to match. The goal of the series is to engage participants in a process of learning about themselves and how their addiction has limited them so that they can make the necessary changes to live successfully with sobriety.

The authors of *Doing Life!* believe that the 12 Steps are the most effective process for dealing with addiction for most addicts. We acknowledge, however, that there are a number of very effective models for change available to recovering people, and have studied and worked with many ourselves. Those who have studied other programs will recognize concepts from those which most influenced us.

The 12 Steps form the core of this work. The 5 Steps to Decisions support the 12 Steps and help participants learn about how their choices affect the quality of their lives. By learning to apply the 5 Steps to Decisions, they enhance their chances of a successful recovery.

Each of the twelve workbooks is a complete module, and follows a standardized format. The workbooks open with a definition of the step to be addressed, and ask the participants to define how they understand the step. Each workbook provides an opportunity for the participants to evaluate their life up to this point. Then, the participants are taken through a series of new concepts and ideas for healthy, sober living. Exercises are used to assist them in seeing how these concepts affect their lives. Each book in the series builds on the previous one(s), and ends with a summary of the step and encouragement to move on to the next workbook. Learning and memory techniques, such as mind mapping and memory anchoring, are taught as skills for completing the workbooks with ease, and for use in everyday living.

This chapter is designed in a similar format to the *Doing Life!* workbooks. We encourage you to participate by completing the exercises as you read. Doing this will give you an idea of the holistic, interactive context of the program.

About Doing Life!

"One who lacks the courage to start has already finished."

—Road to Success

The material in the *Doing Life!* series has been in use in some form since 1935. Cheryl L. Clark, Director of Shock Incarceration (New Your State Department of Correctional Services) has been teaching it to offenders, professionals, counselors, volunteers, therapists, and clergy as a tool for working with addicts or alcoholics and their families since 1973. Mary Bogan, Deputy Superintendent For Programs (Willard Drug Treatment Campus, New York), has been working with the material since 1982.

The *Doing Life!* workbooks represent years of combined experience and learning. The program has evolved from what the authors have learned while working with prisons, schools, private practice, and other agencies, and studying with leading experts in the field. The concepts presented in *Doing Life!* originate from a number of sources, listed here in the order in which the authors learned about them. Each influenced the development of material presented in this workbook series. All are equally important.

- Alcoholics Anonymous
- Transactional Analysis
- Imaginal Education
- Yoga and Meditation
- Reality Therapy
- Virginia Satir
- Neuro Linguistic Programming
- R. Buckminster Fuller
- Control Theory
- Narcotics Anonymous
- Accelerated Learning Techniques
- Loving Relationships Training
- Quantum Learning

Good guides know their territory. To be successful in guiding participants through a 12 Step based program, such as *Doing Life!*, we suggest you familiarize yourself with the basic concepts behind the material. You can learn about the 12 Steps from the following books: *Alcoholics Anonymous* (often referred to as the 'Big Book' by AA members); NA's *It Works, How and Why*, and *Narcotics Anonymous*. These books are available in every library and at AA and NA meetings everywhere.

Doing Life! is . . .

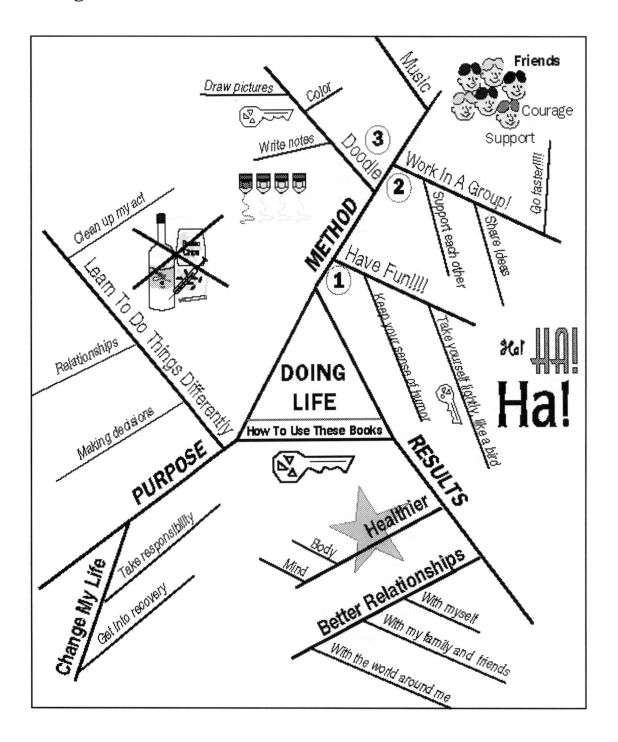

"Free your mind, the rest will follow."
— Funky Divas

The 12 Steps To Recovery

The 12 Steps To Recovery was written by and for members of Alcoholics Anonymous, and came from the experiences, successes and failures of the early AA members. The 12 Steps are a pathway to right living. They are a set of universal or basic truths about living that can assist a person in getting through any problematic situation. Although the 12 Steps are primarily associated with alcoholics, they are valid tools to solving problems in anyone's life.

Bill W. and Dr. Bob were the first alcoholics to push the principles of "one alcoholic helping another." Although they were individually committed to their own sobriety, they had failed many times to stop drinking on their own, losing friends, family, money and health along the way. First-hand experience told them that sticking together was their only hope, and so they created the first "group" to support recovering alcoholics. From there the community of fellowship began and grew. AA has become a worldwide phenomenon with millions of recovering members. Anywhere you go on the planet, you can find a meeting.

Alcoholics Anonymous is the foundation of over fifty 12 Step groups such as Narcotics Anonymous, Overeaters Anonymous, Sex and Love Addicts Anonymous, Gamblers Anonymous, to name only a few. Programs like Phoenix House, Delancey Street, Portage, Weight Watchers and other therapeutic communities and self-help programs owe their beginnings to AA, as well.

In the *Doing Life!* workbooks, the 12 Steps form the structure, or context, for the material presented. Each step has been evaluated to determine the information and skills required to successfully work through the step. The information and skills are then presented in a format that makes the steps "user friendly" and supports successful learning. Recovery through the 12 Steps is presented as an opportunity for a new beginning and exercises are provided as a means to fully engage the participants in integrating these new concepts into their lives.

The 12 Steps have been written with masculine pronouns. Some people are upset by this, but we encourage them to remember that we live in a culture in which "politically correct" language only now is part of our consciousness. That sensitivity was not part of the culture when the Steps were recorded. The authors have chosen to present the steps as they have been presented to addicts since 1935. The authors of *Doing Life!* are women and do not feel that using the masculine pronouns, as they were written, is any reflection on us, nor do we view it as an insult. We feel connected to the long, successful tradition of recovery when we read the steps as they were first written, and to those early courageous members who forged a new path for millions.

The 12 Steps are not a quick cure. With the 12 Steps, the disease of addiction is approached much like diabetes or other diseases that affect a person's lifestyle and require a lot of ongoing care. Recovery is a lifelong process that requires time and attention every day. Addicts cannot afford to forget where they have been and what their addiction has done to them. If they do, even for one day, the disease takes hold again, stronger than before.

As *Doing Life!* progresses, the previous steps are reviewed in relationship to the one currently being addressed, and emphasis is placed on the belief that addicts can never assume they are fully recovered. They cannot afford to forget where they have been or they may end up there again.

The 5 Steps To Decisions

The 5 Steps To Decisions have their origin in the Thresholds program, in which volunteers from the Ecumenical Institute taught the decision making process to inmates in jails and prisons.

During the 1960s, one of these inmates was greatly influenced by the program and became a leader in educating other inmates. When he began teaching the 5 Steps To Decisions, he used a story about a successful "job" he had pulled robbing a bank. The young man was smart, sharp and arrogant, and believed that he was justified in stealing from banks because they had insurance. After this particular "job" was done, he discovered that the teller had given him too much money. He knew the extra money would be taken out of her paycheck, so he boasted that, at great personal risk, he took the extra money back. He told this story to show how strong denial can be. Denial blinds us to reality, to the truth around us. He was addicted to power, the thrill of the con, and this addiction told him that he was smarter than everyone else. His denial convinced him that he would never be caught.

He was caught, however, and went to prison. There, his life was dramatically changed one night as he watched a small, scared, seventeen year old, youth get murdered by a muscle-head. He spent the night in agony because he could not stop the murder. The next day, he talked to his volunteer counselor, who gave him a copy of "You Are Accepted" by Paul Tillich. He made a decision as a result of reading that article to make amends for the wrongs he had done and dedicated the next ten years of his life to teaching volunteers how to teach decision making in prison.

Cheryl Clark met this gentleman in 1973 and worked with him for four years, learning how to teach the 5 Steps To Decisions. The Network Program she developed is based on this decision-making model, along with the principles and Steps of the AA program.

The 5 Steps To Decisions are a simple, straightforward plan for improving the quality of the choices we make. The first step, See Your Situation Clearly, asks us to make distinctions between facts and feelings and to see that in every situation there are both gifts and limits. Step two asks that you Know What You Want in your life. Here we think about the quality of life we want for ourselves and the people who are most important to us. Step three teaches how to Expand Your Possibilities to think about many possible ways to get what we want. Fourth, we must Evaluate those possibilities before we Decide about which ones will work best. Here you will think about the Desirability of each possibility and the Odds, Outcome and Risks (D.O.O.R.) involved. The first four steps are the basis of the fifth, an Action Plan for acting on the decision.

The first six workbooks teach the basics of the 5 Steps To Decisions to help participants start making changes in their lives. In the second six, these steps are renewed to help them make a plan to take control of their lives. Go over the 5 Steps To Decisions below and on the next page.

To get a simplified idea of how they can assist someone in making life decisions, practice using them to work through a decision you currently have to in your life.

A decision I have to make is: _____

_____

Step #1 — My situation: _____

_____

Step #2 — What I want is: _____

_____

Step # 3 — The possibilities are: _____

_____

Step #4 — Evaluate and Decide _____

_____

Step #5 — My action plan is: _____

_____

_____

Integrating The Steps

Doing Life! is designed to help addicts get a grip on their lives, to take control of their thoughts, ideas and feelings so that they can create a life of sobriety for themselves. To do this, they require, not only the information or the "data," they require a new skill set, as well. *Doing Life!* provides both of these things, complementing one with the other, to create a whole learning experience that will prepare them for the rest of their lives.

The first six workbooks are a journey within. They are a guide to exploring the inner self. In them, we ask participants to examine themselves, to look inward to what they did in the past and why they did it. They are encouraged to be completely honest with themselves, as painful as it may be, so that they fully understand the extent of their addiction.

The second six workbooks build on the first six. During steps six through twelve, participants are guided through a process of looking outward, to see that they are not alone, that there is help for them. They examine the way their addiction has affected their loved ones and others in their lives, and they begin to take action to correct any harmful deeds from the past.

In the *Doing Life!* workbooks, the 5 Steps to Decisions are fully integrated with the 12 Steps and follow the internal/external model outlined. These two concepts support each other in providing a strong, solid foundation for living. Both offer skills for successful living and teach us how to be self directed, rather than being pushed around by others or "brainwashed" by fads, advertising or emotions out of control.

Originally, the decision making process was delivered in a 12 lesson format. We have adapted the format to complement the twelve recovery steps.

Taking 12 Steps to the Future

STEPS	... TO RECOVERY	... TO DECISIONS
1	We admitted that we were powerless over our addiction, that our lives had become unmanageable.	See Your Situation Clearly
2	Came to believe that a power greater than ourselves could restore us to sanity.	You Are Accepted
3	We admitted that we were powerless over our addiction, that our lives had become unmanageable.	Know What You Want
4	Made a decision to turn our will and our lives over to the care of God as we understood him.	Expand Possibilities
5	Admitted to God, to ourselves and to another human being, the exact nature of our wrongs.	Evaluate and Decide
6	Became willing to have God remove all these defects of character.	Action Plan
7	Humbly asked Him to remove our shortcomings.	See Your Attitude Clearly
8	Made a list of the people we had harmed and became willing to make amends to them all.	Accept Responsibility
9	Made direct amends to those we had harmed, except when to do so would injure them or others.	Know Your Resources
10	Continued to take personal inventory and when we were wrong, promptly admitted it.	Expand Your Personal Style
11	Sought through prayer and meditation to improve our conscious contact with God as we understood Him, praying only for knowledge of His will for us and the power to carry that out.	Evaluate Your Social Style
12	Having had a spiritual awakening as a result of these steps, we tried to carry this message to others and to practice these principles in all our affairs.	Celebrate In Action

Each of the twelve workbooks addresses one of the steps in detail, providing information and exercises to assist the participant in integrating the principles into their life. *Doing Life!* is based on these two very successful models for change. Any kind of change, big or small, takes a lot of time, effort and energy. We know, from first-hand experience, that all who take the time, effort, and energy to "work" these principles will find that they will work for them, to create the change they want in their lives.

Individual or Group Study

Doing Life! is designed for either individual self-study or for study in a facilitated group environment. Fundamentally, the use of the program is the same, although the dynamics of the two approaches will be different.

In a self-study context, participants can work at whatever speed is comfortable for them. Because much of the work is challenging, and it may be the participants' first instinct to quit, we recommend that they create some sort of support network for discussion of ideas and to help with motivation. This could be another inmate, a group of inmates, a counselor, or a teacher. Whoever is committing to supporting the participant, however, must be clear about the seriousness of this work. They must understand that the participant is committed to turning his or her life around, and that this task will not necessarily be an easy one. The participant will be angry or emotional at different times. He or she may become confused and upset when confronting the past. And when in these states, the participant may be very fragile. If the person supporting the participant is not able to handle these types of situations, he or she may do more harm than good in the long run. If you are suggesting *Doing Life!* to someone for individual study, please address this issue, and suggest ways that they can find a support person or group.

In a structured group environment, *Doing Life!* will typically be part of a curriculum on substance abuse in a treatment program. In many cases, there will be a timeframe within which the workbooks are to be completed, and the participant will complete the series with the group. In this type of study, participants have the opportunity to use the group as their support, and can find motivation and understanding from others who have been in the same position as they have. On the other hand, because they are working at the group's speed, they may not be giving each piece of the series the attention or time that is ultimately required for them personally to derive the most benefit. We encourage you to suggest that the participants spend time outside of the group working on any pieces that they feel are not complete. Also, suggest that the participants find one other person who is doing the program to act as their "study buddy" outside of the classroom. Establish a form at the beginning of each study session to allow for questions and comments that have come up for the participants since the previous session.

As a facilitator, you will require support as well. You will be encountering new, challenging and often emotional situations in your group and may not always know the answers or how to handle the emotions. It is very important that you have someone (or a group) to go to when you need a friendly ear, or when you need to ask questions or discuss ideas. Even though the pattern of addiction is similar for almost everyone, each participant will have his or her own "stories" and perspective. You will have to allow all of these points of view and be able to mesh the lessons together in a manner that works for all the participants. A strong support network will help you do just that.

Getting the Most From *Doing Life!*

Individual Study

- Participants can work at their own speed
- Participants must have a strong reason for doing the program and must be self-motivated to get through all of the workbooks
- Participants require a support person or group to help them be honest with themselves about their addiction and how it has affected their lives

Group Study

- Participants do the program with the group within an established timeframe
- Participants will find motivation and support within the group
- Participants will find that others in the group will have had the same experiences and will be able to see that they are not alone in their addiction
- The facilitator can provide structure and guidance to the participants, helping them through difficult sections of the book, and providing them with feedback on their work

H.O.W. To Facilitate *Doing Life!*

It is not necessary for facilitators themselves to have struggled with addiction, although those who are actively engaged in a recovery program certainly can draw on their own experiences for understanding. Facilitators need only three basic characteristics to be effective. Very simply, a facilitator needs to be, Honest, Open and Willing. Here is what we mean by that:

Honest

Be yourself! If you are a seventy-year-old volunteer from a church group who knows nothing about jails and prisons, that is fine. If you are from the country or suburbs, do not pretend to understand what it is like to grow up in the inner city. If rap music leaves you cold, do not pretend to like or understand it if you do not. You do not have to be an addict to understand that drugs, including alcohol, can be very harmful—just as you do not have to burn your hand on a hot stove to know that gas flames or a red burner will hurt. If you are in recovery yourself, you still have the right to privacy. It is not necessary or important to break your anonymity if you are not comfortable with that. Whatever your situation, stand up for yourself and be yourself!

Open

Second, be Open to the experience. Being Open does not necessarily mean "spill your guts." Participants may try to get you to talk about yourself to get the focus off them. Most addicts are master manipulators, if not masters of anything else. They will try guilt, intimidation, any con they can think of, to make you the focus. Keep the focus where it belongs, on them. It is fine to share a personal example if you are comfortable with that, but not necessary by any means. Being Open means doing the best you can to be nonjudgmental and objective as you facilitate.

Willing

Be Willing to listen and learn. Be Willing to give and receive feedback. Be Willing to learn about the 12 Steps To Recovery and the 5 Steps To Decisions. Prepare yourself to be as effective as you can be. Be Willing to learn from the participants. Be Willing to be flexible and meet the needs of each person during each study session.

And, by all means, keep your sense of humor! The best facilitators are those who enjoy what they do and have fun with it. Your tone will set the mood for the participants in the program. If you get too "heavy," the participants will follow, and with the difficulty of the work they are doing, this would be a hindrance.

New facilitators will run into challenging situations and may make mistakes. Making mistakes is human, and is the way that we learn. Throughout *Doing Life!*, we ask the participants to look at mistakes they made in the past so they can learn what it was that did not work in their lives. We ask the facilitators to do the same. Taking an honest look at mistakes is an opportunity to learn what does and does not work in any situation.

Remember, there is no "right" or "wrong." There are only results. If the results you are getting are not what you want, change your strategy, try something new. And celebrate what you learn from your mistakes.

On the next page, define for yourself the meaning of staying Honest, Open and Willing.

I am . . .

HONEST
OPEN
WILLING

To me, being HONEST means . . .

_____

_____

_____

To me, being OPEN means . . .

_____

_____

_____

To me, being WILLING means . . .

_____

_____

_____

What Makes A Great Facilitator?

One of the books we recommend as reading for facilitators of *Doing Life!*, is *Super-Teaching* (Eric P. Jensen 1988). In it, Jensen gives us a thought that sums up the tone of of the book, "The purpose of teaching is to provide for your students an experience of their own greatness." He has dedicated himself to becoming the most effective teacher he can be, and his work has become a standard in leading edge teaching techniques.

As a facilitator for *Doing Life!*, your job is to provide participants an experience of who they really are, different from who they were in their addiction. It is a challenging task, there is no doubt. The protective shell of addiction is tough to crack. But once you crack it even a little bit, you will see results that overwhelm you. And the participants who experience the crack will be awed at the possibilities that lay ahead for them.

In chapter 2 of *Super-Teaching*, Jensen talks about the different attitudes among teachers, "values or underlying premises . . . how top teachers think of themselves, their job and their students." It is his opinion, and ours, that your beliefs will define your results. If you believe that you can make a difference, you will. If you believe nothing you can do will change anything, nothing will change.

Some of the premises that Jensen believes contribute to a great teaching experience are the following.

- *You are the cause of your own experience.* The choice is yours, and the responsibility for the results is also yours.

- *Reality is personal.* Everyone sees a sunset differently. Allow all participants their points of view and they will allow yours. What they see is valid to them and deserves to be respected.

- *It is your job to enter the student's world.* If you want to give directions to someone who is lost, you need to find out where they are. You will get better results if you find out where your participants are starting from and lead them from there, instead of trying to get them to come to you.

- *There are no failures, only outcomes and feedback.* Believing that mistakes are "bad" or "wrong" is a hoax that our society has created. The truth is, in fact, that the only way humans learn is by making mistakes and correcting them. And if you or they are not making mistakes, you are not stepping out to learn and become a bigger, better human being.

- *There are no resistant or learning disabled students.* This may or may not be true, but if you facilitate from a position that holds this to be true, your results will get better.

How facilitators for *Doing Life!* approach their role is fundamental to the results the participants will achieve. Attitude will determine the outcome. Substance abuse recovery is a difficult topic to lead, and to be a successful facilitator, requires flexibility and patience. Facilitators must stay committed to the goal of providing an opportunity for the participants to experience something other than their addiction.

The Context For *Doing Life!*

In the *Doing Life!* book, the typed information is on the left hand page and illustrations and exercises on the right hand page. The reason for this is to engage both sides of the brain in the learning process as much as is possible.

Human brains are divided into two hemispheres, the left side and the right side. Research shows us that each of the hemispheres is responsible for different aspects of thinking. The left brain oversees logical, sequential, linear, rational thinking processes, and the right brain is involved with random, unordered, intuitive, and holistic processes.

Traditionally, classroom information is presented in words, either verbally or in written form, and stimulates only the left half of the brain. We are expected to read, copy words from a chalkboard, and memorize data. This means that one-half of the brain, the right side, is engaged very little, if at all. Because learning is more successful when both sides of the brain are engaged, it is, therefore, very important that facilitators also create positive stimuli for the right side of the brain.

In a "super learning" or "accelerated learning" process, the environment becomes very important. Special attention is paid to creating external stimuli that will engage the creative, holistic right side of the brain. Even though you may be limited by your facility, there are a number of simple things you can do. Some of them are covered later in this guide.

- *Use color.* Encourage participants to use colored markers or pens. If you can use a flip chart instead of a chalkboard, get colored markers and use them all!

- *Play background music.* Music can be a very useful tool in anchoring an idea or an emotion. If you can, bring a portable stereo to the class, use music to create energy or calm the participants.

- *Take breaks often.* For the brain to work optimally, and for the participants to stay focused, it is important that they are breathing and that their bodies are comfortable. If you feel the participants are falling asleep, or getting stressed out, have them stand up and stretch. We recommend, at minimum, that you break every fifty minutes.

- *Celebrate achievements.* The emotion of a celebration, even one that is just a loud "YAY!" will stimulate the right brain to be more active and will encourage the participants to keep moving through the program. They may be resistant to acknowledging their own or others' achievements at first, but you will find that the positive feedback will become contagious over time.

- *Finally, be prepared.* Ensure that you know the material you are presenting. Read through each workbook and do the exercises yourself. Look up anything with which you are not familiar, or find someone who can give you the information you need. If you can, do some background reading, listen to some of the recommended songs and view any videos or movies that are suggested. The better your preparation, the better your results.

Not only do these types of premises make the learning process more successful, they can make it fun, as well. We encourage all facilitators to learn as much as they can about the super learning and accelerated learning educational styles.

A Final Word

As a correctional officer involved with substance abuse treatment in boot camps, your job is to find or develop and provide the program that will get you the best results. The results you want are people committed to recovery, leading a life of sobriety.

Doing Life! approaches substance abuse treatment from the addict's or alcoholic's point of view, rather than from a clinical perspective. It is a hands-on user program that is designed to stimulate and engage the participant, to keep them on the track of their recovery even in the face of very challenging tasks. It is a substance abuse treatment program model specifically developed for the unique circumstances of the incarcerated population in North America, using language and references that they can understand.

Do your research. Look into the programs that are available across the nation. Read the material you are provided with from the point of view of the addict or alcoholic. Because, very simply, if they cannot relate to it, if they cannot glean an understanding of what you are presenting to them, they will not be "enrolled." If the participants are not "enrolled," the only results you will have will be wasted time and money.

And thank you for being part of the solution!

Boot Camps, Work Camps, and Community Needs: A Restorative Justice Perspective on Correctional Objectives*

Gordon Bazemore, Ph.D.

Associate Professor
Florida Atlantic University
Fort Lauderdale, Florida

Thomas J. Quinn

Visiting Fellow
National Institute of Justice
Washington, D.C.

Introduction

In recent years there has been a widespread interest in the establishment of boot camps as an alternative or supplement to the more traditional corrections' options in many jurisdictions. There is no uniformly accepted definition of "boot camp," although generally such a facility includes: barracks-style housing; platoons (of some form or similar

*Note: This paper is supported by federal grant 95-IJ-CX-0016 from the National Institute of Justice and grant JJ-XX-XX -xx from OJJDP. The views expressed are those of the authors and do not necessarily reflect the views of the United States Department of Justice or any of its agencies.

grouping and phasing of activity); military drill, titles, and protocol; physical activity; labor; and programming of varying types (MacKenzie and Hebert 1996).[1] While early boot camps gave almost exclusive emphasis to militaristic discipline and punishment, more recently implemented boot camps also include treatment and educational components.

Now, we have the occasion to discuss correctional objectives not yet addressed even by the more holistic boot camp models. In considering such new objectives, planners should consider not only correctional exigencies such as cost and political expediency, but also genuine community needs.

One community need that has not been addressed clearly in the boot camp model is the need for reparation of victims or victimized communities. Related to this need is the need for offenders to understand the consequences of their behavior in terms of harm to real people and the need to take responsibility for "making it right" with their victims. This failure to connect the criminal act with the sanction (with responsibility of the offender to make amends) is characteristic of interventions developed with only offender-driven objectives. As such, it is one of the failings of the current criminal justice system that is addressed by an increasingly popular concept in community corrections, restorative justice (Bazemore 1994, Barajas 1995, Bazemore and Schiff 1996).

This paper considers how this restorative justice model can be implemented in boot camps or work camps. This may occur by closely examining what the community wants and expects from such programs. The "lens" of restorative justice provides an important perspective on community needs that can assist planners and current camp administrators to develop objectives, which more clearly address these needs.

What the Public Wants: The Appeal of Boot Camps and the Missing Link

While fiscal and other administrative concerns (such as increasing costs and crowding) are important in considering and planning interventions such as boot camps, their current political popularity ultimately must be squared with community expectations for correctional programs. Public opinion surveys over the past decade show that citizens are generally less punitive toward offenders than policy makers who continue to support the unprecedented expansion of incarceration. These surveys suggest that when given reasonable choices between sanctions for nonviolent offenders, significant majorities choose intermediate sanctions. However, they do not choose just any intermediate sanction. Rather, citizens want offenders to be "held accountable" for their behavior. When choosing among different ways of doing this, often citizens chose reparative sanctions—such as restitution and community service with the requirement that the offender be made to face his or her victim or surrogate victim (Pranis and Umbreit 1992, Schwartz *et al.* 1992). Surveys focused on juvenile offenders also document support for education programs and rehabilitative programs, as well as reparative requirements, but these surveys indicate least support for traditional treatment programs focused on counseling and traditional training schools (Schwartz *et al.* 1992).

What the public resents is the proverbial "slap on the wrist" associated with probation and some treatment programs. What may create a sense of outrage, often expressed as support for incarceration, are programs which appear to provide special benefits to offenders while showing little concern with sanctions or with the needs of victims and communities. Treatment programs emphasizing only recreation, and even those focused only on offender education, may provoke opposition.

Boot camps have reaped the benefit of a windfall of public outrage against traditional correctional approaches. Their political popularity, therefore, is due not so much to community dissatisfaction with prisons as their dissatisfaction with treatment programs and with probation.

By providing discipline and structure, as well as a dose of punishment, boot camps appear to have filled a void between probation and more traditional forms of incarceration. Boot camp is not a "day at the beach." Yet the disappointing research results (MacKenzie and Hebert 1996) as well as increasing administrative costs, suggest that boot camps may provide less bang for the public buck than generally is imagined.

While boot camps address the public desire for discipline and punishment, most often they do nothing to address the need for accountability to victims and the community. As in probation, victims and community remain in passive roles, and the offender, while given structure, remains a recipient of punishment and treatment. Offenders must rise early, march, and obey orders, but most boot camps provide little productive work and service; the public pays and neither community nor victim receive much in return. Whatever one believes about the rehabilitative value of such activities for offenders, the return of the investment in boot camps at best is subject to serious questioning and, at worst, is self-indulgent.

The public is dissatisfied with justice, but the debate on whether to punish or treat the offender is off the mark. When a crime has been committed, someone has been hurt, and the community has been disrupted. A primary purpose of the justice process should be to understand the damage inflicted, to determine who needs to right that wrong, and to make sure it gets done. These principles are central to restorative justice, and the public favors policies and programs embodying these principles. Focus groups in Delaware, Alabama, and Vermont (Doble *et al.* 1991) indicate a clear preference for community service and restitution, and for more direct victim involvement in the justice process. This is consistent with numerous other studies.

Toward Restorative Justice

Victim advocates are demanding and receiving rights and attention. Meanwhile, the dissatisfied public is increasingly demanding notification and involvement. Less formal processes for involving the community directly, and linking the offender with the repair of the harm caused by the crime, are gaining favor in the United States. Simultaneously, policy makers beyond corrections are scrambling for more cost-effective ways of dealing with offenders as increasing portions of state budgets are reserved for retribution.

Other cultures, including many Muslims, American Indians, and Pacific rim societies include restoration of the victim and the community as core elements of justice. In Australia and New Zealand, "family group conferencing," based on indigenous cultures there, has gained some favor in mainstream juvenile justice. It brings juvenile offenders and their families together in a mediated setting with the offenders and their families to discuss the case, including how to repay the damage, and what penalty should apply. This more personal approach is part of the reason juvenile crime went down 27 percent in one jurisdiction.

This version of justice is catching on anew in our own society, beginning with a community justice center started in Elkhart, Indiana by Mennonites in 1978. Now, there are hundreds of programs that provide community-based mediation, which is one example of a program rooted in the restorative philosophy. The victim may request a face-to-face meeting with the offender, who then cannot sit and rationalize away the crime. Victims get answers to questions not available under the traditional system. In a sense, it is a return to a decentralized, more immediate response to crime.

Obviously, this will not be appropriate for all cases. Yet, according to recent research (such as Umbreit 1994), victims who go through mediation are more satisfied, less fearful, and receive more restitution than those who are processed through the traditional court system. Offenders who participated were slightly less likely to commit new offenses and were more likely to view the system as fair. When the dialog takes place early in the process, it also can save valuable time of prosecutors and judges.[2]

For crimes with no specific victim, community service acts as a substitute to repay society for the disruption caused. Imagine a squad of convicted drug dealers cleaning up graffiti and boarding up abandoned houses, helping to improve the appearance of the same neighborhoods they have tarnished in the past. That is justice.

One victim-offender mediation program in British Columbia, evaluated in 1995 by Tim Roberts, deals with more serious cases including robbery, rape, and homicide. Obviously with a very serious case, some of the advantages of restorative justice at earlier stages of the process, such as court resource savings, are moot. However, if a system is to be truly restorative, victims have much to gain from such programs. The desire to know "why" is more intense with cases involving serious injury or death. These cases take more preparatory time and a higher level of training for the staff involved, but the evaluation from British Columbia as well as anecdotal cases from Texas, New York, and Minnesota indicate that victims and offenders both feel the process is valuable; for victims it provides a sense of closure, and for offenders it offers a feeling of self-growth.

An interesting and victim-sensitive adaptation occurs in the face-to-face meeting in this Canadian program. This includes face-to-face dialogs and other less direct exchanges, such as correspondence and a video of victims telling the offender the impact of the crime, or of the offender answering questions posed by the victim or the victim's proxy. This type of creative and flexible approach to involving the victim can go a long way to helping some victims move on with their lives, a goal that too often may be foreign to representatives of our correctional system.

Restorative justice is central to a new approach, the "balanced and restorative justice project" model.[3] The federal Office of Juvenile Justice and Delinquency Prevention is sponsoring demonstrations of this model in three states. Another twenty states have adopted this model in statutes and/or policy statements. In the balanced and restorative justice project model, every disposition must include elements of public safety, accountability to victim and community, and offender competency. The balanced and restorative justice model requires that the juvenile justice agencies focus resources equally on three clients: the victim, the offender, and the community.

Priorities for programs and practices in the balanced and restorative justice model include: restitution, restorative community service, work experience, and other forms of competency development, victim offender mediation, and other victim involvement approaches and preventive capacity building (Bazemore and Umbreit 1995).

Boot Camps, Work Camps, and the Restorative Model

Vermont Community Service Work Camp

The Vermont Department of Corrections has made a deliberate and concerted effort to move toward a restorative or "reparative" model. Based on market research (Vermont Department of Corrections 1995), Vermont discovered that the public wanted the following (see the chapter in this volume on Vermont):

- Safety from violent predators
- Accountability for violators of the law
- Repair of the damage done
- Treatment to assure safe release
- Involvement of the community
- Assurance of quality and efficiency

As a result, they began to overhaul their correctional system and involve the community with "community reparative boards." These boards act as sentencing panels for relatively minor offenders. The Department of Corrections also created a two-track probation system (one risk-management, the other reparative), retrained and reorganized personnel, and created a community service work camp. It is important to understand the correctional context in which the camp operates.[4]

The Vermont Community Service Work Camp shares with more traditional correctional boot camps the movement through levels in three-to-six months, the barracks (two fifty-bed units), the trade-off for time sentenced (day for day), and the structured routine. It does not use military titles or drills, nor is there marching or exercise. The court refers offenders and the Department of Corrections does the screening.

In place of drill is work—initially within the compound and later under supervision in the community. This work is for the needy or the government. It includes such things as cutting wood for welfare recipients for heat and making signs for the state parks. In the process, offenders learn work habits and skills. The work crews are in demand in the community, as nonprofit and church groups seek the assistance of the offenders in building bus shelters, creating dugouts for Little League, repairing old buildings, and the like. Emphasis is on work that leaves a legacy that offenders and the public alike can see for some time.

In addition, victim impact panels periodically offer evening sessions to sensitize camp inmates to the impact of crime on victims; individual victim-offender mediation (with voluntary participation) is anticipated soon. In fact, the staff is designing a mediation approach to be used for disputes and conflicts within the boot camp itself. Leaders hope that the modeling of this approach will help imbue offenders with conflict resolution skills for their own future. For victims, the opportunity to express the impact of the crime on their lives can be helpful in healing.

In Washington State, for example, victim impact panels have reduced recidivism (72 percent) in offenders who participate, compared to similar offenders who did not complete victim impact panel classes (Stutz 1994). It has increased the payment of restitution (29 percent versus 20 percent) and has resulted in fewer parole violations. Some offenders—perhaps most—do not see their victims as individuals. Indeed, they often see themselves as victims. Perhaps, the victim impact panel reaches some of them so they do understand the result of their behavior on other human beings.

Federal Intensive Confinement Center, Lewisburg, Pennsylvania

The only boot camp facility for men in the Federal Bureau of Prisons houses 200 offenders recommended by the court for up to six months each. Programming includes awareness and sensitivity and parenting training, as well as more traditional programs in drug treatment, the general equivalency diploma instruction, English as a Second Language (ESL), life skills, and vocational skill development in such skills as welding.

Parenting training is tied into the victimization, which the offenders have experienced. Selected offenders even serve as surrogate "big brothers" to high-risk youth who they visit regularly. This gives the offenders an opportunity to practice dealing with the younger generation so they may better interact with their own offspring once released; they also can bring up problems faced by the at-risk youth with instructors and others in the parenting class.

A victim awareness and sensitivity component is taught by a community volunteer. The eight-hour class is taught in four segments and covers:

- definition of victimization, as well as trauma, culpability, and restitution

- stress predictors (reaction to adverse life situations, choices/outcomes)

- criminal justice system (from the "other side," victims' bill of rights versus Miranda, legislation and statistics)

- socioeconomic impact of crime (planned versus impulse crime, use of weapons, making it right, and personal choices)

This program sensitizes the offenders while involving victims and the community, who come into the facility to address the inmates and express the impact crime has had on them.

The Loxahatchee Youth Environmental Services (YES) Project

The YES project in Palm Beach County Florida is a community-based collaborative effort of the State Department of Juvenile Justice and the United States Department of the Interior. It uses restorative sanctions and processes (Martinez 1996). Juvenile offenders in residential programs satisfy their community service requirements in a wildlife refuge in the Everglades, working thirty-two hours a week at a variety of tasks, mostly related to exotic plant control. Youth supervised by Department of Interior employees work with other youth and adults to develop a sense of teamwork and become familiar with the habits of fauna, such as sea turtles.

The residents are educated to the ecological benefits of the project while understanding the reality of hard manual labor and learning the use of hand tools. During their tenure, they follow an individualized educational plan with required school lessons along with lessons on punctuality, problem solving, conflict resolution, and other life experiences. Most of the young men are paid a minimum wage for their work beyond the assigned community service hours through a Private Industry Council grant. A large portion of any wages are set aside for restitution and other obligations. Youth also receive victim awareness education during their stay in the facility.

Applying Restorative Justice to the Boot Camp Model

Because the mission of the boot camp should be understood in the context of the overall department and the criminal justice system, leaders should consider including victim restoration and community reparation as primary (or complementary) goals of the camp. Activities then would be designed to accomplish that mission.

Paying restitution should be a requirement and a priority of the camp. Consistent with the restorative justice philosophy, one of the primary objectives of the justice process should be to right the wrong to the individual victim. Further, there is some evidence that offenders who do pay restitution are more likely to remain crime free (Schneider and Hughes 1989). These payments should be tracked and reported as success measures for everyone—the victim, the offender, and the system.[5]

Besides providing a new perspective for the offender, victim awareness education or victim impact panels can help victims heal and involve the community in positive ways. They also fulfill the program component time, providing for a full day of activities.

Gordon Bazemore, Ph.D. and Thomas J. Quinn

Trained mediators (often volunteers from the community) can allow victims in a controlled setting to confront their offenders, express their outrage, get questions answered, and better understand the incident. Research has consistently shown that compared to the traditional criminal justice process, victims who partake in such sessions are less fearful, more satisfied with the process and receive their restitution more completely (Umbreit 1995). It also might be possible to use mediators to help resolve disputes and grievances in the facility as is being contemplated in Vermont.

For victims who are unwilling to directly confront their offender, videotaped comments could be offered, or offenders could be videotaped responding to written questions from the victim. The victim is offered this choice in British Columbia with serious and violent offenders. It provides a way of returning to the victim a sense of control that was lost by the criminal act. In fact, in thirty-nine dialogs involving serious offenses (murder, rape, robbery, and aggravated assault), all the victims and all the offenders indicated that they would repeat the process and recommend it to others.

There is much need in the community that supervised labor by offenders can meet. Besides the value of the help, the connection to the community and the sense of having actually paid back the victim are positive features. The public image benefits also should not be underestimated. However, restorative community service cannot mean simply sending individual offenders to parks to pick up trash or to government agencies which struggle to find useful work for them to complete. Rather, what Bazemore and Maloney (1994) call "service on its highest plane" would have the following characteristics: It would be connected to the overall mission and philosophy of repairing the harm, with some relevance to the specific damage and actions, in a direct or symbolic way (Eglash 1976, Bazemore and Maloney 1994). Mentoring and intergenerational linkages would be encouraged as a way to break down barriers and reconnect youth with adults in a structured way (Shine 1990). Economic development would be considered in selecting community service projects for their maximum visible impact, public support, and community betterment. Citizenship and civic participation would expose youth who may not have been involved in such activities to the sense of shared community and reinforce positive messages about resolving problems without violence.

One of the important advanced steps in recovery for substance abusers is "giving it back"—helping other offenders. Offenders could give to their peers. This also can be an important part of a meaningful and restorative rehabilitation process for other offenders, as well.

To begin implementation, learn more about restorative justice by requesting material from the National Criminal Justice Reference Service, the National Institute of Justice, the National Institute of Corrections, the balanced and restorative justice project, or the National Center for Restorative Justice and Mediation at the University of Minnesota. It also may be helpful to visit existing sites where restorative justice is used. Also, training and technical assistance is available from a number of sources; some of it is free.

The second step is to determine what public opinion research in your jurisdiction indicates is desired and acceptable. This may require conducting new surveys or focus groups and should allow for informed opinions with realistic expectations and cost issues included. There is no magic bullet that will make society crime free, and everything has a cost. In turn, an informed public can better inform its policy makers about the acceptable path to follow and support the efforts required to progress in the desired direction.

Third, find out who is interested in your jurisdiction: legislators, victims, offender support groups, community organizations, church groups, business organizations, other criminal justice agencies, particularly judges, prosecutors, and defense counsel. Wherever the energy and zeal are, build on it. Try to get a core group of professionals and community leaders committed to making a difference and willing to create a new and better reality.

Fourth, form a planning group. Either build on an existing coordinating council or create a new one. This group will drive the planning and act as advisory overseer of the restorative aspects of the operation. Involve representatives from various segments of the community. Agree on a mission for the work camp that fits within the corrections and justice system.

Fifth, analyze services available for victims. Are victims informed of available social services? Do they receive restitution statements? Do they have the opportunity to confront offenders in a mediated dialog, or as part of a victim impact panel? Can violated communities request services?

Sixth, design measurable performance objectives and create a system for monitoring progress and providing feedback. Goals may be focused in any number of directions, but be realistic about what can be achieved. Determine what data or subjective measures will determine whether you are accomplishing your objective, and expect to periodically redirect as needed. Have a feedback/review loop in place to allow that to occur.

Seventh, create a work plan. Depending on the focus, you will need to recruit and train mediators or develop a curriculum. Insure that someone is charged with key responsibilities, set a timeline, but expect delays and unanticipated obstacles.

Eighth, train staff and educate the justice system agencies. Allow the opportunity for questions and ongoing suggestions and feedback. Be flexible.

Ninth, set up a public education/media strategy. Meet with editorial boards, submit "op-ed" pieces to the local newspaper, have representatives on local radio or television talk shows, set up a speaker's bureau that offers to attend service and professional organizational meetings, such as Rotary Club lunches. Invite groups, including legislative bodies, into the boot camp/work camp to tour or hold their monthly meeting.

Tenth, set up periodic quality control/program reassessment to redirect the program and goals as needed.

Conclusion

The public expects the criminal justice system to hold offenders accountable—that is one of the alluring elements of the boot camp model. However, should not offenders also be held accountable to right the wrong directly to those they have harmed? The public expects so, and justice requires it. The next generation of boot camp or work camp models should include in the design restorative principles, which can supplement the punitive approach to balance and humanize the justice process while involving the community in ways that will increase their confidence in our justice process.

Notes

1. See for example, Doble Research Associates Inc., *Crime and Corrections: The Views of the People of Oregon*, prepared for the Oregon State-Centered Project and the Edna McConnell Clark Foundation, Englewood Cliffs, New Jersey 1995; *Crime and Corrections: The Views of the People of Vermont*, a report to the Vermont Department of Correction, Englewood Cliffs, New Jersey 1994; Doble, Immerwahr, and Richardson, *Punishing Criminals: The People of Delaware Consider the Options*, prepared by the Public Agenda Foundation for the Edna McConnell Clark Foundation, New York, 1991.

2. Umbreit's study includes four victim-offender mediation programs in different cities in the United States. Before mediation, 25 percent of victims feared being revictimized; afterwards only 10 percent expressed such fear.

3. Some victim organizations look with suspicion at proposals that call for restorative justice. They fear that the victim angle is a cover for more rehabilitation services for the offender. At the same time, there is some notable movement in the victim community to push for these programs. For example, Dr. Marlene Young, Executive Director of the National Organization for Victim Assistance, recognizes that it is in the interest of victims and the general public alike for offenders who are returning to the community to be better prepared to contribute to society. She calls for victim and community involvement and offender competency development (Young 1995).

4. Researcher Tom Castellano suggests that the boot camp mission statement should clearly define the role of the boot camp vis-a-vis the overall correctional system, and explain how its program components achieve that larger mission. We take that one conceptual step further and suggest that the operation should be considered in the broader context of the overall criminal justice system and its mission. This is obviously a far-reaching and time-consuming recommendation, but the lack of focus among the various agencies of justice is an issue of its own demanding attention. We have addressed this further in the last section of this article.

5. Consideration should be given also to redesign of the restitution process for the rest of the system (which is not well organized in most jurisdictions). For example, officials could request technical assistance from local banks or the National Institute of Corrections to review their system and supply some function that may be absent using inmate labor, such as dunning letters, reminder phone calls, and other labor intensive activities.

References

Austin, J., M. Jones, and M. Bolyard. 1990. A Survey of Jail-Operated Boot Camps and Guidelines for Their Implementation. In MacKenzie, D., and Hebert, eds. *Correctional Boot Camps: A Tough Intermediate Sanction—A Research Report.* Washington, D.C.: National Institute of Justice.

Barajas, Eduardo. 1995. Moving Toward Community Justice. In *Topics in Community Corrections, Annual Issue.* Longmont, Colorado: National Institute of Corrections.

Bazemore, G. 1991. New Concepts and Alternative Practice in Community Supervision of Juvenile Offenders: Rediscovering Work Experience and Competency Development. *Journal of Crime and Justice.* 14 (2), 27-52.

Bazemore, G. 1994. Understanding the Response to Reforms Limiting Discretion: Judges' View of Restriction on Detention Intake. *Justice Quarterly.* 11(3), 429-453.

Bazemore, G., and M. Schiff. 1996. Community Justice/Restorative Justice: Prospects for a New Social Ecology for Community Corrections. *International Journal of Comparative and Applied Criminal Justice.* 20 (1), forthcoming.

Bazemore, G., and D. Maloney 1994. Rehabilitating Community Service: Toward Restorative Service in a Balanced Justice System. *Federal Probation.* 58, 24-35.

Bazemore, G., and M. Umbreit. 1995. Rethinking the Sanctioning Function in Juvenile Court: Retributive or Restorative Responses to Youth Crime. *Crime and Delinquency.* 41 (3).

Byrne, J. 1989. Reintegrating the Concept of Community Into Community Based Corrections. *Crime and Delinquency.* 35 (3), 471-499.

Clarke, S., et al. 1991. *Mediation of Interpersonal Disputes: An Evaluation of North Carolina's Programs.* Chapel Hill, North Carolina: Mediation Network of North Carolina.

Coates, R. 1985. *Victim Meets Offender: An Evaluation of Victim-Offender Reconciliation Programs.* Valparaiso, Indiana: Pact Institute of Justice.

Cronin, R. 1994. *Boot Camps For Adults and Juvenile Offenders.* Washington, D.C.: National Institute of Justice.

Doble Research Associates, Inc. 1991. *Crime and Corrections: The Views of the People of Oregon*. Englewood Cliffs, New Jersey: Oregon State-Centered Project and the Edna McConnell Clark Foundation.

Eglash, A. 1976. Beyond Restitution: Creative Restitution. In J. Hudson and B. Galaway, eds. *Restitution in Criminal Justice*. Lexington, Massachusetts: Lexington Books.

Immarigeon, R. 1994. Family Conferencing, Juvenile Offenders, and Accountability. *The Child Advocate*. Fall.

MacKenzie, D., and E. Hebert. 1996. *Correctional Boot Camps: A Tough Intermediate Sanction - A Research Report*. Washington, D.C.: National Institute of Justice.

McElrea, F. W. M. 1994. Restorative Justice—The New Zealand Youth Court: A Model for Development in Other Courts? *Journal of Judicial Administration*. Vol. 4.

Martinez, L. 1996. Summary of information provided by Lois Martinez, Project Staff, letter March 27, 1996.

Pranis, K., and M. Umbreit. 1992. *Public Opinion Research Challenges Perception of Widespread Public Demand for Harsher Punishment*, monograph. Minneapolis, Minnesota: Minnesota Citizens' Council.

Schneider, A., and S. P. Hughes. 1989. Victim Offender Mediation: A Survey of Program Characteristics and Perceptions of Effectiveness. *Crime and Delinquency*. 46 (2).

Schwartz, I., J. Kerbs, D. Hogston, and C. Guillean. 1992. *What the Public Really Wants*, monograph. Lansing, Michigan: Center for the Study of Youth Policy, University of Michigan.

Sheperd, R. 1995. *Executive Summary—Neighborhood Dispute Settlement: An Evaluation Report*. Harrisburg, Pennsylvania: Neighborhood Dispute Settlement of Dauphin County.

Shine, J. 1990. Working paper.

Stutz, W. 1994. *Victim Awareness Educational Program Evaluation*. Prepared for the Washington State Department of Corrections.

Umbreit, M. 1994. *Victim Meets Offender: The Impact of Restorative Justice and Mediation*. Monsey, New York: Criminal Justice Press, Willow Tree Inc.

————. 1995.Umbreit, M. 1995. *Mediation of Criminal Conflict: An Assessment of Programs in Four Canadian Provinces*. Center for Restorative Justice and Mediation, University of Minnesota, in cooperation with the John Howard Society of Manitoba in Winnipeg.

Van Ness, D. et al. 1994. *Restorative Justice Theory and Practice*. Washington, D.C.: Justice Fellowship.

Vermont Department of Corrections. 1995. Chart outline "Restorative Justice in Vermont."

Walgrave, L. 1993. Beyond Retribution and Rehabilitation: Restoration as the Dominant Paradigm in Judicial Intervention Against Juvenile Delinquency. Paper presented at the 11th International Congress on Criminology, Budapest, Hungary, August, 1993.

Young, M. 1995. *Restorative Community Justice: A Call to Action—Discussion Draft*. Washington, D.C.: National Organization for Victim Assistance.

Boot Camp Aftercare Programming: Current Limits and Suggested Remedies

Thomas C. Castellano, Ph.D.

Associate Professor of Criminal Justice, Center for the Study of Crime, Delinquency and Corrections
Southern Illinois University
Carbondale, Illinois

Susan M. Plant

Researcher, Center for the Study of Crime, Delinquency and Corrections
Southern Illinois University
Carbondale, Illinois

As indicated in many of the preceding chapters, there is a widespread consensus in the field that correctional boot camps without a well-developed and integrated aftercare component are doomed to fail in their quest of producing reformed and law-abiding citizens. Despite this common belief, which tends to be supported by available empirical research, most observers of correctional boot camps have decried the fact that very few boot camps have any meaningful aftercare component. This is not to say that there are not any programs that attempt to ease an offender's return back to the community by providing a continuity of care between what is experienced while an individual is incarcerated in a boot camp and what happens to that person when he or she returns to the community. There are some very strong boot camp aftercare programs in existence, and we can learn much from them. Nonetheless, they are the exception to the rule. Why is this the case? What can be done to improve the situation? Providing some answers to these questions is the goal of this chapter. The last few pages of this chapter offer some experientially based recommendations.

We first examine beliefs about the necessity of aftercare programming for boot camp graduates and what the research tells us about how aftercare efforts may affect offender recidivism and community adjustment. After this, we provide an overview of the levels and types of aftercare programming currently existing in the field and present a typology of aftercare efforts. We then focus on the evolution of boot camp programming efforts and show how the establishment of meaningful aftercare efforts has been a central component of that evolution. We describe two well-developed, intensive, and integrated boot camp aftercare programs: New York State's statewide Aftershock program for adult offenders and Maricopa County Probation Department's program for local graduates of Arizona's boot camp (Shock Incarceration Unit). The final section of this chapter presents detailed recommendations for guiding the development and implementation of boot camp programs that feature cost-effective aftercare efforts.

The Common Sense of Boot Camp Aftercare Programming

The widespread consensus that correctional boot camps without a well-developed and integrated aftercare component are doomed to fail has emerged for a variety of reasons. Common sense is perhaps the greatest reason. Boot camps tend to be very short in duration; most program lengths range from three-to-six months. For many, it is inconceivable that programs of such length—however intensive they may be—will have lasting impacts on young offenders who have a multiplicity of needs and must return to homes and environments that do not provide care, support, nurture, or safety. As John Winn, director of education for the Florida Department of Education, has stated, "A lot of folks say no boot camp unless there's aftercare as well. If you've got a fifteen-year-old who's had thirty-nine arrests since age eight, you're not going to turn him around in three months without some support afterward" (Harrington-Lueker 1994).

In demanding aftercare programming, others have focused on how the "military model" has been incorporated into correctional boot camps. Many observers have noted that most correctional boot camps place a heavy emphasis on a military model that does not comport well with models actually used in the armed services. For instance, basic training in the military is a relatively minor step in a much larger process that results in soldiers being trained for a specific duty assignment and eventually serving the nation in that capacity. Boot camps within this model are designed to reduce trainees to their most elemental and common denominators. Attempts also are made to build on the concept of the "team" ("You're in the Army now"), and to smooth the rough edges created by the basic dehumanizing and rebuilding processes of basic training through advanced basic training and subsequent military assignments.

Yet, most contemporary correctional boot camps feature a process of individual reshaping that is much more limited and truncated than that found in the military. The institutional phase of correctional boot camps does not tend to be followed by analogous subsequent phases used in the military. That is, while correctional boot camps often intend to destroy negative patterns of thought and behavior—to "tear the offender down"—few have the time or the programming to "build the person back up." Much too often, correctional boot camp graduates are released back into their communities without getting the advanced training or other benefits that military recruits receive (including jobs). For these reasons, aftercare is crucial. As Dan Zorich, supervisor of the Maricopa County, Arizona Aftershock program, has said with regard to the rationale for his program, "Boot camp is the start. It strips down the offenders, takes down their defenses, and they become ready for change. The Aftershock program builds them back up . . . it puts on the finishing touches. It helps give them the individual skills they need to survive."

What the Empirical Research Tells Us

Boot Camp Evaluations

To date, the evaluative research on correctional boot camps has been limited. Despite this, fairly persuasive evidence shows that aftercare components are necessary ingredients of a boot camp experience that reduces recidivism.

MacKenzie's multisite evaluation of eight correctional boot camps has been the most important research in this area (MacKenzie and Souryal 1994). This multifaceted study of eight state-level adult boot camps generally found that boot camps do not appear to be reducing offender recidivism rates. The boot camp experience did not result in a reduction in recidivism in five states. In three states, boot camp graduates had lower recidivism rates than comparable inmates who served longer prison terms in conventional prisons on at least one measure of recidivism.

The three state boot camp programs that appear somewhat successful in having a positive impact on the offender recidivism rates had some common characteristics. First, intensive supervision of boot camp graduates is a program component in all three states, while prison releasees were generally not intensively supervised upon release from prison. Second, the institutional phase of these programs tended to be longer, contained a stronger rehabilitative focus, and generated higher in-program dropout rates than the other boot camp programs examined. The analyses could not disentangle the effects of particular program features (such as intensive supervision versus in-prison treatment), but other evidence suggests that the likely cause is the postrelease supervision and services provided graduates. Most of this evidence comes from in-depth internal evaluations of boot camp programs that were part of MacKenzie's multisite study.

Evidence from New York State's adult Shock Incarceration program, which has a very strong aftercare component for program graduates (described later in this chapter), indicates that shock graduates are more likely to abstain from using drugs, are more likely to be employed, and are more likely to stay crime free during the first two years of release than are comparable groups of inmates who did not participate in Shock. The totality of the evidence from that state suggests that the cause of these benefits lie in the intensive services and supervision that are part of its Aftershock component (New York State Department of Correctional Services 1992). Because of these findings, New York's Aftershock program has served as a model for other states. For instance, early internal evaluations of Florida's boot camp indicated that the boot camp was having no impact on offender recidivism. This led corrections officials there to conclude that "Florida's Boot Camp program could be strengthened by an improved follow-up component" modeled after New York's "Aftershock" program (Florida Department of Corrections 1990: 25).

Internal evaluations of Illinois' boot camps found that boot camp graduates were much more likely to be returned to prison within two years than the comparison group for technical violations, but that boot camp graduates were less likely to be returned to prison for the commission of new crimes. Agency reports attribute these differences to the much greater level of supervision provided boot camp graduates (which includes three months of monitoring on electronic detention) than is provided traditional prison releasees who are largely unsupervised (Illinois Department of Corrections 1994: 22-24).

Evaluations of Louisiana's boot camp program have led to the conclusion that it does not appear that the in-program phase of the boot camp experience has had any discernible impact on offender recidivism or community adjustment. The generally more positive adjustment of shock graduates in the community (including their participation in positive social activities) and patterns in failure rates appear most likely to be the result of the intensive supervision component of the program (MacKenzie, Shaw, and Gowdy 1990; MacKenzie and Shaw 1993).

Drug Treatment Research

Support for the benefits of strong aftercare programming also comes from allied research efforts in the drug treatment, intensive community supervision, and juvenile correctional literature. The drug treatment literature is especially relevant to boot camp programming because many boot camps target drug offenders (even if only by excluding violent offenders).

Researchers have found specific therapeutic strategies and program characteristics to produce efficacious results among substance abusing criminal offenders. For instance, Andrews and Keisling (1980), Wellisch, Anglin, and Pendergast (1993), and Peters (1993) have each suggested principles of effective treatment that parallel the principles espoused by the other researchers. A primary principle, based on dozens and dozens of studies that have tracked drug abusers into the community, is that "effective drug treatment programs involve sustained offender participation in substance abuse treatments that last at least three months." Most boot camps do not adhere to this principle because of their limited duration and extensive nontreatment programming. However, other principles of effective drug treatment are germane. For instance, research and experts highly recommend that continuing care during transition and return to the community, and a lengthy period of supervision in the community, be made integral parts of the treatment program. Moreover, early in the program, transition planning for inmates returning to the community should be in place. Finally, community resources must be used to provide services relevant to inmates' needs. All of these principles of effective drug treatment for criminal justice populations are based on a wealth of empirical research. Thus, even relatively short boot camp programs may be effective in dealing with offender substance abuse if these principles guide programming efforts. The key to effectiveness appears to be drug treatment in the community as part of an integrated aftercare program.

Intensive Community Supervision Research

A growing body of literature on intensive probation/parole programs (ISP) has generated fairly negative results. Intensive supervision does not appear to reduce offender recidivism. Some people argue these negative results have tended to result from the overriding emphasis most intensive probation/parole programs have placed on the surveillance, control, and punitive functions of community supervision. They contend that supervision programs that merge control with rehabilitation are more likely to achieve favorable results (see Gendreau, Cullen, and Bonta 1994). Earlier studies that examined intensive supervision and mandated treatment of drug offenders suggest they may be right. Coupled with studies on the effectiveness of intensive probation supervision that indicate probationers who received more treatment as part of their probation performed better on probation than those who received less treatment (Petersilia and Turner 1993), there is some reason to believe that intensive parole supervision programs that demand offender treatment may promote beneficial results in terms of reduced recidivism. Thus, while aftercare for boot camp graduates appears vital, it is also necessary that these aftercare programs go beyond intensive surveillance and result in the delivery of treatment services to offenders.

Juvenile Corrections Literature

Most of the evaluations and literature discussed derive from correctional interventions with adults, but the same issues apply to programs for juveniles, and perhaps even more forcefully. Indeed, the juvenile corrections literature on aftercare is quite consistent with these findings. For instance, the Office of Juvenile Justice and Delinquency Prevention (OJJDP), United States Department of Justice, has recently sponsored the development of a model intensive aftercare program for high-risk juveniles. The model was designed, in part, to address one of the major problems besetting the juvenile correctional system:

> . . . the inability to transition offenders from closely monitored and highly regimented life in a secure institutional environment to unstructured and often confusing life in a community. The difficulties posed in providing continuity of service and supervision between institutional confinement and community living have long plagued efforts to successfully achieve successful community adjustment for juvenile offenders (Altschuler and Armstrong 1994: 7).

In response to this situation, Altschuler and Armstrong have recently developed a prototype intensive aftercare program model for high-risk youth (the type that enter juvenile boot camps). They write: " . . . any attempt to lower rates of recidivism with high-risk juvenile offenders on parole must include a substantial intensification of intervention strategies providing social control and service provision" (1994: 3).

The implications of this research have not been lost on correctional policy makers and program administrators. Partially because of the limits of early boot camps in the area of aftercare programming, we have witnessed a desired evolution in boot camp programming. Much of the progress has focused on the delivery of aftercare programming that goes well beyond basic probation and/or parole supervision. Nonetheless, the field still has a long way to go. These issues are discussed next.

What Do We Mean by Aftercare?

Aftercare is not a term that is commonly used in the world of adult corrections. The term is much more common in juvenile corrections and in addiction's-treatment literature. In both fields, aftercare has been associated closely with rehabilitative ideology, and the notion that treatment interventions that take place within institutions are unlikely to be successful in changing people unless they are coupled and coordinated with treatment interventions in the community. "Aftercare" is thus a term that is generally linked to a rehabilitative goal, and implies much more than traditional parole surveillance and supervision. Concepts such as community-based treatment, continuity of care, offender assessment and classification, and case management are commonly viewed as essential elements of an effective aftercare program. Surveillance, while perhaps a necessary component of an effective aftercare program, is not a defining characteristic of aftercare. Aftercare's essence is care, usually conceived of in terms of interventions that directly tackle the criminogenic needs and characteristics presented by an offender. Surveillance and other forms of external control, while perhaps valuable, alone do not constitute aftercare in the traditional sense of the term.

Some would argue further that because the primary determinants of successful offender adjustments are found on the streets and not in prison, the period of aftercare should be comparable to or longer than the period of incarceration. Moreover, this extended aftercare component should involve a service delivery focus that is even more intensive than when the offender was behind bars.

The Evolution of Boot Camp Programming

These lessons have been recognized and, as a result, we have been witnessing a positive evolution in boot camp programming. The earliest boot camps, sometimes referred to as "First Generation" camps, which came onto the correctional scene in 1983, tended to have a heavy emphasis on military-based program activities but had little treatment or aftercare programming. "Second Generation" boot camps, which began to emerge in the late 1980s and early 1990s, tended to follow the lead of some of the earlier treatment-oriented programs (such as New York's Shock Incarceration program). They toned down the military emphasis and began to increase substance abuse, educational, and cognitive programming. They made attempts to provide boot camp graduates with greater levels of postrelease supervision and services.

Some observers of correctional boot camps suggest that "Third Generation" programs are now beginning to emerge (Parent 1996). These programs involve the search for alternative boot camp models (such as empowerment, leadership, and work ethic) that move away from an emphasis on militaristic program components and which are program rich. Importantly, aftercare programs that are integrated into institutionally based interventions and which emphasize a continuity of treatment and services once the offender reenters the community are a hallmark of these more advanced programs. Unfortunately, these latter programs still are quite uncommon, and especially so in relation to boot camps for adults. To illustrate this point, we present a brief overview of aftercare components associated with boot camps.

The Nature of Current Boot Camp Aftercare Programming

The common denominator in boot camp aftercare approaches appears to be the use of community supervision through probation or parole officers (depending on whether the boot camp program is established as a probation component or part of an incarceration sanction). However, beyond the basic commonality of parole or probation supervision, there is wide variation in the scope and type of services provided to boot camp releasees. Inspection of these differences suggests that aftercare delivery may be categorized into the four levels or program models, which are summarized in Table 1, on the next page.

At the first level, aftercare closely resembles traditional parole or probation supervision. That is, officers act as service brokers referring the boot camp graduates to available treatment programs in the community. This approach relies heavily on existing community programs such as Alcoholics Anonymous and Narcotics Anonymous (12 step programs), community mental health units, Treatment Alternatives to Street Crimes (TASC), and Boys and Girls Clubs. Here, the linkages between the aftercare provider and the boot camp program are informal and loosely structured. Also, the boot camp staff usually have little direct contact or knowledge regarding the offender once he or she graduates from the facility, and the decision authority for aftercare placement comes from the probation/parole agency or the courts, rather than from the boot camp facility.

A second, more structured level of this approach is the use of an intensive supervision model seen in states such as Georgia, Illinois, and Pennsylvania. In this enhanced supervision approach, caseloads are intensively supervised with more frequent contact and additional requirements such as curfew, frequent urinalysis testing, and a more structured treatment referral process. This approach generally provides greater continuity of treatment since the specialized probation/parole officers may be identified as part of the boot camp program, and have more extensive contact with the institutional staff than occurs in

Table 1.: Boot Camp Aftercare Program Models

Brokerage Model	Enhanced Brokerage Model
Traditional parole/probation supervision	Intensive parole/probation
Use of existing treatment resources	*Specialized caseloads or intensively supervised caseloads
Minimal contact between boot camp facility staff and community supervision staff	*Specialized requirement for boot camp releasees (such as curfew, frequent urinalysis testing)
Treatment placement decision rests with parole/probation agency rather than with facility	Use of existing treatment testing resources but with structured referral process
	Parole/probation staff may identify themselves as part of boot camp program
	Treatment placement decision continues to be channeled through parole/probation agency
Contracted Vendors Model	**Comprehensive Models**
Intensive parole/probation supervision	Intensive parole/probation supervision
Contracted treatment vendors are secured to provide services	Integrated program developed and formalized as part of boot camp program continuum
Direct linkage between boot camp facility and treatment provider(s)	*Substance abuse treatment/ relapse prevention
*Formalized agreement exists stipulating treatment parameters (such as type, length, and assessment costs)	*Job development/placement
Formalized mechanisms for placement	*Education/training
	*Housing assistance
	*Life-skills programming
	Established linkages between boot camp facility/program and community services

*Adapted from Cowles, E. L. and T. Castellano. 1995. *Boot Camp Drug Treatment and Aftercare Intervention: An Evaluation Review*. Washington, D.C.: National Institute of Justice.

the more traditional probation/parole scenario. There also may be a concerted effort on the part of the parent agency(ies) to identify the boot camp program as a continuum with both institutional and release components. Still at this level, the provision of services continues to be channeled primarily through referral by the supervising officer to existing community programs on an ad hoc basis.

At the third level, contracted vendors are secured to provide various treatments for boot camp graduates in addition to their community supervision. The difference between this approach and the brokerage, or even enhanced brokerage strategy previously identified, is the direct involvement of probation/parole officers who may be identified as part of the boot camp program, and have more extensive contact with the institutional staff than under the traditional parole/probation scenario. In the brokerage approach, the connection between the facility and the treatment provider is mediated by the supervising officer/agency. In this vendor model, formal agreements are developed between the boot camp facility/agency and the provider(s) stipulating the parameters of treatment (such as treatment length and type, assessment, costs, and other concerns). In addition, the mechanisms for placement of the offenders into the treatment program are formalized. States specifying the use of vendors include Ohio and the juvenile boot camps in Florida.

The fourth and final level of aftercare services might be characterized best as a "comprehensive" model. In this approach, a structured mechanism for the provision of aftercare services is established. This integrates multiple treatment elements which go beyond substance abuse treatment/relapse prevention and parole or probation supervision. These programs emphasize transitional services such as job development and placement, education, housing assistance, and life-skills programming. While the other three levels may essentially achieve this level of programming, the identifying characteristics of the comprehensive program includes the fact that these elements are developed and formalized as part of the boot camp program continuum structure. New York was the first state with extensive boot camp aftercare services reaching this level; and even in this state, the aftercare program servicing offenders from the five boroughs of New York City is much more developed than for other areas in the state.

California has a strong aftercare component (Cronin 1994) in both its adult and juvenile boot camps (Bourque *et al.* 1996). Cronin also notes that juvenile boot camps were more attentive to the aftercare component of their programs, citing Denver, Cleveland, and Mobile programs as having treatment in addition to the supervisory function of parole/probation. This also was supported by the 1996 National Institute of Justice Report (Bourque *et al.* 1996), which clearly demonstrated that the Florida juvenile programs had an elaborate aftercare network.

As might be expected, there are variants on these four approaches to the provision of aftercare services. For programs such as Montana's Swan River Correctional Training Center, aftercare placement is dependent on release status. In Montana, 90 percent of releasees are sent to a prerelease center where they participate in work or training programs and engage in various types of counseling activities. The remaining 10 percent are placed on intensive supervision with electronic monitoring. Their program participation is left to the discretion of the individual probation/parole officers and is dependent on program availability in their county of release.

A more detailed glimpse into the types of aftercare programming used in boot camps can be found in a 1996 National Institute of Justice Research Report (Bourque *et al.* 1996) which provides an inventory of fifty-two state, local, and juvenile boot camps. Aftercare programming in these facilities generally can be broken down into two categories: transitional/residential and "special aftercare" (see Table 2). Fifteen programs offered some type of transitional program, with most involving community residential placement for the first few months following release. These residential programs generally are oriented toward readying the releasee for life in the community, and involve drug counseling and job readiness. California, Texas, and two federal boot camps in Pennsylvania and Texas offer residential work release, and New York and North Carolina offer temporary housing for those releasees who have not secured an acceptable place to live following release.

The Texas (CORE) boot camp offers an interesting example of transitional/residential programming. After spending 105 days in the program, inmates enter a fifteen-day transitional phase in which they work in a government or nonprofit agency. They are not under direct supervision at work, but they do return to the boot camp in the evening. Following this, they are eligible for work release from the institution for the remainder of their sentence (usually sixty days). At this juncture, they can engage in full-time work or education, but they must return to the boot camp in the evening, participate in CORE activities, and pay a daily rent (minimum $5). In this case, the boot camp acts as its own transitional facility.

Special aftercare programming tends to focus on treatment/rehabilitation. Florida, for example, has built a system of juvenile boot camps that provide for aftercare programming at community service centers. Releasees live at home, but are transported daily to the centers, attending school there for the first few months following release. The centers offer a variety of programs, including drug counseling, anger management, life skills, and others. Recent changes in the program involve varying the length of aftercare depending on risk: low-risk youths receive two months of aftercare, minimum-risk four months, and high-risk at least four months (Cass and Kaltenecker 1996).

In summary, there is wide variation in the type and level of aftercare services available to offenders completing a boot camp program. For many programs "aftercare" seems to be fairly traditional probation/parole supervision—sometimes augmented by closer supervision, drug testing, and referral to existing community treatment resources. A small number of jurisdictions have developed more formalized linkages with treatment providers (who generally service noncorrectional populations as well). Fewer yet have extended the continuum of treatment back into the community in a substantial way.

Table 2.: Aftercare Components by Program Types

Transitional\Residential Program Type	Location*/Length Special Requirements
Unspecified/ when appropriate	**AZ** 90-120 days; **OR**
Residential work release	**CA** 60 days **TX** (CORE) 15 day prelease Federal (**PA** & **TX**) during phase I
Halfway house	**KY** 120 days if sub. abuse needs **WI** 80% released for 3-6 months
Prerelease center/ Community residential center/ Transitional facility	**MD** (or home detention) **MT** 1-60 days nonintensive probation cases **FL** 4-6 months **FL** Leon(J)45-60 days; **MI** up to 90 days **OH**(J)
Temporary housing and support	**NY** up to 90 days **NC**
Home visits during day	Federal (**PA** & **TX**) prerelease phase

(Table continues on the next page)

*Unless otherwise indicated by a specific location, programs are state-run. (J) refers to juvenile boot camps.

Table 2.: Aftercare Components by Program Types (Continued)

Special Aftercare Programming (Other Than Transitional/ Residential)	Location/Length Special Requirements
Not Specified	**AZ**/ **MA**/ **NH** biweekly/ 6 months/ **TX** Hidalgo-weekly 1M/ biweekly 6M
Group meeting/acupuncture	**MI** 120 days if sub. abuse needs
Life skills/group support	**TX** Harris
Attendance at Boys and Girls Clubs	**AL (J)** Weekly
Multiple treatments (drug, vocational, counseling)	**CA (J)**/ **FL** Leon, Manatee, Martin, Pinellas (J)/ **NY** (Contracted out)
City Challenge/day treatment program	**NY** South Kortwright (J)
Regular supervision (primarily)	**AL**/ **AR**/ **FL**/ **GA**-Inmate/ **NV**/ **SC**/ **TX**/ **WY**/ **MI**-Oakland/**TX**-Brazos/ **AL**(J)/ **CO**(J)
Intensive supervision/electronic monitoring	**AZ**/ **CA**/ **ID**/ **KS**/ **OH**/ **OR**/ **PA**/ **WI**/ **NY** Nassau, NYC/ **CA** (J)
Combination/other (usually intensive supervision followed by regular supervision)	**CO**/ **GA**-Prob/ **IL**/ **KY**/ **MI**/ **MN**/ **MS**/ **MT**/ **NH**/ **NY**/ **NC**/ **OK**-SIP/ **OK**-RID/ **TN**/ **VA**/ Federal (**PA** & **TX**)/ **CA**-Santa Clara/ **TX**-Harris, Travis, Hidalgo/ **FL**-Leon, Manatee, Martin, Pinellas (J) **OH** (J)/ **NY** (J)

Examples of Strong Program Models

Maricopa County's Aftershock Program

An example of an intensive aftercare boot camp component is Maricopa County Probation Department's Aftershock Transition program. It is designed to provide a smooth transition back into the community for Maricopa residents who have successfully graduated from the Arizona Department of Corrections Shock Incarceration program. Intensive probation is required by statute for all Shock graduates. Probation services are provided by the county probation department in the offender's county of residence.

Soon after the Shock Incarceration Program began in 1989, it was apparent that failure rates among the Maricopa County shock graduates were very high—revocation rates were as high as 50 percent. Over half of the revocations took place within ninety days of graduation. This resulted in more system crowding and suggested that the needs of shock offenders were not being met by the existing intensive probation structure. In particular, probation staff felt that offender problems were centered around their lack of suitable housing, employment, and basic living skills.

The staff created a specialized caseload for shock graduates. They enhanced programming and surveillance and sought to maintain some of the structure experienced in the boot camp. One major premise of the emerging Aftershock program was the perceived necessity of maintaining the group cohesion among Shockers that was started in the boot camp. Probation officers began running "Aftershock" meetings on Wednesday nights. This allowed the graduates to get together and to talk about their common problems. On many occasions, drill instructors from the boot camp would donate their time and attend the meetings to enhance the support function of the meetings. Group activities then expanded to Friday nights, and tended to revolve around recreational events. Saturdays were devoted to community service projects, at which Shockers would work alongside probation officers. Then, job searches took on a team approach; groups of shockers and probation officers would seek jobs together. These efforts proved quite effective, with most Shockers finding employment and employers beginning to view Shockers as reliable and hard-working individuals. Shockers realized this was happening, and their commitment to the group encouraged them not to jeopardize the employment prospects of their peers. Finally, probation staff realized that suitable and supportive housing arrangements were lacking for a good number of Shockers. Thus, staff began a search for a transitional housing facility.

In January 1992, probation staff collaborated with The New Day Educational Center, a local transitional living program, in seeking funds for an Aftershock Transitional Center. External funding was not achieved, but with rent paid by the shock graduates and assistance from the Center, the program was implemented in April 1992. It operated until October, 1993 when it was relocated to Garfield House, which is also the site of an Adult Probation Day Reporting Center.

The Aftershock program thus emerged slowly and as result of perceived inadequacies in existing aftercare services for Shockers. The program was initiated by street level probation staff who had been working with the Shockers. They realized that the increased surveillance, by itself, was not resulting in the beneficial impacts they desired. Accordingly, they began to do more. They incrementally added service delivery efforts to the foundation of intensive probation supervision. The result is an aftercare program that can serve as a model for other jurisdictions. Next is a description of some current program components in the Aftershock program.

A probation staff member (Aftershock Coordinator) assesses each graduate from the Shock Program prior to his graduation and determines which graduates will participate in the Aftershock program. Shock graduates from Maricopa County assigned to other intensive probation supervision caseloads may be transferred to Aftershock if their situation suggests this would be an appropriate assignment.

The Aftershock Coordinator has worked with each offender since before the offender's disposition was made by the sentencing judge, and thus knows each client well. She has personally gone through the Shock Incarceration training process and maintains a regular presence during the four-month program. Information sharing between the Shock and Aftershock staff is strong, providing for durable links between the programs and a continuity of care.

Aftershock "teams" include two surveillance officers and one probation officer. Team staff are encouraged to interact extensively, and to support community service, recreational, and employment searches as a team. There are currently two distinct Aftershock caseloads, one for offenders who are not in the transitional living component (about thirty offenders), and the other for those in residence at the Living Center (maximum of twenty-eight).

Supervision requirements imposed on Shockers are the same as for all intensive probation/parole program cases. Three phases of supervision exist—each averages three months, with required contact levels decreasing as a probationer progresses through the phases. Surveillance expectations are the sole responsibility of surveillance officers. A separate probation officer manages community service requirements while a court clerk monitors restitution orders.

Upon entry into the Aftershock program, the supervising probation officer prepares a case management plan based on risk and need factors. Cases are under the house arrest and supervisory requirements of the intensive probation/parole program. Length of stay generally spans ninety days or more. Successful stay in the program results in transfer to another intensive probation/parole caseload for supervision.

Program interventions include community restitution, community service, educational/vocational activities, general and substance abuse counseling, and random urinalyses. The Aftershock component provides transitional housing for the neediest cases and also emphasizes community service, athletics, and job search skills. There is a strong emphasis on the use of existing community services.

A private drug treatment firm has been contracted to provide Shockers with treatment programming. It has implemented an eleven-week outpatient program that takes a cognitive/behavioral and psycho/educational approach to drug treatment. The program is being delivered by a full-time certified substance abuse counselor. All Shockers are screened and assessed through the use of the Addiction Severity Index when they enter the program. All Shockers must complete an education-only program component. This is for those with a nonsevere drug history. The education program lasts eight weeks and includes three-hour sessions once per week. The core of the program for most Shockers is primary group counseling. Each client is required to complete a total of thirty-three groups (eleven weeks, three times per week, two-hour sessions). Primary group members are also expected to attend three outside AA/NA meetings per week. On completion of the primary group counseling phase, offenders enter the aftercare phase. Two-hour sessions offered once a week are required for twelve weeks. Shockers also are expected to attend AA/NA meetings twice weekly during this phase. Individual counseling is also a drug treatment program component.

This transitional living program component is found in one wing of the Garfield House, and has the capacity to house up to twenty-eight Shockers. It is designed to be a temporary, safe place for shock graduates to reside, find employment, and return to the community being self-sufficient. While in residence, most of the Shockers work during the day and participate in programming during the evening (education, chemical dependency). The goal is to have a resident stay no more than ninety days, but some have stayed up to six months.

Employment services are a very impressive component of aftershock. A job developer on staff helps Shockers set up savings accounts, engage in financial planning, and broker jobs; however, all of the probation staff—including surveillance officers—have prioritized the goal of finding their clients work. They go to prospective employers and try to create jobs for the Shockers. They have been very successful. Almost all Shockers have been able to find steady work.

An educational program is also part of the aftershock intervention. Literacy centers, daytime English as a Second Language (ESL), and general equivalency diploma classes as well as a nighttime English as a Second Language class are offered. The classes are open to the public. Both individualized tutoring and classroom instruction are available. Shockers are in educational programming two-and a half-hours per day four days a week. On Saturdays, they participate in a life skills course for two hours (over a six-week period) and a parenting course for two hours.

New York State's Aftershock Program

New York State's Shock Incarceration program was one of the first, if not the first boot camp program, to be based on the twin pillars: discipline and treatment. Moreover, from the very start, aftercare was perceived as a key element in their successful boot camp venture. Accordingly, in the early planning stages, a joint task force of the Department of Correctional Services and the Division of Parole was created to develop a Shock model that incorporated discipline, treatment, and aftercare. Elements of drill and ceremony, hard physical labor, and education were added to two existing program formats that emphasized life skills/decision making and substance abuse treatment, to form the institutional program core.

New York's program also takes the position that aftercare is an important and integral part of the shock experience. That is, the program encompasses a continuum of care that includes both the incarceration and the community release components. Further, it advocates a comprehensive model of aftercare that combines elements of intensive supervision, education and/or vocational training, job development and placement, some type of continuing program to maintain cognitive and behavior changes initiated in the in-program phase, and continued substance abuse or relapse-prevention treatment.

In New York, the release portion of the program is initiated two or three months prior to an offender's release date. The institutional parole officer puts together a condensed parole summary which is reviewed by the parole board. Information on the offender's planned residence is forwarded to the field offices for investigation. In turn, the field offices report back to the institutional parole office on the suitability of the residence. The offender does not actually appear before the board, but the board must approve the offender's release, which is done routinely.

Shock releasees originally were placed into intensive supervision caseloads of about forty offenders supervised by a team of two officers. In 1995, one officer became responsible for a caseload of twenty-five graduates. The intensive supervision requirements include weekly home visits by the officers, a curfew, and weekly urinalysis testing. After six months under the intensive supervision regime, successful shock parolees are moved to a regular supervision status; however, the board still may place special conditions on the offender.

All New York City shock parolees are guaranteed a job on release. Through an agreement with the Vera Institute's Neighbor Work Program, shock parolees are placed into a structured program working in neighborhood renovation projects. The work is structured as a job development program, with the offender spending four days a week on the job and on the fifth visiting a job developer. The eventual goal of this effort is to move the offender into stable full-time regular employment.

Until 1996, a contract with the New York City Episcopal Mission Society provided a continuation of the institutional program (Network) that emphasizes positive decision-making skills. Each week for a period of three months after release, Shock graduates participate in a community meeting, a four-part meeting, and a clearing meeting. These meetings currently are run by parole officers. Substance abuse and relapse prevention counseling is provided through the Fellowship Center, and includes both group and individual counseling services that are provided during the first six months of release. Additionally, shock parolees are strongly encouraged to participate in AA/NA meetings. A slogan commonly voiced during the institutional program is "ninety meetings in ninety days."

Clearly, New York's aftershock program provides a much greater level of programming and services to graduates from the New York City area than graduates who return to other parts of the state. This tends to be true across the board: boot camp graduates from less densely populated areas do not receive the same level of services as graduates from more urban areas. This pitfall is difficult to overcome.

Recommendations for Practitioners

The New York and Maricopa aftercare examples illustrate a number of lessons. First, there is no single right way to develop and implement a successful aftercare program. In New York, the impetus for aftershock came from the highest levels of the correctional administration and involved early and on-going collaboration between two agencies. The program was initially conceptualized as having two distinct but complementary phases: the first institutional, and the second community based. In contrast, the Maricopa program originated in a totally different manner. Rank and file probation officers saw problems in what was happening to boot camp graduates when they were returning home. They banded together, and with few to no resources and little organizational support, they attempted to remedy the deficiencies of an inadequate program model. While they did receive support from their local administrators and the federal government, the Arizona Department of Corrections—which administers the shock program—was not a formal partner in the aftershock program. This may help to explain the Department's recent decision to close down the Shock Incarceration Unit. Viewed as failing to achieve its goals, the Department apparently did little to ensure the success of the Shock Incarceration Unit.

Based on what we now know, there should be little need to replicate Maricopa's experience. While it can serve as a model to remedy deficiencies with existing programs, New York's approach is preferred if a jurisdiction is contemplating the establishment of a new program. The following recommendations are built on the experience of New York and other jurisdictions which have had some success in establishing bona fide and potentially effective boot camp aftercare programming.

Recommendation #1

Correctional agencies cannot do business as usual if they want to establish effective boot camps. They must be proactive in educating the public and policy makers about what works and what does not work within boot camps.

Agencies involved in the funding, development, and implementation of boot camps must reinforce, both within the organization and externally, the necessity to develop boot camps that have therapeutic integrity. Therapeutic integrity requires meaningful institutionally based treatment programming and a strong aftercare component. Political and correctional demands for programs oriented primarily toward hard work, physical training, and drill and ceremony must be countered by educational efforts that address the fact that such programming structures have not been found to produce the desired outcomes. While more treatment-oriented boot camps facilities that contain meaningful aftercare components have not yet been found to be successful in affecting recidivism rates, they are the ones that are suggested by both current theory and research to be most likely to achieve such results.

Boot camps have expanded throughout the nation--oftentimes without adequate conceptualizing and planning at the local level. Many jurisdictions have implemented boot camps in response to political demands, without adequate input provided by treatment professionals or community corrections experts. This often has resulted in too little being offered too late. While citizens and politicians may feel good about having a boot camp in their jurisdiction, there is often little in place to ensure program success on dimensions of central value (such as reducing recidivism and lowering long-term correctional costs).

For instance, aftercare programming often has been introduced into a boot camp program only as an afterthought or because legislators have felt the need to "punish" the offender more than is allowed by a three-to-six month period of incarceration. Many states have adopted program designs from other states, sometimes with only minor modifications. This is not necessarily desirable. What may "work" there may not be applicable or appropriate to differing legal structures and program environments. Wholesale duplication of programs without adequate consideration of how the programs should be modified and/or tailored to best fit differing environments and offender populations has been an undesirable feature of the boot camp movement. This leads to the second recommendation.

Recommendation #2:
Stronger and more comprehensive planning processes that include the input of community corrections professionals should occur prior to the implementation of a boot camp. All possible efforts should be made to conceptualize and operationalize the boot camp experience as a continuum that includes both an institutional and aftercare phase. This would include extensive enhancements to pre-release and postrelease programming efforts that ensure a continuity of care throughout the respective program phases. Legislative and organizational barriers to such efforts must be addressed and reduced.

The implementation of this recommendation is no easy matter. Historically, corrections has not been a unified field. Prison work and workers have long been considered distinct and different from the work and employees of community corrections. Organizational boundaries have been built and institutionalized; the walls separating the two enterprises are tall and thick—even when a single agency contains both institutional (prison) and field service (parole) divisions. Thus, bringing the two together in the pursuit of a common goal is often difficult, especially now when budgets are shrinking relative to work demands. Nonetheless, successful boot camp programming requires such boundary-spanning efforts. Otherwise, the implementation of aftercare programming that is continuous, seamless, and integrated with institutionally based efforts aimed at promoting offender change is not likely to be successful. Having strong administrative leadership within the involved agencies and a willingness to be "partners" in boot camp programming is a key ingredient of success.

Recommendation #3:

Standardized, comprehensive assessment procedures and case management aftercare systems designed to match inmates to supervision levels and treatment services according to results of the assessment and classification are highly desirable.

Legislative and policy standards often require all boot camp graduates to experience similar levels of aftercare programming and supervision. Aftercare programming seems to be driven to a large extent by general structural and administrative concerns relating to boot camps, rather than by offender needs or risks. For instance, it appears that the predominant mechanism for placement of boot camp graduates into specific postrelease supervision levels or treatment programming comes not through an individual assessment of risk and need, but rather through a legally mandated or nonindividualized decision process. In many states, all boot camp graduates are required by statute to be placed on intensive supervision for a certain period of time. All graduates of some boot camps are required by internal policy to attend monthly group meetings, despite the fact that they may not benefit from the meetings and the meetings pose considerable inconvenience (for example, attendance requires a two-hour drive, loss of work time, and other issues).

In other instances, the parole board may require all persons convicted of a drug offense to receive substance abuse services in the community. These requirements tend to waste valuable aftercare resources; yet, they appear to be common. Without the aid of a decent classification system that is actually tied into a case management system that drives intervention decisions, even the strongest service delivery system will result in the wrong offenders receiving the wrong services at the wrong time. While it is nice to think that all boot camp graduates require intensive supervision or a wide array of treatment services—that aftercare is necessary for everyone—research tends to indicate this is not true and perhaps even counterproductive in outcome. Thus, costly aftercare interventions should be individualized and allocated judiciously.

Recommendation #4:

Aftercare staff members should be cross-trained with institutional staff members, have frequent and intensive contact with the facility and its staff, and, if at all possible, be employees of the same organization/subunit that administers the boot camp.

Oftentimes, community correctional staff who supervise and provide assistance to boot camp graduates know little about the institutional phase of the program. Programming philosophies, interventions, and prerelease programming efforts are not made known to such officials, and they have few organizationally based incentives to become familiar with such things. To avoid this common situation, aftercare agents should be fully exposed to all institutionally based activities. Staff crosstraining, required aftercare agent presence at the facility (especially in terms of prerelease and transitional programming), and common employment structures are methods to promote effective aftercare provisions. Combinations of these have been achieved at many boot camp programs and should be emulated by newly emerging programs and programs attempting to enhance current aftercare programming.

Recommendation #5:

Boot camp and aftercare administrators must not sell the program short. Effective aftercare programming is costly, and necessary expenditures must be made. Pursuit of extra-corrections dollars for the delivery of services is often necessary to supplement agency funds, but such attempts can be and often are successful (such as funds from federal and state entitlement programs). Further, aftercare agents must be advocates for their clients and seek out community resources. This involves developing partnerships with other criminal justice and social service agencies that can aid in providing needed services to boot camp graduates. A full array of services that address criminogenic needs should be available, including housing, substance abuse treatment, mental health counseling, and educational and employment services. The service and treatment provisions should be emphasized at least co-equally with surveillance.

Many boot camp advocates argue that treatment and aftercare programming is not very costly. This is not necessarily the case. The presence of highly qualified and competent staff who are better able to meet client needs because they have manageable caseloads requires the expenditure of considerable personnel dollars. Contracts with community-based treatment providers also tend to get quite expensive. Yet, they are essential elements of effective aftercare programming. The lack of an adequate budget to deliver the necessary staff and services to boot camp graduates will result in program failure, regardless of whatever else has been accomplished.

Accordingly, program administrators and budget officials must be creative in accessing the funds necessary to deliver needed program services. This may include seeking funding external to the involved corrections agencies, and closely monitoring expenditures to weed out those costs that are not promoting goal achievement. Perhaps most importantly, as revealed by prior research, it is absolutely necessary that aftercare efforts address the basic needs that resulted in the offender entering the boot camp in the first instance.

While adherence to these recommendations may not ensure the establishment of a successful boot camp aftercare component, it is fairly clear that aftercare efforts lacking these qualities are those that tend to be unsuccessful. The challenges and obstacles are daunting; yet, we have been witness to programs that have prevailed nonetheless. We encourage others to follow their lead.

References/Further Reading

Altschuler, D. M., and T. L. Armstrong. 1994. Intensive Aftercare for High-risk Juveniles: Policies and Procedures. Washington, D.C.: Office of Juvenile Justice and Delinquency Prevention, United States Department of Justice.

Andrews, D. A., and J. J. Keisling. 1980. Program Structure and Effective Correctional Practices: A Summary of the CAVIL Research. In *Effective Correctional Treatment*. Ross and Gendreau, eds. Toronto: Butterworths.

Anglin, M. D., and Y. Hser. 1990. Treatment of Drug Abuse. In *Drugs and Crime*. M. Tonry and J. Q. Wilson, eds. Chicago: University of Chicago Press.

Bottomly, K. A. 1990. Parole in Transition: A Comparative Study of Origins, Developments, and Prospects for the 1990s. In *Crime and Justice: A Review of Research*, M. Tonry and N. Morris, eds. Vol. 10. Chicago: University of Chicago Press.

Bourque, B. B., M. Han, and S. M. Hill. 1996. *An Inventory of Aftercare Provisions for 52 Boot Camp Programs*. Washington, D.C.: National Institute of Justice.

Cass, E., and N. Kaltenecker. 1996. The Development and Operation of Juvenile Boot Camps in Florida. In *Correctional Boot Camps: A Tough Intermediate Sanction*. MacKenzie and Hebert, eds. Washington, D.C.: National Institute of Justice.

Cowles, E. L., and T. Castellano. 1995. *Boot Camp Drug Treatment and Aftercare Intervention: An Evaluation Review.* Washington, D.C.: National Institute of Justice.

Cronin, R. C. 1994. *Boot Camps for Adult and Juvenile Offenders: Overview and Update.* Washington, D.C.: National Institute of Justice.

Florida Department of Corrections. 1990. Boot Camp: A Twenty-five Month Review. Unpublished report by the Bureau of Planning, Research, and Statistics. Tallahassee, Florida.

Gendreau, P., F. T. Cullen, and J. Bonta. 1994. Intensive Rehabilitation Supervision: The Next Generation in Community Corrections? *Federal Probation.* 58(1): 72-78.

Harrington-Lueker, D. 1994. Are Boot Camps the Answer? *American School Board Journal.* December.

Illinois Department of Corrections. 1994. Impact Incarceration Program: 1993 Annual Report to the Governor and General Assembly. Springfield, Illinois.

MacKenzie, D. L., and J. W. Shaw. 1993. The Impact of Shock Incarceration on Technical Violations and New Criminal Activities. *Justice Quarterly.* 10 (3): 463-488.

MacKenzie, D. L., J. W. Shaw, and V. B. Gowdy. 1990. An Evaluation of Shock Incarceration in Louisiana. Unpublished final report submitted to the National Institute of Justice, August.

MacKenzie, D. L., and C. Souryal. 1994. Multisite Evaluation of Shock Incarceration. Washington, D.C.: National Institute of Justice.

National Institute of Corrections. 1991. Intervening with Substance-abusing Offenders: A Framework for Action. The Report of the National Task Force on Correctional Substance Abuse Strategies. Washington. D.C.: United States Department of Justice.

New York State Department of Correctional Services and New York State Division of Parole. 1992. The Fourth Annual Report to the Legislature: Shock Incarceration-Shock Parole Supervision. Unpublished report. Albany, New York. The Division of Program Planning, Research and Evaluation and the Office of Policy Analysis and Information.

———. 1996. The Eighth Annual Shock Legislative Report. Unpublished report. Albany, New York. The Division of Program Planning, Research and Evaluation and the Office of Policy Analysis and Information.

New York State Division of Parole. 1989. Shock Incarceration: One Year Out. Albany, New York. Unpublished report by the Office of Policy Analysis and Information.

Parent, Dale. 1996. Presentation made at the Office of Justice Programs, United States Department of Justice sponsored workshop on correctional boot camps. Dallas, Texas, April.

Peters, Roger. 1993. Drug Treatment in Jails and Detention Settings. In *Drug Treatment in Criminal Justice*. J. Inciardi, ed. Newbury Park, CA: Sage Publications.

Petersilia, J., and S. Turner. 1993. Evaluating Intensive Supervision Probation/Parole: Results of a Nationwide Experiment. Research in Brief. Washington, D.C.: National Institute of Justice

Ringel, C. L., E. L. Cowles, and T. C. Castellano. 1994. Changing Patterns and Trends in Parole Supervision. In *Critical Issues in Crime and Justice*. A. R. Roberts, ed. Newbury Park, California: Sage Publications.

Turner, S., and J. Petersilia. 1992. Focusing on High-risk Parolees: An Experiment to Reduce Commitments to the Texas Department of Corrections. *Journal of Research in Crime and Delinquency*. 29, 34-61.

Wellisch, J., M. D. Anglin, and M. L. Pendergast. 1993. Treatment Strategies for Drug-abusing Women Offenders. In *Drug Treatment in Criminal Justice*. J. Inciardi, ed. Newbury Park, California: Sage Publications.

Staff Training: Foundation for Success

John F. Wertz

Commander, Pennsylvania Department of Corrections
Quehanna Boot Camp
Karthaus, Pennsylvania

Ronald D. Griffith

Deputy Commander, Pennsylvania Department of Corrections
Quehanna Boot Camp
Karthaus, Pennsylvania

Introduction

This chapter on staff training takes the correctional practitioner through the necessary steps to establish and maintain a credible boot-camp training program. It does not outline what to teach but focuses on how to teach or instruct, and why. This procedure will allow agencies with existing programs as well as those just starting out with the framework necessary to insert specific training subjects into their curriculum.

Overview

In the early eighties, corrections departments throughout the nation began to embrace a new concept of behavioral modification, strict military discipline combined with drug and alcohol therapy, and education in a correctional setting. The first correctional boot camps were born from this grand experiment. Throughout the eighties, boot camps grew in popularity. No longer considered a correctional fad, boot camps now are accepted by reasonable correctional practitioners as a necessary and viable sentence alternative. Yet, as a result of the wait and see attitude taken by some notable professionals, specialized training designed to meet the needs of the men and women who run these boot camps was an afterthought more than a prerequisite. This chapter remedies this problem and address-es the importance of training for boot camp staff from the practical standpoint of what works.

The Training Triad

Regardless of the subject, the success of any training program depends in large part on three components: staff selection, quality of instruction, and in-service training. We refer to these components as the "training triad."

Staff Selection

The selection of staff is vital to the overall success of any boot camp program. Without the flexibility to "hand pick" the staff, all other factors shrink to insignificance. The ability to orally communicate is essential. Military experience should be given serious consideration but should not be a prerequisite. Remember, you are selecting staff to be instructors, you are not just filling a duty post. A core group of your staff should have a solid correctional background. This will insure that fundamental penological standards are maintained without the necessity to address them in this specialized training.

Physical fitness should play a role in the selection of line staff, and you should adhere to clearly defined minimum standards. The Armed Forces Physical Fitness Test is an excellent and simple standard that can be implemented with little difficulty. It is age and gender friendly. It consists of push-ups, sit-ups, and a timed two-mile run. It is a reason-able assessment tool, which has stood the test of time.

All candidates for employment should undergo an interview process that emphasizes verbal skills, decision making, and personal appearance. During this process, the program goals and objectives should be explained to each potential candidate. Experience has taught us that some candidates seek out boot camps for the wrong reasons. The initial selection process should be designed to identify inappropriate candidates and weed them out. The success of any boot camp rests with staff who are committed to setting the exam-ple and leading by it. Boot camp programs that require all staff to follow a role model concept (in other words, inmate does push-ups and staff does push-ups) are the most effective and substantially reduce the potential for abuse. Therefore, it is important at the beginning of the selection process to let candidates know that staff who do get hired will be expected to follow higher standards and must agree to this arrangement.

Preservice Training

Quality of Instruction for the Trainers

Quality of instruction, the second component in the training triad, is of vital importance. The axiom of any potential instructor must follow the concept, Be, Know, Do (United States Army F.M. 22-100).

- **Be:** The professional you want others to emulate (appearance, attitude, articulation).
- **Know:** The mission goals and objectives and their proficient execution.
- **Do:** Demonstrate on a continuous basis what you are trying to teach your students/inmates.

Instructor confidence and credibility ensures that what is taught is retained and applied. To this end, we recommend a train-the-trainers program that establishes standardization and trainer certification.

The Rehabilitation Training Instructor Course taught at Fort McClellan, Alabama, meets this need. This two-week program is accepted nationally as the national training program for boot camp employees. The program is free (except for travel) to any agency requesting its employees' participation. The training is designed to provide correctional staff with the knowledge and skills required to handle the operations within a boot camp environment. Training consists of United States Army drill sergeant's techniques that are designed to maintain a consistent level of stress control and discipline needed to alter human behavior. The subjects include counseling (fourteen hours), leadership development (twelve hours), drill and ceremony (twenty-six hours), physical fitness training (thirty hours), suicide prevention (one hour), stress management (two hours), drug and alcohol abuse awareness (four hours), and methods of instruction (three hours). This course requires strenuous physical activity and students are credited with ninety-eight academic and training hours. After successful completion of the course, each student may be certified as a corrections drill officer by their facility.

The instructor is as important as the message taught. The instructor must meet measured performance standards for instructor certification. The established standards of any training program must be obtainable but not set too low. Any credible training program must have a failure rate factored into it. "Show up and graduate" programs destroy instructor credibility and undermine confidence. Just as boot camps are not for every inmate, boot camp training programs are not for every employee.

Course grading should be on a "Go," "No Go," or pass/fail basis. So called outcome-based programs sensitive to individual self-esteem do little to build confidence or credibility and should be discarded. As referred to earlier, the role model concept becomes an essential link in building a very necessary alliance between the instructor and the inmates. Training programs that require the instructor to instill this philosophy lay the foundation for programmatic success.

The quality of any instruction involves a much talked about but frequently misre presented element, leadership. Leadership is of two types: direct and indirect. For training purposes, the primary focus should be on direct leadership. Direct leadership is used primarily at the line level. The proportion of influence, in other words, instructor to students, should be used for training. Leadership in training must provide purpose by addressing and answering the question "Why?" When the instructor instills a sense of purpose in the students based on training needs, the first steps toward building a rapport or alliance occurs.

This dynamic should be used as a source of motivation that can provide a positive learning environment. Once this foundation is laid, direction should be provided to influence and reward students in the proficient execution of training tasks. This can be accomplished by using student demonstrators and acknowledging their proper performance in front of the group. The importance of developing the training alliance cannot be overstated. Providing purpose explains why training under stressful circumstances develops self-confidence in students. Direct leadership meets this need and insures the technical standards of training are met.

Direct leadership has proved to be the most effective form of leadership in a training situation. Since the mission of most boot camps is primarily to teach, we recommend direct leadership. Unit management still may be applied to the overall facility, but taken solely from a training perspective, direct leadership instills the will, creates the initiative, and places the responsibility for it at the instructor's level.

Four major elements must be considered systematically in training: the leader (instructor), the led (students), the situation (what is being taught), and communication (method of instruction). Any new training task will require more direct supervision, and the instructor should employ the step-by-step method of instruction. Students with low confidence require support and encouragement. Students who display hard work and competence on training tasks should be singled out and praised. The instructor should place more responsibility on them and use them as peer group coaches.

The correct assessment of a class is essential to any successful training program. You need to know what your potential trainers can do. Since a great deal of training is presented orally, it is essential to rehearse what to say. To this end, standard oral "teach backs" should be employed. Effective communication is not just the exchange of information from the instructor to the student (the potential instructor); the student and instructor must understand what the other is saying.

The quality of the instruction is directly linked to the instructor's ability to communicate in a way that builds a relationship and creates a bond between the instructor and the student. Instructors must be aware that emotions are part of communication. Regardless of content, how the message is delivered is a key in training.

Students can be molded into an effective team only when they trust and respect the instructor and view themselves as trained professionals who understand the importance of their contributions. There are eleven universal leadership principles that are the cornerstone of any training program:

- Know yourself/seek self-improvement

- Be technically proficient

- Seek responsibility and take responsibility for your actions

- Make sound and timely decisions

- Set the example

- Know your students and look out for their well being

- Keep your students informed

- Develop and nurture a sense of responsibility in your students

- Ensure the training task is understood, supervised, and accomplished

- Teach in accordance with your student's capabilities

- Build your class around these principles

As the training alliance grows between the instructor and the potential instructor, values begin to emerge. As corrections moves into the twenty-first century, values, or the lack of them, have become a heated topic of discussion. Instructors' values, beliefs and norms are an essential component that further defines them. Boot camp instructors are attempting to influence and change behavior. With that mission in mind, a systematic set of values, beliefs and norms must be established within the training program so that the instructors can buy into them.

Values are attitudes about the worth or importance of people, concepts, or things. Values influence behavior and should be used to decide between alternatives to what is taught. Strong values are what you put first, define most, and want to give up least. Values such as truth, human rights, justice, and compassion are consistent with acceptable social behavior regardless of an individual's background or life experience. Individual values can and will conflict at times with a training program, and in this situation, the student's values on truth versus self-interest may collide. The instructor must emphasize that it takes moral courage to correct mistakes based on these individual values, and what the students value most will guide their course of action.

The four individual values all boot camp instructors should possess include:

- Courage

- Candor

- Competence

- Commitment

If these four values are applied and emphasized, a strong training alliance will develop.

As an instructor who will be teaching people from all walks of life, it is important to recognize that the participants' various belief systems will have an impact on how the training is received. Beliefs are assumptions or individual convictions that you hold to be true. These beliefs can be very deep seated, such as religious beliefs or the fundamental principles on which our nation was founded. The instructor's commitment to the mission of the program must be unwavering and absolute. From a train-the-trainers perspective, the instructor should understand that while one student may perceive duty as putting in time, another may believe in selflessly serving the agency or facility. Students generally behave in accordance with their beliefs. Similarly, the beliefs of the instructor impact directly on the cohesion, discipline, and effectiveness of those being trained. These four individual values impact on training.

Courage

Courage takes two forms, physical, and moral. Physical courage is overcoming fears of bodily harm while doing what must be done. An obstacle course is designed to meet this training need. When students encounter physical objects that require them to negotiate and overcome these barriers, fears such as height can be dealt with by being put into perspective.

Moral courage occurs when people stand firm on their values, principles, and convictions. Students should understand that it takes moral courage to support unpopular decisions that are ethically correct. There will be times when other staff may encourage slightly unethical solutions as the easiest or most convenient option. The instructor must convey the need to stand firm and, as a leader, not ease the way for others to do wrong. After all is said and done, one axiom holds true: if after consideration and sober judgment you believe you are right, hold your position.

Candor

Candor is being frank, open, honest, and sincere with students, peers, and supervisors. As a trainer, you should always teach your students what they need to know and avoid teaching students what they want to hear. The instructor must be aware that emotion is part of oral communication. Never undermine the program or authority with a negative attitude. Any credible training program must involve interaction between the trainer and the students. The instructor should select the right time and place to offer advice or criticism. An instructor's rule of thumb in this area should be, praise in public, correct in private. When pointing out a training deficiency, the instructor should provide a solution as well as demonstrate the correct way. Students should understand that input, while valuable, should end when a decision is reached.

Competence

Competence is proficiency in required professional knowledge and judgment skills. An instructor must display the commitment to teach and ensure all training standards are met. Competence is essential to insure the quality of instruction. The lead-by-example concept referred to earlier demonstrates this to the students. As it relates to the boot camp instructors, competence in job skills and presentation of these skills breeds confidence in students and inspires a can do attitude.

Commitment

Commitment is the desire and the will to uphold the standards taught on a consistent basis. As an instructor, it is critical that a degree of tenacity be instilled in students and that excellence becomes the standard, not just an option.

Student norms are the final area of importance. Norms are policies or procedures that are based on agreed on beliefs that the instructor and student follow to ensure that training is duty realistic and in harmony with the overall goals and training standards. There are two categories of norms, formal and informal.

Formal norms are official standards, policies, or laws that govern behavior. As an example, an instructor may use traffic signals, federal and state laws, training policies, or standards in describing formal norms to students. The importance of understanding norms and how they are developed empowers students not to fall prey to tunnel vision. To explain this, the instructor should rely on the students to provide the answer. For example, why should we obey traffic rules? An instructor should insure that students view their role as it relates to the overall program and the big picture.

Informal norms are unwritten rules or standards that govern behavior and should be identified in training. At the root of this norm, instructors share their value about the importance of caring about what they teach, how it is taught, and the lesson students derive from it. Common examples of informal norms include: "you are not permitted to cry 'fire' in a crowded theater," or "don't spit into the wind." Once students have identified some informal norms, the instructor then can address the ones that are applicable to the boot camp training program. The instructor then should attempt to provide the students a greater sense of self-assurance and comfort by knowing that their efforts are appreciated and recognized. In short, as an instructor, your actions show students you care! Instructors should recognize that they have the power to influence the beliefs and values of students by setting an example. In a training environment, it is important that the instructor recognize behavior that supports and strengthens professional beliefs. Effective training occurs when the instructor and students mutually experience realistic and common sense conditions that prepare them as a team for challenges that this sentencing alternative provides.

In-service Training (follow-up training)

We discussed the specifics of preemployment boot camp training. However, training retention will be in direct proportion to the quality and quantity of in-service or follow-up training that is done.

This third and final component of the training triad, in-service training, must be completed on a scheduled periodic basis throughout the year. Once an instructor earns drill certification, it is vital that the methods of instruction and standards of training that are employed be consistent and be maintained systematically.

The Training Officer

Each facility should have a sole point of contact regarding training. Although titles vary from state to state, most correctional agencies have adopted this approach. This staff member should be responsible for the coordination of all training, including preservice, in-service instructor certification, and that training needed to ensure performance standards are met for recertification. The specialized training subjects applicable to boot camps should be included within the mandatory training guidelines for any correctional facility that is established by the facility's governing agency. For example, Pennsylvania requires forty hours of training per year for all contract employees. The subjects range from the use of force, to the right to know, to cardiopulmonary resuscitation and first aid, among others. Within these training requirements, specialized training requires additional training time. Boot camp employees with drill certification are required to undergo an additional twenty hours of training that is job specific to boot camps. The subjects include drill and ceremony, physical training, role model concepts, and mental control of adolescent behavior.

The staff member who coordinates the in-service training is a critical link to the overall success of any boot camp program. By using a preplanned systematic approach to this training, continuation of training and quality assurance at the instructor level is insured.

The pivotal role of preplanning the training year can be accomplished by "time lining" each subject on a training calendar that identifies for each month the subject to be taught, the instructors, and the area where the training will be held. This mode of preparation is known as strategic planning and is designed to clearly outline in a logical sequence of events the in-service training for the year. Strategic planning should always be in "broad strokes." Put simply, this process answers four training questions, What (training subject), Who (the instructor), Where (training area), and When (month-day). The fifth and final question, How, should be the instructor's responsibility.

There is an additional benefit of applying strategic planning to the training process. This method avoids having the training officer overwhelmed by details such as training aids, classroom set up, scheduling time (hours), and attendance. This should be the responsibility of the primary instructor and can be accomplished in what is known as "tactical planning."

Tactical planning should be conducted two weeks prior to the first training session and should focus on the details. We recommend that all mandatory boot camp subjects employ the "team teaching" approach with a primary instructor identified. Tactical planning should be detailed and cover all areas not addressed in the strategic planning process, including hours and students to be trained. This planning session also should identify any training aids required, classroom set up/break down, and the documentation required for maintaining instructor certification and class attendance. During this tactical planning session, the subject to be taught should be reviewed and rehearsed by using the approved lesson plan.

Staff Burnout

Burnout describes or possibly explains why staff cannot maintain acceptable levels of performance. Correctional practitioners have wrestled with this problem primarily from a cause and effect standpoint for years, and as a result of this limited approach have proposed one-dimensional solutions to a multidimensional problem. Correctional programs that require a high degree of technical proficiency and meticulous performance standards combined with a positive attitude cause a greater potential for burnout. Of all correctional programs, boot camps are at the top of the potential "burnout" list as a direct result of their inherent nature and structure. To reduce this potential threat, the leaders, supervisors, and managers must understand that the intensity of training and raised performance standards do not cause burnout. However, lack of input into policy development, pyramid management, permanent duty assignments, "chair-borne" supervision, and overuse of staff discipline sew the seeds for burnout to grow.

As a program, boot camps succeed or fail based on the instructor's ability to inspire, motivate, and maintain performance standards. The greatest resource that managers possess are the staff who drive the operation. Boot camps are program driven, and staff drive the program. With this undisputed fact in mind, here are some techniques to keep the fire burning.

- Flexible schedules allow for longer periods away from work. Consider permitting staff to trade days and shifts. Provide as much cross training as possible. Practice horizontal management when developing policies and procedures. This can be accomplished by creating small Policy Action Committees (PACs) consisting of line staff employees. These PACs should develop draft policies and procedures. Importantly, promotions should come from within. Reward the staff with career incentives based on performance.

- Listen to what your staff is saying and encourage them to propose solutions.

- Get out of the chair, but stay out of their hair, in other words, lead by example. As a manager, there is always a tendency to let your position define who you are. Take steps to separate your profession from who you are as a person, and most important, share this with your staff. "Corrections is what we do, not who we are."

- Lesson plans or any specifics regarding in-service training are available on request.

In the final analysis, a boot camp operates more like a military training company than a correctional facility. Therefore, it is essential that the administration of any boot camp establish and maintain this mind-set. After all of the details of your training program have been accomplished and you are ready to train, remember: One person can make a difference and together we can achieve anything. By approaching the training mission with this philosophy, we have learned that the boot camp concept has worked in Pennsylvania, and it can work for others, too.

Mission Statement

The Pennsylvania Department of Corrections recognizes and accepts its public responsibility to maintain a safe and secure environment for both the incarcerated offenders and the staff responsible for them.

We believe that every inmate should have an opportunity to be constructively engaged and involved in a program of self-improvement.

Authority exercised over inmates will be fair and professionally responsible.

We recognize our responsibility to be open to and provide access to inmate families, religious groups, and community volunteers.

We are sensitive to the concerns of victims and their need for inclusion in the correctional process.

We recognize that our greatest source of strength lies within our human resources—the men and women and their families who are the Pennsylvania Department of Corrections.

Philosophy

The Pennsylvania Department of Corrections, Quehanna Boot Camp, will provide a secure, safe, and humane alternative to standard incarceration. This voluntary six-month program is designed to enforce positive life building skills in a regimented, disciplined environment in concert with intensive drug and alcohol therapy and educational classes. The goal of this program is to provide each inmate with the opportunity and mental tools for positive change. Each staff member is committed to the ideal, "One person can make a difference, and together we can achieve anything." For the staff of Quehanna Boot Camp, "Excellence is not an option; it is our standard."

Staff Selection and Training

Ronald W. Moscicki

Superintendent
Lakeview Shock Incarceration Correctional Facility
Brocton, New York

Correctional boot camps are no longer a national experiment but are now a national phenomenon. At their core is the hope that the prisons and detention facilities administered under this heading can be a wholesome treatment environment, safe for both the staff who will work in them and inmates who reside there. At an April 1996 conference on Boot Camps sponsored by the Office of Justice Programs, lively discussions revolved around the "kinder gentler" boot camp with de-emphasis on military aspects and a corresponding increasing emphasis on treatment, including decision making skills, cognitive restructuring, education, and substance abuse counseling. An increasing emphasis is being placed on the importance of aftercare and the need to monitor and evaluate programs.

The federal government is committed to marshaling the "best and the brightest" in corrections and getting them to focus their attention on "reforming" the nation's boot camps. To this end, researchers in social learning theory and juvenile reintegration were asked to speak about their specialties in the context of boot camps. Similarly, the sponsors of less coercive programs such as the New York State Youth Leadership Academy and Abraxas were highlighted for their innovation in juvenile boot camp programs. (See the chapters in this book on each of these programs.)

Some of the most telling discussions of the new generation of boot camps is the recognition that despite the evidence to date, at best boot camps may be somewhat more costly and may not have long term effects on recidivism, they are still being embraced as a treatment vehicle that can be sold to politicians who wish to continue on the road of "getting tough on crime." Despite evidence to the contrary, boot camps are being oversold as to what they can do. Legislators, governors, mayors, and county boards of supervisors are still demanding that this type of correctional environment be tried as an alternative.

There is very little discussion of the economics involved in starting and maintaining a program. Given the push to fund the expansion of adult and juvenile boot camps, it is clear that the small size of many programs may prohibit any real cost avoidances or reduction on demand for bed space. This is particularly of concern in those jurisdictions where municipalities are increasingly cash strapped. The likelihood that a boot camp will be funded by local or state revenues if it cannot show a bed savings or a reduction in the size of the inmate population, by reducing return rates, is diminished. Thus, there needs to be an emphasis on documenting what a well run boot camp consists of and determining what other outcome measures can be quantified.

The current state of knowledge about adult boot camps comes from the National Institute of Justice funded multisite study. For juveniles, it comes from the Office of Juvenile Justice and Delinquency Prevention demonstration sites data. The results of these two major research efforts have not been as promising as hoped. Despite these findings, we have not been able to answer what, if anything, works about boot camps. Aside from the anecdotal data about how the boot camp environment should work, we have no information about the causes of relapse among program graduates, nor if it has anything to do with exposure to the program. In fact, we do not even know why successful program graduates are making it on the streets. The small sample typology study conducted by New York State indicates that those who are successes already had more going for them to begin with than those who failed, and that they followed the conditions of their parole more closely than those who failed. Despite these seeming differences, there was little, if any, variation about both the program's successes and its failures, or about the positive nature of the shock environment among the staff and the program components.

Despite this lack of knowledge, there are special groups in Shock programs about whom we are now asking questions. Can the military component be modified in such a way as to be sensitive to the needs of women, younger offenders, violent offenders, older offenders, or offenders with disabilities?

There is a great deal of variation between programs based on the type of offender, the method of participant selection, and the relative program size. The best practices of a small juvenile facility may not be applicable to a larger multisite program for adults. This, too, needs to be recognized. Even within one jurisdiction, a program for adult males, age eighteen-to-thirty or higher, may not be applicable for female offenders in the same program. In particular, we need to recognize that there are special needs' populations who would be better served by having some additional programming to help them get the most out of this treatment.

We applaud this increasing focus on treatment in these programs. Since 1987, when Shock Incarceration began in New York, we have emphasized the need for intensive substance abuse treatment, academic education, decision making, and life skills in the program. Research on the success of our graduates, postrelease has consistently demonstrated far lower rates of parole violations or return to prison for new crimes, then comparison groups of offenders similar to the Shock population. We believe that a comprehensive holistic approach to working with young, nonviolent offenders is far more effective than longer periods of incarceration, especially when program budgets are limited.

Yet, to be effective, boot camps have to be staffed properly, with the right people, in the right jobs. It takes a team. Drill instructors are important in a boot camp, but teachers, counselors and support staff are equally important in an effective operation. Drill instructors include people with this title as well as all uniform or security staff. Security has to work cooperatively with program and administrative staff.

There must be standards for all employees that are clearly delineated. In a unionized system, you may not have the option to specially select staff for the boot camp. That is not necessarily a drawback. Staff in New York have seniority transfer, and shift and post bidding rights. They understand that when they choose to transfer to a Shock Facility, they must agree to abide by (Employee Standards) and participate in the four and one half week staff training program. All employees, regardless of discipline, from superintendent to clerks, participate in training together.

The following is excerpted from the *Shock Incarceration Program Procedural Manual*, describing employee standards and the staff training program.

Employee Standards

In every case, staff are role models for everything taught in Shock. A role model demonstrates a way of acting. Staff are expected to live up to both the community standards and the philosophy of Shock Incarceration and to lead inmates by example.

While we are clear that because of the nature of the program, we hold to higher standards of performance, the underlying philosophy which governs Shock Incarceration holds to these high standards because of the nature of the program. At all times, all staff are expected to model the discipline, motivation, and teamwork inherent in Shock Incarceration.

Performance Expectations

- Complete successfully four and one-half weeks Shock training
- Maintain physical and psychological fitness
- Conduct yourself according to strict military protocol

- Maintain positive attitude
- Demonstrate continued willingness to accept new responsibilities

Grooming Standards

All staff who work in Shock facilities are expected to maintain military grooming standards consistent with the Shock environment. Staff are models of standards expected from inmates.

Male Grooming Standards

- Hair will be neatly groomed and tapered and will not fall over the ears or eyebrows or touch the collar except for the closely cut hair at the back of the neck.
- Sideburns will be neatly trimmed and will not be of the muttonchops or flared type. The base of the sideburns will be clean-shaven on a horizontal line and shall not extend below the lowest part of the exterior ear opening.
- Beards of any type are prohibited.
- Mustaches will be kept neatly trimmed and shall not extend beyond the corners of the mouth or fall below the center line of the lips.

Female Grooming Standards

- Hair will be neatly groomed; female officers will wear their hair up and tied back, off the collar if long. Hair clasps should be appropriate for uniform. No colored nail polish.

Security Staff

- Grooming standards for males and females: No jewelry is allowed with the exception of one watch, one wedding ring, one engagement ring, one religious medal which should be out of sight. No earrings, medallions, or necklace type chains are allowed.
- The standard attire for security staff is a Class B uniform which will be pressed with military creases, collar brass, name tag, whistle and chain, web belt, black shined boots, and campaign hat. Nothing will be worn in the shirt pockets except for one pen and/or pencil in the left front shirt pocket. All buttons will be buttoned except for the top shirt button.

Civilian Staff

- The standard attire for all noncustodial males in this category is a business suit, sports jacket or sweater, pressed trousers, dress shirt, and tie.

- Female personnel in this class may wear an appropriate dress or skirt and blouse or sweater, or slacks and blouse of their choice, as long as it is considered in good taste and consistent with the Shock setting.

- Clothing should be appropriate to duties, conveying a professional image consistent with military grooming standards for the uniformed staff.

- Shoes should be polished.

Maintenance Staff, Commissary, Store Clerks

- These personnel may wear neat presentable clothing suitable to their tasks.

Shock Incarceration Staff Training

Since we recognize that Shock is not corrections as usual, it is important that staff who work in the program understand the program, the theory behind it, and what is expected of the inmates. One important way to ensure program integrity is through staff training. All staff who work in a Shock Incarceration facility in New York State are required to attend a comprehensive, highly structured, rigorous four-week training program. The training program has a regimen that is similar to the Shock program for offenders. The goal of the training is to familiarize all correctional employees, regardless of discipline, with the concepts, goals, and structure of the Shock program.

Prior to the opening of a Shock facility, all staff assigned there are required to attend this training before they have any contact with Shock inmates. The training is based on the model first introduced in 1979, when interdisciplinary teams were being trained to staff Network units. That training was an intensive two-week course in providing therapeutic community concepts as applied in a correction's facility. Shock staff training has been expanded to four weeks to include physical training, drill and ceremony, and introduction to alcohol and substance abuse treatment (ASAT) in addition to the principles of the therapeutic community, and to familiarize staff with decision-making skills as taught in Network.

To familiarize correctional employees with the concepts, goals, and structure of Shock Incarceration, each candidate must attend a comprehensive, highly structured, rigorous four and one-half week training program, which includes physical training (calisthenics and running), classroom instruction, drill and ceremony, substance abuse treatment, ways to teach decision making and life skills, accelerated learning techniques, and participatory exercises in group dynamics. This program offers a regimen that is similar in structure to that which inmates follow.

The training is designed to help employees obtain a better understanding of the inmates they will work with in Shock. It leads to an improved understanding of the interrelationships among security, programs, and administration. It also has provided a chance for employees to increase their understanding of themselves and others. Group unity and teamwork are emphasized as staff are placed in platoons and work together throughout the training in an experiential approach to learning how to teach inmates.

The Course Content

The following items are taught: control theory, leadership skills, training in teaching decision-making skills, the alcohol and substance abuse treatment curriculum, drill and ceremony, physical training, and military bearing. The emphasis in training for all staff is on teaching inmates all aspects of the program. An interdisciplinary approach to working with inmates is emphasized throughout. The training scheduled is based on a modified version of the Shock day for inmate participants, beginning with physical training each morning and concluding with community meetings in the evening. Each day includes drill and ceremony and is designed to cover some aspect of the six-month treatment curriculum. As with the full inmate program, all of the content of the staff training is taught using accelerated learning strategies. For the staff to work at a Shock facility, they must agree to undergo this rigorous training. As a result, the staff at Shock tend to be very committed to the program goals and highly motivated.

As of October 1995, more than 3,000 New York State Department of Correctional Services employees have been trained in Shock methods during twelve sessions. In addition to conducting staff training in New York, staff trainers have also provided training for other states and localities.

Expected Outcomes of Training

These outcomes include:

- A better understanding and knowledge of the inmates who the employees will be supervising

- A better understanding of the inter-relationship between security, programs, and administration

- The opportunity for learning or developing personal confidence and responsibility

- Self-respect and respect for the attitudes and value systems of others

- Group unity and teamwork

The Importance of the Drill Instructor

Command Sergeant Major Joshua Perry (Retired)
Course Director
Rehabilitation Instructors Training Course
Fort McClellan, Alabama

When I was a young, raw recruit back in 1961, still wet behind the ears, my drill sergeant took me in hand and set the direction for the rest of my life. He insisted on the best from me and would not settle for anything less. If you took a gun to my head today and said, "Josh Perry, you've got thirty seconds to tell me the name of the Commanding General and the Command Sergeant Major at Fort Leonardwood, Missouri when you were in basic training or I'm going to shoot you." I would have to say, "OK, go ahead and kill me. I'm gone, I can't remember." But ask me the name of my drill sergeant, and I'm good to go. I will never forget him. That man saved my life.

For thirty years, I was privileged to serve my country in the United States Army. Most of my career was spent in leadership positions responsible for guiding and teaching recruits, soldiers, and drill sergeants. When I retired in 1991, I was asked to direct the

Rehabilitation Instructors Training Course at Fort McClellan, Alabama. Since that time, more than thirty-three states have sent drill instructors to be trained in the Rehabilitation Instructors Training Course.

Quality correctional boot camp programs have much to offer. However, there are criticisms and controversy surrounding these programs. For example, an editorial in *The Anniston Star* on June 13, 1995 criticized the "boot camp" system established to treat first-time, nonviolent youthful offenders. The blanket condemnation of all such programs based solely on the failure and closure of one such camp seems unfair. Across the country, a number of similar programs are successful. One thing is clear. This country has a serious problem with youthful offenders and teenage crime. Some very complex social-economic and cultural dynamics are at the core of this problem.

After spending more than thirty years in the military, this author takes issue with some of these boot camps because the term "boot camp" implies that they are modeled after the military. When soldiers graduate from boot camp, they have been trained for a job. They are faced with a service obligation to the military; they are subject to the Uniform Code of Military Justice, and they are assigned to a unit where they have a cadre of people who are concerned about their being at the appointed place at the appointed time, doing what they are told when they are told. Contrast that with some of these so-called civilian boot camps, which put youngsters through ninety days of an intense, grueling program, then return them to the same crime-infested environment with no job and no education. Then, we wonder why juveniles resort to doing the only thing they know—how to survive. Here are three options for society to deal with this issue.

Societal Options

Option One: Do nothing

We are a violent society, and we get our full measure of violence in our neighborhoods, schools, movies, and on television. General Hines, the former commander of Fort McClellan, once mentioned what he observed in a grade school classroom in Anniston, Alabama. Two little boys were vying for space at the chalkboard when one punched the other in the face and then continued writing. As General Hines relates the incident, there was nothing personal in the attack. It was just "normal" business as usual. We have come to accept the idea that violence is normal and read about it or watch it happen. However, many people believe that doing nothing is not an option.

Option Two: Throw them all in jail

"You do the crime, you serve the time." That will keep criminals off our streets, right? Wrong. Our jails and prisons are already bulging at the seams. By October of 1994, the United States incarcerated more than 1 million inmates. Not only is it financially impossible to build and staff enough prisons to warehouse all criminals, but on any given day, hundreds of inmates complete their sentences and are released back into our neighborhoods. They are not rehabilitated to be productive members of society—they are just older, wiser criminals, still without the means and skills to earn an honest living. This option does not solve the problem.

Option Three: Invest in programs to curb criminality and rehabilitate offenders

The boot camp system falls into this category. It is an attempt to solve criminal behavior by dealing with it early enough to exert a positive influence that might alter youthful offenders' antisocial behavior. The more successful programs attack the problem from various levels. They have well-trained, professional staffs that care deeply about their responsibilities. They know you do not rehabilitate by tearing down people. They know you cannot abuse or scare these youth straight. Most of these young people, in their short lives, have been exposed to more mistreatment and scary situations than you can imagine. You do not change people by punishing them, nor are these programs a quick fix. The more successful programs are longer in duration. In New York, the program lasts almost one year.

The more successful programs also provide follow-up monitoring. You cannot place these youths back in their old environments and forget about them. The weaker ones will quickly succumb to bad influences. You must give them a fighting chance to secure a job. States with successful programs sometimes subsidize minimum-salary wages, if employers give them a chance. An effective aftercare program is essential to a successful boot camp. The solution is not as simple as some would have you believe. Take a young person exhibiting extreme antisocial behavior, place him in a boot camp for two months to give him a taste of some old-fashioned military discipline and presto: a model citizen. It is not as easy as that. It takes time, effort, and commitment. It also takes money. The other options are more terrible and costlier in the long run. Do we have a choice? This is a situation where we pay now or we pay with interest later. Boot camps are an investment in our youth and in our society. Properly executed, they are an investment that will pay our society great dividends.

Because we are committed to the development and operation of quality correctional boot camps, we provide an intensive staff training program for drill instructors at Fort McClellan. We teach standards for staff who will teach inmates skills that will help them escape the "revolving door" of prison. Drill instructors or drill sergeants must be leaders, teachers, and counselors, and have a wide range of skills and abilities. The most important ability they must have is to care about the people with whom they work. The following are basic standards for drill sergeants in correctional boot camps:

- Set the example—Drill sergeants must be able to consistently conform to the values of the institution (boot camp). They must be able to encourage inmates to be committed to the same values.

- Set and enforce standards—They must be able to maintain discipline. They must encourage inmates to perform duties in the absence of orders.

- Treat inmates with respect—Drill sergeants must treat inmates with dignity and be concerned about their welfare. Drill sergeants must have compassion, be able to listen effectively, and respect the inmates. The obverse, respect for drill sergeants by the inmates, is important.

- Physically fit—Drill sergeants must be fit, mentally and physically. Drill sergeants who are physically fit are most likely to handle stress better. They must be the proper height and weight. Most importantly, drill sergeants must present a trim and sharp appearance and be able to pass a physical fitness test with higher standards than those required for most correctional departments.

- Integrity—Drill sergeants must have integrity of the highest level. Drill sergeants must be able to report serious offenses, including excessive force involving their peers, particularly if it involves inmate abuse. They must be able to supervise, counsel, develop confidence, and instill discipline into inmates.

- Proper background—Drill sergeants should have a corrections' background and graduate from a drill instructor school, such as the Rehabilitation Instructors Training Course.

The following is a description of the Rehabilitation Instructor Training Course at Fort McClellan, Alabama and the Shock Incarceration training in New York. These two programs are among the most comprehensive in the country and are available for boot camp staff of any jurisdiction.

Rehabilitation Training Instructor Course (RTIC)

The objective of the training is to assist the National Drug Control Strategy by providing instructor training to federal, state, and local civilian correctional officers who have adopted a military boot camp program for the rehabilitation of nonviolent youthful drug offenders.

Scope

The training is designed to provide civilian correctional officers with the knowledge and skills required to rehabilitate youthful drug offenders who are confined in a shock incarceration environment. Training will consist of United States Army drill sergeant techniques designed to maintain a constant level of stress, control, and discipline needed to alter the behavior of adolescents. The training includes counseling; evaluating; developing leadership and discipline; performing drill and ceremony; physical fitness training; preventing suicide; managing stress; developing alcohol and drug abuse awareness, and learning various methods of instruction. This course requires strenuous physical activity and all students, regardless of age, must be cleared by medical personnel prior to arrival at Fort McClellan and have written proof of this clearance during processing.

Prerequisites

Students who attend this course will have a minimum of one year of experience in the corrections' field or other related field as determined by their supervisor. Each student must possess a minimum of a high school diploma or a general education diploma. Students who have prior military service must have an honorable discharge.

Course Content

The physical training component is thirty hours in length. It includes the following elements:

- **Fitness Components and Principles:** The components of physical fitness and key principles of exercise apply when designing a fitness program and conducting fitness training; students apply the F.I.T.T (Frequency, Intensity, Time and Type) principles. These determine how often fitness training occurs a week, for how long, and what exercises are conducted on which days.

- **Fitness Training Procedures:** These procedures include changing from a standard company/platoon formation to the extended rectangular and circle formations and returning back to standard formations for conducting training. We use the three-step teaching method in demonstrating a calisthenic exercise: introduce the concept, demonstrate it, then have trainees do it. We instruct drill instructors in how to teach and conduct warm-up, stretching, and cool-down exercises and provide precautions to them as well as offer different stretching techniques.

- **Partner Resistance Exercises:** These procedures address how to teach and conduct partner resistance exercises with an emphasis on exercises which improve individual's push-up and sit-up ability.

- **Aerobic/cardiorespiratory (CR) Training:** We address the principles of aerobic training and cardiorespiratory exercises, including the importance of training heart rate in cardiorespiratory conditions; minimum intensity and time needed to achieve cardiorespiratory training; the importance of the warm-up and the cool-down period; and improvement techniques for the two-mile run test.

- **Circuits and Relays:** We demonstrate various types of circuits and relay training and show drill instructors how to implement them in the inmate environment. We emphasize two basic types of circuits—free and fixed—and show drill instructors how to monitor this program.

- **Army Physical Fitness Test:** The drill instructors learn how to organize, administer, and use the Army physical fitness test as an evaluation tool to determine fitness levels prior to designing a fitness program for inmates.

- **Grass Drills:** Drill instructors learn how to conduct and execute grass drill; the four basic grass drill positions and grass drill exercises, and how to use proper exercise formations.

- **Guerrilla Exercises:** The last component helps drill instructors learn how to conduct and execute guerrilla exercises for physical training and how to use the correct training formations.

Drill and Ceremony lessons are provided for twenty-six hours. These include:

- *Drill and Commands:* We offer an explanation of drill terms and demonstrate their correct use, including proper inflection, cadence, snap, and distinctiveness.

- *Stationary Drill*: We teach procedures for teaching the position of attention and rest positions at the halt and use of the "talk through" teaching method.

- *Facing Movements at the Halt:* We demonstrate procedures for teaching right face, left face, and about face; and the the use of the "by the numbers" teaching method.

- *Steps and Marching:* We teach drill instructors the procedures for teaching the thirty-inch step from the halt and marching in place using the "step-by-step" method of instruction.

- *Group Drill Terminology and Rules:* Instruction includes counting off, opening and closing ranks, marching the small group, and changing the direction of a column.

- *Small Group Drill:* This segment consists of aligning the small group at normal and close interval, and changing the direction of a column from the halt.

- *Marching the Platoon:* The potential drill instructors learn how to march the platoon from one location to another using proper voice inflection, cadence, snap, and distinctiveness.

The Leader Development and Assessment component lasts for twelve hours. It includes a Leaders' Reaction Course. This physically demanding and challenging course gives students an opportunity to lead peers in overcoming obstacles and completing specific missions. Then, students observe United States Army drill sergeants leading and motivating basic trainees through their daily schedule using the same techniques of the Rehabilitation Instructors Training Course that students learn.

Professional sensitivity and awareness training takes seven hours. It includes stress management instruction which covers its definition, causes, effects of excessive stress, stress prevention, and management techniques.

The alcohol and drug abuse component provides information on the danger of abuse, background of inmates with a history of abuse, ways to deal effectively with such inmates, and latest information on illegal substance abuse trends within the country.

There is training on suicide prevention and crisis intervention. Students learn how to identify the risk factors, symptoms, causes, and danger signals of suicide.

For fourteen hours students learn counseling techniques. In the introduction to counseling, students are provided with a basic understanding of the counseling process and its impact on performance, general skills, types of approaches, effective communication, and verbal and nonverbal means of communication. In the personal counseling segment, students learn interviewing techniques to be used with new inmates, identifying personal problems which interfere with inmate performance, and counseling to resolve problems. Students conduct counseling focused on periodic performance appraisals of the inmates. Students also learn motivation techniques and methods to establish positive and realistic goals for inmates. Finally, students receive training in leadership styles, attributes, and the duties of corrections officers. This includes instruction in methods to enforce discipline, basic leadership methods in a corrections environment, positive reinforcement, counseling, and standards set by role models (corrections officers).

Students receive three hours of training in Instructional Methods and Techniques. This includes information on presentation and communication. Students receive basic fundamentals and techniques of instruction, including effective communicating and questioning techniques. Students learn about the availability and use of training aids, and their value to assist in instruction. In performance-oriented training, students hear an explanation of the components of performance-oriented training (learn by doing), and both perform and watch demonstrations by students.

Students receive six hours of training on Administrative Requirements. The three modules include introduction of key personnel and support available, equipment and book issues, and course critiques and graduation issues.

Student Instructions

Introduction

The length of the course is two weeks, or ninety-eight academic hours. In Phase 1/Week 1, the drill instructors introduce the students to the rigorous and physically demanding boot camp style environment. Emphasis is on drill and ceremony, leadership and discipline, physical fitness, performance counseling, instructional methods, and alcohol and drug abuse awareness.

In Phase 2/Week 2, students demonstrate their skills as they lead and inspect their peers; plan, coordinate, and conduct training; and maintain the same demanding boot camp environment. Students are evaluated by both drill instructors and peers. Emphasis of this student-led instruction is on drill and ceremony, physical fitness, and counseling techniques.

Physical Fitness Requirements

Students participate in a daily fitness training program, which follows the fitness techniques taught in the United States Army master fitness trainers' course. Students take a diagnostic physical fitness test during the third day of the course. This test will determine their general physical condition, and will assist them in establishing fitness goals. The test consists of three events: the push-up, the sit-up, and a two-mile run. Students take a final physical fitness test prior to graduation. The test documents the progress within the course and allows them an opportunity to conduct a formal physical fitness test.

Small Group Instruction

Students are be assigned to groups of ten-to-twelve personnel. Each group is assigned one drill instructor who is responsible for each student's development through the course. Small-group leaders enhance the student's learning and are available for additional instruction or retesting of material. Because of the small group method, each student has every opportunity to succeed. Simply put, each student attains 100 percent mastery of course objectives.

Counseling System

During the first day of the course, each student receives initial counseling. This counseling ensures that students understand what is expected of them during the course. Rules and regulations which apply to them are addressed. When any student receives "No Go" on a performance test, the drill instructor conducts a counseling session.

Student Leaders

All students have the opportunity to perform as leaders during the course. They are responsible for some instruction, inspecting of personnel and billets, developing training schedules, coordinating some of the training, and maintaining the training facilities.

Performance Examinations

Standards for performance examinations are explained in each task group (such as drill and ceremonies, physical fitness training, and others) provided to the student in the form of evaluation criteria. These are used by the drill instructor and peers to assess the performance of the student-instructor. Students receive the evaluation criteria prior to the performance examination. Students are given three attempts on each performance examination to receive a "Go." If a student fails for a third time to receive a "Go" on a performance examination, the commandant may allow a fourth and final attempt. The commandant will use the total student concept (the student's overall performance and demonstrated motivation while at the course) in making this decision. Each student will be granted a fourth attempt to pass a performance examination only once during the course.

Student-led Instruction

Training for the second week requires student-led instruction. All students coordinate their presentation with drill instructors prior to presenting it. Students are provided with all training materials, including approved lesson plans and evaluation criteria. Subject areas include: physical training, drill and ceremony, motivation in correction, suicide prevention, crisis intervention, and management training. All students receive drill instructor and peer evaluations.

Course Curriculum/Objectives

The Rehabilitation Instructors Training Course is a "Controlled Entry - Group Exit" course of instruction. The course is divided into six major subject areas. All areas require successful completion before a graduation diploma is issued.

Inspections

A drill instructor and student leader conduct an in-ranks inspection each day. Uniform, time, and location are noted on the training schedule. All leather footgear will be brush shined. Only shoe polish will be used. Other means, such as paints and sprays, are not authorized. All clothing will be neat, clean, and serviceable (no holes or rips). All pockets which can be buttoned or snapped will be buttoned or snapped. No bulky materials or pens/pencils will be visible. Students will maintain haircuts and mustaches as prescribed by their department requirements. Drill instructors and students will conduct daily inspections of billets.

Complaints and Grievances

The chief, advanced law enforcement training division is available to receive complaints or grievances. Students will coordinate their interactions through their drill instructors. In many instances, the drill instructors or course manager will be able to address the issue.

Bulletin Boards

Students will read the class bulletin boards twice daily to monitor training schedules and receive any other critical information.

Leaves and Appointments

Leaves may be granted for emergency situations (death or serious illness requiring hospitalization of a family member). The corrections officer's supervisor will confirm the situation prior to the departure of the student. The leave will be coordinated through the drill instructor. Students who miss eight hours or more of training may be subject to dismissal from the course. Appointments must be approved by the drill instructor.

Sick Call

Students must report to the drill instructor or student leader prior to the first formation of the day for sick call. Sick call is available at Noble Army Hospital, Fort McClellan. Emergency sick call is available at all times. Coordination is through the drill instructor or student leader.

Course Completion

When the students have received a "Go" on all performance examinations, they are eligible for the graduation diploma. They will receive their diplomas at the graduation ceremony on the last training day. After graduation, all students must "out process" with their drill instructors to satisfy the administrative requirements and turn in any government equipment.

Saturdays and Sundays are purposely left open for students to coordinate schedules, prepare training, or to retrain or retest on "No Go" areas. Students also must present their classes to the drill instructor prior to their scheduled instruction.

Dress Code

Only departmental uniforms are authorized (less weapon), complete with boots and cap during training. Students from the same department will wear the same uniform. All awards (and decorations) and name plates will be worn on the departmental dress uniform.

Only personal wristwatches, wedding bands, and identification bracelets are authorized for wear while in uniform. Medical alert bracelets/necklaces also are authorized. Religious medals may be worn if they are not exposed or do not present a safety hazard. Except for valid medical reasons, only prescription sunglasses are to be worn during training. Fad or designer sunglasses are not authorized.

Due to the short duration of the course, mail is discouraged. Military telephones are not authorized for personal use, except in emergencies. Students have access to a civilian phone. Coordination for military phone use is through the drill instructor. Students are authorized to bring privately owned vehicles, but must register them with the Fort McClellan Provost Marshal's Office.

A military dining facility is designated where all breakfast, lunch, and dinner meals will be served. The course is resident and the billeting is located at Fort McClellan. Each room is a double occupancy room. Students share a common latrine. Female corrections' officers are billeted with separate latrine facilities. Spouses, other family members, or guests may not accompany students in billets. Cleaning and maintenance is the responsibility of the student leaders. Cleaning supplies are provided.

While students are enrolled in the Rehabilitation Training Instructor Course, they are authorized to use the post exchange, the trade winds, the bowling alley, post theaters, barber shop, and the gyms. Students are not allowed to purchase alcoholic beverages, tobacco products, or military uniform items.

Students are expected to maintain the highest standards of conduct, both during training and on off-duty hours. Failure to do so may result in dismissal from the course. Further questions on appropriate conduct may be addressed to the drill instructors. Students may be released from the course for administrative and/or medical reasons. If released, students' records will be forwarded to their agencies. Students released from the course may apply for readmittance if their removal was for other than disciplinary reasons. Application procedures are the same as for initial enrollment.

A service school academic evaluation report is forwarded to the student's sponsoring agency. It portrays the attitude, capabilities, accomplishments, and academic progress of the student. Each student is given a copy at graduation. Each student must complete critique sheets prior to graduation. A second sheet is sent to the graduate after course completion for further comments. The sheets result in changes to the course and help create the best possible training environment.

Male Required Clothing List

- 1 - Bag, laundry
- 4 - Uniforms, Departmental, Work
- 1 - Belt, Trouser, Black (if one is worn)
- 2 - Shoes, Departmental, Work
- 4 - Pairs of Socks for Uniform
- 1 - Gloves, Black (seasonal)
- 1 - Nameplate, Pin on (if one is worn)
- 4 - Socks, Cushion Sole, White, Pair
- 6 - Undershorts, (Boxer or Jockey), White
- 4 - Undershirts, White
- 3 - Towels
- 3 - Washcloths
- 1 - Physical Training Uniform, Gray (top and shorts/sweatshirt and sweatpants - seasonal)
  No writing or design on pants and shirt
- 1 - Athletic Shoes, Running
- 1 - Lock, Combination or Key
- 2 - Undergarments, Cold Weather "Long Johns" (seasonal)
- 1 - Coat, Cold Weather, Departmental (seasonal)

Female Required Clothing List

- 1 - Bag, laundry
- 4 - Uniforms, Departmental, Work
- 1 - Belt, Trouser, Black (if one is worn)
- 2 - Shoes, Departmental, Work
- 4 - Pairs of Socks for Uniform
- 1 - Gloves, Black (seasonal)
- 1 - Nameplate, Pin on (if one is worn)
- 4 - Socks, Cushion Sole, White, Pair
- 6 - Undergarments, (Brassieres and Panties) Pair, Panties will be either cotton or have cotton crotch
- 4 - Undershirts, White
- 3 - Towels
- 3 - Washcloths
- 1 - Physical Training Uniform, Gray (top and shorts/sweatshirt and sweatpants - seasonal)
  No writing or design on pants and shirt
- 1 - Athletic Shoes, Running
- 1 - Lock, Combination or Key

- 2 - Undergarments, Cold Weather "Long Johns" (seasonal)
- 1 - Coat, Cold Weather, Departmental (seasonal)

Other Items: (Men and women)

- Medical Records
- Medical Alert Identification Tag (if appropriate)

Attendees from the same correctional facility who attend this course together will wear the same style work uniform and the same style physical fitness training uniform.

There are height and weight criteria for correctional officer candidates. The federal correctional officer physical standard states only that weight must be in proportion to height. This broad criteria resulted in inconsistent interpretation and application of the standard. To correct this, the desirable weight tables shown below were developed in conjunction with the medical director of the Bureau of Prisons, who is also an Assistant Surgeon General with the United States Public Health Service. The tables were extracted from the *Physician's Handbook* and have been increased by 30 percent in each category.

Maximum Desirable Weights for Male Correctional Officer Candidates

Height (Feet)	Small Frame	Medium Frame	Large Frame
5'2"	156	168	183
5'3"	160	173	187
5'4"	164	177	192
5'5"	168	181	198
5'6"	173	186	203
5'7"	178	191	209
5'8"	183	198	216
5'9"	189	203	221
5'10"	195	208	226
5'11"	200	215	233
6'0"	205	221	239
6'1"	211	228	246
6'2"	217	234	252
6'3"	222	241	259
6'4"	228	247	265

Maximum Desirable Weights for Female Correctional Officer Candidates

Height (Feet)	Small Frame	Medium Frame	Large Frame
4'10"	127	139	155
4'11"	131	143	159
5'0"	135	147	163
5'1"	139	151	166
5'2"	143	155	170
5'3"	147	159	174
5'4"	151	164	179
5'5"	155	169	185
5'6"	160	176	190
5'7"	165	181	195
5'8"	170	186	200
5'9"	176	191	205
5'10"	182	196	212
5'11"	187	202	218
6'0"	192	207	225

If You Don't Take Responsibility, You Take Orders

Ronald W. Moscicki

Superintendent
Lakeview Shock Incarceration Correctional Facility
Brocton, New York

Boot camps often seem to begin with the assumption, "If it ain't rough, it ain't right." Most people think that "rough" is sweaty drills, "in your face" and bulging muscles. They never associate "rough" with inmates sitting in a circle in white shirts and ties, with counselors and drill instructors leading a treatment group or academic classes, teaching inmates how to read and write.

The Military Component is NOT the Toughest Part

This writer believes that treatment is the toughest part of this program. The military component is what scares the inmates, and some staff, away. In truth, the military part is the easiest because it is constant repetition. Once the inmates' muscles stop aching, and they realize they can survive being ordered about, they get it. Once they get it, they've got it. Repetition leads to skill.

The military components in our programs teach inmates how to listen. They learn how to listen by hearing our orders and following them. Once they know how to listen, the next step is to teach them to think before they act. If all we teach them is how to follow orders, we will not be able to turn our backs on them, and we certainly cannot let them out of our sight. If all we expect from our inmates is that they follow orders, we will have good inmates. Inmates, even good ones, belong in jail.

Effective treatment and education teach inmates how to think for themselves, solve problems and take responsibility for their lives. Once they learn how to "take responsibility," we don't have to worry about what happens when we are not around to make them "take orders." The sign over the front door of the school at Lakeview says, "Knowledge is Power." We teach our graduates how to have power in their lives after they leave us. That is the measure by which we are judged. The first, sometimes the only question any of us ever gets asked about how effective we are is "What is your recidivism rate?"

We have seen programs that think they are tough because their drill instructors are all 6'2", with bulging muscles, veins popping out from their necks, who engage in loud cursing, punishing, and talking down to inmates. Not so coincidentally, we also have noticed that their inmates are late for the mess hall, up before reveille, their lockers are a mess, their boots are not shined, and their clothes are not pressed. The "tough guys" scorn the opposite extreme, the soft talking social workers who try to motivate inmates into formation instead of giving orders. Neither extreme has clear goals or direction for inmates. They have high dropout rates. If you turn up the heat too fast, inmates jump out of the pot; too slow, and they drown.

There is No Staying Power on the Drama Triangle

These programs have much drama, but they do not produce a lot of change and have no staying power. Inmates in the "tough" programs do what they are told as long as they are being watched. Inmates in the "soft" programs act out, get in trouble, and are confused. Both of these extremes have lots of fights, misbehavior reports, and problems. Both have inmates who figure out quickly what we want and give it to us. They are masters of survival. Either they are rigidly locked up at attention, screaming "Sir, yes Sir!" at every opportunity, or they are crying in every group, wallowing in the heartbreaking misery of their lives. Both learn our favorite jargon quickly and tell us what we want to hear.

We call that being on the drama triangle. There are only three types of people in those programs: victims, rescuers, and persecutors. They are in every program. Staff caught in drama undermine each other, bad mouth and complain, often in front of the inmates. Rescuers get mad about how mean persecutors are to the "kids." Persecutors are disgusted by rescuers always wanting to "hold their hands and pat them on the head." Victims get to play each off against the other, laughing if they are big enough to get away with extortion, scared to death if they are little, weighing in at ninety pounds soaking wet. Everybody loses in that game. It is a set-up for failure. The drama triangle keeps everybody off balance.

The bottom line is that everybody, both staff and inmates, buy into the idea that inmates cannot think for themselves or they "can't help it" because they were "born that way, bad to the bone, just plain lazy, stupid, poor, poor dears, disadvantaged, deprived, emotionally disturbed, or no damn good." The triangle is drawn point down to show how easily the system can be tipped over. Everyone on the triangle blames everyone else for their problems and justifies their own behavior by making excuses.

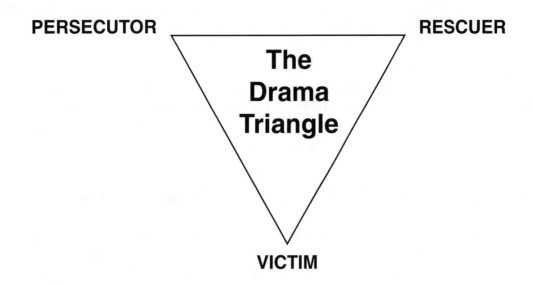

Drama Blinds Us

In one program we visited, the budget was tight and there were not any chairs, so inmates were given five-gallon buckets to sit on for groups and community meetings. The staff, who were committed to doing a good job, asked us to come to assess their unit and tell them what was wrong. When we got there, inmates were milling around, talking. The drill instructor called them to community meeting, so they mobbed over to the dayroom area and sat down. The big guys each had three five-gallon buckets to sit on, the little guys were sitting on the floor, the mid-sized ones sat on one of those open-weave milk cases, which we found out later they were not supposed to take out of the mess hall. When we asked the drill instructors why everyone did not have a five-gallon bucket, they were surprised, saying that everyone had been issued one when they started. It should not surprise you to discover that race was another deciding factor for who got to sit on what.

The staff were willing, but like many programs do, they were selected because they were young, could leap the obstacles on the confidence course they ran twice a day without breaking a sweat, liked physical training and drill and ceremony. None of them knew inmates or how to talk to them. None of them had any experience in corrections. They were not following the plan we had laid out for them. When we pointed out that we had not let them move to community meeting or groups any old way in training, the lights went on; they realized that there was method to our insistence on strict adherence to military bearing at all times. They were so upset about not having chairs for the inmates that they forgot to have an established location for everyone's five-gallon bucket, so when they conducted inspections, there would be one for everyone, all in the same place. Drama blinds us. When we are caught on the triangle, we cannot see clearly.

A video we saw of another program shows drill instructors throwing inmates off the bus onto the ground and into walls, shoving their faces into a fence, screaming and calling them "scumbags." The thing that bothered us even more was that the judges and politicians interviewed endorsed this abusive behavior as "very effective." It was not. It was abuse. We were told that the public likes it so much that the news channel in the area shows it three or four times a year.

This writer is a strict disciplinarian who expects his staff to hold the line, not to lose control. One thing my staff noticed when they saw the video, was that most of the inmates were scared, a couple were fighting or crying, but all the drill instructors were sweating. They laughed because my advice is, "Never let them see you sweat."

Knowing When You Are Playing on the Drama Triangle

A clue that you are on the drama triangle is when you are working harder than the inmates, whether it is to "save" them or to "get their attention." Drama gets us all a bad name and is a bad way to do business. As Command Sergeant Major Perry says, "Violence begets violence." There is no excuse for abuse or playing with inmates because you can.

People who want to fight with inmates in these programs never have been in a yard when the inmates stopped playing basketball, stopped talking, stopped lifting weights, and started squaring off. They have never been hit over the head and have never been thrown down a flight of stairs. One thing this writer has figured out in the last twenty-three years is that the inmates kept getting younger, and he keeps getting older. The goal is to do this program smarter, not harder.

So, How Do You Get Off the Drama Triangle?

To get off the drama triangle, set the tone from the beginning. When our first platoon arrived at Monterey on September 11, 1987, this author's orientation speech said, "Things are different here. We have no hair. We have no packages. We have no fights. We have no threats. We have no gangs. We DO NOT make good inmates here. We have fifty-eight jails in this state that can make "good" inmates. Here in Shock, we make "good citizens." Nothing has changed since then, except now we have sixty-six other prisons in the state and four Shock Incarceration Correctional Facilities.

How Do We Make "Good Citizens"?

As administrators, you have got to reverse the triangle, introduce stability into the system by planning, through training, monitoring, and supervising. The model we use for our planning is a critical path model, introduced by R. Buckminster Fuller. Quality systems have gotten much play in recent years. Fuller taught the principles from 1927 until he died in 1983. W. Edward Demming tried to teach managers a variation of this system at about that same time, but American business was not ready to hear it, so he went to Japan. He helped them take "Made in Japan" from a joke to being the most sought-after products in the world. The design is one that this writer operated intuitively even before he studied the model, because it just makes sense. It is easier to follow a plan when you can see it. Here is the basic structure:

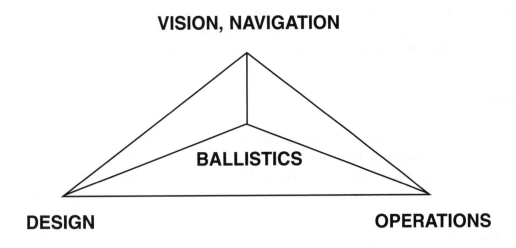

VISION, NAVIGATION

BALLISTICS

DESIGN   **OPERATIONS**

Vision, Navigation

Everything starts from the top. As a leader, you set the tone. You have to start from a vision of where you want to go. This is how you navigate through the rough waters that are sure to come with taking responsibility for these programs. That is the responsibility of leadership. One personal hero, General George S. Patton said, "Leadership is the art of getting your subordinates to do the impossible." He must have had us in mind when he said that. Anybody crazy enough to start a boot camp in prison knows how to do the impossible. We believe that the impossible just takes more work and a little more time.

The team that put Neil Armstrong on the moon had a vision. To achieve that vision, they had to plan ahead before they set off in the direction they wanted to go. On the way to the moon, they estimated that they were off course 99.5 percent of the time, but through constant correction, by holding their vision, they were able to stay on course. They had about twelve seconds worth of fuel left when they landed the LEM module on the moon, but they kept their eyes on the goal and got there. They stayed focused. At the same time that you are focused on your goal, be prepared to make constant course corrections.

It is no accident that the top of the tetrahedron is where we put "vision." Leadership demands that you risk standing out from the crowd. Taking responsibility is not easy. Some of us would rather take orders, too. Many of our subordinates, managers, supervisors, and staff, would prefer to take orders. That way "It is not my fault." There is always somebody else to blame. Like Eichmann, "I was just following orders," becomes their defense.

The trap for those of us who are willing to lead, is that we may not trust our subordinates to take charge. We may resort only to giving orders. We think, "It is easier and quicker to do it myself." You get ulcers and they want to kill the chief. Letting them hide in the crowd turns them into snipers and us into targets. If you are going to take responsibility for this program, make sure you have a strong, cohesive team to back you up. The best mountain climbers have a precision support team that is as skilled, or more so, than they are. The leader may be first, but the whole team has to be high and tight, together all the way for the climb to the top of the mountain to be successful.

Design

You have to have a map when you start out in new territory. You need a blueprint to build a strong, solid structure. You need a plan that clearly spells out your goals to have a high quality program and to be effective. Follow the guidelines you write. Do not stray off course. If you do, make corrections early, frequently, and quickly. Do not overcorrect. Fine tune.

Demming defined "quality" as "maximum consistency, minimum deviation." When you buy Sony, Honda, Toyota, or other brand names, you are buying them because you know what to expect. People will bypass great little local restaurants in an unknown area to go to McDonald's, because they know what to expect. Know what you expect and work to ensure consistency.

Your policies and procedures have to be clear and spelled out in black and white. Your schedules must include a balance of treatment, education, and discipline. You need good, treatment-oriented, security-conscious staff. Our best staff combine those qualities, regardless of role. Each discipline has its specialty though. We do not want our counselors playing drill instructor and forgetting about treatment, or our drill instructors forgetting their role in favor of their best imitation of what they think of as counseling. Staff have to respect each other's views and listen to each other, especially when they disagree.

Your schedule needs to be tight, and it has to make sense. There is a reason to get inmates up early. You have to get your work crews out on time or get them to school for classes. You do not want them up too late, or your treatment staff is working too late at night. Everyone needs rest to be effective. A structured, balanced routine provides stability and safety.

Your physical training program and obstacle course should be designed to build confidence and fitness, not stronger, faster criminals. Physical training is the first event of the day. It sets the tone. Physical training should motivate inmates, help them get fit and healthy, not be punishing and grim. Know your audience. We are working with drug addicts, dealers, and streetwise kids who hang out in gangs because there is safety in numbers. The military uses ability runs and timed exercises now. We do not. If we did that, all of the Young Lords, Latin Kings, Néta, Skinheads, Arian Brotherhood, Neo-Nazis, Crips, Bloods, F.O.I. and others would be running together, each looking to corner the other gang, out of sight of the staff.

We want inmates to learn to pay attention to the people around them, to support each other. We cannot afford to let racial differences become a problem. They will, if we do not pay attention and structure groups to reflect a racial balance. We tell them that they cannot do it alone, that they need each other to make it through the program. Every event of the day is designed to reinforce that philosophy.

Operations

Most of our correctional agencies have three divisions: security, programs, and administration. Security runs the jails, programs take care of inmates, and administration provides support, maintenance, materials, and supplies. Our Director of Shock Incarceration, Cheryl Clark, and this writer came from two different specialties, programs and security. We each had been very effective in the Department, which is why our Commissioner assigned us to this project. He wanted the best of the discipline and rock-solid control which this writer had with our Corrections Emergency Response Team at Attica; and the best of the Network therapeutic community model which she designed for the department and had implemented in twenty-nine of our prisons.

The Commissioner knew the combination would be effective. We were not so sure about that when we met in 1987. Ms. Clark was afraid that Shock Incarceration could become a place where "free beat-ups on inmates" were okay. The Commissioner assured her that this writer would not tolerate that from officers. This writer was afraid that she might want officers "holding hands with inmates." The Commissioner said that the discipline, order, and officer involvement in establishing the tight norms of Network, were what she could bring to Shock. If this writer had had his way when we started, the result would have been a sweet little jail, but no results. Over the years, she has taught him and our staff about the power of effective treatment and education. This writer has taught her about jail: security and operations, what to look at and how.

Together we have developed a team that we will take anywhere. They are committed to excellence. Like us, they are absolutely committed to teach everyone how to operate with the same precision, determination, and dedication that has made Shock in New York the program to model. We want every program in this country to be the best. All you need is commitment, stamina, and a plan. Then, you have to stick to your plan.

If the treatment and education components are doing their job, the longer inmates are in the program, the tougher it gets. A good counselor, drill instructor, or teacher should be challenging inmates to think before they act, to adapt, adjust, and overcome until day 190 and after they leave us, too. Staff are turning up the heat more and more each month, expecting the inmates to confront their attitudes, feelings, and each other.

Ballistics

When this writer was in Vietnam, his platoon sergeant was always drilling the platoon on ballistics. He demanded strict attention to detail:

> Change your socks. Clean your weapon. Stay off the trails. Read the signs. Watch for footprints, for matted grass. Look for cooking fires. Leave the area the way you found it. The information is there for you. Gather intelligence. Rely on your training. Maintain your discipline. Stay alert and increase your chances of survival.

Exacting attention to every detail could be the difference between life and death. When this writer worked in Attica, the old timers said:

> Look like you're in charge. I know you're new kid, but the inmates shouldn't. Act like you know what you're doing. Hold your head up. Know your inmates. Don't hang around the coffee pot, smokin' and jokin'. The inmates don't need to know about last night's bowling scores or any other scores you might have made. Watch your inmates. Do their pockets bulge? Are they wearing two sweatshirts and a winter coat when it's 90 degrees in the yard? Pay attention. Listen for their nicknames. Watch for patterns. Gather intelligence. Rely on your training. Maintain your discipline. Stay alert and survive.

When this writer became an "old timer," he told the new guys, "The state planned for everything, they even thought about giving us baggy pants, so the inmates wouldn't see our knees shake." When he taught defensive tactics, he told the officers that it was okay to be scared, but the inmates could not know it. They had to "act as if." When he trained the Corrections Emergency Response Teams, he relied on paying attention to detail, discipline and vigilance. "You fight like you train. You train like you fight." If anybody broke discipline or failed to maintain the standard, they relinquished the right to be on the team.

It is not any different in this program. You have to plan, gather intelligence, rely on your training, stick together, maintain your discipline, set and hold to standards to increase your chance of survival. We are always telling our staff:

> Shock does not work unless you do. Move like you're in charge. You can't do Shock with microwaves and jelly doughnuts. Don't hang around smokin' and jokin'. The inmates don't need to know about your personal life. Never let them see you sweat. Know your inmates. Pay attention. Watch for patterns. The information is there for you, gather intelligence. Rely on your training. Read the manual and follow it. Maintain your discipline. Stay alert and survive.

Ronald W. Moscicki

One of the problems we face is that Shock makes you lazy. Staff get so used to "Sir, Yes Sir!" that they forget basic jail. They get complacent and forget that these are inmates. They forget their training, and they forget to pay attention. One of our units was having a problem. The staff could not figure it out. The squad bay had recently been repainted. The only place where the paint was chipped was the spot right behind the officer's chair. You cannot do this program kicked back in a chair with your foot in the drawer.

The inmate who gives us exactly what we want by day two is also a problem, a big one. They are still selling their product. They want us to buy their dope. Shame on us if we let them run our program. It is a constant balancing act. This writer used to drive Ms. Clark crazy when he said it was all "just theatrics." The last time she let him get away with that comment was when Maria Shriver came to film us in 1988. Ms. Shriver asked this writer, "How much of this is just theatrics?" I snapped back, "All of it." From her background as a drama major, Cheryl Clark knew how much work good performances take, and did not want our excellent work dismissed lightly.

The difference between a grade-B movie and an academy-award winner, an amateur act and a professional performance, is hard work, repetition, good direction, continuous improvement, and fine tuning. You have to be "on your mark," and on time for the production to work effectively. Practice makes permanent. At the same time, you have to make it fresh every day. You cannot afford to get stale and comfortable. Amateurs get people hurt. Professionals set exacting standards and work to improve their performance all the time. We are professionals in a demanding business. Let us be the best we can be.

Repetition builds skill, but routine makes you lazy. It is difficult to get complacent at Lakeview, with 1,100 inmates on site, drafts of fifty moving in daily, filling platoons somewhere in the state weekly, and getting the disqualified inmates out as soon as we can locate a bed. Despite that pace, some people manage to be lulled into complacency. In our smaller 250-300 bed places, everybody knows everybody, platoons arrive once a month; it is a slower pace and sometimes people get comfortable. That is the first slip on a downhill slide. Recently this writer had occasion to remind all of our managers to stay on point. They received the following reminder:

> Every morning in Africa a gazelle wakes up.
>
> It knows it must run faster than the fastest lion or it will be killed.
>
> Every morning a lion wakes up also.
>
> It knows that it must outrun the slowest gazelle or it will starve to death.

It doesn't matter whether you are a lion or a gazelle.

When the sun comes up, you had better be running.

Remember: if you don't take responsibility, you take orders.

A Critical Look at Boot Camps for Women

Voncile B. Gowdy, Ph.D.
Senior Social Scientist
National Institute of Justice
Washington, D.C.

Issues for the Development of Boot Camp Programs for Women

There should be greater emphasis on concerns and programs for women offenders, not only due to the increasing numbers of women in jails and prisons, but because women's needs differ significantly from men's. And a unitary boot camp program for men and women may not offer full benefits for women. In the last ten years, the number of women committed to state prisons has increased at a rapid pace, reaching 57,263 by 1994. An increase in the number of women in jails also has become noteworthy. By the early 1990s, the number of incarcerated women in prison or jail at any one time was approaching 75,000 (Immarigeon and Chesney-Lind 1992). A current national estimate of the number of women incarcerated is 100,000.

Rapid growth in the number of incarcerated women, recognition of their unique needs, and longstanding awareness of gender differences in prison and jail programming have resulted in considerable concern about gender equality in the development of institutional programs. Traditionally, women have been the "silent minority" within the penal world, and correctional systems have provided fewer and less varied programs for women than for men (Shover 1991, Morash and Bynum 1995).

Boot camp programs are generally designed for young, nonviolent offenders at their first felony conviction. Because participants have been overwhelmingly male, correctional officials did not immediately adopt boot camps for women. These facilities were developed for men, and the admittance of women to boot camp programs began, in many instances, as an afterthought. The continued growth in the female population in prisons, coupled with an interest in parity for incarcerated women, underscore a need for correctional officials to take a hard look at meeting the needs of this special population.

In the interest of parity, programs for women should provide for effective programming (*Glover v. Johnson* (1979), *Craig v. Borne* (1976), Lown and Snow 1980, Smart 1989, MacKinnon 1987, Rafter 1990). Morash found in her study on programs for women that parity differed from equivalence and requires that officials address women's and men's program needs with the same level of program variation, availability, intensity, and duration (Morash and Bynum 1995). These needs may not be addressed necessarily by the same program, however.

Data from studies (Rafter 1990, MacKenzie and Donaldson 1996, Crawford 1988) on the current adequacy of programs for incarcerated women, including boot camps, identified three primary areas of concern: (1) Women's access to programs in correctional settings is less than that of men. (2) Shaped by the stereotypical beliefs about women's lives, programming for women is qualitatively different. (3) This inept programming fails to address the unique needs of women.

Boot Camp Programs

Current research suggests that much remains unknown about "what works" in boot camp programming for female offenders. However, the following issues may serve as a framework for consideration when planning, modifying, or evaluating your boot camp program for women. These include:

- How are the female offenders identified for participation in boot camp programs?

- Do female offenders have an equal opportunity to participate in the program? If not, what changes are needed?

- What are the needs of women in your boot camp?

- Are their needs being addressed? How do you know?

- What are the advantages for women who participate in boot camp programs?

- Does your boot camp cause female offenders any harm? This includes analysis of demeaning or condescending staff performance, as well as linkage with family, including the women's children.

- Does the aftercare component effectively meet the needs of women offenders?

- What are the best practices or ideal models for female boot camps, or for women in coed boot camps? Is a treatment model appropriate for your population?

Do Boot Camp Programs Address the Needs of Women?

Very limited literature is available on the needs of women participating in boot camps, beyond the multisite evaluation study of state correctional shock incarceration (MacKenzie and Souryal 1994). Only in the last few years have women's demands for equal programming in boot camps and the growing interest of correctional officials and researchers warranted an assessment of the suitability of women's participation in boot camps.

The National Institute of Justice conducted a multisite evaluation of boot camp programs that began with a 1989 survey of fifty state correctional jurisdictions to determine what specific program components seemed to work best and for what types of offenders. In thirteen of the twenty-five states with boot camps, women were participating in their programs (MacKenzie and Souryal 1994). Significant findings from those surveyed are outlined:

- Wide variation was found in the number of beds allocated for women participating in boot camp programs ranging from 8 to 150; the majority ranged between 8 and 60.

- New York had the highest number of women involved in boot camp programs (see the following chapter by Cheryl Clark).

- In states with boot camp programs, the capacity allocation for female offenders was consistently smaller than that for male offenders.

- Some programs integrated women into the programs with male offenders. In this case, women were housed at male boot camps or in nearby women's prisons.

- Women participated with the men in almost all activities.

- A vast majority of female offenders had children, and most planned to live with them after their release. There were no visitation programs to encourage the continuation of mother-child relationships however.

- Most of the participants in boot camp programs were serving sentences for nonviolent crimes (drugs, theft, or fraud).

- Many participants in boot camp programs had substance abuse problems and histories of abusive relationships.

When female offenders are placed in boot camp programs only for reasons of equality, merging women into a program designed for male offenders does not create an equal situation. Such programs did not take into consideration the special needs nor the physical stamina of women. Placing women in environments where most of the participants and staff were men created additional stress for them (MacKenzie and Donaldson 1996).

Merry Morash and Lila Rucker (1990) argue that integrating women offenders into programs designed for men without prior determination of the women's needs may be harmful. That is, the programs may be inappropriate for women or have unintended consequences that are destructive for the female inmate. For instance, MacKenzie found that in correctional boot camp programs that combined women and men that: the drill instructors are harsher; the stress is greater; activities are restricted; and there may be problems with sexual behavior (MacKenzie, Elis, Simpson, and Skrobron 1996). The goal then becomes to match or develop the program activities that address gender-specific needs.

If you have women in your boot camp or plan to have women in your boot camp:

Questions for Consideration

- How do you determine their needs?
- How do you evaluate whether you have met those needs?

What are the Ideal Characteristics of Boot Camp Programs for Female Participants?

Earlier research noted that boot camp beds for women were not operating at capacity. However, the few women who entered boot camp programs were apt to drop out (MacKenzie and Souryal 1994). Lack of policy by correctional officials that supports the often differing emotional needs of women, and their failure to provide programs to meet women's needs for drug treatment, and vocational training have all contributed to the small numbers of women participating in boot camp programs.

The typical boot camp program combines women and men. Problems associated with commingling frequently cause a high level of stress to women. For instance, some women in boot camps report a high level of stress around their unique health needs. They reported that due to these needs, males made them feel inferior. Additional emotions surrounding abusive relationships contributed to their difficulties relating to men in power, such as the drill instructor. Scars obtained by female boot camp offenders from this experience could be irrevocable and cause permanent trauma.

Restrictions around age could be another factor that limits the availability of female participants in boot camp programs. Although these programs are designed generally for young nonviolent offenders, women who have participated in boot camp programs have had a tendency to be older than their male counterparts (MacKenzie 1994). Do age restrictions limit the number of females in you boot camp? Assessment of the age factor should be made to determine if it eliminates otherwise eligible women.

Questions for Consideration

- How are female offenders identified for participation in boot camp programs in your jurisdiction?

- What accommodation or change do you need to make to reach this? Develop a timeline for achieving your goals.

- Are there advantages for women to participate in boot camp programs in your jurisdiction? If so, what are they?

Model for Future Boot Camp Programs for Women

Considering the public and political interest in boot camps, they are likely to expand. We believe that the allocation of funds for this correctional option will continue and that programs should be planned to meet the needs of all populations. With the passing of the 1990 Crime Act, the Bureau of Prisons established a boot camp program for women in Bryan, Texas, and it is likely that more will be planned. Careful attention should be given to the design, and all aspects of boot camp programs for women.

Many models including leadership, hybrid, treatment, militaristic, and juvenile are being experimented with around the country (Parent and McDonald 1995). However, given the unique needs of women, the treatment model may be the most compatible with women's needs.

The first step in any model is to identify the goals, including objectives, of the program. Understanding what the program is trying to achieve guides the development of the next phases. The treatment model is appropriate because many women in prisons were found to have:

- emotional and drug-related problems

- been juvenile runaways

- been the victims of sexual or physical abuse

- attempted suicide or

- had serious drug problems (American Correctional Association 1990, Morash and Bynum 1995).

The desire to have these needs met underscores the development of a treatment model program. A female boot camp program that provides treatment and services would be ideal for this population. One goal of the boot camp may be to "rehabilitate" offenders, in other words, provide assistance to help them change their behavior and thereby to reduce the prison population.

In general, the second step is targeting the right offenders for the boot camp program. This step is critical to the success and the completion rate of inmates who participate in boot camp programs. The need for proper selection becomes even more of a requirement if implementation of the treatment model is to be used as a foundation for designing female boot camps. Parent and McDonald (1995) suggest that any subgroup of offenders can be targeted for participation in a treatment boot camp, as long as they share a particular problem which can be altered through the use of a treatment intervention, or service provided by the program. Female boot camp programs need to be designed to provide treatment and services to remedy some of the problems this population shares. For ongoing boot camp programs, a further step is matching the needs of women with the types of programming existing in specific boot camps.

Voncile B. Gowdy, Ph.D.

How female offenders are screened and selected is crucial to the achievement of program selection and success. Traditionally, placement and release decisions vary (Parent 1989) and may be made by judges, corrections department administrators, or members of parole boards.

All programs consider security as a basic concern when placing offenders in boot camp programs. The treatment model, however, suggests the screening out of offenders who do not need the treatment regimen provided, or who are not motivated to enter and succeed in treatment (Parent and McDonald 1995). Using this screening format, allows correctional practitioners to select those persons genuinely interested in participating in the program. It allows for the selection of female boot camp offenders by a multifaceted team of criminal justice practitioners including the department of corrections, mental health experts, the judge, and security risk staff.

Because the treatment model is an option that is promising and could meet the needs of female offenders, components of that model are discussed:

- **Program Length**. Program length is the first issue that a jurisdiction must address in developing a boot camp program. The programs range in length from three-to-four months for the confinement phase, and up to a period of one year for the community phase (MacKenzie and Souryal 1994, Parent 1989). Recently, an increasing number of jurisdictions are reevaluating this position. For example, the treatment boot camp model should provide a longer confinement phase than designated in earlier boot camp models to include several gradations that yield increasing reductions in surveillance levels for participants who demonstrate good adjustments.

- **Mandatory Participation**. Mandatory participation in boot camp programs is more likely to reduce prison populations than those operated under capacity (MacKenzie and Piquero 1994, MacKenzie and Souryal 1994). The treatment model is designed to let the inmate volunteer, and thus, increase the use of existing boot camp programs for women.

- **Confinement Phase**. Boot camp programs should be located in a specialized facility or within an institution in a unit separate from the general population. A thorough assessment, including physical, dental, and mental health evaluations, should be completed on all woman entering boot camps. This assessment should be used to develop a case management plan that identifies problems for which services and treatment will be delivered during the institutional and aftercare phases.

- **Discipline and Removal of Offenders**. Procedures for discipline and removal of offenders from the program should be built into a boot camp's model program design from its inception. Some type of management system that rewards participants for good behavior and punishes them for misconduct should be implemented. First-generation boot camps were cautioned about the misuse of power and derogatory language when addressing inmates. This behavior should be avoided, and practices that humiliate women should not be tolerated.

Officials should make it difficult for offenders to leave a boot camp under the treatment model. Existing research findings show that of those boot camps that prohibit or restrict voluntary withdrawals, 80 to 90 percent of the inmates complete the program versus 60 to 70 percent in boot camps that let inmates withdraw at any time (Parent and McDonald 1995).

- **Treatment and Services**. The treatment and services component is a key element in developing an effective treatment model. Although boot camp programs are multifaceted, a significant amount of time during the scheduled day should be set aside for treatment programming—probably about five hours. In the multisite study, three sites, where return to prison rates for boot camp graduates were lower than they were for comparisons groups, the boot camps allowed significant time for treatment and services (MacKenzie and Souryal 1994). Treatment programs should provide for an array of women's needs identified during early program assessments.

- **Aftercare and Community**. Research on boot camps has revealed the necessity for correctional officials to include well-developed aftercare components and to strengthen the boot camp and aftercare links. Some women who complete the program later may have their positive attitudes eroded and some participants eventually return to substance abuse and other criminal behaviors. To address this void, new boot camp models expand and develop aftercare programs emphasizing drug treatment, life skills development, job training, employment, counseling, and family support.

The community intervention portion of a boot camp program should be tailored to match the specific intervention strategy employed by the institution. One technique for reinforcing and monitoring a graduate who returns to the community is to continue to implement the individualized case plan developed in the institution (Altschuler and Armstrong 1994).

Conclusion

The problems and concerns with female boot camp programs may not be resolved in the near future. Because of the issues and concerns of women, the use of a treatment model could provide a foundation for adequate program development for a boot camp program for women. Because correctional officials are on the cutting edge of designing boot camp programs that are responsive to the needs of special populations, the author believes that this information is timely.

References

Altschuler, D. M., and T. L. Armstrong. 1994. *Intensive Aftercare for High-Risk Juveniles: A Community Care Model.* Washington, D.C.: United States Department of Justice, Office of Juvenile Justice and Delinquency Prevention.

Voncile B. Gowdy, Ph.D.

American Correctional Association. 1990. *The Female Offender: What Does the Future Hold?* Laurel, Maryland: American Correctional Association.

————. 1993. *Female Offenders: Meeting Needs of Neglected Populations*. Laurel, Maryland: American Correctional Association.

Austin, James, Michael Jones, and Melissa Bolyard. 1993. *The Growing Use of Jail Boot Camps: The Current State of the Art*. Research in Brief. Washington, D.C.: National Institute of Justice.

Bureau of Justice Statistics. 1991. Women in Prison. Washington, D.C.: Government Printing Office, March.

Chesney-Lind, Meda. 1992. Rethinking Women's Imprisonment: A Critical Examination of Trends in Female Incarceration. Unpublished paper. April.

————. 1987. Women's Prison Reform in Hawaii: Trouble in Paradise. *Jericho*. 45: 6-7.

Crawford, J. 1988. *Tabulation of a Nationwide Survey of State Correctional Facilities for Adult and Juvenile Female Offenders*. College Park, Maryland: American Correctional Association.

Dobash, R., and S. Gutteridge. 1986. *The Imprisonment of Women*. New York: Basil Blackwell.

Immarigeon, Russ and Meda Chesney-Lind. 1992. *Women's Prisons: Overcrowded and Overused*. San Francisco: National Council on Crime and Delinquency.

Lown, R. R., and C. Snow. 1980. Women, the Forgotten Prisoners: *Glover v. Johnson*. In G. P. Alpert, ed. *Legal Rights of Prisoners*. Beverly Hills, California: Sage Publications.

MacKenzie, Doris L. 1990. Boot Camp Prisons, Components, Evaluations, and Empirical Issues. *Federal Probation*. September, pp. 44-52.

MacKenzie, Doris L., and Heidi Donaldson. 1996. Boot Camp Prisons for Women Offenders. Final Report. Unpublished document. National Institute of Justice.

MacKenzie, Doris L., Larry A. Gould, Lisa M. Riechers, and James W. Shaw. 1993. Shock Incarceration Rehabilitation or Retribution? *Journal of Quantitative Criminology*. 7(3): 213-236.

MacKenzie, Doris L., and Dale G. Parent. 1992. Boot Camp Prisons for Young Offenders. In James M. Byrne, Arthur J. Lurigio, and Joan Petersilia, eds. *Smart Sentencing: The Emergence of Intermediate Sanctions*. Newbury Park, California: Sage Publications.

MacKenzie, Doris L. and Alex Piquero. 1994. The Impact of Shock Incarceration Programs on Prison Crowding. *Crime and Delinquency*. 40:2.

MacKenzie, Doris L., James W. Shaw, and Voncile B. Gowdy. An Evaluation of Shock Incarceration in Louisiana. Research in Brief. Washington, D.C.: National Institute of Justice.

MacKenzie, Doris L., Lori Elis, Sally Simpson, Ph.D., and Stacy B. Skrobron. 1996. Boot Camps as an Alternative for Women. In MacKenzie and Herbert, eds. *Correctional Boot Camps: A Tough Intermediate Sanction*. Washington, D.C.: National Institute of Justice.

MacKenzie, Doris L, and Claire C. Souryal. 1994. Multisite Evaluation of Shock Incarceration, Evaluation Report. Washington, D.C.: National Institute of Justice.

MacKinnon, C. 1987. *Feminism Unmodified: Discourses on Life and Law*. Cambridge, Massachusetts: Harvard University Press.

Morash, Merry and Timothy Bynum. 1995. Findings from the National Study of Innovative and Promising Programs for Women Offenders. National Institute of Justice. Unpublished document.

Morash, Merry, Timothy Bynum, and Barbara A. Koons. 1996. Findings from the National Study of Innovative and Promising Programs for Women Offenders. National Institute of Justice. Unpublished document.

Morash, Merry and Lila Rucker. 1990. A Critical Look at the Idea of Boot Camp as a Correctional Reform. *Crime and Delinquency*. Vol. 36: 204-222.

Parent, Dale. 1989. *Shock Incarceration: An Overview of Existing Programs*. Washington, D.C.: National Institute of Justice.

Parent, Dale and Douglas McDonald. 1995. Goals and Measures for Future Boot Camps. Abt Associates. Unpublished document.

Rafter, Nicole Hahn. 1990. *Partial Justice: Women, Prisons and Social Control*. New Brunswick, New Jersey: Transaction Books.

Shover, N. 1991. Institutional Corrections: Jails and Prisons. In J. F. Sheley, ed. *Criminology: A Contemporary Handbook.* Belmont, California: Wadsworth.

Smart, C. 1989. *Sociology of Law and Crime: Feminism and the Power of Law.* London: Routledge.

"Sisters Are Doing It For Themselves": Women in Correctional Boot Camps

Cheryl L. Clark
Director of Shock Incarceration
New York State Department of Correctional Services
Albany, New York

Women In Boot Camp Programs

In their upbeat song, "Sisters Are Doing It For Themselves," Annie Lennox and Aretha Franklin belt out the message, "Now there was a time when they used to say, that behind every great man, there had to be a great woman. In these times of change, you know that that's no longer true, we're coming out of the kitchen, to say these words to you: Don't you know that sisters are doing it for themselves! We're standing on our own two feet and ringing our own bells."

At Lakeview Shock Incarceration Correctional Facility in New York, where almost one third of the women in boot camps in the United States participate, the women have turned that anthem into a cadence. As they run together at 6:30 in the morning, their drill instructors remind them that they are strong women who have the right and responsibility to move through life with pride and dignity. They encourage each other to keep going throughout the demands of an intensive sixteen-hour day. Most of them are mothers (approximately 75 percent) and they speak about, " . . . Doing this so I can get home to my kids sooner."

Correctional boot camps, like the military and corrections of old, were the exclusive domain of men when they were first developed. In the interest of parity, women began to be included in these high intensity, early release programs, but often without much attention to the differing needs of women. This has led to criticisms of boot camps for women and the deep concern of some that boot camps are not appropriate for women. While even critics believe that women should be offered the same option for early release as men, they feel that the strict military regimen and mostly male drill instructors are damaging to women who have a history of abusive relationships with men.

There is some research available now on women in boot camp programs. If your agency is planning to include women, or if you are currently operating a boot camp for women, read the research available and talk to those experienced with operating boot camp programs for women *before* you embark on this venture. It is also recommended that you study the general literature on women's needs and that a task force, which includes women knowledgeable about these issues, be involved in planning for a boot camp for women.

Those of us who have been working with women in these programs for a number of years believe these programs have much to offer when they are properly designed and are responsive to women's needs. We have also seen evidence that when special needs of women are not considered, the programs can be damaging. In those cases, the results for women are not impressive and one might be tempted to dismiss boot camp programs for women as of little value. Women who have participated in successful programs in New York and other places would strenuously object. Graduates say they owe their success to having had the opportunity to learn the self-discipline and empowerment skills taught in Shock.

At a recent presentation to the Association of Women Judges in New York, women graduates of the New York State Department of Correctional Services Shock Incarceration program and of the STEP Program for women at Rikers Island in New York City, credited those programs with getting them started on the road to sobriety and success. They attested to the benefits of the military bearing, physical training, and discipline of the programs in improving their health and even more importantly, with getting and keeping their attention, so they could focus on the drug and alcohol treatment, decision making, life skills, parenting, and academic classes also required by these programs.

One young woman spoke of how she called her sentencing judge two years after her release, to thank him for sentencing her to two and a half to five years, so she could be eligible for Shock. She had been arrested more than ten times throughout her six years as a crack addict. At the time of her last conviction, she was twenty-two years old, pregnant, and living with a drug dealer who was using her as a mule. Eight years after graduation, she is a professional counselor, working two jobs, going to college at night, and raising her son alone. He is first in his class. Had she not been arrested and incarcerated, she says he would have been a crack baby. Her mother, who had given up on her, refusing to let her come home even after graduation from Shock, is proud of her daughter's accomplishments today and helps out by sitting for her grandson while her daughter attends college classes. A dynamic speaker, she is far from alone in her impressive record of successes.

Two of the other women were both HIV positive from intravenous drug use when they were arrested. Their health was so bad when they entered Rikers, that they were afraid they would not be accepted in the program. They credit the physical training, drill and ceremony and focus on self-discipline with saving their lives. Today they are both living with HIV, as contributing professional women. Both talked about the other treatment programs they had been in to avoid jail sentences, prior to entering STEP. There was nothing wrong with the programs, they said, except that the other programs taught them that they had to want to change, giving them the option to participate when they were ready. Imagine that! They were not ready and say they never would have been. STEP demanded change from them and insisted on a standard of participation that tolerated no excuses.

All three of these women, as well as many others who have spoken about the benefits of boot camp programs in their lives, told the judges that they knew they would be dead without these programs; dead, or in prison for the rest of their lives. "Nothing would have stopped me from using, it was the most important thing in life to me." It is stories like these, more than a thousand in New York alone, that convince us that well designed boot camps for women can add immeasurable value to their lives and in the lives of those affected by their recovery.

This chapter will focus on design issues relative to including women in boot camps and is not intended as a research report of boot camp programs for women. Excellent studies are available from several sources, most recently in *Correctional Boot Camps: A Tough Intermediate Sanction*, edited by Dr. Doris Layton MacKenzie and Eugene E. Hebert (1996). One of the studies included in that National Institute of Justice Research Report, is "Boot Camps as an Alternative for Women." In March of 1992, Dr. MacKenzie headed a research team of four women who examined the involvement of women in boot camps. They conducted a survey of boot camp programs in the country and found that at that time, thirteen of twenty-five states included women in boot camp programs. Seven of the programs they found combined men and women in the same program, six had either separate or semi-separate programs for women. Their research addressed several issues important for anyone operating or planning to operate a boot camp for women:

- Do women offenders have an equal opportunity to enter and remain in the boot camps?

- Do the camps address the needs of women offenders?

- Are boot camps potentially harmful for these offenders?

- What are the potential advantages for women?

- Are there alternative correctional programs that would be more appropriate?

These issues are important considerations for those operating or planning to implement a boot camp program for women. In the same National Institute of Justice Report, Carole Sanchez Knapel discusses the "Santa Clara County PRIDE Program: A Local Boot Camp" which examines the purpose, methods, and preliminary findings of a jail boot camp programs for women in California. The Federal Bureau of Prisons also operates one of the larger boot camp programs for women at the Intensive Confinement Center at Bryan, Texas. These programs and New York's three are the largest boot camp programs for women in the country. Oklahoma includes women in their boot camp programs and is among those, like New York's Shock Incarceration program, operating for the longest period of time. All have similar findings about the women's issues which must be addressed for boot camps to be effective for women. Additionally, the Office of Justice Programs has a great deal of information to offer through the Violence Against Women project in Washington, D.C.

The New York Programs for Women

In New York, the first 250-bed Shock Incarceration facility opened in September 1987 and was for men only. We knew that it was important to offer women the same opportunity for early release as men, but were concerned with learning how to operate the program first, before introducing another variable in our learning curve. In March of 1988, New York opened a second 250-bed Shock facility for men, and in April of that year, began planning in earnest for the women's program. A task force, which included women leaders from several state and private agencies, was convened to discuss the issues of including women in Shock Incarceration. As a result of the work of the men and women on that task force, the first women entered the six-month Shock Incarceration program in December of 1988, graduating in June 1989. All eligibility criteria were the same for men and women. Women comprise less than 5 percent of the total prison population in New York State and represent 10 percent of the Shock population.

Presently, there are 160 beds for women at Lakeview Shock Incarceration Correctional Facility, in Brocton, New York including twenty beds for intake, reception, and orientation. New York has the largest Shock Incarceration program for women in the country. It operates as a semi-separate program within a 1,000-bed facility which includes 540 beds for males in Shock.

In 1990, staff and agency heads from New York City Corrections contacted the Department of Correctional Services for assistance with developing the HIIP program for men and the STEP program for women at Riker's Island Correctional Facility. After a series of meetings, training staff from New York City Corrections attended a two-week staff training program conducted by the New York State Shock Incarceration staff in December of 1990 and began implementation of HIIP and STEP early in 1991. These programs are sixty- to ninety-day programs for both sentenced and pretrial offenders and include military bearing, physical training, drill and ceremony, and substance abuse education and counseling.

In October of 1995, a specialized, ninety-day drug treatment program, for second felony offenders and parole violators, based on the Shock model, opened at the Willard Drug Treatment Center in Ovid, New York. Established by legislation as part of the Governor's Initiative, the drug treatment center is a 750-bed facility for men and women, with approximately eighty women participating at any one time. Operated by the New

York City Department of Correctional Services, the program was jointly developed by the Department of Correctional Services, the New York State Division of Parole and the Office of Alcoholism and Substance Abuse Services. Staff of the department of correctional services and division of parole provide treatment and educational services in the program, with consulting and monitoring by the Office of Alcoholism and Substance Abuse Services. The Director of Shock Incarceration and the Supervising Superintendent for Shock are responsible for the operations of the drug treatment center. The ninety-day treatment curriculum has been adapted from Shock, with even more of an intensive focus on substance abuse treatment because of the shorter duration of the program.

Second-felony offenders can be sentenced to a term of parole supervision, to commence at the drug treatment center, in lieu of a longer term of incarceration for offenses related to drugs and alcohol, or they can be technical parole violators who would be returned to the Department of Correctional Services for longer periods of time for these same violations. In every case, offenders in the program are prison-bound. Failure in the program can result in serving at least a full minimum term of incarceration in prison. The facility can accommodate as many women as are eligible, generally about 10 percent of the population.

Housing units and most program activities are separate for men and women at both Lakeview and Willard, although program space is shared and staff work with both men and women. In New York, security staff have seniority shift and post bidding rights. There is no preference based on gender for most assignments, so both men and women staff work with the women in the program. Program staff work as assigned, but are involved in decisions relative to assignments. Interest in working with women is considered in their assignments. Staff training addresses differences in approaches to working with women and men. Since we train all staff, (security, program and administrative) together, staff are assigned to training groups to ensure diversity. Women staff are also about 10 percent of the facility complement, so both men and women staff work with women in Shock. There are male and female drill instructors, drug and alcohol counselors, teachers, nurses, cooks, and work supervisors working with the women.

Should Men And Women Participate Together Or Separately?

Initially, when we first began including women in Shock Incarceration in New York, they were housed separately but participated in program activities with the men. A number of factors influenced us to change our approach, not the least of which was the distraction of relationships between the women and men. While inmates are closely supervised, in a population as starved for affection and attention as are these young men and women, the temptation to "fall in love" was just too great and distracted them from focusing on themselves and their own growth and change. This is not to imply that there is no longer that temptation with them separate, yet within the same facility. Unfortunately, the attraction is there and must be anticipated in programs where men and women are confined in the same facility. The creativity of their attempts to contact each other is impressive. Channeling this creative energy into positive pursuits is a challenge.

Another reason for separating program activities was the need for women and men to address their unique issues apart from the other group. Participants would posture for the opposite gender or avoid dealing with some problems because they were uncomfortable with sharing some things with them. On the other hand, there were some advantages with a mixed groups in certain cases. Each was able to address issues they had with the other in groups designed for that purpose. They were able to see themselves as the opposite gender saw them.

This is not to imply that in every program men and women should not participate in classes together. Some programs have as few as two-to-six women participating. It is simply not practical to offer separate activities in those cases. The cost alone is prohibitive, to say nothing of the isolation of the women. While an ideal situation may be to have separate programs for men and women, most agencies do not have that luxury. Most boot camp programs have so few women eligible, that separate facilities are not practical. In programs where there are very few women, their needs must be a primary consideration, even though they represent only a very small percentage of the participants.

Programs like the boot camp for women at the Intensive Confinement Center operated by the Federal Bureau of Prisons in Bryan, Texas are able to provide a separate program for women. The disadvantage noted by the Bureau of Prisons is that women from all over the country are sent there for the program, so they have no direct contact with families and children throughout their participation. This is offset by the shorter duration of the program, as women committed to the Bureau of Prisons would be separated by distance from families because of the location of Federal Correctional Centers, in any case. There are no easy answers to this question. The form a boot camp for women takes, as stated previously, must flow from the circumstances the agency has to deal with in combination with the purpose of the program for women.

What About Male Drill Instructors?

Some critics of boot camps for women cite women's histories of abusive relationships as the reason male drill instructors are inappropriate for women. A majority of the women who are incarcerated have a history of physical, emotional, and psychological abuse. There are differences in physical strength, perceived power, and other inequities; however, critics usually focus on men's abuse of women, even though the women have also been abused by other women in their lives. Incarcerated men, although often less likely to talk about it, also tell of abuse by men and women. Abuse is a key issue in any corrections program, particularly boot camps, because of their high intensity and basis in an authority-based, hierarchical model. We believe these issues are as critical for the men in our programs to deal with as they are both the abused and often the abuser.

By definition, boot camps are high intensity, short-term programs. For this reason, they are also highly confrontive. Being highly confrontive does not, and should never, mean abusive, neither for men nor women. Staff who are abusive have no place in corrections, let alone a boot camp program. If you have the ability to select staff, by all means use whatever screening devices you have to assist with the selection process. Psychological testing and other screening instruments are not necessarily absolute measures, but they can help. When staff selection is not an option, then qualifications, careful training, duty descriptions and evaluations for staff working with women need to be addressed. In any case, there are stresses associated with working in the corrections' settings which affect staff. Continued training, monitoring, and providing support services for staff are critical, especially in situations of cross-gender supervision.

As discussed elsewhere, women frequently have defined themselves and their self-worth in the past by their power to attract a man. Because of abusive relationships, alcohol and drugs, many are co-dependent, giving up their sense of self to others who use and abuse them. They use manipulation as a survival tool. It is an unconscious skill. They are masters at it. Women will flirt with their drill instructors, act "cute" and coy, attempt to "trade favors" and use other forms of manipulation which have helped them to negotiate difficulties in the past. At the opposite extreme are women who have been so damaged that anger is their first response to any situation. Even a drill instructor who is thoughtful and reasonably confident about his or her abilities will have problems with women who routinely respond with anger and upset to stressful situations. Being in prison is stressful; the intensity of the boot camp environment may magnify that stress, especially in the early days of the program when women are getting used to a new routine, and attempting to meet challenging physical, mental, and psychological demands.

Women tend to act on their emotions more readily and are more often likely to act out when upset than men in the program. Female participants will scream, cry, and hit more readily than the males in the program, especially when they think they have an audience. This is part of the manipulation they learned as children. We believe that one contributing factor when drill instructors are harsh with women in boot camp programs is their own discomfort with handling this manipulation. Specialized training in "games people play" is critical for this staff.

However, we have found that thoughtful, professional male drill instructors have been very effective with women in the program. Because most of the drill instructors, counselors, and teachers who work in the New York State and City programs are male, they bid on posts that supervise women. At graduation, during presentations and in letters written back after release, women often thank their drill instructors for teaching them how to be proud, strong women of dignity. "D.I. ____ taught me to expect the most from myself and others, that I am worth respect. . . . He taught me that I have the right to be treated with respect and dignity" is a regularly expressed sentiment. Obviously, whenever possible, we assign female staff to work with the women in the programs. Women staff who are confident and clear about who they are as women are invaluable role models for female offenders. It does not follow, however, that all women staff are clear and confident about themselves as women, any more than supervision by male staff is abusive. Effective monitoring and ongoing staff training is critical in these programs.

Program Components For Women

The majority of women participating in boot camp programs are mothers. In general, they are raising their children alone, without the children's fathers to assist and support them. Given their history of abuse, it is almost inevitable that their parenting skills are poor, and that they have perpetuated the cycle of neglect and abuse with their own children which they learned when they were children themselves. This cycle has been discussed repeatedly in research about child abuse, domestic violence, and other issues contributing to dysfunction.

This author spent the first ten years of her career working with abusive, dysfunctional families. As a supervisor of child protective services in two agencies and a psychiatric social worker for a juvenile treatment facility, she learned first hand, the hard way, how powerful and compelling early learning is in abusive families. All abusive parents had themselves been abused as children. There were no exceptions. Since the majority of women in corrections, by their own admission have been abused, teaching them parenting skills is critical to working effectively with these women.

Most often, they have had children either because they did not know how to protect themselves from unwanted pregnancies or because they wanted someone to love them and a baby seemed the answer. Babies, for many, are like playing with dolls; they do not understand that the baby would have needs too, and that they could not put the infant down when they were tired of playing. They have not been taught how to bathe, diaper, properly feed and care for infants. Often, they do not know how to cope with their children when they cry, are upset or sick. One young woman, horribly scarred and mutilated by abuse in her past, tearfully told how she and her sister had accidentally killed her baby when they were high and could not stop her crying. She was never charged with a crime because they were homeless at the time it happened and the baby was an unknown. She could not remember what they had done with the baby, just that they "got rid of it."

These types of stories are far too usual among women inmates in corrections. Parenting skills are critically needed. Any boot camp program for women must focus on parenting, issues of abuse, and domestic violence. Health and nutrition are equally important. Most women have badly neglected their health. They are very likely to have neglected themselves during pregnancies, have sexually transmitted diseases, and be HIV positive. They are out of shape and physically weak. Many are either overweight or malnourished from neglect and poor nutrition and do not know how to take care of themselves. In general, they are babies of babies. It is not unusual for a seventeen year old to have more than one child, living with a thirty-two year old grandmother. Indeed, many of the women, less than thirty-five years old in Shock, older in the Drug Treatment Center and STEP, are grandmothers themselves. Preparing these young women to be good parents to their children is an important contribution for boot camps to offer.

One approach to parenting skills in Shock is the children's reading program we developed to teach mothers and fathers how to select books appropriate for reading to their children. There is a children's book corner in the prison library and children's stories are used to reinforce some of the concepts we teach in the program. For example, *The Little Engine That Could* is read and discussed during zero weeks. *Amazing Grace* is one we find particularly useful for the women. Grace's nana tells her, "You can do and be anything you want." Many of these young women missed having stories read to them as children and are excited by the whole new world opening up to them.

Another program is a Trooper Toys For Tots workshop operated out of Lakeview. Women repair toys donated by toy companies all year and prepare them for shipment at Christmas. Women and men work on packing and shipping toys and work as Santa's Elves and Toy Soldiers during the Christmas season. The women are learning how to repair toys, and it gives them a sense of contact with their children. These types of community service activities are invaluable tools, not only for the community served, but for boosting the women's sense of pride and accomplishment.

"Sisters" Can Do It!

We believe that carefully designed boot camps for women have much to offer, physically, mentally, and spiritually. They must include all of these dimensions and be staffed with people who genuinely care about teaching women to take positive control of their lives. These programs have the potential to build self-esteem in women who learn that they can accomplish positive things. Many talk about the thrill of becoming physically healthier and stronger as contributing to their positive self-image. They are proud of their accomplishments in the program and report that their children and families are proud of them too.

Bibliography

Adams, Bronte and Trudi Tate, eds. 1991. *That Kind of Woman*. New York: Carroll & Graf Publishers, Inc.

Burkhart, Kathryn. 1973. *Women in Prison*. New York: Popular Library, Doubleday and Co.

Boston Women's Health Book Collective. *Our Bodies, Ourselves*. 1996. 25th anniversary edition. New York: Simon & Schuster.

Chernin, Kim. 1983. *In My Mother's House*. New York: Harper & Row, Publishers.

Clark, Cheryl L. 1978. Network Program Plan. Unpublished document of the New York State Commission of Correction. Albany.

———. 1979, revised and updated: 1981, 1983, 1985. Network Program Procedural Manual. Unpublished document of the New York State Commission of Correction and the Department of Correctional Services. Albany.

———. 1987, 1988. Shock Incarceration Program Procedural Manual updates with R. W. Moscicki, 1989, 1991, 1994. Unpublished document of the New York State Department of Correctional Services. Albany.

———. 1995. Willard Drug Treatment Center Program Plan. Unpublished document of the New York State Department of Correctional Services. Albany.

Clark, Cheryl L., David Aziz and Doris MacKenzie. 1994. Shock Incarceration in New York: Focus on Treatment. National Institute of Justice.

Cooper, Mildred and Kenneth H. Cooper, M.D., M.P.H. 1972. *Aerobics for Women.* New York: Bantam Books.

DePorter, Bobbi with Mike Hernacki. 1992 *Quantum Learning: Unleashing the Genius in You.* New York: Bantam Doubleday, Dell Publishing Group, Inc.

Fifteen Women Doctors. 1990. 4th edition. EveryWoman's Health: The Complete Guide to Body and Mind. New York: Doubleday, Inc.

Foley, Denise, Eileen Nechas and the editors of *Prevention Magazine*. 1993. *Women's Encyclopedia of Health and Emotional Healing.* Emmaus, Pennsylvania: Rodale Press, Inc.

Friday, Nancy. *My Mother, Myself.* New York: Dell Publishing Company, Inc.

Glasser, William, M.D. 1965. *Reality Therapy.* New York: Harper & Row Publishers.

———. 1969. *Schools Without Failure.* New York: Harper & Row Publishers.

———. 1984. *Control Theory.* New York: Harper & Row Publishers.

———. 1986. *Control Theory in the Classroom.* New York: Harper & Row Publishers.

Harris, Jean. 1988. *They Always Call Us Ladies: Stories from Prison.* New York: Zebra Books.

King, Laurel. 1989. *Women of Power, 10 Visionaries Share Their Extraordinary Stories of Healing & Secrets of Success.* Berkeley, California: Celestial Arts.

LaRouche, Janice and Regina Ryan. 1984. *Janice LaRouche's Strategies for Women at Work*. New York: Avon Books.

MacKenzie, D. L. 1990. Boot Camps Grow in Number and Scope: National Institute of Justice. November/December, 6-8.

MacKenzie, D. L., and D. B. Ballow. 1989. Shock Incarceration Programs in State Correctional Jurisdictions—An Update. Washington, D.C.: National Institute of Justice.

MacKenzie, D. L., L. A. Gould, L. M. Reichers, and J. W. Shaw. 1989 Shock Incarceration: Rehabilitation or Retribution? *Journal of Offender Counseling, Services and Rehabilitation*. 14(2), 25-40.

MacKenzie, D. L. and Eugene E. Hebert, eds. 1996. *Correctional Boot Camps: A Tough Intermediate Sanction.* Washington, D. C.: National Institute of Justice.

MacKenzie, D. L. and Claire C. Souryal. 1991. Boot Camp Survey: Rehabilitation, Recidivism Reduction Outrank Punishment as Main Goals. *Corrections Today*. October: 90-96.

New York State Department of Correctional Services. 1988. First Platoon Graduates from Shock Incarceration. *D.O.C.S. Today*. April 1:12.

———. Shock Incarceration Not For Men Only. *D.O.C.S. Today.* December 2:7.

———. 1992. Shock Incarceration Five Years Later. *D.O.C.S. Today*. 4:3.

New York State Department of Correctional Services and New York State Division of Parole. 1989-1996. The . . . Annual Report to the Legislature: Shock Incarceration in New York State. Albany. Unpublished report by the Division of Program Planning, Research and Evaluation and the Office of Policy Analysis and Information.

New York State Division of Program Planning, Research and Evaluation. 1993. Characteristics of Inmates Under Custody: 1985-1992. Albany: New York State Department of Correctional Services.

Parent, D. G. 1989. Shock Incarceration: An Overview of Existing Programs. Washington, D.C.: National Institute of Justice.

Paulsen, Kathryn and Ryan A. Kuhn, eds. 1976. *Woman's Almanac: 12 How-To Handbooks in One.* New York: An Armitage Press / Information House Book, J. P. Lippincott Company.

Rush, Anne Kent. 1973. *Getting Clear: Body Work For Women.* New York: Random House.

————. 1976. *Moon, Moon.* New York: Random House, Moon Books.

Schenkel, Susan, Ph.D. 1984. *Giving Away Success: Why Women Get Stuck and What to Do About It.* New York: McGraw-Hill Book Company.

Stephens, Autumn. 1992. *Wild Women, Crusaders, Curmudgeons and Completely Corsetless Ladies in the Otherwise Virtuous Victorian Era.* Berkeley, California: Conari Press.

Violence Against Women Project. Washington, D.C. Senior Policy Specialist Catherine Pierce, (202) 723-6666.

Walker, Barbara G. 1985. *The Crone: Woman of Age, Wisdom and Power.* San Francisco, California: Harper and Row, Publishers.

Boot Camp Standards—Can They Help Officials Plan a Facility?

Carole Sanchez Knapel

Consultant
Capitola, California

Introduction

Too often in jurisdictions throughout the country, the word comes down to the department of corrections that the elected representatives want to have a boot camp program in their jurisdiction. Even more distressing, they want the program to start up immediately!

In recent years, the popularity of boot camp programs has skyrocketed. Programs have been developed at every jurisdictional level for all types of inmates, both adults and juveniles. There are many theories about why this is so, but even though there is much disagreement in corrections about the effectiveness of such programs, one conclusion is shared by most: the number of boot camp programs is continuing to increase.

Corrections officials must respond to the ongoing demand to develop boot camp programs—and they want to do this by creating an effective program. The American Correctional Association, recognizing the need for information on boot camp programs, has developed standards for the operation of both adult and juvenile boot camp programs.

To accomplish this task, in 1993, the American Correctional Association brought together corrections officials, medical advisors, representatives of state and local governments and organizations, and corrections researchers. The group met over the course of two years, examining both research findings on effective boot camp programs and operational procedures from jurisdictions throughout the country. The result of the effort was a separate set of standards for both adult and juvenile boot camp programs. As is the case with all standards developed by the American Correctional Association, the boot camp program standards provide for the accreditation of the individual boot camps. As always, accreditation offers several benefits, including the demonstration of a jurisdiction's efforts to improve conditions of confinement, maintain a safe and humane environment for all corrections personnel, and establish measurable criteria for monitoring and improving programs and personnel on an ongoing basis.

Program Planning

In addition to the straightforward benefits of the use of standards and participation in the accreditation process, the boot camp standards provide critical assistance for the planning of a boot camp program. Because boot camp programs are relatively new, in developing the standard, we obtained critical information from research on programs in operation. These research findings have been incorporated into the standards in several key areas.

During the process of developing the boot camp standards, the research provided insight in areas which are critical in the operation of a boot camp. The research, which has been completed and published, has focused on practical operations issues such as program goals, program effectiveness, and staff selection and training. As a result, corrections officials who are planning boot camp programs can use the research findings through the standards to create an effective program.

The following key issues have been addressed in the standards which made use of research findings. These areas are critical for the jurisdictions which are determined to commence a boot camp program.

Key Planning Issues

1. Purpose and Mission

Goal: To have a written body of policy and procedure that establishes the facility's goals, objectives and standard operating procedures and establishes a system of regular review.

All standards developed by the American Correctional Association begin with the need to establish a mission. The Boot Camp Program standards also indicate that the program must establish a mission. However, the research indicates that initially, the mission of a boot camp may be difficult to identify.

In part, the difficulty of establishing a mission arises out of the need for the program to satisfy a variety of needs. Among the most frequently cited reasons for establishing a boot camp program are the following:

- reducing crowding in traditional corrections facilities
- reducing the cost of corrections
- rehabilitating the offender/reducing recidivism
- protecting the public/deterring crime
- addressing public concerns with increasing crime/punishment of offenders

While each of these goals can be important, programs cannot be effectively developed to address all of these goals equally. That is, it is not possible for a single program to have equally important goals of rehabilitation of inmates and punishment of inmates. The planning of a boot camp program requires a very clear decision about the program's mission. Out of this early decision, all programming will follow.

For example, inmate rehabilitation frequently is indicated as a goal for boot camp programs. Corrections officials who determine to address this goal may choose to provide program components of education, job training, or substance abuse counseling or treatment. However, officials who choose to address a primary goal of inmate punishment may not see these programs as useful.

Further, for a boot camp program to be effective, it must be based on a mission which is attainable. Many programs, for example, focus on the need to reduce crowding in a corrections facility. To emphasize this goal, corrections officials must develop a program which significantly reduces the length of time an inmate spends in custody from the time that an inmate would spend in the traditional corrections facility. A boot camp program developed by a state jurisdiction has a potential opportunity to significantly reduce in-custody time for sentenced inmates. A local jurisdiction, however, might have a more difficult task if this is a primary program goal because inmates generally are not in custody for significantly long periods.

2. Size, Location, Organization

Goal: To have a facility that affords flexibility, creativity, and innovation in meeting the concerns for effective programming, safety, and quality of life for both staff and offenders.

The American Correctional Association's boot camp standards indicate that the physical facility should allow for flexibility in the program. Although this is a standard that also is used for other facility types, nowhere is it more useful than in the boot camp programs. Because the boot camp concept is relatively new, it is important that the program provide the flexibility for change.

The original boot camp program concept most often included a heavy emphasis on a harsh environment, physical training, military precision, and ceremony. As more programs have developed, some have incorporated education, job training, and substance abuse counseling. Much of the change has been driven by ongoing assessment and evaluation completed on existing programs. As evidence of evaluation results accumulates, corrections officials have incorporated these findings into their operation.

As a way of meeting this standard, corrections officials should incorporate monitoring and assessing of programs into their program planning process. In this way, the jurisdiction will have data to demonstrate program effectiveness, make program adjustments as indicated, and continue to further the collection of corrections data for use by officials throughout the country.

To effectively use limited resources, corrections officials must have an understanding of the effectiveness of all programs. The collection of program data, combined with the establishment of a flexible, creative program will allow for the best use of available resources.

3. Training and Staff Development

Goal: To have a written body of policy and procedure that establishes the facility's training and staff development programs, including training requirements for all categories of personnel.

Whatever the stated mission and goals of a particular boot camp program, all boot camp programs are unique within their own correctional systems. Given this fact, it is critical that the staff fully understands their own program theory and philosophy. Even more than traditional programs, boot camp programs must have specific staff training requirements. Such training should address the interrelationships of security, programs, and administration.

Further, the training of staff for boot camp programs must provide for the opportunity for staff to build unity and teamwork in a way that will provide for these concepts to be demonstrated to the inmate population. Jurisdictions which have developed staff training have included courses in leadership skills, physical training, control theory, demonstrations of training methods to develop decision-making skills, and concepts of substance abuse education, treatment, and counseling. This type of staff training assists in the emphasis on a multidisciplinary approach to the boot camp program concept.

Research findings provide important information on issues of staff training and development. Some programs indicated that corrections staff initially have been hesitant to work in a boot camp program because they were not comfortable with punitive aspects of some programs. Other jurisdictions have indicated that they have had overly zealous staff who may not clearly understand the delineation between exercise of authority and abuse of that authority. Still other jurisdictions have indicated that the training of corrections staff for boot camp programs has been difficult because the nature of the program required that staff learn new roles.

To address these issues, the staff training program must be carefully planned. The training must begin with a basic understanding of the concepts of boot camp programs, in general, and the jurisdiction's specific boot camp programs, in particular. Therefore, training must include an opportunity to better understand inmate needs, the interrelationships of security and programs, group unity and teamwork, and provide an opportunity for staff to develop personal confidence which can be passed on to the inmate participants.

In addition to the initial training, the American Correctional Association's standards address the need for annual training. Again, the intense nature of boot camp programs requires constant monitoring to ensure that staff and inmates focus on the true goals of the program. Without such a monitoring and retraining effort, the program can move away from the central goals of the program.

4. Rules and Discipline

Goal: To ensure that all discipline is Specific, Measurable, Attainable, Realistic, and Time limited (SMART), and that the facility's rules of conduct, sanctions, and procedures for violations are defined in writing and communicated to offenders and staff.

Disciplinary procedures are to be carried out promptly and with respect for the offenders. Boot camp programs are based on regimented behavior and discipline. Despite the stated goals and mission of individual programs, surveyed programs indicate that these program components are key.

Even with the focus on discipline, however, boot camp programs must address the more general corrections' goals of reasonable and fair sanctions. Boot camp programs, by their nature, can develop informal procedures which are contradictory to these types of general corrections practice. Under the model used by many programs, the sanctions for violations often are relatively severe and immediate. The concepts of review and appeal may not appear to be consistent with these objectives.

Research on boot camp programs also has examined this issue. Many researchers as well as corrections officials have suggested that a program based on fear, which is used to modify criminal behavior may not be effective. At the same time, boot camp program standards require that boot camp programs adhere to the general corrections practice. Conformance with this boot camp standard can provide for disciplinary procedures while also maintaining reasonable and fair standards.

Issues of offenders' rights follow closely the issues of rules and discipline. That is, the boot camp program cannot abandon general corrections practice which requires a balance between the expression of individual rights and the preservation of order. For example, boot camp program participants must continue to have access to courts and counsel. Further, the inmate must be protected from harm. Sanctions which affect the offender's health, physical, or psychological well-being should be prohibited.

In addition, the boot camp program must provide an opportunity for all inmates. This is of particular concern when the program offers an opportunity for a shorter period of incarceration for those who participate. Federal law requires that within the requirements of facility security, all inmates must be provided the same access to programs if they meet the program requirements.

Program planners need to take this requirement into account in the development of programs. For example, female inmates must be provided an opportunity to participate in a program even if the original concept was developed for male inmates. Inmates with physical disabilities also should be provided an opportunity to participate. They cannot be prohibited from participation solely because of a disability.

Conclusion

The American Correctional Association's standards for the operation of a boot camp program provide valuable assistance for those jurisdictions which have commenced the planning of a program. Because the standards were developed based on research findings, as well as on a review of effective programs, the standards provide planning guidelines.

Boot camp programs are unique in corrections in several key ways.

1. The development of a program depends initially on the development of a clear mission.

2. The unique nature of the boot camp program requires specialized staff training and a continuous training program.

3. Inmate rules and discipline also present unique challenges in the creation of a boot camp program.

The standards, which have been developed for boot camp operations, address each of these issues. The process used for the development of these standards suggests that effective program planning can result if a planning agency adapts these operational standards as a planning guide.

Note: A list of boot camps accredited by the American Correctional Association is in the Appendix. These programs all met the standards established for boot camps.

Illinois' Impact Incarceration Program: Evaluation and Implementation Issues

Robert J. Jones

Research Scientist, Planning and Research Unit
Illinois Department of Corrections
Springfield, Illinois

Introduction

During the 1980s, like other state correctional systems, the Illinois Department of Corrections was experiencing an astronomical population growth. In 1990, the adult prison population had nearly doubled over the past seven years. The Illinois prison population far exceeded rated capacity despite the building of eleven new medium- and minimum-security prisons during the 1980s, which were designed to house 9,555 additional inmates.

Increases in offenders incarcerated for violent crimes with long prison sentences was one reason why long-term offenders were stockpiling in the state's prisons. Moreover, an unprecedented volume of offenders sentenced to prison for manufacture or delivery of controlled substances resulted in the processing of hundreds of drug offenders through the reception and classification centers on a weekly basis. Residential burglars were receiving mandatory prison sentences, while younger offenders convicted of burglary, motor vehicle theft, retail theft, and other property crimes were taking up increasing numbers of prison beds.

At the end of 1990, over 7,500 property offenders were in prison (27 percent of the prison population). Almost half of these inmates would return to prison within three years of their release. More strikingly, there were only 851 inmates incarcerated for a drug offense in 1985. Yet, in 1990, there were 4,681 inmates, a 450 percent increase; they served a mere thirteen months in prison.

As the decade was coming to a close with Illinois' prisons full of young, nonviolent drug and property offenders, legislators and prison administrators began to seriously explore the use of alternatives for these offenders. One choice was a shock incarceration program. Like most shock incarceration programs, Illinois' prison boot camp program, termed Impact Incarceration Program, instills a structured environment to address the multiple problems young street-oriented men and women have which lead to their criminal activity. The Impact Incarceration Program was one of the first prison boot camps to incorporate extensive residential program service elements plus an intensive supervision aftercare component.

The Impact Incarceration Program focuses on offenders at risk of continued criminal activity because of substance abuse, poor social skills, and other related problems. The intent is to build character through order and discipline, encourage a sense of maturity and responsibility, and promote a positive self-image that will motivate the offender to be a law-abiding citizen. The ultimate goal is to increase public safety by promoting and reinforcing lawful behavior of the youthful offender. At the same time, the Illinois Department of Corrections hopes to save valuable bed space for higher-risk inmates.

The Task Force on Crime and Corrections in 1993 recommended expanding the Impact Incarceration Program's legal eligibility criteria, largely due to the boot camp's preliminary success in reducing recidivism and prison crowding. A new law allows for offenders age seventeen to thirty-five, sentenced up to eight years, and incarcerated as an adult for a second time to be eligible for the Impact Incarceration Program. Prior to this,

offenders eligible for the program had to be age seventeen to twenty-five, with a prison sentence of five years or less, and incarcerated as an adult for the first time.

This chapter focuses on the importance of planning of all phases of program activities. This includes: reporting and evaluating procedures, designing and measuring outcomes, and designing special program components.

Impact Incarceration Program Services

Two facets of the Impact Incarceration Program programming phase were particularly distinctive when the program was developed in 1990: a three-tiered substance abuse education/treatment program and aftercare.

Substance Abuse Education and Treatment

Due to the documented drug and alcohol abuse histories of the majority of criminals, we placed emphasis on a continuum of substance abuse treatments. The process begins at admission and continues through PreStart supervision. The Impact Incarceration Program provides a unique opportunity for treating substance abuse and breaking the cycle of drugs and crime.

During orientation, inmates are fully assessed and evaluated; they provide a social history; a diagnosis is made, and a treatment plan is discussed with the client. As a result, approximately 70 percent of Impact Incarceration Program participants are identified as probable substance abusers. From the assessments conducted by licensed substance abuse professionals, inmates are classified into three categories.

Level I inmates are designated as those with no probable substance abuse problem and receive two weeks of education. Participants discuss communication and daily living skills; the effects of inhalants, hallucinogens, narcotics, stimulants, depressants, marijuana, cocaine, tobacco, and alcohol; and tuberculosis and AIDS. Inmates learn to make identifications and distinctions between different types of drugs and their effects. A post-test is given at the end of the two weeks to determine the change in the client's knowledge base.

Level II inmates are considered to be probable substance abusers. In addition to drug education, these inmates receive drug treatment in which, among other topics, denial and family support issues are discussed in group therapy. Inmates determined to have probable drug addictions are placed in Level III group services. Topics of discussion include relapse, co-dependency, behavioral differences, and addicted families, along with the role that the inmate plays within the family. During the final two weeks of the boot camp, inmates designated Level II or Level III meet with substance abuse counselors to arrange referrals for treatment on release. This approach allows appropriate treatment for each inmate in need of intensive services.

Substance abuse services are provided by independent contractors. Services are given during afternoons and evenings, ensuring that program participants receive their therapy as diagnosed in their treatment plan. We have established an extensive referral system to substance abuse personnel so that treatment can continue to be provided after release. This also enables staff to monitor activities and conduct follow-up inquiries.

Postrelease

On release from the boot camp phase, offenders participate in an intensive community supervision program, Phase II of the PreStart program. Aftercare supervision is designed to closely monitor the releasee's activities so that controls can be tailored for diversion from previously conducted negative activity.

The primary focus of the aftercare component is to provide education and assistance to releasees in securing community-based services. Releasees are under electronic monitoring and violation procedures, and for some, a special drug program. Field staff provide community reintegration, referral, support, and follow-up services. Thus, we provide more complete service delivery while ensuring the safety of the public. Released inmates who demonstrate positive adjustment may be recommended to the prisoner review board for early discharge from supervision.

We use electronic detention during this phase to gradually release the offender from the totally structured and controlled environment to the free community. The PreStart staff must approve a schedule outlining the graduate's activities outside the home. Face-to-face contacts are frequent. They place emphasis on achieving beneficial programming of employment, education, substance abuse counseling, and training. Through intensive supervision, drug usage is closely monitored. Frequent drug testing quickly identifies any relapses.

Program activities for Impact Incarceration Program releasees include education, work or job service, public service or volunteer work, substance abuse counseling or support groups, group therapy, and family group therapy. Releasees with limited work histories, or who have no viable vocational skills, are encouraged to enroll in a training program. We require functionally illiterate releasees to enroll in a literacy program. We also require releasees to register with the local Job Service and work with them until they find a job. We mandate drug and/or alcohol counseling for those with a substance abuse history. With the exception of medical restrictions, no releasee is allowed to sit at home idly.

The Importance of Planning

The success associated with a smooth and timely implementation of the Impact Incarceration Program is due to thoughtful planning.

Planning Committee

Planning should begin before serious consideration is given to operating a boot camp program. Many program descriptions and evaluations are now published. Those interested in establishing and running a boot camp must read the literature to determine if a boot camp will solve their prison crowding issues.

For example, if long-term violent offenders are causing a jurisdiction's prisons or jails to be filled while equal numbers of property and drug offenders are simply replacing each other in the system, the shortened prison stays of a boot camp program will not combat the real issue. If recidivism rates are high because of the recycling of the same drug dealers, burglars, and thieves, the shock incarceration of a military-style boot camp may have little effect. If older, less vulnerable and less agile offenders are finally coming to prison after years of revolving through the probation-jail-periodic imprisonment system, a system of exercise, basic education, and life skills will not have the impact it would have on relatively unsophisticated criminals who would benefit most by the style of the impact incarceration setting. Then, if a jurisdiction believes that shortening an offender's stay in prison will save them money, a careful budgetary review may reveal unanticipated financial problems associated with increased costs for food, clothing, tools, additional staff and vehicles, and other expenses associated with operation of a boot camp.

Furthermore, to open and operate a boot camp, a great deal of assistance is required from the legislative and executive branch of government. Judges may not accept the concept and may not agree to sentence a sufficient number of youthful offenders to the military-style environment. Legislators may be led falsely by political motives to open a program which may not increase public safety. However, by regularly surveying the key decision makers and keeping them informed, you build a constituency for your program that provides a bulwark against later resistance to the program. Additionally, by careful early planning, you eliminate many of the obstacles that would threaten or defeat your program.

Once the administration decides to explore the use of a boot camp program more seriously, an abbreviated formal planning committee should be selected to meet regularly to develop an implementation plan. Experienced staff and resources from primary interagency divisions should be made available to consult in the planning and implementation of the shock incarceration program. Based on Illinois' experience, the following groups should be part of the planning process:

- executive staff and wardens who provide experience in the administration and planning for opening of correctional facilities and related programs, as well as provide input on staff training needs and potential inmate issues

- a legislative liaison to assist in writing and enacting appropriate legislation

- legal services to identify and examine legal issues

- architects and engineers to assist in the planning, building and/or conversion of the boot camp facility

- clinical services to provide information on program services and inmate movement issues

- a transfer coordinator to assist with regulations for inmate movements and classification

- line staff to give impressions of what to expect from inmates based on their population; this includes correctional officers with and without military experience

- health care experts to address medical, mental health, dietary, and environmental issues, and substance abuse needs

- a representative from the school district to establish the basic education curriculum

- members of the treatment staff to coordinate the instruction of life skills and substance abuse programs, and to provide individual assessments and counseling; we recommend contracted service providers from a certified local agency

- representatives from the juvenile division to provide recommendations for managing youthful offenders in an institutional setting and in the community

- parole staff members to develop strategies for release preparation and to coordinate the postrelease supervision system

- representatives from the policy and directives section of the state government to establish policies and procedures and to coordinate efforts with the legislative liaison and legal services staff

- representatives of inmates to focus on and develop policies regarding inmate privileges and grievance procedures

- personnel to coordinate labor relations and handle central screening concerning employee issues

- the training academy representatives to help prepare a specialized boot camp curriculum and training manual

- representatives from planning, research, and evaluation of the state government to provide background information on strategies used by other correctional authorities; they would prepare grants and determine the data needs to monitor the program's developmental progress

- data processing to identify and analyze data needs, develop or update the database, and prepare automated periodic reports

- a public information officer to inform the media and criminal justice professionals of program concepts, activities, and merits

- union representatives, if applicable, to prepare for any staffing issues during the hiring stage and disciplinary hearings

Initial Planning Procedures

Prior to receiving input from the large group described above, the planning committee must prepare for their first meeting. This is done by a review of research publications, evaluations, training manuals, and the regulations of boot camps in other jurisdictions. Because shock incarceration programs have been operational across the country for well over a decade, jurisdictions should build on the experiences of other agencies. You can use their ideas and learn from their mistakes. There is no longer a need to "reinvent the wheel" in planning the details of a prison boot camp.

Later, committee members experienced in corrections as well as the military, educators, treatment professionals, and community service experts should have the opportunity to express their ideas and concerns. They should note how a shock incarceration program would affect both positively and negatively their responsibilities and those of the entire correctional department.

During these planning meetings, the committee should define a concept and a philosophy. At this time, it is important to write a formal mission statement for the program. It should address the degree to which discipline, physical activities, labor details, and military bearing will interplay with program services, including instruction and after-care supervision. The mission statement is vital. All other programmatic decisions stem from this focus.

After establishing the general purpose and program philosophy, it is necessary to set program goals and objectives. Achieving these goals depends on determining measurable objectives which can be evaluated. Devise a timetable for monitoring specific goals and objectives, and for documenting achievements as they are met.

Legislation

Development of a prison boot camp program most likely will require changes in state or local statutes. Correctional department staff must work with key legislators to draft legislation. The legislative process can be long and arduous. Expect constant revisions in the language used to describe the program and political concessions. Compromise is necessary as staff from many branches of corrections and the state government express their concerns for issues.

The Illinois legislative process began in February 1989. The Impact Incarceration Program was established in July 1990.

Site Visits

In establishing your own boot camp program, it is essential that your department of corrections' staff visit and discuss shock incarceration programs with experienced administrators and line staff before and after program implementation. The exchange of ideas will yield meaningful information on the successes and failures of other programs. Planning committee members and program administrators can then apply these vital factors to refining their specific philosophy and developing a program whose procedures and operations are supported by other programs. In the long run, this saves time and energy and means fewer problems will be confrontational.

Site visits to existing prison boot camp programs allow staff to see first hand the movements and feel the atmosphere of this intense program. We recommended that agency administrators, legislators, and future boot camp staff visit sites for approximately three days, and at least one day from reveille to lights out. Key staff may wish to stay up to two weeks, so they can witness all phases of the program's operations, review program documents, and interview experienced line and programming staff. Researchers who go on site can discuss shock incarceration evaluation strategies. Visits can be funded by grant funds, particularly technical assistance monies from the National Institute of Justice.

For those hosting such visits, as well as for staff training, it is wise to develop videos on operations. Such videos may be shown in training sessions or staff meetings for central office personnel, correctional officers, and a range of support staff including dietary officials, educators, substance abuse counselors, secretaries, and others.

After a boot camp is open for six months, staff, now experienced in the implementation and operation of a boot camp program, can observe functions at other longer-running boot camp facilities. At this point, staff will be able to evaluate further the implementation progress of their program. On their return, they will be better able to discuss unforeseen ideas on program components, philosophy, operations, and facility design.

Staffing

We are concerned about two staffing issues. The first issue is the experience of security staff. Some administrators argue that officers should have military experience; others do not want that influence to be conveyed to criminal offenders with serious substance abuse problems and antagonistic histories with authority. We encourage a diversity of experiences, combined with consistent training methods. Further, we believe security staff should have at least one year of correctional-officer experience and an understanding of the philosophy of a conventional prison. Thus, by the time they begin work at the boot camp, they will have practical experience combined with specialized boot camp training.

Second, all staff should be required to maintain themselves in good physical condition. We recommended that officers lead the inmates in exercise and drills, and, as leaders, they cannot fall behind. Staff medical examinations and psychological screening should be mandatory. Such procedures may have to be negotiated with employee unions.

Selection Decision Authority

There are also two key issues regarding inmate selection. First, the decision makers must determine who selects offenders to participate in a boot camp program: judges, corrections department officials, or a combination. This factor may influence whether the program "widens the net" to include offenders who otherwise would not have been incarcerated; or whether the sanction is used strictly as an alternative to longer-term incarceration, in which case, it would result in reduced prison crowding.

Probably, prison admissions will increase if sentencing judges are allowed sole discretion. Most likely, judges will sentence those offenders to boot camp who would normally receive probation, in hopes of frightening young impressionable offenders with "shock incarceration" to deter the need for future punishment. On the other hand, disallowing judicial discretion may hinder any existing cooperation between the courts and already crowded correctional systems.

Illinois legislators concluded that the sentencing judge would recommend a statutorily eligible inmate for placement in the program. Then, Illinois Department of Corrections staff would review the case further to ensure all eligibility requirements have been met and determine if the inmate would pose a safety or security risk. This system allows a series of criminal justice professionals to review each inmate's circumstances to select the lowest-risk candidates. On the other hand, with all denied offenders transferred to prison, this increases the likelihood of some net widening.

Second, adult inmates should be given the opportunity to volunteer to participate. This philosophy will reduce the probability of escape, as inmates are free to leave and do not have to face the unknown consequences of "running" when they get scared or realize they can no longer undergo the program's military-based rigorous activities. Inmates most often cite unfair treatment, medical problems, general philosophical differences, or willingness to serve their court-ordered sentences followed by regular community supervision as reasons for quitting.

Informing Judges

Sentencing judges must be made fully aware of the criteria, components, and philosophy of the shock incarceration program during the planning stages. It is important that corrections officials talk to judges early in the planning stage. The Illinois Department of Corrections has made numerous ventures to inform judges so that their recommendation are knowledgeable. The staff work with the administrative office of the Illinois Courts to inform judges during judicial training sessions. Copies of the Impact Incarceration Program reports are mailed to judges to keep them informed of the progress of the program.

To publicize the program, we made a video of the Illinois Impact Incarceration Program available prior to program inception. It was distributed to judges and other interested parties. Then, we prepared and distributed a second video which displays program activities after the Illinois Impact Incarceration Program began operations.

Informing Impact Incarceration Program Candidates

Inmates often are given poor information about correctional programs. Court personnel and attorneys usually provide limited facts about the prison environment. With up to

400 inmates admitted to the Illinois Department of Corrections every week, a correctional counselor's time is limited. To allow for a detailed, visually displayed explanation of the Illinois Impact Incarceration Program, staff prepared a video specifically designed for inmates, in a language which they could understand. The video explains the concept of the Impact Incarceration Program for recommended offenders who have not yet volunteered to participate.

To address boot camp issues, counselors at the most active reception and classification center at Joliet Correctional Center have set aside one day per week to process recommended Impact Incarceration Program candidates so they could explain the program more fully and answer specific questions. Illinois' experience shows that reception counselors should be trained to provide consistent, reliable information to potential candidates. Any forms which inmates will review while making their decision to enter a boot camp should be made available in both English and Spanish. Inmates must be informed of all consequences before they sign any forms. A review of an orientation manual at the reception center may assist inmates in making their decision.

Temporary Housing

While approved inmates should be transferred immediately to the boot camp to begin their program, in several instances, inmates may be temporarily housed at a traditional adult facility, although separate from the general population. First, inmates may have a medical problem, which delays their approval. Second, there may be confusion regarding the legal paperwork which accompanies the inmate. A statement of facts may not be available to inform staff of the specific circumstances of the offense, or an outstanding warrant or detainer may exist. Until all court documents and warrants can be reviewed, the inmate cannot be approved for the boot camp.

Third, the number of projected judicial recommendations may increase beyond expectations. It may be difficult to determine the number of eligible inmates for the program, who will be selected and approved by court and corrections personnel, and who will volunteer to participate. In Illinois, at one time the backlog reached 224 inmates, waiting an average of four months to enter the program. This increased their prison stay and reduced expected cost savings.

The admittance delay contributed to a number of inmates being declared ineligible because they either refused to enter the program or acquired disciplinary infractions while awaiting transfer. Many approved inmates revoked their consent to participate for two reasons. First, the inmates discovered the lengthy timeframe for entering the Illinois Impact Incarceration Program after expecting to be admitted immediately after processing at the reception center. Second, with the inmate's release becoming imminent, the traditional prison and regular parole options became feasible alternatives without having to undergo the strenuous nature of the program along with intensive supervision.

Logistical and security problems are enhanced at a designated pre-boot camp holding facility. In Illinois, keeping the Impact Incarceration Program inmates separate from the general population caused shuffling of institutional schedules. For example, Impact Incarceration Program inmates had their recreational periods at night, when the other inmates were sleeping or confined to their cells. Also, there were confrontations among inmates, as general population inmates taunted and ridiculed inmates in the holding unit. Most importantly, housing pre-shock inmates in a traditional prison environment will affect the intention of the shock concept.

Orientation Manual

An inmate orientation manual should be prepared for the inmates. Our orientation manual includes our mission statement, program expectations, daily schedules, formal procedures regarding care of personal items, inmate grooming standards, dress codes, foot locker maintenance requirements, a narrative describing expectations and program activities, written rules for disciplinary procedures, and a description of the inmate grievance process.

Graduation Ceremony

Graduations are an excellent public relations tool to demonstrate the positive, self-fulfilling experience of successfully completing the 120 days. Some planners and Impact Incarceration Program staff opposed the graduation ceremony because it was a deviation from the formal regimentation. Yet, we included formal graduation ceremonies in the Impact Incarceration Program's original design to reflect a positive ceremonious display of accomplishment. At the ceremony, the boot camp staff congratulate the graduates indi-

vidually and give them a diploma. We invite former graduates to return to demonstrate to their fellow inmates how they have learned respect for authority and have achieved the ability to work with others. The graduates encourage the inmates who are just beginning program activities or contemplating voluntary termination from the program.

Media Exposure

Boot camp programs are presented by the electronic and print media as punishing and threatening treatment for criminals. Citizens are certainly supportive of this perspective, so the media portrays prison boot camps in this manner. However, the Illinois Department of Correction's Public Information Office has used the media to inform citizens and criminal justice professionals of significant accomplishments and noteworthy achievements. A notable example of positive media exposure took place during the midwest flood relief efforts in 1993. Although correctional staff and inmates statewide participated in the cleanup, the Impact Incarceration Program received particular notice. Boot camp inmates often were shown assisting local residents trying to save their homes and communities.

The Illinois Impact Incarceration Program received televised news coverage in Illinois and Missouri. *Newsweek* and *The New York Times* carried accounts of the clean-up efforts, as well as did CBS *This Morning* and the *48 Hours* program. The Cable News Network showed boot camp inmates at work on *The World Today*. Since then, boot camp inmates have become involved in projects to cleanup after numerous tornados struck central Illinois. This alternative depiction of a boot camp program was accomplished through good media relations and innovative presentations.

Program Evaluation

The Illinois Department of Corrections has made a commitment to conduct periodic reviews and to monitor the program continuously due to the initial requirement by the National Institute of Justice to evaluate the Impact Incarceration Program. We submitted an annual report documenting the program's progress to the governor and the general assembly.

The evaluation research design includes four areas of emphasis that describe how the boot camp operates and determines the impact of the program on participants and on the Illinois Department of Corrections. We offer descriptive statistics, process evaluation, analyses of impact measures, and cost analyses. Research methods and data collection instruments that were developed as part of a National Institute of Justice Multisite Study of Shock Incarceration assist our evaluation staff. An automated database makes match-group comparisons and analyzes demographic, criminal history, and outcome data. Preliminary evaluation results allowed the state department of corrections to objectively make decisions and recommendations for expanding the program and the eligibility criteria.

Descriptive Statistics of Recommended Offenders

Since the opening of the first facility at Dixon Springs, we have tabulated descriptive statistics to provide the Illinois Department of Corrections with a profile of the offenders who are eligible for the Illinois Impact Incarceration Program but not recommended by judges, those denied participation due to legal concerns and Department criteria, and those admitted. We track those admitted, the number of graduates, movements to court writs or medical facilities, quitters, and terminations due to either a series of minor violations (program reviews) or a serious incident (adjustment committee hearing).

Movement data are recorded manually, and verified in the Department's Offender Tracking System database. Recently, we added transfers between boot camps because some inmates were relocated to another facility for administrative reasons (boyfriend/girl-friend, enemies). The transfer coordinator's office maintains weekly summaries of inmates recommended by the courts. This office is responsible for approving, assigning, and transporting inmates to the Illinois Impact Incarceration Program facilities. These descriptive statistics are included in the Department's Monthly Population Summary. Statistics are aggregated on a fiscal year basis, and a cumulative table is produced for the annual reports to the Governor and the General Assembly. Ad hoc requests for specific information can be provided within the hour.

Denial Statistics

All reports of the program's progress include data on inmates denied entry into the program. We then conduct analyses to see what factors distinguish between offenders who are admitted to the Impact Incarceration Program and those who are denied.

Inmates can be denied entry for a number of reasons, which are documented. These data are evaluated by the state department of corrections administrators, and this information is used to improve the approval process. The sentencing court may find errors or administrators may make discoveries of unreported or falsely provided eligibility criteria, escape risk, or outstanding warrant information. Continually informing court personnel of errors and problems which arise in the review process ensures that up-to-date, accurate information is available at the time of approval.

We constantly inform medical personnel and psychologists at the reception and classification centers to be aware of people with asthma, existing injuries, old wounds, or psychological issues which would result in an approved inmate later being removed for these preexisting problems. Our program evaluators keep track of any backlogs of inmates awaiting transfer, and notify administrators regularly so plans for any necessary additional facilities can begin in a timely manner. As part of the process evaluation, evaluators also interview inmates who refuse to participate, and they inform administrators of the reasons they cite.

Impact Incarceration Program Females

We evaluate female boot camp inmate issues very closely since the first intake in October 1990. Then, ten beds at the Dixon Springs Impact Incarceration Program were available to females. Due to expansion of statutory criteria, the number of female beds was expanded in 1994. During this period of adding new beds, we renovated the female dormitory to house a larger population.

We used grant funds to allow females to participate in boot camp programs. In August 1995, we received a grant from the United States Department of Justice for $697,500 to renovate the boot camp to accommodate more female inmates. The state provided matching funds of $232,500 bringing the total available to $930,000. We will use these funds to add twenty-six more beds to the female housing area, modify and expand classrooms, and upgrade electrical, lighting, and fire exits. After renovation, our new female capacity will be fifty beds.

Process Evaluation

The process evaluation helps us to determine if the program is operating the way it was originally designed. Implementation data is collected through observation, interviews, and reviews of written materials, then compared to the design and timelines of the planning committee. We discuss discrepancies with boot camp administrators.

We use our evaluation plan to direct the researchers' observations. As the research progresses, we make refinements of questions, employ close-ended questionnaires, and structure observation schedules. In addition to observing classes in progress, our evaluators also observe staff-to-staff as well as staff-to-inmate interactions. We conduct interviews with all program staff, security staff, administrators, and inmates. Interviews are directed toward acquiring information that cannot be obtained while observing classroom sessions.

We employ at least three researchers at the boot camp on varying days, times, and classes. After each period of observation or interview, they dictate and type their field notes. These data are used to illustrate and support the conclusions drawn from this stage of research. We set quotes off by quotation marks. We put any interpretation or comments about the observation or interview in parenthesis.

To complete our evaluation, researchers also collect all relevant materials that are used for instruction and assessment. We obtain any guidelines or manuals developed as part of the course curriculums, as well as evaluation forms, in-class assignments, reading materials, and tests which are used to document the progress of inmates. We review inmate records, with assessments matched with referrals to note if appropriate action is being taken to prepare the inmate for using community resources after release. A final report summarizes all data, draws conclusions, and makes recommendations for each specific area of inquiry.

The results of our evaluatiion has provided the Illinois Department of Corrections with a comprehensive understanding of the implementation and development of Illinois' program. We examined each function of the daily operations: orientation, program services, disciplinary methods, and physical activities. External areas of evaluation included: security staff training procedures, the reception and classification process, administrative problems at the pre-Impact Incarceration Program holding facilities, and the intensive supervision program. Observations also focused on the relations between security and program staff. As a result of the process evaluation, the Illinois Department of Corrections opened two additional Impact Incarceration Program facilities with greater ease.

We gave high priority to examination of the program service components (substance abuse, education, life skills, and release preparation). We conducted interviews with staff on their formal and informal roles and duties in relation to programming. We also interviewed inmates about what they viewed as beneficial.

A common problem in participant observation and unobtrusive methodologies is that people being evaluated will act differently, unnaturally, as they think the observers want them to behave. At Dixon Springs, we assigned a researcher to make occasional visits to the facility to collect data and inspect operations. When the formal process evaluation was to take place, we brought in a second researcher to record data. Inmates were oblivious of the observations taking place, but security staff became well aware. Even though the researchers were well informed by their supervisor, they could not combat the Hawthorne Effect brought on by the staff's presence. They made initial observations, but the research staff did not have confidence that reliable, consistent data were being recorded.

To increase reliability, we assigned one researcher to spend more time at the facility and have staff become more comfortable with his presence. In addition, we brought in three other researchers, posing as Illinois Department of Corrections staff, interested in the specific activities of the program, for occasional visits. These researchers collected data at random periods to assist in determining evaluation areas that had been overlooked, and to provide objective (unbiased) suggestions that may have hindered research goals due to continued observation of Impact Incarceration Program operations by the on-site researcher. They took no notes in front of staff; they recorded field notes in private after a period of observation. Those evaluators had to remember more, and surely some detail was lost, but the recorded data were more reliable as staff were unaffected by researchers' presence.

This method was most successful in evaluation of two program elements: the intake process and training. The first intake contact by boisterous staff on naive inmates is interesting, and somewhat entertaining. Security staff were accustomed to being observed by a number of people, and had little or no knowledge of which staff were recording their actions. Therefore, researchers who posed as interested observers, instead of as data collectors, allowed staff to act naturally during intake.

To study the training methods, a researcher posed as a staffer who was partaking in the training as a new Illinois Department of Corrections' employee. It is a common procedure that all staff associated with the program undergo training. Thus, as the researcher went through the training, he inconspicuously recorded notes relating to the lessons and methods used to teach those procedures to the Illinois Department of Corrections' personnel. This method, along with interviews and review of training materials, led to a very detailed evaluation of the preservice training methods used for boot camp staff.

General Equivalency Diploma Attainment

A very effective method of using quantitative data in a process evaluation relates to the percentage of Impact Incarceration Programs participants who obtained a general equivalency diploma while in the program. Inmates serve a relatively short period of time in the Impact Incarceration Program, and most of their day is spent with physical activities. They have three hours in the evenings for programming, only part of which is for school.

The process evaluation began qualitatively with a brief description of the educational and assessment processes. Areas of instruction include math, English, science, social studies, literature and arts, and reading comprehension. Study times are available outside of the classroom, and we offer tutoring by other inmates.

Quantitatively, we measure success by calculating the percentage of inmates who take the general education development test and pass. We compare these rates to "graduation rates" of inmates in traditional institutions. As of June 30, 1995, 810 inmates had taken the general education development test while participating in the Impact Incarceration Program, and 704 (87 percent) received a passing grade. Rates have been just below 80 percent for other inmates, who have an average stay of approximately 1.7 years. Then, for those inmates who leave the Impact Incarceration Program without a general equivalency diploma, we conduct another assessment prior to release and help them make plans to continue their education so that they can obtain their general equivalency diploma in the community.

Attitude Survey

Finally, as part of the Multisite Study of Shock Incarceration, Illinois was asked to participate in a survey to measure inmate's attitudes toward authority at admission and also after graduation from the Impact Incarceration Program. We attempted to replicate the methodology of the other states, but due to a backlog of inmates held in a holding facility, this period of incarceration, in a conventional prison, contaminated any measures of attitudes.

Results of the Process Evaluation

During nearly six years of operation, we made several programmatic changes as a result of impact and process evaluations. We altered the program's design since the initial implementation. Following a year of initiation, in the second fiscal year we made programmatic changes, including expanded program service hours and revised disciplinary procedures. We later expanded the program service hours to include afternoon sessions. We wanted to emphasize the rehabilitation aspects based on the achievements of the general equivalency diploma examination and enhancement of the substance abuse curriculum taught by certified, experienced professionals. We now conduct a disciplinary review process more frequently to review each inmate's personal development.

A significant program modification occurred in November 1992 when the Illinois Department of Corrections removed part of the aftercare component. Under previous policy, Impact Incarceration Program graduates spent at least ninety days on electronic detention plus at least ninety additional days on intensive supervision prior to being placed under regular parole (PreStart) supervision. We abolished the intensive supervision requirement due to low recidivism rates for commission of new offenses by Impact Incarceration Program graduates, to date. We based this on a comparative analysis conducted with inmates released from traditional institutions who had similar demographic, criminal history, and sentence characteristics.

In 1993, we opened a second boot camp in Greene County because of the success of the Dixon Springs Impact Incarceration Program, and an increasing backlog of approved inmates awaiting entry into the program. The correctional facility was a newly constructed work camp. We made additional renovations to accommodate boot camp inmates. In August 1994, we opened a third facility at DuQuoin.

Impact Measures

Recidivism is the most requested measure of boot camp effectiveness. Illinois Department of Corrections administrators foresaw the importance of analyzing recidivism outcomes, particularly because of the commitment to the drug treatment and aftercare phases which centered around breaking the cycle of drug use and crime. The Illinois Department of Corrections maintains recidivism data encompassing an extensive follow-up period, starting with the first graduate in February 1991. At the close of Fiscal Year 95, we had adequate data to analyze three-year recidivism rates for boot camp graduates. Illinois Impact Incarceration Program return rates could be studied along with established Illinois Department of Corrections recidivism data (see Jones, 1994 Statistical Presentation).

Defining Recidivism

The Illinois Department of Corrections uses a standard operational definition of recidivism. First, we considered the philosophical concept of what recidivism actually measures. When the Illinois Department of Corrections planning and research staff developed their operational definition in 1986, they knew that the recidivism rate was a common statistic used in corrections, but that many consequences result from this inconsistently reported percentage. Some suggested recidivism measures the degree of success in rehabilitating an inmate. Others said it measures the level of "policing" done by parole agents and other law enforcement agents with ex-inmates. The latter suggestion became relevant when reviewing return rates of boot camp graduates who technically violated their parole.

Second, we measure a recidivism event by reincarceration. We do not gather recidivism data until the releasee is readmitted to a correctional institution. A true measure for a corrections agency is not merely re-arrest nor conviction for an offense which carries a less severe probation or jail (misdemeanor) sentence. Furthermore, Illinois arrest and conviction data placed into the State Police database to create "rap sheets" have been unreliable, incomplete, and difficult to interpret (Illinois Criminal Justice Information Authority 1995, Cowles and Gransky 1996).

Third, a conventional obstacle in the designs of recidivism analyses is waiting for a reasonable follow-up period to elapse. Traditionally, a three-year follow-up rate is used in the Illinois Department of Corrections. At the time we developed the operational definition, a review of the literature revealed that "(w)hile the classic studies by the Gluecks (1930, 1939) utilized a five-year plan, Laulicht (1962) reports that a three-year period provided 81 percent of the total number of recidivists found in a seven-year follow-up period. Glaser (1964) found that a three-year follow-up included about 90 percent of probable future returns to prison. The conclusion, then, is that a study of recidivism should employ a follow-up period of at least three years" (Martin and Barry 1969). Furthermore, any criminal activity occurring after three years of crime-free behavior theoretically could constitute a transformation in the offender to warrant a "new" criminal perspective in his or her life. Some studies ignore a time "limit" and control for time on release mathematically, using such techniques as survival analysis; inmates with varying time periods in the community can be studied together (MacKenzie 1994).

Recidivism Data

These findings were all incorporated into the design of the outcome study for Illinois' boot camp program. All Impact Incarceration Program graduates and a comparison group of inmates released from traditional prison during Fiscal Year 91 and Fiscal Year 92 were tracked through June 30, 1995 so that each releasee had undergone a full three-year follow-up period.

We faced some methodological obstacles, however. During this time, changes had occurred which were not in place when the releasees being studied were in the boot camp. Through Fiscal Year 95, none of the graduates from Greene County and DuQuoin facilities had been released for the full three years; therefore, all recidivism data were from Dixon Springs Impact Incarceration Program graduates. One- and two-year rates were published, but comparisons could not be made to traditional rates until a three-year period had passed. In addition, no Illinois Impact Incarceration Program graduates in the first three-year study were admitted prior to the law enacting the expanded statutory criteria. Therefore, the impacts of the expanded criteria had to wait over three and a half years after enactment to measure its full effects. The same held true for Illinois Impact Incarceration Program graduates who were released to a shortened ninety-day intensive supervision component implemented in 1992 (see Illinois Department of Corrections 1993).

Comparison Groups and Sample Selection

Recidivism rates can be calculated for the program inmates, but the data are meaningless without a representative group of persons (cohorts) to which comparisons can be made. In research, the performance of one treatment group often is compared with that of another group. These groups of subjects differ on a variety of characteristics which may influence the results. It is essential that as many traits as possible be the same between groups, so that the only difference between them is that one receives the treatment and the other does not. The second group is used as a control for common occurrences which happen during the treatment, such as historical events, aging of subjects, new laws, and political and policy changes. Selection for a comparison group must be designed to increase reliability and improve validity.

Designs

With quasi-experimental designed studies, there are no guarantees that inmates would be matched on other important overlooked characteristics related to criminal activity. Over time, changes will occur for which the researcher has no control, such as community policing in the neighborhoods in which the releasees return, increases in drug dealing arrests, seasonal employment opportunities, and others. It must be the boot camp experience and aftercare services which cause changes in the dependent variable.

Few programs, all relatively small, are allowed the luxury of evaluating recidivism with randomly assigned experimental and control groups. There are many reasons why this type of methodology has not been used in large scale correctional research. First and foremost, it is seen as an unethical approach to incarceration. Inmates "unfortunate" enough to be assigned to the control group would have to serve a longer prison term in a more dangerous environment. They also may not be awarded the programming options available at boot camps. It may be difficult to convince inmates to volunteer for a study with serious unknown consequences. Many correctional administrators fear lawsuits, even if inmates volunteer to take the chances associated with this type of experimentation.

However, we must take precautions to reduce the liability to the offenders who may not be allowed to participate. Any offender in the eligibility selection pool must be fully aware of the experiment and all of the foreseen consequences and must volunteer by signing a detailed consent form. Assistance from a university's human subjects' committee and the agency's legal staff is helpful in designing the consent form. Incentives, such as a reduced sentence in a "safer" correctional facility such as a lower-security facility or a work camp, could be offered to those not selected for the boot camp.

In Illinois' design, the comparison releasees were group matched based on the original Impact Incarceration Program selection criteria: age, prior incarcerations, offense, and sentence length. A very important selection decision was made regarding sentence length. Although the old statutory criteria stipulated a one- to five-year sentence range, only 2 percent of the Impact Incarceration Program graduates had a two-year sentence or less; thus, those inmates were excluded from the comparison group.

These short-term inmates were not volunteering for the more rigorous program, and represent a much less serious group of incarcerated offenders. Excluding them produced a more reliable comparison group. Moreover, we made no attempt to exclude inmates denied Impact Incarceration Program participation or Impact Incarceration Program failures. Therefore, these inmates may be part of the comparison group because they possess characteristics used for selection. Any inmate released from traditional prison would be eligible for comparison to Impact Incarceration Program graduates. This group had experienced prison, despite some who may have spent some time in the Impact Incarceration Program.

Comparison Recidivism Data

The data for Fiscal Year 91 and Fiscal Year 92 releasees indicated that Impact Incarceration Program graduates returned to prison with fewer new crime offenses (21 percent within three years) than the comparison group (34 percent). However, Impact Incarceration Program graduates are returned to prison with a technical violation of their release agreement more often than those with traditional prison exits. Eighteen percent of the Impact Incarceration Program graduates were returned to prison for a technical violation while only 3 percent of the other releasees were returned for this reason. The number of technical violations for Impact Incarceration Program graduates is driving the aggregate Impact Incarceration Program recidivism rate to a slightly higher rate than that of the traditional releasees, 39 percent for the Illinois Impact Incarceration Program graduates and 37 percent for the comparison group.

With the PreStart program in operation, except for Impact Incarceration Program graduates, we place little emphasis on returning releasees to crowded prisons for technical violations. For traditional releasees, PreStart staff concentrated on providing services, and we direct few active law enforcement procedures toward releasees. Since we used dissimilar supervision strategies for the experimental and control group subjects, comparisons for this variable are misleading.

However, when scrutinizing recidivism results, technical violations of the Illinois Impact Incarceration Program graduates may be considered part of the program strategy. A brief return to prison for possession of drugs or paraphernalia, not being at home as detected by the electronic monitor, or failing to attend substance abuse treatment is part of the discipline. Strict supervision takes place in the boot camp, and any negative actions are punished. The same philosophy is carried over into the community, where these released graduates are expected to obey the orders of their PreStart agents, participate in treatments, continue their education, and obtain meaningful employment. Future misbehavior can be deterred by such intermediate actions at the beginning of their release period.

As stated earlier, if recidivism is measuring the level of "policing" done by parole (electronic detention) agents, which is the case for Impact Incarceration Program graduates for the first three-to-six months after release, technical violation rates cannot be considered a valid measure of recidivism, especially when compared to a group of releasees who are not "watched" in the community. Therefore, the only comparable measure of recidivism for Impact Incarceration Program is return to prison for a new felony within three full years of release.

Additional Recidivism Analyses

Additional analyses can be applied when reporting recidivism rates. First, statistical tests can be conducted to determine whether the three-year recidivism data are statistically significant. In contrast to the comparison group, Illinois' results showed that Impact Incarceration Program graduates have a statistically significant lower new offense rate; however, the graduates were significantly more likely to return to prison with a technical violation. Significant differences carry more influence for administrators when presented with lower return rates for correctional program completers.

Second, time in the community must be examined to analyze intervals before violators return to prison. This is very important when studying boot camp graduates. These offenders are often more prepared to leave prison and return to their home community and their friends. Their attitudes are very positive, their self-esteem has been raised, and they return home with all intentions of finding a job, staying off drugs, and remaining crime free. In addition, in Illinois, they are in the electronic (home) detention program, under close scrutiny by field agents.

On the other hand, recidivism statistics for traditional releasees reveal that, of those who do violate, 50 percent return to prison within nine months of release. The pressures of the streets affect the typical releasee fairly quickly. Therefore, in theory, boot camp graduates would return to prison later in their supervision term. Survival analysis, a statistical method which looks for differences in time periods of "surviving" after treatments, can be used to yield more valid results on the effects of boot camps.

Other than the recidivism data reported yearly in the Impact Incarceration Program Annual Reports, the Illinois Department of Corrections has cooperated with several independent research projects on the Illinois Impact Incarceration Program. Each study has attempted to increase understanding of the Impact Incarceration Program's recidivism data by broadening the scope of analyses. The Illinois Department of Corrections participated in the Multisite Evaluation of Shock Incarceration as the Illinois Impact Incarceration Program was being implemented. Preliminary recidivism data were analyzed using survival time procedures. After extensive follow-up data were available, another survival time analysis was conducted in a separate study (Karr 1995). Further, the Illinois Criminal Justice Information Authority sponsored a postrelease evaluation of Impact Incarceration Program graduates according to in-program assessed substance abuse treatment levels (Gransky and Jones 1994). Impact Incarceration Program and research staff have cooperated in numerous surveys and studies from such agencies as the Corrections Services Group, the United States General Accounting Office, and Southern Illinois University (see Gransky, Castellano, and Cowles 1995).

Cost Savings

Costs of incarcerating an inmate in the Impact Incarceration Program can be reduced for two reasons. First, inmates spend less time in prison. In Fiscal Year 95, Impact Incarceration Program inmates spent an average of 6.3 months of incarceration, including more than two months awaiting transfer and the four-month stay at the Impact Incarceration Program facility. Given their imposed sentence and allowing for average good time reductions, these inmates would have served an average of twenty months in prison.

The formula used in Illinois to calculate cost savings takes into account that all Impact Incarceration Program graduates released in Fiscal Year 95 saved an average of 427 days from the time they would have served given their full sentence. Therefore, the 1,530 graduates saved a total of 653,310 days.

Cost savings are determined by using a marginal annual per capita cost of $3,143 per inmate at institutions. This amounts to the extra money which is needed to house each additional inmate. The marginal cost includes the food, clothing, medical, and other basic costs of incarceration. It excludes the cost of construction, extra security, and other related expenses which would be required if a new prison were needed. This marginal cost amounts to $8.61 per day. Calculating this daily rate by the 653,310 days saved totals $5,625,000. This is the money saved by the state to operate the Impact Incarceration Program for the graduates of Fiscal Year 95. Cost savings are not formulated for program failures since they serve their remaining sentence in prison.

However, the cost of processing the graduates who return to prison for a technical violation occurring while on electronic detention or PreStart must be taken into consideration. The 108 technical violators who returned in Fiscal Year 95 for an average of ninety-five days cost the Department $88,339 plus undetermined processing expenses. Therefore, the net cost saving for Fiscal Year 95 was an estimated $5,536,661.

The Fiscal Year 95 savings was the highest one-year total to date. This was due to the presence of three Impact Incarceration Program facilities housing up to 624 inmates, and the allowance of expanded eligibility criteria. With the more extensive use of the six- to eight-year sentences and minimal use of one- to two-year sentences, savings to the Department will continue to escalate.

Through Fiscal Year 95, the gross cost benefit for the Impact Incarceration Program totals $13,999,008, saving 1,625,901 days of incarceration for the 4,079 graduates. With the 659 technical violators returned since the first graduation, and an estimated ninety-three day average stay in prison, the net savings for the Impact Incarceration Program has been approximately $13,471,327.

Grant funds used for support services both in the Impact Incarceration Program and PreStart expenses had not been calculated into the cost savings to this point. These dollars should be figured into cost savings, because the programs paid for by grant funds eventually will have to be paid from the state's general revenue.

Second, there are added cost savings from having Impact Incarceration Program graduates employed in the community. Working graduates are earning money to support themselves and their families, paying taxes, removing themselves from public assistance roles, and remaining busy and productive. To determine these cost savings, figures must be calculated from estimates of the number of graduates who are working, the length of their employment, taxes they paid based on salary estimates, and the number removed from public assistance as a result of obtaining a job. These calculations are not part of the current Impact Incarceration Program savings formula, but anticipated database matches with the Illinois Department of Employment Security may provide reliable data.

Finally, business administrators must take several budgetary factors into account. Most likely, boot camp inmates will eat more food than traditional prison inmates. Also, clothing and laundry costs may be higher for boot camp inmates; inmates may soil multiple sets of clothing throughout the day. Business administrators may have to purchase foot lockers and other equipment exclusive to a boot camp, in addition to tools and vans for work details. Walls may need to be refreshed with paint to connote a clean atmosphere; supplies for insignias and motivational graphics may need to be purchased. Floors will need to be waxed and buffed on a regular basis. All of these may be unforseen when planning a boot camp program.

Summary

We have developed and implemented the Illinois Department of Corrections' Impact Incarceration Program to operate with the assistance of numerous devoted correctional professionals. After establishing a basic philosophy, we evolved a cohesive program with the ultimate goal of educating young prison-bound offenders, to build self-esteem and encourage their lawful, responsible behavior and respect for authority by providing substance abuse, academic and life skills instruction. At the same time, the Illinois Department of Corrections reduces prison bed space through shorter prison stays while preserving public safety.

We have spent numerous hours writing and revising legislation; obtaining outside funds; developing an evaluation plan and procedures for site selection, inmate selection, and criteria; informing judges and offenders; and outlining program components. We have discovered that implementation of a shock incarceration program involves a series of administrative planning sessions, research and site visits, and development of policies and procedural documents.

We also discovered that department staff at all levels must participate in the planning process and offer continued suggestions after implementation. As a result of our efforts, we learned that we should make improvements only after carefully considered choices, based on sound objective evaluations, so that our program will be advantageous to the correctional department as well as the young men and women who will benefit most from the experience.

References

Cowles, E., and L. Gransky, L. 1995. An Exploratory and Descriptive Review of Incarcerated Illinois Class 4 Felony Offenders: Are Alternative Sanctions Appropriate? Unpublished report.

Glaser, D. 1964. *The Effectiveness of a Prison and Parole System*. New York: Bobbs-Merrill.

Glueck, S., and Eleanor T. Glueck. 1930. *500 Criminal Careers*. New York: Knopf.

————. 1939. *One Thousand Juvenile Delinquents*. Cambridge: Harvard University Press.

Gransky, L., T. Castellano, and E. Cowles. 1995. Is There a 'Second Generation' of Shock Incarceration Facilities?: The Evolving Nature of Goals, Program Elements, and Drug Treatment Services in Boot Camp Programs. In Smykla and Selke, eds. *Intermediate Sanctions: Sentencing in the 1990's*. Cincinnati: Anderson Publishing Company.

Gransky, L., and R. Jones. 1995. *Evaluation of the Post-release Status of Substance Abuse Program Participants*. Chicago: Illinois Criminal Justice Information Authority.

Illinois Department of Corrections. 1992. Impact Incarceration Program: 1992 Annual Report to the Governor and the General Assembly. Springfield: Illinois Department of Corrections.

Illinois Criminal Justice Information Authority. 1995. *A Comprehensive Examination of the Illinois Criminal History Records Information (CHRI) System*. Chicago: Illinois Criminal Justice Information Authority.

Illinois Revised Statutes. 1991. Chapter 38, paragraph 1005-8-1.1.

Illinois Task Force on Crime and Corrections. 1993. Final Report. Unpublished report.

Jones, R., 1993. *1992 Statistical Presentation*. Springfield: Illinois Department of Corrections.

Jones, R. and S. Karr. 1995. Impact Incarceration Program: 1995 Annual Report to the Governor and the General Assembly. Springfield: Illinois Department of Corrections.

Karr, S. 1995. Recidivism and Illinois' Impact Incarceration Program: A Survival Time Analysis. Unpublished Master's Thesis, Southern Illinois University.

Karr, S., and R. Jones. 1994. Impact Incarceration Program: 1993 Annual Report to the Governor and the General Assembly. Springfield: Illinois Department of Corrections.

Karr, S., and R. Jones. 1996. The Development and Implementation of Illinois' Impact Incarceration Program. In MacKenzie and Herbert, eds. *Correctional Boot Camps: A Tough Intermediate Sanction*. Washington, D.C.: National Institute of Justice.

Laulicht, J. 1962. A Study of Recidivism in One Training School: Implications for Rehabilitation Programs. *Crime and Delinquency*. 8:161-171.

MacKenzie, D., J. Shaw, and V. Gowdy. 1990. An Evaluation of Shock Incarceration in Louisiana. Unpublished manuscript. Final report to the National Institue of Justice.

MacKenzie, D., and C. Souryal. 1994. *Multisite Evaluation of Shock Incarceration*. Washington, D.C.: National Institute of Justice.

Martin, P., and J. Barry. 1969. The Prediction of Recidivism: A Review. *Journal of Correctional Psychology*. 3:6-15.

U. S. Government Accounting Office. 1993. *Prison Boot Camps: Short-term Costs Reduced, but Long-term Impact Uncertain*. Washington, D.C.: U. S. Government Printing Office.

Can Boot Camps Save Dollars as Well as Souls?

David W. Aziz, Ph.D.

Program Research Specialist III
New York State Department of Correctional Services
Albany, New York

Paul H. Korotkin

Assistant Director MIS Research
New York State Department of Correctional Services
Albany, New York

Whenever a reporter, student, legislator, or a correctional colleague becomes curious about the boot camp experience, there are inevitably two questions that get raised in some form: "What's your recidivism rate?" and "How much does it cost?" Both Cronin (1994) and the United States General Accounting Office (1993) reported that reducing crowding and costs were one of the many goals that state corrections officials had in mind for their programs.

Efforts at standardizing the methodology for calculating the answers to either question have not yet been established, leaving it up to each jurisdiction to use their own local definitions and calculations. This chapter is a discussion of the elements that need to be considered in any cost savings model. It uses information from the New York State experience as an example. This chapter raises some cost-related issues relevant to jurisdictions trying to justify new programs or to jurisdictions trying to assess their program's ability to reduce crowding and costs. The issues raised here can be used as a benchmark for all jurisdictions with boot camps to determine if these program goals are attainable.

States such as New York (1989,1990,1991,1992,1993,1994,1995,1996), Louisiana (1990), Florida (1990), Georgia (1991), and Oregon (1994) developed their own models for boot camp cost savings. (See the prior chapter on cost saving in Illinois). Although program components differed, the end results were similar. When used as an early release mechanism, boot camps can save beds and money.

The methodology for determining how many beds boot camps save has been examined in national forums by Doris MacKenzie and Dale Parent in a variety of their writings. They recognized that these programs may not be fiscal winners for all jurisdictions at all times. The Multisite Evaluation of Shock described a model for determining the ability of jurisdictions to save beds. Of the five jurisdictions which provided data for analysis, only two (New York and Louisiana) were able to document their ability to save beds. At the time of the study, the impact on two of the other participating jurisdictions (South Carolina and Georgia) resulted in the need to increase the number of prison beds to accommodate the program (MacKenzie and Souryal 1994:43).

The General Accounting Office examination in 1993 concluded that boot camps manage to save money not by being less expensive to run, but by releasing inmates earlier than what otherwise would have been possible. The report found that the per diem cost was greater to house shock inmates, but the number of days inmates were incarcerated was substantially shorter.

Admittedly, cost avoidance or "saving bucks" is not as high a priority as "saving souls" among the many jurisdictions entering the boot camp arena. This seems to be particularly true of the newer entries into this intermediate sanction. As recently as the Boot Camp Planning workshop held in Dallas, Texas April 9-11, 1996, by the United States Justice Department, many participants who obtained federal funds for planning or construction indicated that despite some disappointing evidence on these programs' abilities to attain bed savings or lower return rates, the belief that shock was a better treatment environment for both staff and inmates continued to motivate them to proceed with their projects.

The Costs Of Shock—A National Perspective

A report by Dale Parent (1989) that provided a national overview of shock programs examined fiscal information from four states which run shock programs and stated:

> In all four states officials said that the SI [shock incarceration] program costs for food, clothing and consumables were about the same as for regular prisons. Nonetheless, more intensive demands on custodial and/or rehabilitation staff in many SI programs led to higher daily costs per inmate, as compared with regular prison inmates.

The Corrections Yearbook for 1995 reports that the average daily costs reported by twenty-eight jurisdictions operating shock programs in January 1995 ranged from a low of $29.85 in Mississippi to $141.83 in Wisconsin. The average cost for these jurisdictions was $53.48 (Camp and Camp 1995). The range of these costs is due to a number of factors including program size and comprehensiveness, and whether the program is conducted in stand-alone facilities or as part of a larger prison site.

New York is one of the few states that runs all of its shock facilities as stand-alone facilities. Many other states have shock programs operating as part of an existing prison. These states have been able to use the resources of the larger facilities as a way of cutting costs. However, running these programs as part of another facility can make it more difficult to disaggregate the program expenditures made exclusively by the boot camp component.

In states where judges control which inmates are sent to the program, or where shock incarceration is used as an alternative to probation, the reported savings accumulated by releasing inmates early must be offset by the inevitable net-widening effects of judges' decisions on whom to send. This net-widening effect occurs when convicted offenders, who would not have been incarcerated for their offense, get sentenced to a shock incarceration program because of its perceived benefits. Even in New York, where judges do not directly sentence offenders to shock, a survey of the judiciary in 1990 indicated that 5 percent of the judges gave prison sentences to young offenders rather than jail or probation to assure that they would be program eligible.

Recognition of New York's Shock Program as an Effective Cost Savings Strategy

One of the stated goals of New York's program is the reduction of demand for bed space as a way of addressing prison crowding issues in the state. According to MacKenzie and Parent (1991), for shock programs to be successful in this effort, it requires:

1. a sufficient number of eligible inmates who are recommended for the program

2. a large enough number of offenders completing the program

3. a true reduction in the length of time offenders spend in prison

4. offender participants who are drawn from those who would normally be incarcerated rather than those who would normally be sentenced to probation (or no net widening) (MacKenzie and Parent 1991, p. 8).

New York has fulfilled all of these requirements and as a result it is acknowledged that "New York . . . may have a large enough number of graduates to have an impact on crowded prisons . . . this is not the case in most states" (MacKenzie 1990, p.49).

In remarks made to a National Institute of Corrections Intensive Skills Workshop presented at the American Correctional Association Congress in the summer of 1991, Dale Parent cited the New York State Department of Correctional Services boot camp operation as a model which contains all the features necessary if boot camps are to have the capacity to reduce prison bed space needs and, hence, to cut both operational and capital costs. The United States General Accounting Office review of boot camp programs concluded that these programs reduce overall corrections costs and systemwide crowding. The report also noted that of the jurisdictions studied, "New York is the best example of reported cost savings" (United States General Accounting Office 1993, p. 25).

New York State's shock incarceration program has been widely cited in the limited literature on the topic of boot camps because of three factors. They include the treatment-oriented program content; the size of the program, with an annual capacity of over 3,100 inmates; and the existence of a consistently thorough evaluation effort that has been associated with the program. In fact, the General Accounting Office review of boot camp programs indicated, " . . . the most extensive evaluation process was done in New York, which publishes an annual report on its boot camp program" (United States General Accounting Office 1993, p.22).

When modeling the costs of shock incarceration, we have been asked, "What would it cost the department if the shock program did not exist and all shock graduates since the start of the program had to serve out their complete sentences in a nonshock facility?" The resultant model was constructed as a way to measure the program's ability to reduce the demand for bed space and result in a cost avoidance for the agency as the result of its operation. The model consists of two distinct components:

- Savings due to reduction in the need for care and custody of shock inmates
- Savings due to the avoidance of capital construction costs

Dale Parent and Doris MacKenzie (1991) introduced another cost savings model for boot camps in Louisiana. This model grew out of the work they were involved in on both the multisite study of shock incarceration and the evaluation of the program run by the Louisiana Department of Correctional Services Boot Camp. Their model has some limitations in that it calculates bed savings without attaching dollar estimates to those beds. Additionally, the model has three other limitations. First, it assumes that all shock beds are filled to capacity at all times. This is not the case in New York State due to removal and limited backfilling of empty beds. Second, the model does not allow for bed savings that are cumulative over time. Third, the model does not take credit for the operational savings that occur when graduates are released before their court-mandated minimum period of incarceration.

Still, the Parent/MacKenzie model is useful as a catalyst for a variety of jurisdictions which run shock programs to think about their programs and the factors involved in obtaining bed savings. For this reason alone, it should be considered by all shock programs as a starting point in understanding the benefits and liabilities of running their boot camps.

The New York State Cost Avoidance Model

Since the New York model examines the fiscal impact of the program from its inception, dollar savings are considered to be cumulative. To construct the model there were at least nine factors to be considered. These include factors which are all used in the development of the cost savings model for the department of corrections shock incarceration program:

1. the fiscal year expenditures for shock facilities

2. the fiscal year expenditures for general confinement facilities where shock inmates could be housed if the program did not exist

3. time to earliest parole release from custody of shock program graduates

4. the security level of shock program graduates at reception

5. the amount of time shock graduates spent in the department of corrections custody before their release to parole supervision

6. the proportion of shock inmates who would not be released to parole supervision at their first opportunity and the average duration of their stay in prison if shock did not exist

7. the costs for constructing medium- and minimum-security prison beds in the jurisdiction

8. the average number of vacant beds in the shock program

9. the number of inmates removed from shock before their completion of the program

There also should be some tangible evidence that the jurisdiction was involved in either a prison construction effort or was resorting to some double bunking/celling to address the issue of crowding. This would provide assurances that they would definitely have spent additional money to house shock participants if the shock program did not exist. For example, in 1982, there were thirty-seven New York State correctional facilities housing 34,710 inmates. Yet, between 1983 and 1994, an additional thirty-one facilities were opened housing an additional 29,570 inmates (New York State 1995). This is clear evidence that prison construction on a large scale was occurring during the period when the shock facilities were opened. Even though the size of the inmate population increased during the period when the shock program was being introduced, the program has had an effect on slowing the growth of the inmate population.

Fiscal Year Expenditures of Shock Versus Nonshock Facilities

There are differences between the operation of a shock and a nonshock facility. There are fiscal implications resulting from shock facilities having intensive rigorous programs run under strict discipline. Since program rigor has made it necessary to have inmates transferred out of shock, either because of their behavior or because the program proved to be too tough for them to complete, the shock facilities are not always running at full capacity.

The overall per diem costs for shock and the comparison facilities can be categorized into four major areas: support services, supervision services, health services, and program services. An examination of some of these expenditures helps to explain the higher costs of the boot camp. The differences in supervision expenditures are attributable to security concerns. Security staffing levels are different at shock because the role of the drill instructor is unique to these facilities. Additionally, since many shock programs are required to have a hard labor component, most of the shock platoons are supervised in work crews during the day when they are working at locations outside the facility.

Because all inmates in shock are fully programmed during their entire stay in shock, the cost for program services may be more than at the comparison facilities where full program participation is not mandated for all inmates. The most significant component in the cost of health care at shock is due to the unique screening and orientation functions that are present. After initial medical screenings at reception centers, medical staff may order additional tests for medically marginal inmates before determining if they can participate in the program.

It costs more to feed shock inmates because the rigorous nature of the program means that inmates are burning more calories. Inmates in shock do not receive packages, and food is not available for purchase in the inmate commissary. The food provided by the facility is all the food that shock inmates have available to them. All meals are mandatory, and the food taken by inmates must be eaten. This is very different from the food, package, and commissary policies of most nonshock facilities. Yet, the per diem costs are only part of the fiscal story of the shock program. Money is being saved due to the early release of shock graduates.

Cost Savings Due to Shock Incarceration

The starting point for placing a dollar value to the bed savings component of the cost avoidance model is the actual expenditure data for your shock facility. The cost should then be compared to the cost of operating a nonshock facility where these inmates would be housed if there were no shock program. To be useful, this data has to be translated into per diem costs per inmate for each of the shock and the comparison nonshock facilities. This is accomplished by using the actual fiscal year expenditures for each facility divided by the average daily inmate population for those facilities for the fiscal year. That amount is then divided by 365 to obtain the per diem rate per inmate. This per diem data is needed because the model examines the differences in the costs of the shock and nonshock facilities while also considering the difference between the number of days that the shock and nonshock inmates are being housed.

If you have data going back over a number of years, this model can average the costs of the shock and the comparison nonshock facilities and apply these averages to all the inmates released from both the shock and the comparison facilities. This averaging of per diem costs over time smooths out the variation in fiscal expenditures from year to year. An averaging of the costs presents a more accurate picture of expenditures over the entire period of the program's operation.

Operations: Care and Related Custodial Costs

In New York State, the successful completion of shock incarceration has become a systemic way in which inmates are released to parole supervision prior to the completion of their court-mandated period of incarceration. Thus, bed space savings for shock graduates are due to their spending less time incarcerated.

In the New York example, if the program did not exist, each of the 13,360 shock releases through September 30,1995 would have spent an average of 545 days in prison from the date they were determined to be shock eligible until their earliest possible parole board release dates. In fact, these 13,360 shock releases actually spent an average of 222 days in the Department of Corrections custody from the date they were determined to be shock eligible until they were released to parole supervision. Thus, for each shock graduate, there was an average saving of 323 days or 10.6 months between their actual date of release from shock to what would have been their earliest possible release at their court-determined parole eligibility date. The program requires inmates be no more than thirty-six months from their parole eligibility date at admission. Some program graduates have saved as much as thirty months while others have saved little or none as a result of having gone through the program. Thus, in New York, for every 100 inmates who graduate from shock, there is a savings of $1.46 million because we have housed them for less time. These savings are due exclusively to the early release of inmates prior to their parole eligibility dates.

Since New York is a state with indeterminate sentencing, the fact is that not all inmates get released at their parole eligibility date. The board of parole may determine that despite their involvement in programming, some inmates need to spend a longer time incarcerated. In New York, the proportion of inmates approved for release at their initial parole hearing since March 1988 is 63 percent, while virtually all (98 percent) successful completers of the shock program have been granted parole releases at their initial hearings. Thus, if shock were not available, 63 percent of the graduates would be released at their parole eligibility date, while 37 percent would be given additional time, which is estimated to be ten months. This additional calculation adjustment would not be necessary for jurisdictions with determinate sentencing as their calculation for time and dollars saved need not be modified.

The department estimates the annual operational and administrative costs per inmate at $19,455. Therefore, ten months, or 83.3 percent of a year of incarceration, costs $16,213. For our purposes, that is an additional saving of $599,867 for the thirty-seven inmates who would not have been released after their parole eligibility date if shock did not exist.

So, for every 100 shock releases, it is estimated that the New York Department of Corrections saves $2.05 million, which it otherwise would have had to expend for the care and custody of these inmates. Thus, for the first 13,360 releases from shock, as of September 30, 1995, there was an estimated savings in program costs of $273.2 million.

These savings must be offset by the cost of housing and programming inmates who started the more expensive shock program but did not complete it. As of September 30, 1995, 7,501 inmates spent an average of sixty-six days in the program before being removed. Instead of spending these sixty-six days at either a medium- or minimum-security facility at $53.30 per day, these inmates spent this time at shock facilities at a cost of $65.75 per day. The difference in costs for housing these inmates in shock for sixty-six days was $825.07. This difference multiplied by 7,501 removals results in an offset of approximately $6.1 million. Thus, the revised savings estimate for the care and custody of shock inmates is $267.1 million.

To summarize the operational savings portion, the model indicates that on a per diem basis, shock is a more expensive place to house an inmate; the number of days spent incarcerated is substantially smaller than what would have been spent in either a medium- or minimum-security facility if the program did not exist; and there is an offset to any savings because some inmates programmed and housed at the more expensive rate are removed from the program and then spend the rest of their sentences in less expensive general-confinement facilities.

Capital Savings: Bed Savings and Associated Costs

An additional set of savings from shock incarceration, separate from the operating costs, are the bed savings, which translate into the capital construction costs avoided as a result of not having to house shock graduates. The calculation of this savings is a bit more difficult to construct as it requires information that may not be readily available to jurisdictions. Where relevant, estimates of these numbers can be used.

To start with this process, we must understand the components of a capital savings portion of the model. Initially, the researcher must answer the question, "At any particular time, if the program did not exist, how many of the people who graduated would still be in custody?" The prescribed methodology to answer this question will be different for jurisdictions with determinate sentencing than for those with indeterminate sentencing. This is because in a determinate-sentencing jurisdiction, there is no need to estimate any additional incarceration time due to parole board decision making.

David W. Aziz, Ph.D. and Paul H. Korotkin

An even tougher question must be considered by researchers from jurisdictions where the judge sentences individuals directly to a boot camp program. In this instance, it would be necessary to determine whether an individual would have been incarcerated at all if the boot camp did not exist, and if the individual would have been incarcerated, how long would that imprisonment be. In jurisdictions which have this process, we advise researchers to profile the criminal history, gender, age, and most serious prior charge on current arrest of all the people sentenced to shock. Then, we compare this data with the sentences of similarly situated convicted felons received prior to shock's existence in the jurisdiction. After the researcher determines how many people would have been incarcerated and for what sentences, the next question is, "How long do these similarly situated inmates serve?" For a determinate-sentencing jurisdiction, the researcher would calculate the average sentence length of all shock successful completers to date, calculate the average amount of jail time credits for shock completers; apply a good time proportion to the distribution of determinate sentences received by graduates, and compare the graduates' anticipated release date without shock to the date being used for the bed savings estimate.

For jurisdictions with indeterminate sentencing practices, like New York, incarcerated individuals do not have a known or preset date of release when they enter the system. Instead, an external agency, such as the Board of Parole in New York, determines when the inmate is capable of returning to the community. The researcher, therefore, must estimate each shock graduate's date of release to the community if there were no shock program.

The researchers in New York have accomplished this by (1) arraying the number of shock graduates by month; (2) calculating the time saved from the parole eligibility date for all shock graduates (that is parole eligibility date minus the shock graduation date in months); (3) creating a corresponding frequency distribution for time saved to parole eligibility date; (4) multiplying step number one by step number three to obtain the number of graduates who would have been eligible for parole as of the target date for each month's graduates; (5) creating a frequency distribution for the probability of release by month following the parole eligibility date (this can be created by arraying release date minus parole eligibility date for an annual cohort of shock-like inmates just prior to the opening of the program). The researcher will then determine, as of the target date, the number of inmates from each monthly graduate cohort that would still need to be housed if shock did not exist.

In our example (see the table on Shock Bed Savings) Column 1 is a monthly accounting of the number of shock graduates. Column 2 is a historic distribution of the number of months saved from parole eligibility date for the graduates. While 6.11 percent of the graduates saved fifteen days or less from their parole eligibility date, 10.91 percent saved up to forty-five days, 17.74 percent up to seventy-five days, and 25.37 percent saved up to 105 days. Column 3 represents Column 1 multiplied by Column 2, or the number of graduates in a given month who would have reached their parole eligibility date by September 30, 1995.

Column 4 is the probability of release by the board of parole for those individuals who would have reached their parole eligibility date. This probability accounts for the fact that

Table: Shock Bed Savings as of September 30, 1995

Month	Actual Shock Releases (Column 1)	% of Inmates Who Would Have Reached Parole on	Number Who Reached Parole as of 9/30/95 (Column 3)	% Who Would Have Been Released by Parole on 9/30/95 (Column 4)	Number Who Would Have Been Released Under EEP	Beds Saved as a Result of Shock Program (Column 6)
3/88 to 4/93	7,912	100.00	7,912	99.89	7,903	9
5/93	149	99.83	149	98.69	147	2
6/93	202	98.77	200	98.60	197	5
7/93	165	96.64	159	98.46	157	8
8/93	135	94.28	127	98.36	125	10
9/93	247	92.05	227	97.75	222	25
10/93	182	89.93	164	97.29	159	23
11/93	177	88.26	156	96.78	151	26
12/93	228	86.55	197	96.78	191	37
1/94	167	84.75	142	96.61	137	30
2/94	173	82.86	143	96.41	138	35
3/94	143	80.96	116	96.15	111	32
4/94	160	79.10	127	95.32	121	39
5/94	187	77.69	145	94.63	137	50
6/94	198	75.57	150	93.43	140	58
7/94	177	71.35	126	92.85	117	60
8/94	146	66.29	97	91.99	89	57
9/94	202	62.29	126	90.97	114	88
10/94	203	58.95	120	87.40	105	98
11/94	204	55.92	114	85.35	97	107
12/94	201	52.47	105	81.81	86	115
1/95	158	47.29	75	79.79	60	98
2/95	211	41.87	88	75.32	67	144
3/95	215	37.56	81	73.32	59	156
4/95	200	33.79	68	67.61	46	154
5/95	211	30.67	65	65.91	43	168
6/95	232	25.37	59	63.95	38	194
7/95	163	17.74	29	62.82	18	145
8/95	264	10.91	29	62.82	18	246
9/95	148	6.11	9	62.82	6	142
Totals	13,360		11,304		10,999	2,361

David W. Aziz, Ph.D. and Paul H. Korotkin

some of the individuals might have reappearances before the board if shock did not exist. For example, the September 1994 factor is almost 91 percent compared to the 63 percent factor for September 1995 because some of the 126 individuals from the September 1994 graduates who would have reached their parole eligibility date by September 1995, might have been turned down by the board at their initial board hearing, but they were seen by the board again and were released.

Column 5 represents Column 3 times Column 4, or the number of individuals that researchers estimate would have been released even without a shock program. Column 6 represents Column 1 minus Column 5, or the bed savings attributable to shock.

As can be seen in the table, the proportion of graduates eligible to be released on the target date increases for inmate graduates in earlier months. This proportion of possible releases to be applied to each month's graduates is based on the time-savings' calculation.

As previously stated, the case can be made that with the department's history of prison construction, it would not hesitate to have these beds constructed. The cost of constructing these 2,361 beds would be based on portions of the estimated costs for building both medium- and minimum-security facilities. A standard 750-bed medium-security facility would cost approximately $64.95 million, while a standard 250-bed minimum-security facility would cost approximately $13 million. By using an estimated breakout for the initial security classification of shock inmates, 40 percent of the 2,361 inmates (or 944) would be housed in medium-security facilities, while the remaining 60 percent (or 1,417 inmates) would be housed in minimum-security facilities.

Using the amount of $86,600 as the cost of one medium bed and $52,000 as the cost of one camp bed, our capital costs involved in housing these 2,361 inmates would amount to $155.4 million. This amount is what the department has saved by not having to build space for these shock graduates.

This estimated bed savings does not take into account that a certain portion of shock beds are vacant because the program structure does not routinely backfill platoons when inmates are removed from the program. On average, since the start of the program, the number of vacant beds has been calculated at 266 for the four shock facilities. The model assumes that these 266 beds would be filled if the shock program did not exist. Thus, they must be subtracted from the 2,361 bed savings for a total bed saving of 2,095. This adjustment reduces the dollar savings to $137.8 million, which is a more accurate representation of the construction avoided because of the shock incarceration program. By using these figures, the saving for the Department of Corrections through September 30, 1995 for the 13,360 released graduates is equal to $404.9 million, which includes savings in the provision of care and custody and savings in the cost of capital construction.

The reader should be aware however, that the costs and benefits of the shock program are not limited to the Department of Corrections. For example, this cost avoidance model does not consider the money that employed shock graduates contribute as tax-paying citizens, nor does it consider the additional expenditures that the division of parole incurs to provide intensive supervision and services to the graduates for their first six months in the community.

The cost avoidance model has been refined over the years to make it the most accurate estimate available, and the cost avoidance figures outlined represent "front end" dollars that are accrued as a result of the department's running of the incarceration phase of the shock program. Thus, the shock incarceration program is capable of reducing the demand for bed space and saving the state money, despite the fact that it is expensive to provide this intense level of programming.

Community Service Products: Selling the Program to the Citizens

Another substantial cost benefit to the taxpayers from the shock incarceration program involves the community service work that is performed by inmates. Community service work often has been used as an effective penal sanction and an alternative to incarceration, and has a successful track record. Services provided by shock inmates to New York State communities represent more than $7 million annually.

One of the legislative mandates for the program was that it had to involve inmate participants in an intensive regimen of physical labor. One of the most innovative ways to fulfill this mandate has been to involve inmates in performing community service projects for the towns, villages, and state parks that border the shock facilities.

Each year, supervised crews of shock inmates perform thousands of hours of community service as part of the daily routine of the facilities. As a result, the shock program is providing cash-strapped municipalities, religious organizations, and community groups with the manual labor needed to complete a variety of projects that, otherwise, would not get done. Based on information provided by the facilities, we estimate that in calendar year 1995 inmates from shock facilities performed approximately 1.2 million hours of community service (this is the equivalent of 1,000 inmates working six hours per day, four days per week for fifty weeks). If the municipalities that were helped had hired laborers at a federal minimum wage rate of $5.25 per hour to accomplish these tasks, it would have cost approximately $6.3 million to complete these projects.

The opportunity for shock inmates to perform these much needed community services helps the program to meet two of its objectives by fulfilling the hard physical labor component of the program and providing inmates with positive and altruistic community experiences. Additionally, the positive behavior exhibited by inmates providing these community services is supportive of one of the twelve steps to recovery used by shock inmates, that is, to make direct amends for past destructive behavior, wherever possible. The program's involvement in community affairs also helps build strong local support for shock and its accomplishments.

Summary

Along with the increasing popularity of boot camps comes additional scrutiny. Jurisdictions involved in running such programs are going to be held increasingly accountable for their decisions. The two strands that seem to apply to these programs are recidivism rates and cost avoidance. The discussion of a cost avoidance model in this chapter presents some ideas for those who operate boot camps or those who plan to operate one in the near future with some techniques for documenting program costs or savings that result from the program. These are front-end savings. This is not a complete cost benefit analysis. The cost avoidance figures outlined represent "front end" dollars that are accrued as a result of the department's running of the incarceration phase of the shock program. Some additional areas to consider are higher parole costs, and the costs of returning failing shock graduates back to prison. Although boot camps as treatment vehicles can appeal to liberals and conservatives, they also should be seen as vehicles to allow correctional agencies to account for their treatment dollars.

References

Aziz, David, Paul Korotkin, and Donald Macdonald. 1990. Shock Incarceration Program Follow-up Study, May 1991. Albany, New York: Unpublished report by the Division of Program Planning, Research and Evaluation.

Camp, George M., and Camille Camp. 1995. *The Corrections Yearbook.* South Salem, New York: Criminal Justice Yearbook.

Clark, Cheryl L., David W. Aziz , and Doris L. MacKenzie. 1994. *Shock Incarceration In New York: Focus on Treatment.* Washington, D.C.: National Institute of Justice.

Clark, Cheryl L., and David W. Aziz. 1996. Shock Incarceration In New York State: Philosophy Results and Limitations. In Doris L. MacKenzie and Eugene E. Hebert, eds. *Correctional Boot Camps: A Tough Intermediate Sanction.* Washington, D.C.: National Institute of Justice.

Cronin, Roberta, C. 1994. *Boot Camps For Adult and Juvenile Offenders: Overview and Update.* Washington, D.C.: National Institute of Justice.

Florida Department of Corrections. 1989. Boot Camp Evaluation and Boot Camp Recommitment Rate. Unpublished report by the Bureau of Planning, Research and Statistics.

Flowers, Gerald T., and R. Barry Ruback. 1991. Special Alternative Incarceration Evaluation. Georgia Department of Corrections. January 15.

Georgia Department of Corrections. 1989. Georgia's Special Alternative Incarceration. Unpublished report to Shock Incarceration Conference, Washington, D.C.

MacKenzie, D. L. 1988. Evaluating Shock Incarceration in Louisiana: A Review of the First Year. Unpublished report by the Louisiana Department of Corrections.

———. 1990. Boot Camps: Components, Evaluations and Empirical Issues. *Federal Probation*. September.

MacKenzie, D. L., and Dale Parent. 1991. Shock Incarceration and Prison Crowding in Louisiana. *Journal of Criminal Justice*. Vol. 19, pp. 225-237.

MacKenzie, D. L., and Claire C. Souryal. 1994. *Multisite Evaluation of Shock Incarceration. A Final Summary Report.* Washington, D.C.: National Institute of Justice.

New York State. 1995. Statistical Yearbook.

New York State Department of Correctional Services and New York State Division of Parole. 1993. The Fifth Annual Report to the Legislature: Shock Incarceration in New York State. Albany: Unpublished report by the Division of Program Planning, Research and Evaluation and the Office of Policy Analysis and Information.

_____. 1994. The Sixth Annual Report to the Legislature: Shock Incarceration in New York State. Albany: Unpublished report by the Division of Program Planning, Research and Evaluation and the Office of Policy Analysis and Information.

_____. 1995. The Seventh Annual Report to the Legislature: Shock Incarceration in New York State. Albany: Unpublished report by the Division of Program Planning, Research and Evaluation and the Office of Policy Analysis and Information.

_____. 1996. The Eighth Annual Report to the Legislature: Shock Incarceration in New York State. Albany: Unpublished report by the Division of Program Planning, Research and Evaluation and the Office of Policy Analysis and Information.

Parent, D. G. 1988. Shock Incarceration Programs. Address to the American Correctional Association Winter Conference. Phoenix, Arizona.

_____. 1989. *Shock Incarceration: An Overview of Existing Programs. Issues and Practices Report.* Washington, D. C: National Institute of Justice.

United States General Accounting Office. 1993. Prison Boot Camps: Short Term Prison Costs Reduced, but Long Term Impact Uncertain. Report to the Subcommittee on Intellectual Property and Judicial Administration, Committee on the Judiciary, House of Representatives. April.

Contributors

(in Alphabetical Order)

We appreciate the contributions made by each of the authors and evaluators of this text. They worked under impossible deadlines. Most of these individuals would be willing to consult and provide further information to help others establish or modify a boot camp program that is correct for their jurisdiction.

David W. Aziz, Ph.D.

Dr. Aziz is currently a research analyst employed by the New York Department of Corrections in Albany, New York. He has been responsible for monitoring and evaluating the New York State Department of Correctional Services Shock Incarceration program since 1987. He and Mr. Paul Korotkin were principally responsible for creating the cost-avoidance model used for the Shock program in New York.

Gordon Bazemore, Ph.D.

Dr. Bazemore is Associate Professor in the School of Public Administration at Florida Atlantic University. His primary research interests include: juvenile justice, youth policy, corrections, community justice, and crime victims. He serves on the Victim's Committee of the American Correctional Association. Dr. Bazemore is the author of numerous articles, book chapters, and other publications on these topics. He is currently editing a book on international juvenile justice reform, tentatively titled: *Restoring Juvenile Justice*. Recent publications appear in *Justice Quarterly*, *Crime and Delinquency*, the *Prison Journal*, and the *Journal of Sociology and Social Welfare*. Currently, he is the principal investigator of a national action research project funded by the Office of Juvenile Justice and Delinquency Prevention to pilot systemic reform based on restorative justice principles in several jurisdictions in the United States. He also has directed several recent evaluations of juvenile justice policing, and minority overrepresentation programs funded by the United States Department of Justice, the Florida Department of Health and Rehabilitative Services, and the Annie E. Casey Foundation.

William S. Beers

Mr. Beers has served as superintendent of the Shutter Creek Correctional Institution in North Bend Oregon since 1990. Prior to this, he was the superintendent for the Parole Violators' Prison run by the Oregon Department of Prisons. He is responsible for the opening of four correctional facilities, including their initial planning and budgeting, staff hiring and training, and ensuring compliance with zoning and utility regulations. He is responsible for the community's acceptance and support of Shutter Creek. He implemented the Oregon SUMMIT boot camp/cognitive program, including the development of rules, policies, procedures, goals, plans, program evaluation, and budgets. He was selected the Oregon Department of Corrections' Correctional Officer of the Year in 1991, 1992 and 1993. He has his bachelor of science degree from Western Oregon State College and graduate credits in public administration from Portland State University.

Jackie Campbell

Ms. Campbell is the superintendent of the Washington State Department of Corrections Work Ethic Camp at McNeil Island. Prior to this, she was the director of a pilot program to integrate offender education and employment within the prison system. Her past experience is primarily in employment and training programs. Before joining the Department of Corrections, she was a deputy assistant commissioner with the employment security department responsible for statewide job training programs. She was also the administrator of Corrections Clearinghouse, the state provider of offender employment and training programs inside institutions and in the community. Her degree is in correctional administration.

Thomas C. Castellano, Ph.D.

Dr. Castellano is Associate Professor of Criminal Justice at the Center for the Study of Crime, Delinquency, and Corrections at Southern Illinois University at Carbondale.

His research interests include the criminal justice policy formation and implementation process, socio-political factors influencing criminal sanctioning decisions, and the effectiveness of correctional sanctions. He is currently conducting a multisite evaluation of innovative boot camp-type programs. This study is funded by the National Institute of Justice and is associated with his recent Visiting Fellowship at the National Institute of Justice, which also involved supporting the formulation of rules and regulations to implement the corrections' provisions of the 1994 Crime Act. He also has recently completed an implementation and impact analysis of parole reform in Illinois and a nationwide study of the drug treatment and aftercare components of shock incarceration programs. He received his Ph.D. in criminal justice from the State University of New York at Albany in 1986.

Cheryl L. Clark

Ms. Clark has been the Director of Shock Incarceration for the New York State Department of Correctional Services in Albany, New York, since its inception in 1987. Previously, she served as director of staff development for the New York State Division of Parole. In 1990, she received the Governor's Productivity Award for her outstanding contribution to state government. She began her career as a social worker and has been a psychotherapist in private practice. She has been working in the human services field since 1966 and criminal justice since 1974. She is internationally recognized as a leader in her field and an expert in Shock Incarceration. In 1995, the American Correctional Association acknowledged her outstanding contributions to Shock Incarceration as "Best in the Business." She also has designed, and now directs and is the principal instructor for the only dedicated staff training program for Shock Incarceration across the country. This four-week intensive program includes military bearing, drill and ceremony, physical training, Network (therapeutic community that she developed), alcohol and substance abuse treatment, instructor development, and group training skills. She has trained more than 3,000 staffers locally and nationally in therapeutic community methods, skills of conflict resolution and decision making, instructor development, supervision, and management. The Network program has expanded to twenty-nine facilities in New York and was adopted in Vermont as the Vanguard Program used in their correctional facilities. In 1995, she developed and directed the implementation of an innovative ninety day substance abuse treatment program for parole violators. It is located in a 750-bed facility in central New York and is based on the Shock model. She has a master's in science degree in educational psychology and training in clinical psychology. She is a Ph.D. candidate in the School of Health and Human Services at Columbia Pacific University.

Colonel Thomas H. Cornick, U. S. A. (Retired)

Col. Cornick was born and raised in Gloversville, in upstate New York. He was graduated from Middlebury College in 1960 with a bachelor of arts in history. He holds a master of arts degree in international relations from the Maxwell School of Syracuse University, and has completed his course work for his Ph.D. in public administration from the State University of New York at Albany. He was commissioned in the regular United States Army from the Middlebury Reserve Officer's Training Corps. He served in the Army as a military police officer for twenty-seven years, then spent five years in the reserves. He served a combat tour in Vietnam as an intelligence advisor in the Mekong Delta area. Military assignments include extensive training in management assignments in the field of criminal justice. He was command-selected battalion commander of the 504th Military Police Battalion in San Francisco, Provost Marshal of the Presidio of San Francisco, commander of the United States Army recruiting battalion in Eastern New York and Western New England. He is a professor of military science at Sienna College and inspector general of the New York National Guard. Because of his background, he was selected to initiate New York's first juvenile boot camp, designated as the Sergeant Henry Johnson Youth Leadership Academy in South Kortright, New York, in 1992. Simultaneously, he initiated the City Challenge aftercare day placement program in Brooklyn, New York. He has three daughters.

Ernest L. Cowles, Ph.D.

Dr. Cowles is the Director of the Center for Legal Studies and associate professor at the University of Illinois at Springfield. His background covers a wide spectrum of the criminal justice field as a practitioner, researcher, academician, and administrator. His current interests focus on correctional policy issues including: offender treatment, long-term incarceration, and alternative sanctions. He also is involved in assessing the impact of substance abuse on various aspects of the criminal justice system. Dr. Cowles has been active in the policy areas on both a state and national level and has served as a consultant to a number of agencies including the Federal Bureau of Prisons, the Bureau of Justice Assistance, the National Institute of Corrections, and the National Institute of Justice. He received his Ph.D. from the School of Criminology and Criminal Justice at the Florida State University.

Chris Duval

Ms. Duval is the program manager at Shutter Creek Correctional Institution and the Oregon SUMMIT (boot camp) Program in North Bend, Oregon. She began her employment with the Oregon Department of Corrections in 1988, assisting in the opening of the minimum-security Bay Area Work Center in North Bend, and later the opening of the medium-security parole Violators' Prison. In 1990, she assisted in the opening of the minimum-security Shutter Creek Correctional Institution. In cooperation with Superintendent William Beers, Ms. Duval implemented the Oregon SUMMIT Program at Shutter Creek, which opened in March 1994. She holds a bachelor's degree in sociology from the University of Washington and her background includes work in the counseling and legal fields.

Voncile B. Gowdy, Ph.D.

Voncile B. Gowdy, Doctor of Public Administration, is a Senior Social Scientist at the National Institute of Justice in Washington, D.C. She manages the Institute's Corrections Research Program, specializing in the area of community corrections, boot camps, intermediate sanctions, privatization, and issues related to women.

Ronald D. Griffith

Deputy Commander Ronald D. Griffith began his career in 1982 at the State Correctional Institution at Camp Hill as a corrections officer. He was promoted to sergeant in 1985. In 1990, he was promoted to the rank of lieutenant at the Department's training academy and developed Pennsylvania's first statewide Correctional Emergency Response Team (CERT). In 1992, he was promoted to captain and appointed the deputy commander at the Quehanna Boot Camp in Karthaus, Pennsylvania. Deputy Commander Griffith has studied at New York University and Penn State University.

Robert J. Jones

Mr. Jones has been a research scientist in the Planning and Research Unit of the Illinois Department of Corrections in Springfield, Illinois, since 1981. He has assisted in the development and evaluation of parole and work release classification, electronic detention, the Impact Incarceration (boot camp) Program, as well as the department's drug and sex offender treatment programs. He also analyzes the department's sentencing, length of stay and recidivism data as well as most criminal justice-related legislative bill analyses. He also teaches the research methods class in the criminal justice program at the University of Illinois at Springfield. He holds a master of science degree in criminal justice research from Southern Illinois University at Carbondale and has a bachelor of arts degree in the administration of justice from the University of Illinois at Chicago.

Carole Sanchez Knapel

Ms. Knapel, a consultant in Capitola, California, has worked in criminal justice analysis and planning for more than eighteen years. She has worked with a variety of local agencies in the planning, design, and construction of correctional facilities. In 1992, she was appointed a Visiting Fellow at the National Institute of Justice. During that time, she worked with the American Correctional Association in the development of the adult and juvenile boot camp standards. For ten years, Ms. Knapel worked in Santa Clara County, California, where she was responsible for a wide range of projects, including the development and evaluation of alternative sanction programs, inmate population projections, and an inmate population management plan.

Paul H. Korotkin

Mr. Korotkin has been the director of research and evaluation for the New York State Department of Correctional Services in Albany, New York, since 1988. He has worked extensively in the area of inmate population projections and on the impact of legislative policy on the demands for prison beds.

Doris Layton MacKenzie, Ph.D.

Dr. MacKenzie is an associate professor in the Department of Criminology and Criminal Justice at the University of Maryland in College Park, Maryland. Prior to this position, she earned her doctorate from Pennsylvania State University, was on the faculty of the Louisiana State University where she was honored as a "Researcher of Distinction," and was awarded a visiting scientist position at the National Institute of Justice. As visiting scientist, she provided expertise to federal, state, and local jurisdictions on correctional boot camps, correctional policy, intermediate sanctions, research methodology, experimental design, statistical analyses, and evaluation techniques. As an expert in criminal justice, Dr. MacKenzie has consulted with state and local jurisdictions and has testified before committees of the United States Senate and House of Representatives. She has an extensive record of publications on such topics as examining inmate adjustment to prison, the impact of intermediate sanctions on recidivism, long-term offenders, methods of predicting prison populations, and boot camp prisons. She directed the "Multisite Study of Correctional Boot Camps" and a "Descriptive Study of Female Boot Camps." She has completed nine sponsored research projects and is currently director of the National Institute of Justice-sponsored grants to study "Probationer Compliance with Conditions of Supervision," and "Substance Abuse Treatment Using Cognitive Behavior Therapy."

Susan W. McCampbell

Ms. Campbell is Director of the Department of Corrections and Rehabilitation for the Broward County Sheriff's Office in Fort Lauderdale, Florida. She was named to this post in January 1995. The Department has 1,400 employees and an average daily inmate population of 3,500 soon to expand to 4,200 inmates. It operates a range of pretrial and posttrial programs, including a military-style boot camp, therapeutic living community, and a 254-bed forensic unit. Prior to this, she was Assistant Sheriff in Alexandria, Virginia (1983-1994). While in Alexandria, she was involved with the National Institute of Corrections in designating Alexandria's jail a mental health unit as one of the two model programs in the United States. Prior to working in Alexandria, Ms. McCampbell was a project director for the Police Executive Research Forum in Washington, D.C. She holds a bachelor of arts from the School of Government and Public Administration at American University, and a master of city and regional planning from the School of Architecture and Engineering, the Catholic University of America, in Washington, D.C.

Lisa Matheson

Ms. Matheson is cofounder and managing director of Doing Life International Inc. and Doing Life Organization Consulting LLC, in Sunderland, Ontario, Canada, which provides substance abuse treatment consulting and recovery program materials to institutional and private sector organizations. She has fifteen years' experience in the marketing and communications industry. As production manager for one of North America's largest retail agencies in the mid-1980s, she supervised the production of print, electronic media, and point of purchase materials for clients. In 1991, Ms. Matheson with her partner created Canada's largest and most successful home inspection businesses. Currently, she consults with organizations in the development, production, and delivery of corporate training programs and materials.

Ronald Moscicki

Superintendent Moscicki is the supervisor for the Lakeview Shock Incarceration Facility in Brocton, New York, for the New York State Department of Correctional Services. He served on the task force that designed Shock Incarceration in New York. He directed the first training program for staff working in Shock. He was promoted to Superintendent at Monterey in less than a year. He was next promoted to superintendent at Lakeview Shock Incarceration Correctional Facility in 1989. Lakeview is the largest Shock facility in the United States with 720 beds devoted to Shock, including 160 for women. It also serves as the reception center for all Shock facilities. He has trained more than 2,000 staffers in program methods nationally. In 1995, he worked on the design and implementation of the 750-bed drug treatment center modeled after Shock Incarceration. He began his career as a correctional officer at Attica Correctional Facility in 1972. He worked his way up the supervisory ranks, was in charge of discipline at Attica and commanded the Corrections Emergency Response Team at that facility.

Corby A. Myers, Ed.D.

Dr. Myers is currently the Director of the Abraxas Leadership Development Program, a 105-bed boot camp for delinquent males, ages fourteen to eighteen, in South Mountain, Pennsylvania. It consists of a fifteen-week high impact, military-style program combined with an Outward Bound wilderness adventure experience. Before joining Abraxas, Dr. Myers was employed for eight years as the Director of the York County Youth Development Center, including 1994 when the Council of Juvenile and Family Court Judges named it the "outstanding detention facility." He has twenty years of experience in the human services profession, including serving as a teacher for socially/emotionally disturbed youth in the York First Chance Program, and as a counselor/family therapist with York Catholic Social Services. He served as the secretary of the Juvenile Detention Centers Association of Pennsylvania and received their distinguished service award, and the educator of the year award from the Central Pennsylvania Planned Parenthood. He serves on the Commonwealth Detention Task Force and is a member of the Juvenile

Detention Standards Project Advisory Board. His bachelor's degree in psychology is from York College of Pennsylvania, his master's degree from the Fels Center of Government at the University of Pennsylvania in governmental administration, and he recently completed his doctorate in adult education at Temple University. His dissertation was on occupational stress among 224 direct-care workers in juvenile detention facilities in Pennsylvania. He is an adjunct faculty member at Harrisburg Area Community College.

John G. Perry

Mr. Perry has been the Director of Planning for the Vermont Department of Corrections in Waterbury, Vermont, for fourteen years, and has worked in corrections since 1978. Prior to coming to corrections, he was a guidance counselor and teacher in rural Vermont. He is the author of the Bureau of Justice Assistance Corrections Options grant to restructure corrections in Vermont, creating a two-track system of correctional services and integrating the concept of reparative justice.

Command Sergeant Major Joshua Perry (Retired)

Command Sergeant Major Perry (Retired) is a training specialist at the United States Army Military Police School, Fort McClellan, Alabama, where he is course manager for the Rehabilitation Training Instructors Course for drill instructors working in correctional boot camps throughout the country. He has trained correctional staff from more than thirty states and jurisdictions in leadership supervision and instruction skills for correctional boot camp programs. He retired from the United States Army in 1991 after thirty years of distinguished service, including three tours in Germany, one each in Korea and Vietnam, and several stateside assignments. He has an extensive background in corrections in addition to his impressive military experience. He was the Command Sergeant Major for the United States Army Disciplinary Barracks at Fort Leavenworth, Kansas; the Regimental Command Sergeant Major, Military Police Regiment; Command Sergeant Major United States Army Military Police School; and Commandant United States Army Military Police School Noncommissioned Officer Academy, all at Fort McClellan. He earned an associate's degree in law enforcement from Northwestern State University, and has additional military education. His awards include: the Bronze Star, Legion of Merit, Meritorious Service Medal (five Oak Leaf Clusters), Army Commendation Medal, and many others.

Susan M. Plant

Ms. Plant is a graduate of Rutgers University School of Criminal Justice and is currently conducting research at Southern Illinois University at Carbondale. She is a co-principal investigator of an Illinois Criminal Justice Information Authority grant, which is aimed at continuing an earlier evaluation of that state's new prison prerelease program, PreStart.

Thomas J. Quinn

Mr. Quinn received his bachelor's degree from Dartmouth College and his master's degree from the State University of New York at Albany. He worked three years in Philadelphia and its suburbs before a twenty-year career with Delaware's Criminal Justice Council, where he served as staff director for the last decade. During that tenure he also filled the role of staff coordinator for Delaware's Sentencing Accountability Commission. He has been an adjunct instructor at the University of Delaware from 1990-1995. He served as president of the National Criminal Justice Association in 1988-1989. In 1995, he began a fifteen-month fellowship with the National Institute of Justice in Washington, D.C. It is centered around restorative justice, an emerging philosophy which puts the community and the victim at the center of the justice process.

Andre B. Rosay

Mr. Rosay is a graduate student in the Department of Criminology and Criminal Justice at the University of Maryland at College Park. His primary research interest includes the use of statistical models in the areas of delinquency and corrections.

John F. Wertz

Commander John F. Wertz began his career in 1975 at the State Correctional Institution at Camp Hill as a correctional officer. In 1979 he was promoted to chief of training and oversaw the largest expansion of the Department's training academy to that date. From 1988-1991, he served as the academy manager and was responsible for all basic training. In June of 1991, he was appointed commander of Pennsylvania's first and only motivational boot camp at Quehanna in Karthaus, Pennsylvania. The commander holds a bachelor's degree in secondary education, a master's degree in theology and a doctoral fellowship.

Appendix
Adult and Juvenile Boot Camps

Accredited by the
American Correctional Association as of May 2, 1996

Adult Boot Camps

Arkansas Department of Corrections

Wrightsville Unit
Clifford Terry, Warden
P.O. Box 1000
Wrightsville, AR 72183
(501) 897-5806

Esmor, Inc.

Tarrant County Community Correctional Center
John Renfroe, Director
651 Justice Lane
Mansfield, TX 76063
(817) 473-1324

Federal Bureau of Prisons

Intensive Confinement Center
J. D. Lamer, Warden
R.D. #5
Lewisburg, PA 17837
(717) 523-1251

Louisiana Department of Public Safety and Corrections

Elayn Hunt Correctional Center IMPACT Program
Marty Lensing, Warden
P.O. Box 174
St. Gabriel, LA 70776
(504) 642-3306

Massachusetts Department of Corrections

Boot Camp Program
Jake Gadsden, Administrator
2 Administrative Road
Bridgewater, MA 02324
(617) 727-1507

New York State Department of Correctional Services

Camp Gabriels
James Murphy, Superintendent
Route 86, Box 100
Gabriels, NY 12939
(518) 327-3111

Camp Georgetown
John Hoxie, Superintendent
R.D. #1
Georgetown, NY 13072-9307
(315) 837-4446

Moriah Shock Incarceration
Correctional Facility
Walter Thorne, Superintendent
P.O. Box 999
Mineville, NY 12956-0999
(518) 942-7561

Summit Shock Incarceration Correctional Facility
Gary Filion, Superintendent
HCR 2, Box 56
Summit, NY 12175
(518) 287-1721

Oklahoma Department of Corrections

Dr. Eddie W. Warrior Correctional Center
Debbie McLaffey, Warden
P.O. Box 354
Taft, OK 74463-0354
(918) 683-8365

William S. Key Correctional Center
Macy Punches, Warden
P.O. Box 61, William S. Key Blvd
Fort Supply, OK 73841-0061
(405) 766-2224

Tennessee Department of Corrections

Wayne County Boot Camp
Malcolm Davis, Warden
P.O. Box 182
Clifton, TN 38425
(615) 676-3345

Juvenile Boot Camps

Alabama Department of Youth Services

Autauga Campus
Keith Duck, Superintendent
P.O. Box 671
Prattville, AL 36067
(334)361-9161

Thomasville Facility
Samson Crum, Superintendent
P.O. Box 695, Baski Road
Thomasville, AL 36784
(334) 636-8100

New York State Division for Youth

Sgt. Henry Johnson Youth Leadership Academy
Col. Thomas H. Cornick, Director
Route 10, Box 132
S Kortright, NY 13842
(607) 538-1401